SCANDINAVIAN MISADVENTURE

Frontispiece: *HMS Eskimo* (Commander Micklethwait after being torpedoed by the destroyer *Thiele* (Captain Wolff) in the second battle of Narvik. *IWM*

SCANDINAVIAN MISADVENTURE

Maurice Harvey

SPELLMOUNT LIMITED
TUNBRIDGE WELLS · KENT

First published in the UK in 1990 by
Spellmount Ltd
12 Dene Way, Speldhurst
Tunbridge Wells, Kent TN3 0NX
ISBN 0-946771-44-8

© Maurice Harvey 1990

British Library Cataloguing in Publication Data
Harvey, Maurice
  Scandinavian misadventure: the campaign in Norway 1940.
  (Clash of arms series; 2)
  1. World War 2, Norwegian campaign
  I. Title II. Series
  940.542181

ISBN 0-946771-44-8

Typesetting by Vitaset, Paddock Wood, Kent
Printed in Great Britain by Biddles Ltd, Guildford, Surrey

Contents

In the Spellmount Military list:

The Territorial Battalions – A pictorial history
The Yeomanry Regiments – A pictorial history
Over the Rhine – The Last Days of War in Europe
History of the Cambridge University OTC
Yeoman Service
The Fighting Troops of the Austro-Hungarian Army
Intelligence Officer in the Peninsula
The Scottish Regiments – A pictorial history
The Royal Marines – A pictorial history
The Royal Tank Regiment – A pictorial history
The Irish Regiments – A pictorial history
British Sieges of the Peninsular War
Victoria's Victories
Heaven and Hell – German paratroop war diary
Rorke's Drift
Came the Dawn – Fifty years an Army Officer
On the Word of Command – RSM's pictorial history
Kitchener's Army – A pictorial history
A Medal for Life – Captain Leefe Robinson VC
Marlborough – As Military Commander
The Fall of France
Epilogue in Burma 1945-48

In the Military Machine list:

Napoleon's Military Machine
Falklands Military Machine
Wellington's Military Machine

In the Nautical list:

Sea of Memories
Evolution of Engineering in the Royal Navy Vol I
1827-1939
In Perilous Seas

In the Aviation list:

Diary of a Bomb Aimer
Operation 'Bograt' – From France to Burma

List of Illustrations

List of Maps

Acknowledgements

I would like to thank the many people who in their various ways have assisted in the preparation of this book. In particular, I wish to acknowledge Air Cdre Henry Probert and his staff at the Air Historical Branch of the MOD, the Head Librarian of the MOD Central Library, and the Librarian of the Royal United Services Institute for their unfailing help in directing me towards source material. The staff of the Public Record Office at Kew were also very helpful. I received valuable assistance from many Regimental Associations and/or their museums. In particular, I would like to mention the South Wales Borderers and Monmouthshire Regimental Museum and Brigadier Charles Cox, the Light Infantry Office (Yorkshire), Regimental Headquarters The Green Howards at Richmond and the Central Library and Arts Centre, Rotherham, which houses the archives of the York and Lancaster Regiment. I would also like to thank Captain Fjeld of the Defence Museum, Akershus, Oslo and Wing Commander Stewart Cresswell, the Air Attaché in Norway in 1986, who gave me much valuable assistance.

The photographic record of the campaign in Norway is poor, but the staff of the Imperial War Museum and the Royal Air Force Museum were very co-operative in sorting-out what was available. I also owe a debt to John Merriman who helped with the reproduction of my own photographs. I would particularly like to thank Andy Potts, who drew all the maps, and Kay Mullett and Vanessa Kingstone who did the typing, no small task.

I would like to thank the following publishers for allowing me to quote from their books: Cassell (Winston Churchill – *The Second World War* – Vol 1), Jonathan Cape (Dudley Clarke – *Seven Assignments* and Carton de Wiart – *Happy Odyssey*), Wiedenfeld and Nicholson (W. Warlimont – *Inside Hitler's Headquarters 1939-1945*), Gale and Polden (D. J. L. Fitzgerald – *History of the Irish Guards in the Second World War*), W. Clowes and Sons (D. Erskine – *The Scots Guards 1919-1955*) and HMSO (S. W. Roskill – *The War at Sea* – Vol 1). Although efforts have been made to trace the present copyright holders, the publisher apologises in advance for any unintentional omission or neglect and will be pleased to insert the appropriate acknowledgement to companies or individuals in any subsequent edition of this book.

I am particularly grateful for writing the Foreword to General Sir Geoffrey Howlett, KBE, MC, who was Commander-in-Chief Allied Forces Northern Europe between 1986-89, and thus very familiar with the area described in this book. I also owe a debt of gratitude to my publisher, Ian Morley-Clarke.

Finally I would like to thank my wife who was supportive throughout, accomplishing many of the tasks in house and garden which my conscience tells me should really have been mine.

Foreword

*by General Sir Geoffrey Howlett KBE MC
Commander-in-Chief, Allied Forces
Northern Europe, 1986-1989*

It is now 50 years since the campaign in Norway
of 1940. It may well have been only a side show
judged by other larger and longer campaigns in the
1939-1945 War, but the lessons learnt from those few months from April to June 1940
have been far reaching, both politically and militarily.

I also believe that an interval of about 50 years is a very proper gap with which to
look back on history. There are still, God be praised, many survivors alive to tell their
tales, but time has tempered judgement and a more realistic appraisal of the lessons
learnt emerges.

I believe that Hitler's invasion of Denmark and Norway, and their comparatively
speedy occupation for five years, has produced the major moral and political reasoning
behind those two countries' decision to become and remain members of NATO whilst
Sweden remains neutral. The very geographical positions of Denmark and Norway
make both countries early targets for seizure in any conflict, not only between Western
and Eastern Europe but one in which North America is involved too. Neutralism is
possibly practical in Sweden or Switzerland; I doubt that it is an option for Denmark
or Norway, whatever changes the next decade or so will give us in needs for mutual
defence.

The lessons of 1940 have I believe been learnt and if I have a criticism of Norwegian
military thinking today, and I am a great admirer of the Norwegian fighting man, it is
that the lessons may have been too well learnt. There are dangers in a belief that the
next war will be similar to the last one.

In Norway in 1940 the Allies, as opposed to the Germans, had no clear strategy and
little aim. They reacted to events and that slowly and inadequately. There was little
co-operation between the Allies and even less between each Service, especially that
between the Royal Navy and the British Army. Aircraft were in short supply, but that
does not excuse the woeful shortage of reconnaissance aircraft in particular. Above all
the preparedness of men and equipment was lamentable, and Command was split and
unclear.

Even the Germans though perhaps did not think through the full implications of
their occupation of Norway, though this is always easier in hindsight. Of course they
gained many miles worth of well hidden ports and fiords and impressively quickly
constructed airfields to help in the battles for the North Atlantic and north Russian

convoys. They had the advantage of some valuable raw materials, especially Swedish iron ore, though this was never decisive. In return an occupation force of 300,000 men may well have been very decisive when the full economic and manpower might of the Allies was turned on against Germany. Even before this the comparatively heavy losses to the German Navy during the campaign probably played a major part in the abandonment of the invasion of Britain.

Today there is a fully integrated tri-service military Command structure in Norway, and this ties in with the European and Atlantic NATO Commands. Civilian assets are co-ordinated with the military under the Total Defence concept. NATO reinforcements from the United States, the United Kingdom, the Netherlands, West Germany and occasionally others, exercise regularly in Norway, including the harsh winters, on the land, on the sea and in the air and they do this together. Norway's armed forces may not be particularly modern or sophisticated, but for a population of just over 4 million a mobilization strength of 350,000 or 8% of the population is impressive. The United Kingdom would produce 1.1% and the United States 1.5%.

This willingness to defend largely stems from 1940 and will I hope and believe remain a principle even if Glasnost stretches further and wider. This very well researched book which is humanly and uncomplicatedly written gives the historical military reasoning for so much that goes on today in Norway and the Northern European Command which I had the privilege to serve so recently.

Geoffrey Howlett

March 1990

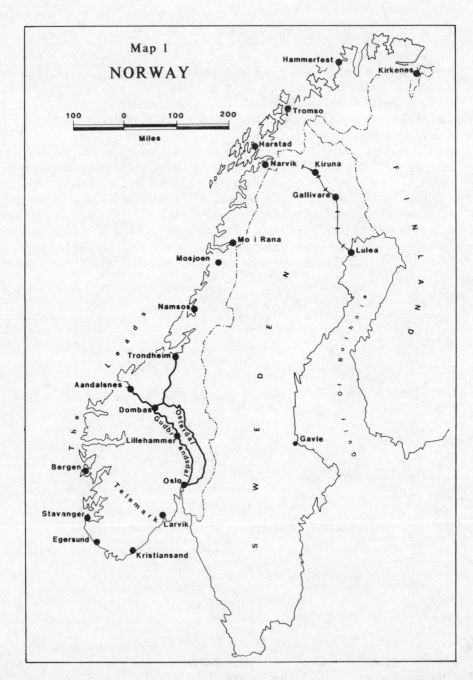

Map 1

NORWAY

Land of the Midnight Sun

'This is the land of the boundless. Everything is different from conditions in other European countries. There are huge mountain masses, separated by deep valleys, almost entirely cut off from one another and ending in dominating snow covered plateaux, cliffs overhanging the winding fiords that pierce their way into the land like writhing dragons.'

Marcel Brion 1952

That Damned Daylight!

At midnight in Narvik in June, there is more than adequate natural light to comfortably read a book. The sun has set in a blaze of colour over the sea, but after a few brief hours of twilight, is again ringing the mountain rims to the north east, shimmering on the snow which still caps the peaks and providing a vivid contrast with the fresh green of the newly awakened birch trees which clothe the lower slopes. The snow in the gullies and ravines, shaded from the sun, is melting quickly now, disgorging in torrents into the dark, dense waters of the fiord. The diminutive wooden houses with their bright red roofs cluster round the little bays in the fingers of the fiord adding yet more variety to the tranquil beauty of the summer landscape.

But the mood changes. Dark clouds gather menacingly over the mountain peaks worn smooth by glaciation, and the still waters of the fiord are disturbed into a frenetic array of rolling whitecaps. The small motor boats – locally called 'puffers' – which had looked so secure on the unruffled surface now speed for safety in the calmer waters of the side fiords. The mountains seem much larger now and more forbidding, looming majestically over the small fishing villages and the bustling little town of Narvik. The rusty piers of the iron ore crushing plant and the jangling cacophony from the overhead railway do not now seem quite such a monstrous intrusion on the benign landscape.

'Land of the Midnight Sun' is a tourist appellation reflecting just one aspect of this uniquely attractive country. But to the men of the 24th Guards Brigade, bemused by a climate and topography which most of them had never encountered before, it was a label which had a more sinister ring. No longer would the sun sinking below the horizon herald the end of the day's campaigning. The steady monotonous rumble of a formation of Heinkel He 111s or Junkers Ju 88s could breach the brooding silence at any hour of the day or night, their target no longer obscured by the shroud of darkness. After a days fighting, the soldier could not put his rifle aside and relax for a few hours secure in the knowledge that no sensible enemy would contemplate trying to gain an advantage in this inhospitable terrain during the protective hours of darkness. An assault could appear at any moment in the 24 hours of the interminable daylight. Beyond the Arctic Circle, time is more meaningfully measured by the clock than the passage of day and night.

The most striking and perhaps least well appreciated feature of Norway is its size. At 125,000 square miles, it is greater in area than both Great Britain and Italy. It stretches over 13 degrees of latitude: Oslo is closer to Vienna and Paris than it is to the North Cape, the most northerly point of Norway. The country is long and narrow. At Hellemofiord between Bodo and Narvik, no more than four miles separates the head of the fiord from Sweden. The bottleneck widens at the top where the Arctic wastes of Finnmark eventually give way to the plains around Kirkenes where modern Norway looks uneasily across the Soviet border towards Petsamo (now Pecenga) and Murmansk. Similarly in the south, Norway again broadens to encompass the lower lands surrounding Oslo, but the predominance of a mountain landscape is maintained in the bulbous base of the Telemark Peninsular thrusting down towards the Skagerrak.

The country is dominated by mountain and sea. The Caledonian mountain range stretches almost 1000 miles along the western edge of the Scandinavian peninsular. The mountains rise to 8000 feet, and over half the land area is above 2000 feet. Over the years, glacial erosion created the dramatic fiords which penetrate far into the hinterland, their probing fingers marking the main barriers to communication between north and south. Even today it is not possible to drive the length of Norway without taking to the ferry – in 1940 there were many such interruptions to an advancing army. At that time, the road north from Oslo ended at Bodo. Beyond stretched a featureless high plateaux, virtually uninhabited, until another small enclave of population appeared around Narvik, some 100 miles to the north. The Arctic Circle lies well to the south of Bodo, running appropriately across a bare, windswept, snowbound tundra that was to become only too familiar to the men of the Scots Guards. In stark contrast, immediately to the north and south lie well wooded, cultivated valleys which in summer are temperate in climate and character.

Further south, in Central Norway, although the rigours of the climate were less extreme, the nature of the ground still played the most significant role in the conduct of military operations. The dominant physical features often provided good natural defensive positions where the lines of advance and communication were concentrated in narrow defiles containing the river, road and railway, flanked by steep and densely wooded mountain slopes. But such apparently impressive defensive positions are so often vulnerable to aggressors who are willing and capable of taking to the mountains to bypass the bottlenecks. The Greeks found the same problem in 480 BC during the Persian Wars when Xerxes neatly turned a seemingly impregnable stronghold at Thermopylae by sending his troops over a little known mountain path, and thus opened the door to Athens. Furthermore, the permafrost even in the lower slopes of the valleys made digging-in difficult and sometimes impossible. Denied the traditional refuge of the infantryman, the soldiers were forced to construct whatever makeshift sangars they could with loose stones and logs, leaving them vulnerable to artillery and mortar bombardment.

The climate in Norway, strongly influenced by the moist prevailing westerly winds of the Atlantic, is not extreme compared with the hinterland of Scandinavia, the seasonal difference in temperature ranging over only 14°C. It is very wet, and as the bulk of the precipitation falls in the winter months, is mostly in the form of snow. There is little evidence of the transitional seasons; the sudden thaw, in May in Central Norway and early June further north, heralds the advent of the short and often sunny summer. In winter, the snow covers all the peaks, and lies deep in the many valleys and gorges streaming down to the fiords. Most of the time the Allied troops were in Norway it remained intensely cold overnight, and with a savage wind often accentuating the chill factor, the risk of frostbite, particularly in the Narvik area, was ever present. But many of the days were quite agreeable, particularly on the valley slopes which were open to the sun. The sudden thaw brought even more problems than the snow. The loose surfaced roads, already attacked by the frost, broke-up and quickly became impassable even for the light vehicles generally used by the opposing forces in Norway.

As one would expect in a maritime climate, the country is well wooded, forests covering a quarter of the land area. Deciduous trees, predominantly birch, clothe the lower slopes with the ubiquitous conifer clinging precariously wherever it can gain a foothold higher up the mountain sides. The dense forest was another constraining factor on military operations, curtailing fields of fire and exacerbating the difficulty of recognising friend and foe.

Norway's people and its economy were both orientated towards the sea. The Vikings had acquired a well earned reputation for exploration, trading and piracy on the high seas, and the Norwegian mercantile marine, the fourth largest in the world, had perpetuated the maritime tradition. Fishing and the associated processing industries were also prominent, but agriculture was almost restricted to the flat areas around Oslo and Trondheim, and in small farmsteads scattered along the lower slopes of the main valleys.

Naturally, all of the large towns and many of the smaller settlements were concentrated by the water, but often at the head of deep fiords many miles from the open sea. The major towns were all ports, Oslo, Kristiansand, Stavanger, Bergen, Trondheim, Bodo and Narvik. Most of them were seemingly well protected lying deep within their fiords and should have been easily defensible against the larger warships, out of their natural element in the restricted waters. This was to prove, except in one case, a serious miscalculation. Norway remains today, as it was in 1940, one of the most sparsely populated countries on the continent of Europe. The total population in 1940 was around three million, the majority of whom lived within sight or sound of the sea, and gained their livelihood from it.

The modern capital Oslo is the hub of southern Norway with roads radiating to the other main centres of population, the medieval capital Trondheim, Bergen and Stavanger. Further north, direct links in 1940 between the main centres of population, Tromso, Narvik and Bodo were more tenuous. Narvik itself, which will feature prominently in this narrative, developed from a small isolated fishing community in the last century as an outlet for the iron ore from the rich fields across the border at Gällivare in Sweden. A railway constructed in 1902 from Kiruna descends steeply through massive earthworks and nineteen tunnels to deposit the ore on the quayside at Narvik where, after crushing, it was loaded on to vessels of many nations, but predominantly those flying the flag of Germany.

Even where roads existed, they were usually narrow, tortuous and rough surfaced. A cursory glance at the map, even today, gives little indication of the difficulty of travel overland in many parts of Norway. The railways were as underdeveloped as the roads and in 1940 did not extend far beyond Trondheim. The aeroplane is now the natural means of travel, particularly within North Norway, but in 1940 there were few airfields, and they hardly existed at all in the far north. The natural lines of communication were formed by the sea and the fiords and here Norway had a major advantage. Along almost the whole length of its western boundary lies a long string of islands, or skerries, which protect the small steamers ploughing up and down the coast as well as the larger merchantships and tankers. Known as the Leads, they were to have a major political as well as geographical importance to Norway in the early years of the war.

Such was the country, beautiful, but hard and uncompromising, that was soon to be thrust into the forefront of the new European war. Experience was to show that the Germans were to adapt to its rigours rather more readily than the Allies.

Neutrality Exposed

Despite a lack of natural resources, Norway was a surprisingly prosperous country on the outbreak of war in Europe. Its small population, capitalising on its strengths and unencumbered by a wasting industrial heartland, was a model of liberal democratic traditions. The Norwegians were proud of their independence, but anxious to live in reasonable harmony with their neighbours.

Britain and Norway had always had a friendly if not a particularly close relationship. They had an obvious affinity as nations which looked naturally towards the sea rather than the continental landmass, and their forms of government and social structures had developed in parallel through the nineteenth and early twentieth centuries. The Norwegian people, however, were generally more knowledgeable about and felt a closer association with Britain, particularly Scotland, than the reverse – to an Englishman, Norway was a land of wild and mystic beauty, but one only rarely visited because of the unpredictable weather.

Norway also had important trading links with Germany, second only to those with Britain, but politically and culturally the relationship was more distant. Norwegian volunteers, in alliance with Denmark, had fought Germany for the control of Schleswig-Holstein in the middle years of the nineteenth century, and since independence, Germany's close relationship with Sweden was often a source of mistrust. In the First World War the unrestricted submarine campaign waged by the Germans, in which many Norwegian seamen lost their lives, had scarred the personal relationship between the people of the two countries. Although the efficiency and authority of Hitler's Germany was respected, even admired, in comparison with the rather bumbling and amateurish reputation of Britain, the instinctive, ingrained sympathy and goodwill of the majority of the people inclined across the Norwegian Sea towards their maritime neighbour.

But whatever the inclination of their subjects, all Norwegian governments had clung tenaciously to a policy of neutrality since the final break with Sweden in 1905. This stance had been maintained with some difficulty during the First World War, particularly as the sympathies of the Left Party, which provided the government, and those of the majority of the people lay with the liberal administrations of the Allies. Fortunately for Norwegians, both sides calculated that their interest would best be served by keeping Norway neutral. In fact, the early years of the war brought a period of enhanced prosperity for the Norwegians as they cautiously traded with both protagonists without disastrously upsetting either. But such a tortuous balancing act could not last, and after August 1916 a more belligerent attitude by both sides placed neutrality under increasing strain and the economy under severe pressure. The end of the war arrived just in time to save at least the outward probity of their neutral status.

Nothing deterred, all the Scandinavian countries embraced neutralism with even greater fervour in the post war years. The creation of the League of Nations provided the platform for promoting the Utopian ideal of internationally guaranteed freedom, and at the same time furnished the excuse for allowing national defences to recede almost to extinction. There was of course a certain intellectual, if naive, force in the argument that if you are incapable of defending yourself against aggression by the super powers of the period, then you might just as well ignore the inevitable and enjoy the good life whilst it lasts.

The 1930s also saw a steady increase in electoral support for the Labour Party at the expense mainly of the Conservatives and the left wing parties. In common with other socialist parties in Europe, the Norwegian Labour Party had an instinctive distrust of the military, and a misplaced confidence in the powers of diplomacy. Nevertheless, when the Labour Party came to power in 1935, the seeds of the eventual military disaster had been long sown.

Norwegian defence policy was based on a small cadre of permanent officers and NCOs backed by the gradual mobilisation of reserve forces in periods of tension. Such a policy was perhaps inevitable at that time in a country with the limited population and resources of Norway, but most of the ingredients for successful implementation were missing. The permanent cadre was too small, the training of recruits too short, and the provision of equipment for the mobilised forces inadequate. Even the policy for the use of force was ill-defined and indecisive and the mobilisation plan untested. In common with other countries in Western Europe, a late spurt, or perhaps more accurately an increased trickle, of defence spending after 1936 attempted to redress the balance, but as elsewhere it was too little too late. There was a misguided belief that the nature of the country with its tortuous coastline, formidable mountains and poor communications would be a sufficient deterrent to invasion. And even if an aggressor had the temerity to ignore this constraint, Norway would be a relatively easy country to defend. In the background, pyschologically at least, was the overwhelming power of the Royal Navy. Surely Britain would not stand by and allow the borders of a small defenceless democracy to be violated by an aggressive, greedy dictator.

In September 1939, therefore, the Norwegian armed forces were in a significantly worse state than they had been at the outbreak of World War I when Norway had 197,000 men under arms. The permanent cadre of the Army consisted of only 1900 officers and NCOs with an annual call-up of about 12,500 men for 84 days training. There were five divisional headquarters spread around the country, but the only formation which was permanently mobilised was the Polar Division in the far north guarding the frontiers of Finnmark against possible intervention by the Russians. Arms and ammunition for the remainder of the reserve forces were scattered in depots throughout the country: many were to be captured by the Germans before their contents could be dispersed.

The Air Force had about 24 aircraft, only six of which were fighters, and was not a significant factor. But the Navy, as befits a maritime country, was fully mobilised at the outbreak of war. Even so, most of its ships were antiquated, one in commission dating as far back as 1858. Its largest vessels, known as coast defence ships, were nearly 40 years old. There were in addition seven destroyers, two minesweepers and two submarines, none of which played a significant role in the disaster that was shortly to descend on the country.

Although not clearly recognised by either the Government or the people, Norway's future now lay in the hands of others. For both Britain and Germany had interests in Norway which almost inevitably, sooner or later, would shatter the fragile neutrality under which the country so uneasily rested.

The Scandinavian 'Problem'

'When men counsel reasonably, reasonable success ensues; but when in their counsels they reject reason, God does not choose to follow the wanderings of human fancies.'

Themistocles

Where Shall We Fight The War?

The main characteristic which distinguished wars in the first half of the twentieth century from their predecessors was their totality. Whilst in past centuries the objectives may have been far reaching, the means of attaining them were limited. Armies fought battles, usually in alliance with those of like-minded powers and often far distant from the territories of the participants. On other occasions, differences were settled by actions confined to the seas. After a more or less decisive encounter, the protagonists would meet and share-out the spoils, and the winners would impose terms of settlement upon the losers which would usually mean that the conflict, often between a different combination of powers, would sooner or later break-out again. Whilst all this was going on, the civil populations of those countries involved, whilst their emotions could be easily stirred to fever pitch by propaganda, generally remained physically remote from the privations and rigours of the fighting itself.

But the pattern began to change in the First World War and the process was complete by 1945. The advent of the aeroplane meant that civil populations could no longer remain immune from the conflict, and that the two main elements of warfare, the sea and the land, were brought together by the unifying element of the air. In many respects, the implications of this change went unrecognised in 1918, leading to developments in military thinking and equipment in the inter-war years which left those who were destined to pick-up again the cudgels in 1939 sadly ill prepared for their task. But the learning process for both sides was soon to be rekindled, for their respective campaigns in Norway in 1940 exemplified the new truth – that land, sea and air forces would henceforth have to operate in co-operation and harmony with each other, a failure in one could have a decisive impact on the efficiency and capabilities of the others. The era of joint warfare had arrived.

Very few people in Britain, probably even less in France, were thinking of Scandinavia on that sombre day in September 1939 when the British Prime Minister, Mr Neville Chamberlain, told the nation that Britain was at war with Germany. For many, the wailing air raid sirens which shattered the stunned silence in London shortly after this historic announcement were a clear portent of the nature of the war to come. Some perhaps envisaged, without much enthusiasm, that the British soldier would be going to the aid of his new found comrade in arms in Poland. But although Poland had filled the headlines for some weeks before the outbreak of war, most people in Britain recognised that they could no more provide direct assistance to Poland than could have been given to Czechoslovakia a year earlier.

But where was the war to be fought? It was unthinkable that the Allies could contemplate another slogging match in the trenches; the memories of that bitter, degrading and so wasteful conflict were less than a generation old and reminders of its aftermath, the great depression, were etched even more sharply on the mind. Hitler, and even more his generals in the Wehrmacht, would have preferred not to be at war with Britain and France at all. Despite the massive build-up in Germany's armed forces since Hitler became Chancellor in January 1933, there were still substantial gaps in the Reich's overall military capability. On the Allied side, the neglect and omissions of the interwar years had severely curtailed the options for taking the offensive in the first few months of the war.

The dramatic, if inevitable, collapse of Poland did not help to answer this question. As their generals were only too well aware, the Wehrmacht was spread rather thinly on the Franco/German border at the outbreak of war, but the French, with their Maginot Line mentality, were unready to undertake an offensive in the Saar even if they had been of a mind to do so. Britain's traditional arena, the oceans of the world, was one possibility, and most of the early encounters between the opposing forces were at sea. The superior strength of the Royal Navy and Germany's need to import essential raw materials suggested that an economic blockade was the most profitable course for the Allies to pursue, and it was in this context that Scandinavia suddenly assumed unexpected importance in the early months of the war.

After the fierce German onslaught on Poland, the war had appeared to go into recess. The British Expeditionary Force had gone to France to take up positions on the Belgium frontier at the northern extremity of the Maginot Line, but apart from a few skirmishes in the Saar, all had been quiet. Italy was not yet in the war, Mussolini had made it quite clear to Hitler before the outbreak of hostilities that he would not be ready to join his Fascist ally until 1942. Japan was also still watching events from the sidelines.

The war at sea on the other hand had been anything but quiet. By April 1940 over 150 merchant ships had been sunk along with the ancient battleship Royal Oak and the aircraft carrier Courageous. Surface raiders, the advent of the magnetic mine, but most of all the depredations of the U-boat had alarmed both government and public alike. There had been isolated successes to relieve the gloom, most spectacularly the battle of the River Plate which had led to the pocket battleship Graf Spee being scuttled by her own crew off Montevideo.

Nevertheless, the prevailing mood of the nation was that it was a 'phoney' war, and would be so until armies, and perhaps air forces, began to grapple with each other in earnest. Winston Churchill, the First Lord of the Admiralty in Chamberlain's War Cabinet, was never slow, at least after 1939, to sense the mood of the nation, and it is not really surprising that, with his characteristic impetuosity, he was in the van of those anxious to extend the boundaries of the war. Furthermore, he clearly saw that with an army still mobilising and an air force impotent until new aircraft could be delivered, action at sea was the most viable method of grasping the initiative: '. . . the search for a naval offensive must be incessant' he wrote on 20th September.[1]

In many respects of course this lack of enemy activity except at sea was an unexpected bonus, providing an opportunity to put right at least some of the omissions in defence planning and rearmament of the pre-war years. It enabled the Army to catch-up with training, particularly of the territorial battalions which were sorely in need of a concentrated work-up period before seeing action. The Royal Air Force also had much to achieve, both in re-equipment and training, to prepare for the struggle ahead. But for the more restless spirits in both Britain and France, the seeming inaction became increasingly frustrating. The progression of the war became an end in itself irrespective of the strategic value or feasibility of the action proposed. There was also a suspicion that Germany might be making better use of this lull in activity than the Allies.

The familiar historical perception of the campaign in Norway in 1940 is of a minor military disaster, but one which had no real relevance to the mainstream of the war, and which was almost an aberration on the part of the Allies who should have had more important matters upon which to concentrate their attention. However, paradoxically, it was the absence of more substantial issues in the first months of the war which led to so much time being devoted to discussion of the Scandinavian 'problem'.

There were of course more material reasons than simply frustration at the slow pace of the war for the Allies recurrent interest in Scandinavia, but the political atmosphere in early 1940 was an uncomfortable amalgam of uncertainty, impulsiveness and prevarication which became increasingly less conducive to logical and coherent strategic planning. The urge to do something – to get on with the war – added an emotional dimension to the debate which led to the Allies belated and ultimately disastrous attempt to become involved in Norway in April 1940.

Expressed in its most simple form, the Scandinavian 'problem' in 1939 was iron ore: its excavation in Sweden, its export through Norway, and its importance to the German war economy. In the early months of the war, the opportunities for waging economic warfare figured strongly in the minds of the Allied leaders. In particular, the imposition of an economic blockade of Germany assumed the same importance it had in the last years of the First World War which had culminated in a plan to install a continuous mine barrier between the Orkneys and Norway.

Germany needed to obtain from abroad two key products to sustain her war effort – oil and iron ore. The oil was obtained largely from Romania and Russia, but for geographical and political reasons, it was difficult to interfere with the flow of oil to Germany in the early part of the war. Iron ore was a different matter. It was calculated by the Ministry of Economic Warfare that Germany would need to import nine million tons of iron ore from Sweden during the first year of the war to avert a major industrial breakdown. Most of the ore came from the Kiruna-Gällivare district in the north of Sweden and was exported to Germany through two main outlets – Narvik in the far north of Norway and Lulea in the Gulf of Bothnia. But Lulea was closed by ice from December to mid April and thus the only available outlets for the ore during the winter months were the ice free port of Narvik and the smaller ports of Oxelösund and Gävle on the Baltic coast of southern Sweden. There was not much immediate scope for restricting the flow through the Baltic Sea which was controlled by the German Navy, but the cessation of supplies through Narvik would mean that, even in the most favourable circumstances, the Germans could receive a quarter of a million tons per month less than their minimum requirements until Lulea opened again in the Spring. After the war, the British estimates were largely confirmed from German sources: Admiral Raeder had told Hitler that the loss of the Narvik route would result in a shortfall of between two and a half to three and a half million tons annually. Whilst depriving the Germans of the Narvik ore alone would not have been decisive, it would have been a serious setback to German industrial output.

The superiority of the Royal Navy in the North Sea would have made the transit of iron ore from Narvik to Germany extremely vulnerable but for one factor: for most of the voyage the ore carriers could remain inside the string of islands off the Norwegian coast and thus gain the protection of Norwegian territorial waters. Whilst well aware of the security the German merchant ships gained from remaining within the Leads, the Norwegian Government was naturally very sensitive to any suggestion from the Allies that they should in any way restrict the passage of civilian ships through these waters. It was not only their strict interpretation of neutrality, but also a fear of the German reaction if they should succumb to Allied pressure to constrain in any way this vital German import. On the other hand, Norway was very dependent on the Allies for other aspects of her economic life. Vital imports, one third of her exports, and the employment of her large mercantile fleet all depended on continuing Allied co-operation. Sitting on the fence seemed the best policy and prevarication the best way of achieving it. Thus it was not until March 1940 that Norway signed a War Trade Agreement with the United Kingdom, just one month before the German invasion nullified the benefits to both sides. The Allies for their part also obtained raw materials from Scandinavia, including some iron ore from Sweden; but unlike the ore exported to Germany, these were not considered to be essential to the war effort.

It was not of course only ships carrying iron ore that used Norwegian territorial waters as a safe haven as the Altmark incident was to demonstrate in February 1940. Germany imported other products from Norway including timber, wood pulp, fish products and non ferrous metals, and German and neutral ships carrying imports to Germany from other countries used the Leads for safe passage whenever practicable.

Another reason why Norway was so important to both protagonists was the considerable benefit the Germans would gain from the occupation of ports and airfields along the 1000 miles of Norwegian coastline. Egress from the North German and Baltic ports was vulnerable to attack by both aircraft and submarines, and refuelling and replenishment facilities at Norwegian ports would greatly facilitate the operation of both submarines and surface raiders against Allied trade routes in the Atlantic. Use of the airfields, although few in number and poorly equipped, would greatly enhance the radius of action of German aircraft in the North Sea and reduce the effectiveness of the Royal Navy in enforcing the economic blockade. They would also compound the problems of the air defence of Great Britain as a new line of approach would be opened-up to German bombers and new targets fall within range. But it was the Swedish iron ore that was the immediate cause of concern and which led to a constant hankering on the part of the Allies to do something about this gnawing hole in the economic blockade.

It is not surprising therefore that Norway evoked so much interest on both sides in the early months of the war. They both had good reasons for retaining Norway's benevolent neutrality, but differing interpretation of this fragile policy was always likely to lead to dispute and confrontation. In the last resort, however, Germany needed a compliant Norway more than the Allies, and if the latter threatened the status quo, it was always likely that Germany would intervene to safeguard her vital interests. Both sides also had to take account of the probable attitudes of Sweden and Russia to any intervention in Norway. Would it be possible to decouple Sweden from Norway if Norwegian neutrality was infringed? What would be the reaction of Stalin? In addition, the Allies had to consider the reaction of other neutrals, particularly America. It was a tangled web of interacting relationships which provided the material for interminable discussion of the Scandinavian 'problem' on both sides of the North Sea.

The Scandinavian Government's attitude towards both belligerents who so obviously threatened their peace and continued prosperity was understandable. Individually or collectively they were helpless against any determined move by either Germany or Russia to violate their territory. They had failed before the war not only to maintain their own defences, but also to establish an effective means of mutual support and co-operation. Any lingering hope that Germany and Russia would deter each other from attacking the Scandinavian countries seemed to have disappeared with the Russo-German Non-Aggression Pact of August 1939. On the other hand, they had reason to expect that the liberal traditions of Britain and France would preclude their instigating any form of military action against the interests of a neutral and democratic country. After all, democracies pledged to fight tyrannical dictatorships which paid no heed to the rights of their weaker neighbours could hardly themselves adopt the same ruthless approach. In the event they were proved right, but not before much agonised debate by the Allies. In the circumstances prevailing in 1939, the Scandinavian countries had no alternative but to avoid unduly antagonising both Germany and Russia even though the political sympathies of their governments and people lay preponderantly, but not exclusively, with the Allies. To put it more succinctly, if with less finesse, they were more afraid of Germany and Russia than they were of Britain and France.

The Machinery of Government

Many of the strategic and military decisions, and perhaps more accurately the absence of such decisions, in the lead-up to and during the Norwegian campaign have been widely criticised in later years, and it may be helpful therefore to briefly describe the machinery of political and military decision making in 1939-40.

Britain and France, mindful of the failures of co-operation in 1914-18, had given much thought immediately before the outbreak of war to securing effective political co-ordination between their two Governments. Likewise, their respective armed services had held staff discussions on mutual assistance and co-operation. The British Prime Minister, Neville Chamberlain, and his counterpart in France, the President of the Council, M Edouard Daladier, had agreed in the summer of 1939 that there was to be a Supreme War Council consisting of themselves and one other Minister on each side, supported by Permanent Military Representatives to provide technical advice. The Council had no executive authority, this was reserved for the individual Governments, but it served as a valuable forum for the discussion of an overall strategic policy for the Allies until the fall of France in June 1940. If it was less than totally satisfactory, it was because the two Prime Ministers were sometimes less resolute within their own cabinets than they had been in joint session. Liaison missions were also established between the three armed services of the two countries.

In Great Britain, the War Cabinet which took over the responsibilities of the Committee of Imperial Defence in September 1939 was the main decision making body of government. In addition to the Prime Minister, it consisted of eight senior Ministers including the Minister for the Co-ordination of-Defence, Admiral of the Fleet Lord Chatfield, and the three Service Ministers, of which the most able, experienced and outspoken was Mr Churchill at the Admiralty. The War Cabinet made all the major political and strategic decisions on the conduct of the war, but strategic planning and the progress of operations was considered in more detail by the Military Co-ordination Committee, chaired by Lord Chatfield until his resignation on the 3rd April 1940, and consisting of the three Service Ministers supported by the three Chiefs of Staff. The Chiefs of Staff Committee was made-up in 1939 of Air Chief Marshal Sir Cyril Newall, Chief of the Air Staff (CAS), Admiral Sir Dudley Pound, First Sea Lord and General Sir Edmund Ironside, Chief of the Imperial General Staff (CIGS). The Chiefs of Staff Committee at this stage of the war was not an entirely harmonious group which reduced their collective influence. The Army and the RAF quarrelled acrimoniously over the employment and control of air power in support of ground operations and the First Sea Lord showed little interest in other than naval matters.

The Chiefs of Staff often attended the War Cabinet and it was their normal practice to meet every morning at 1030 prior to the Cabinet meeting at 1130. Although in theory orders for each Service emanated from its own Department, the Chiefs of Staff Committee increasingly became an executive body as the war progressed, sending orders directly to commanders in the field. Conversely, single Service Departments sometimes issued orders on matters which affected all three Services without any consultation between them. The chain of command was also complicated by the fact that some Commanders-in-Chief were appointed directly by the War Cabinet. For example, CinC British Expeditionary Force, General Lord Gort (who had previously been CIGS), when ordered by the Army Council to withdraw the 5th Division from the line in France for service in Scandinavia haughtily replied that he had been appointed by the War Cabinet and could not recognise the authority of the Army Council.[2] Even within a single Service, the chain of command could be surprisingly obscure. The Admiralty frequently ignored the normal chain of command in ordering individual operations at sea, much to the confusion of the CinC Home Fleet and his subordinate commanders, and the latter were not immune to bypassing levels of command themselves. Joint Service Commands were almost regarded as heresy even though forward thinking minds like General Montgomery had espoused the concept in 1938 (provided of course that he was the joint commander).[3]

There were two more inter-Service bodies: the Joint Planning and the Joint Intelligence Sub-Committees which were staffed by officers of each Service holding executive posts within their own Service Departments. All these bodies were served by a single secretariat which was intended to avoid duplication and misunderstandings between the various committees it served. As we shall see, this worthy aim was not often achieved in practice.

The machinery of government and the chain of Service command was thus far from well defined, let alone well oiled, in those early days of the war. Changes were made and the machinery developed even as the war in Norway progressed, but not before a number of unfortunate, if not deplorable, misunderstandings had occurred which were to have a decisive impact on the conduct of the campaign.

Considering the Options

The importance of a friendly Norway was well recognised in Britain even before the war started. In August 1939, the Chiefs of Staff at the behest of the Foreign Secretary, Lord Halifax, had prepared an appreciation of the attitude Britain should adopt towards Norway in the event of a German attack on that country.[4] Some of the assumptions which clouded subsequent Allied thinking and strategy were already apparent in this report. The Chiefs of Staff concluded that Germany's interest lay in maintaining a neutral Norway unless the latter adopted such a sympathetic attitude towards the Allies that the iron ore supplies were threatened. The report also 'dismissed as impracticable' the possibility of German amphibious operations against Norway's western seaboard, a miscalculation of critical importance which had equally misled the Norwegians as well. More accurately, the Allies inability to prevent air attack on southern Norway was recognised at this early stage and it was concluded that only a naval response was feasible against German intervention in Scandinavia. Although a secret intimation of support for Norway in the event of German aggression was sent to Oslo, it did not, predictably, elicit a Norwegian response.

Mr Churchill was well aware of the importance of the northern flank from the moment he re-entered the Admiralty on 3 September 1939. Just three days after the outbreak of war he had discussed with Admiral Pound the possibility of a naval foray into the Baltic to dominate the sea routes between Germany and Scandinavia. By the 12 September he had drafted an outline plan which was given the codename 'Catherine'. Led by two or three 15-inch gun battleships to deal with the only two German ships of comparable power, the *Scharnhorst* and the *Gneisenau*, the task force would remain in the Baltic for up to three months. Churchill optimistically hoped that this would persuade Norway, Sweden and Denmark to enter the war on the Allies side and would overawe the Russians. The operation was timed for March 1940 when the pack ice cleared in the Baltic. 'Catherine', however, was a rather longer term project. Was there any other action the Allies could take more quickly to restrain the transhipment of iron ore to Germany?

There were three main options open to the Allies. Two were restricted to naval action alone, but the third was more far reaching. The naval options were either to mine the Leads in convenient locations to force merchant shipping into the open seas where they could be subjected to contraband control, or to send surface ships into Norwegian territorial waters for the same purpose. The latter was considered to be a more selective option and therefore politically less damaging. The more radical alternative was to obtain effective control of the port of Narvik and/or the iron ore workings themselves, either by economic or military means.

Throughout the next seven months, the debate ranged widely over the subject in the Supreme War Council, the War Cabinet, the Chiefs of Staff Committee and other government departments, particularly the Ministry of Economic Warfare. The French, in an attempt to deflect German interest away from the Low Countries and France tended to adopt a more aggressive stance, but the British usually wavered, more aware of the potential damaging effect on neutral opinion, particularly in America. By the time a decision on positive action was taken in March 1940, the importance of Narvik as an ice-free port had disappeared for the summer, and the German invasion force for Norway was almost ready to sail.

Mr Churchill, the most restless spirit in the Cabinet during these months of the 'phoney' war, first raised the issue of the iron ore on 19 September 1939. Although his Cabinet colleagues at this stage were still very wary of violating neutral rights, he directed the Admiralty to prepare a plan for the mining of the Leads which could be activated, with Cabinet approval, when the War Trade Agreements with Norway and Sweden had been completed. On 29 September he presented a more detailed memorandum on the subject to the War Cabinet, but the transhipment of ore from Narvik to Germany had all but ceased throughout September because of the reluctance of the merchant ship's crews to put to sea under war conditions. This was sufficient excuse for the Cabinet to delay making any decision, and it was not until the end of November that they formally directed that the military and economic aspects of closing the iron ore route from Narvik should be examined in conjunction with the wider issue of laying a continuous mine barrage from the Orkneys to the Norwegian coast south of Bergen. However, almost immediately, the unexpected invasion of Finland by Russia on 30 November added a new dimension to the discussion.

A New Tyrant – Stalin Strikes at Finland

The Russo-Finnish problem had been simmering since the 5 October when the Finnish Minister in Moscow was informed that 'owing to changes brought about by war, certain political questions needed to be resolved between their two countries'.[5] In the light of Russia's blatant aggression against Poland a month previously and her swallowing of Lithuania, Latvia and Estonia, the probable outcome of such talks could be readily perceived, not only in Helsinki, but also in Paris and London. The Russian demands were the cession of territory in the Karelian Isthmus, certain islands in the Gulf of Finland and the Finnish parts of the Kola peninsular, as well as other concessions and demilitarisation of the frontier. In return Russia would cede territory of no strategic value to Finland. Almost alone in the War Cabinet, Mr Churchill argued that Russian bases in the Gulf of Bothnia should be encouraged: they posed no threat to Britain, only to Germany. In the meantime, planning for 'Catherine' was forging ahead and could be implemented, with Cabinet approval, after 31 March 1940.

The Finns went some way to meet the Russian demands in talks which continued throughout October and November. But there were inevitable sticking points, and a carefully engineered border incident on 26 November led to Russia renouncing the Russo-Finnish Non-Aggression Treaty of 1932 and the breaking-off of diplomatic relations three days later. On the 30 November Russian troops and aircraft attacked across the border: it was yet another example of brutal expansionism. Neither the Finns nor the British Chiefs of Staff had expected the Russians to invade during the winter months, and in the first few weeks of the campaign the Russians themselves had good reason to question the wisdom of their precipitate action.

There was widespread international sympathy for the Finnish cause and indignation that Russia had again followed the example of Germany and perpetrated a ruthless and unprovoked violation of a weaker neighbour's territory. But as in the case of Czechoslovakia and Poland, there was little direct assistance that the Allies could immediately provide in such a distant and remote country. However, the invasion rekindled interest in Scandinavia within the War Cabinet and encouraged them to consider the more radical option of cutting off the supply of Swedish iron ore to Germany at source whilst at the same time providing support for Finland. These two objectives were to become inextricably entangled in the ensuing months. The sinking of two British and one Greek ship in Norwegian territorial waters in early December gave further impetus to the gradual swing in Cabinet opinion in favour of more positive action in North Norway.

On 16 December, Mr Churchill made a further attempt to persuade the Cabinet to curtail the supply of Swedish ore to Germany by mining the Leads and by other undefined methods at Lulea and Oxelösund. In fact, his undeclared intention was that a minefield should be laid by submarines in the Gulf of Bothnia. He considered the likely Norwegian and German responses to such action and concluded that Britain would have more to gain than lose by a German attack on Norway or Sweden. He had already decided that given the prevarication of his Cabinet colleagues, provoking a German intervention in Norway was the best means of persuading them to action.

Mr Churchill concluded his memorandum by a masterly review, which is worth quoting in full, of the moral aspect of infringing another country's neutrality which had so vexed the Cabinet over the last three months.

> The effect of our action against Norway upon world opinion and upon our own reputation must be considered. We have taken up arms in accordance with the principles of the Covenant of the League in order to aid the victims of German aggression. No technical infringement of International Law, so long as it is unaccompanied by inhumanity of any kind, can deprive us of the good wishes of neutral countries. No evil effect will be produced upon the greatest of all neutrals, the United States. We have reason to believe that they will handle the matter in the way most calculated to help us. And they are very resourceful.
>
> The final tribunal is our own conscience. We are fighting to re-establish the reign of law and to protect the liberties of small countries. Our defeat would mean an age of barbaric

violence, and would be fatal not only to ourselves but to the independent life of every small country in Europe. Acting in the name of the Covenant, and as virtual mandatories of the League and all it stands for, we have a right, and indeed are bound in duty, to abrogate for a space some of the conventions of the very laws we seek to consolidate and reaffirm. Small nations must not tie our hands when we are fighting for their rights and freedom. The letter of the law must not in supreme emergency obstruct those who are charged with its protection and enforcement. It would not be right or rational that the Aggressor Power should gain one set of advantages by tearing up all laws, and another set by sheltering behind the innate respect for law of its opponents. Humanity, rather than legality, must be our guide.

Of all this history must be the judge. We now face events.[6]

Although the War Cabinet had this paper on the 18 December, no action was taken pending a meeting of the Supreme War Council which had been convened in Paris for 19 December especially to review the Scandinavian problem. At this meeting, rather like a rabbit out of a hat, M. Daladier produced a paper written before the war for Hitler by the German industrialist Fritz Thyssen stressing the importance of iron ore to the German war effort and even going so far as to suggest that the war would be won by the country which secured control of the Swedish ore. This paper does not appear to have been subjected to critical examination, but it nevertheless made a deep impression on the attitudes of both the French and British Governments. The French also proposed in the Supreme War Council that a joint note be sent to Norway and Sweden pledging Allied support against aggression from either Russia or Germany.

The War Cabinet met again on 22 December to consider Churchill's *tour de force* of the 18th along with the French memorandum produced at the Paris meeting and the Chiefs of Staff report requested on 30 November. As was not unusual under the conciliatory regime of Lord Halifax, the Foreign Office poured a douche of cold water on Churchill's impassioned plea for action, and the Cabinet could not be persuaded either to take any naval action against the iron ore traffic or to provide direct support for Finland. Instead they agreed to send to the Scandinavian countries a note drafted by the French pledging that the Allies would protect their independence and integrity if they in turn provided direct assistance to the Finns. In effect, Norway and Sweden were being invited to declare war on Russia under the protection of an Allied umbrella. In the light of Czechoslovakia and Poland, they could hardly be expected to view this paper guarantee with enthusiasm. In addition, the Chiefs of Staff were instructed to examine further the available options for British intervention and to set in hand the planning of various contingency measures. Words rather than action were still very much the order of the day, but as time passed they possessed less and less credibility.

In the meantime, quantities of war materials, including precious fighters and bombers which could hardly be spared from the Home Front, were authorised for despatch to Finland. Fortunately, access to Finland was so difficult that very little equipment was lost into this bottomless drain.

The Interminable Discussion

Two possible objectives had now emerged from the War Cabinet deliberations during their meetings in December. The lesser plan was that which had first been broached by Churchill on 19 September, that is to take some form of naval action to interrupt the carriage of iron ore from Narvik. This was a straightforward objective which would not have directly involved Sweden or Russia, and whilst it would antagonise Norway and Germany, it could have been easily reversed if political or military considerations made this expedient.

The wider plan was the provision of direct military support to Finland which would of necessity have to be routed through Norway and Sweden. Thus far this proposal had a basis of international respectability under Article XVI of the Covenant of the League of Nations, but that hardly extended to the real motivation of the plan which was to take advantage of the right of passage to seize control of either the ore workings themselves and/or Narvik, the port of exit. It was really a rather naive plot in that it was hardly one that Norway or Sweden would welcome, but it was nevertheless pursued with varying degrees of enthusiasm until the fall of Finland over two months later. It would certainly precipitate direct confrontation with Russia and Germany and risk alienating Sweden and Norway, possibly even to the extent of driving them into the German camp.

This wider objective therefore had far reaching implications and could not be easily reversed without a major loss of face. It is thus not surprising that the War Cabinet continued to tread warily. In preferring the wider plan for which they hoped to obtain the support of both Norway and Sweden, they neglected to pursue the relatively simple, but nevertheless important immediate objective of denying the iron ore to Germany. The year therefore drifted to a close in a mood of hesitancy and indecision. Most members of the War Cabinet were now in favour of doing something in Scandinavia, collectively they had authorised nothing.

Mr Churchill returned to the charge in a note to the War Cabinet on 29 December.[7] He proposed a five point timetable of action: an immediate promise of support for Norway and Sweden followed on 1 January by notification to Norway of our intention to retaliate for the German sinkings in Norwegian territorial waters. These would be followed on 3 January by the departure of naval flotillas for the Norwegian coast, which on the following day would begin arresting German ships in territorial waters. Finally, at the end of the month at the latest, measures should be taken against the iron ore transit facilities at Oxelösund. The War Cabinet again found no difficulty in resisting this call for action.

The Chiefs of Staff reported to the War Cabinet again on 2 January 1940. The proponents of a land expedition, ostensibly to help the Finns but in reality to obtain control of the ore fields, were now gaining ground over those who favoured a naval action against shipping in the Leads. But this proposal still required the co-operation of both Sweden and Norway, and there were no good grounds for believing that this would be forthcoming from Governments still determined to cling to neutrality at all costs. For a while, even the Admiralty's preference for mining the Leads was subordinated lest it should prejudice the wider objective. The First Lord himself was less sanguine:

But is there any prospect of Sweden and Norway actively co-operating with us of their own free will to bring about a series of operations which, as is well set out in the paper, will –

(a) Ruin the trade of their iron field and the shipping which carries it.

(b) Involve them in war with Germany.

(c) Expose the whole southern part of both countries to German invasion and occupation.

Left to themselves they will certainly refuse, and, if pressed diplomatically, they will protest loudly to the world. Thus the minor operation is knocked out for the sake of the bigger, and the bigger is only declared practicable upon conditions which will not occur.[8]

German counter-action to an Allied intervention in Scandinavia was now the Prime Minister's professed area of concern. Occupation by the Luftwaffe of airfields in southern Norway would, he claimed, open-up a whole new avenue of approach for air attacks on Britain which the RAF at this stage of the war would be hard pressed to counter. Whilst true, one inevitably gains the impression that Chamberlain, at heart, was reluctant to commit Britain to a Scandinavian adventure. The discussion rambled on, Ministers and their advisors even contradicting themselves as they wrestled with a problem, the political and military interactions of which seemed intractable. Inevitably no decision was reached.

On 3 January the War Cabinet rehearsed the same arguments at even greater length. Opinion continued to move in favour of more positive action, but only if the Norwegian response was favourable. The concensus was that the Germans would be unlikely to invade Norway, at least during the winter months, but the Cabinet nevertheless set in train planning for the occupation of Trondheim, Bergen and Stavanger to forestall German retaliation if this should materialise.

A more forthright message to Norway, with a complimentary copy to Sweden, was delivered on 6 January. This stated that as a result of the action of German naval forces in Norwegian territorial waters, it was the British Government's intention to prevent by naval action the passage of German ships and trade within those waters. The Swedish response to an earlier Anglo-French message at the end of December had already been received on 4 January and was not encouraging. But the Norwegian response to the latest message was unexpectedly robust, stating that alleged infractions of neutrality by one belligerent were no excuse for another belligerent to perpetrate the same acts, and accused Britain of wishing to drag Norway into the war. The latter was of course palpably correct, but nonetheless unwelcome in London for all that. Although slightly less strenuously, Sweden supported the Norwegian view, but suggested that if the British still intended to go ahead, they should do so without publicity or prior announcements. This was sound advice, for the Allied drum beating was stirring up emotions in Scandinavia and neutral countries as well as alerting the Germans to their intentions.

Over the next few days, with Mr Churchill the main dissenting voice, the War Cabinet slowly talked itself out of any positive action in Scandinavia. The naval plan was dropped because it would prejudice the wider objective, which itself was not proceeded with because the essential acquiesence of the Scandinavian countries was not forthcoming.

Mr Churchill's impatience with the vacillations of the Government boiled over in a letter to the Foreign Secretary on 13 January:

My disquiet at the decision taken [to take no action in Scandinavia] was due mainly to the awful difficulties which our machinery of war-conduct presents to positive action. I see such immense walls of prevention, all built or building, that I wonder whether any plan will have a chance of climbing over them.

Just look at the arguments which have had to be surmounted in the seven weeks we have discussed this Narvik operation.

First, the objections of the other Economic Departments, Supply, Board of Trade, etc. Secondly the Joint Planning Committee. Thirdly, the Chiefs of Staff Committee. Fourthly, the insidious argument, 'don't spoil the big plan for the sake of the small', when there is really very little chance of the big plan being resolutely attempted. Fifthly, the juridicial and moral objections, all gradually worn down. Sixthly, the attitude of neutrals, and above all, the United States. But see how well the United States have responded to your démarche. Seventhly, the Cabinet itself, with its many angles of criticism. Eighthly, when all this has been smoothed out, the French have to be consulted. Finally, the Dominions and their consciences have to be squared, they not having gone through the process by which opinion has advanced at home.

All this makes me feel that under the present arrangements we shall be reduced to waiting upon the terrible attacks of the enemy, against which it is impossible to prepare in every quarter simultaneously without fatal dissipation of strength.[9]

Waging war in a democracy was indeed a tedious business.

By 17 January, Mr Churchill was proposing that Britain should mount an expedition to take control of the ore fields even against Norwegian and Swedish opposition, but he was a lone voice. As ever, the Foreign Office believed, or professed to believe, that the exertion of diplomatic pressure, particularly on Sweden, would eventually persuade the Scandinavian countries to the British way of thinking. But it was a futile exercise, the Scandinavian Governments were far more afraid of Germany than of Britain, except in so far as Britain could drag them into a war they so desperately wished to avoid. Whilst there was any prospect of walking the tightrope of neutrality, they would do nothing to antagonise the Reich.

Their ingenuity in maintining this posture can be seen clearly, for example, in a speech by the Norwegian Foreign Minister, M Koht, on 19 January in which he said:

When a ship is blown up and the crew are killed, we have no proof left of who is responsible, and we cannot address our complaints to any one Government; we can only blame the war itself.[10]

As those so far destroyed in the Leads were British or belonged to nations friendly to Britain, this was, to say the least, a somewhat ingenuous explanation.

It is easy to disparage the weakness of the Scandinavian Governments in the light of subsequent events – after all the British prediction that they would fall under the Fuehrer's thumb if they rejected Allied support proved only too correct, at least in the case of Norway, within a matter of months. But the Scandinavians simply did not believe that the Allies could act in sufficient time and with adequate force to forestall the German retaliation which their intervention would provoke. Events were to prove that this prediction was equally valid. Nevertheless, it was determined at the end of January that the best way of influencing the Scandinavians would be to demonstrably prepare such a force to convince them of both the Allies will and ability to act.

Finland meanwhile, was surviving remarkably well. The Russians had attacked at six points on Finland's 1000 mile eastern frontier, but the main thrust had been mounted against the Mannerheim line at the northern end of the Karelian Isthmus just to the north of Leningrad. Only the attack against Petsamo in the far north had made satisfactory headway, and those directed against the eastern border had proved disastrous. The Finns simply retired slowly in the deeply wooded, snow bound country, and then fell furiously on the Russian lines of communication with startling success. Twelve Russian divisions were hurled against the Mannerheim line, but frontal assaults were also thrown back with heavy losses.

The rest of the world rejoiced at the Finn's success and knowingly confided that the heart of the Russian Army had been destroyed by Stalin's purge of its officer core in the 1930s. Many believed, as Churchill wrote, 'it indicated that the inherent rottenness and degradation of their system of Government and society was now proved'.[11] Hitler, too, had noted the apparent Russian weakness, and it doubtless influenced his decision to turn against his erstwhile ally eighteen months later. Finland stood firm throughout January, but more percipient minds were not misled by this apparent Russian weakness. It was inevitable eventually, certainly as soon as the weather and ground conditions improved, that the overwhelming Russian might would prevail unless direct support as well as material aid was provided to the brave, but increasingly hard pressed Finns.

Hesitantly Forward – The Army Prepares for Action

The Chiefs of Staff reported to the War Cabinet on 28 January on the scale of resources that would be needed to install an effective force in Norway and to mount operations into Sweden. It is notable that their report no longer made reference to aid for Finland, the real reason for the intervention, the suppression of the iron ore flow to Germany, was now fully exposed. The plan proposed a landing at Narvik and the securing of Trondheim, Namsos and Bergen before launching a force towards the Swedish Baltic coast. The French, more idealistic than their allies, were still anxious to help the Finns, and proposed a landing at Petsamo, an idea never embraced with any enthusiasm by the more pragmatic British.

In addition to troop transports, the force requirements included up to forty escort destroyers, an Anglo-French force of 100,000 men (five divisions and two brigades), three fighter squadrons, one and a half army co-operation and two bomber squadrons. The support of four bomber squadrons operating from British bases would also be necessary. The operation had to be mounted by 20 March in order to forestall the re-opening of Lulea and assumed the co-operation of the Scandinavian countries. Even so, the Chief of the Air Staff expressed concern, as well he might, on the size of the opposing German air forces, now estimated to contain 1300 bombers capable of penetrating into Norway as far north as Trondheim.

The War Cabinet accepted the Chiefs of Staff report, but for presentational reasons allied it to intervention in Finland even though all eyes were now focusing on solving the iron ore problem which had become something of a running sore within the

Cabinet. The plan was discussed at a Supreme War Council in Paris on 5 February and the French gave qualified support, agreeing at least for the time being to drop their Petsamo proposal which the British regarded as politically and militarily impracticable.

But the problem remained as ever – how to obtain the support of the Scandinavians? A scheme was hatched for Finland to make a public appeal for Allied assistance which it was hoped would be sufficient to quell the continuing opposition of Norway and Sweden to foreign troops passing through their territory. In other words, to shame them into acquiesing to the plan lest they attract the blame for Finland's defeat. It is difficult to understand how the Allied Governments, against all the evidence, could still persuade themselves that such agreement would ever be forthcoming unless Norway or Sweden was attacked directly. Indeed, it is doubtful if the French ever really did subscribe to such a transparent plot. Nevertheless, it brought an air of unreality to the whole planning process: whatever sympathy Norway and Sweden had for the Finns, it did not extend to the inevitability of embroiling themselves in a war they were so anxious to avoid. The writing had been on the wall as early as December in the League of Nations when they refused to support either sanctions against the Russians or action to expel them from the League.

But on 5 February, after two months of indecision and vacillation, the two Governments at last directed their military chiefs to formulate detailed plans for a landing in Norway by the third week in March. The delicate problem of securing diplomatic agreement from Norway and Sweden would meanwhile be postponed until the planning was complete.

Deliberations within the War Cabinet continued during the first three weeks of February with an optimism which in retrospect borders on fantasy. The attitude of the Swedes and Norwegians was hardening almost daily as details of the Allies' intentions were leaked in the Scandinavian press. The consequences of such open discussion on German planning and intentions does not appear to have been considered within Britain, except perhaps by Mr Churchill and some of his closest colleagues who by now realised that the deadlock could be broken only by provoking Germany to invade Scandinavia, thus giving the Allies the excuse they needed to intervene themselves. Another aspect which received scant attention at this time was the danger of frittering away forces on the flanks of Europe which might well be required for a decisive struggle on the Western Front within a matter of weeks when the weather would be suitable for a grand offensive.

The suitability of the troops themselves for the operations envisaged was also largely ignored. Whilst the French had their Chasseurs Alpins who were trained in winter warfare, it was estimated that in Britain less than 400 soldiers were able to use skis. The formation of the 5th Battalion of the Scots Guards as a specialist winter warfare unit is a good example of the almost Gilbertian absurdity of some of the British military planning at this time.

In January 1940, volunteers who could ski were asked to join a new battalion that was to be formed at Bordon in Hampshire. Unfortunately, skiing was an expensive and exclusive sport in 1940, and by the nature of the composition of the British Army at that time, most of those who could ski were officers. The majority of the volunteers who arrived at Bordon during the first week of February to join the newly formed 5th Battalion of the Scots Guards were therefore officers, over 700 of them. But the battalion required only 19 officers, and so the commanding officer, Lieutenant Colonel J. S. Coats MC, himself a notable skier, having selected his officers, asked all the other officer volunteers to temporarily relinquish their commissions and serve as NCOs and Guardsmen. This rapidly diminished the enthusiam of the majority of those who had come forward, but even so 173 officers accepted this unprecedented offer, including many such as David Stirling and F. Spencer-Chapman who were later to make their mark in Special Forces. There were also about 180 civilian volunteers who could ski but had no military training, and 72 officer cadets, most of whom had some skiing and a little military experience. The Battalion complement was made up by a regular Scots Guard Company of experienced soldiers, but none of whom had skiied before.[12] This bizarre Battalion therefore consisted of a mix of officers demoted to private soldiers, civilians who could ski pretending to be soldiers, and real soldiers with no skiing experience whatsoever.

They had been given less than a month to prepare themselves for action, and although they had not been told where they were going, Finland seemed a pretty good bet. At first it appeared that the gamblers had lost their money as the Battalion headed south, but their destination proved to be Chamonix in France where it was intended they should hone-up their skiing expertise, or in the case of the regular company, to learn to ski from scratch. They had just a week of this rather acceptable diversion under the tutelage of the Chasseurs Alpins before they were recalled to England whence they travelled north immediately to Scotland and embarked on the Polish ship Batory.

Very little attention had been given to the logistic support of this hastily formed unit, and it was therefore their great good fortune that it was by now 15 March and the Finnish war was over. The 5th Battalion of the Scots Guards was therefore disbanded without ever seeing action. It is very unlikely that this eccentric formation would have made any significant contribution to the Finnish cause; and in the process, a substantial number of promising young officers who before long would be so badly needed elsewhere might have perished.

Nevertheless, the idea was basically sound. Troops experienced in winter warfare were to be sorely needed in Norway within little more than a month. But it would have been far more sensible to have taken regular, or even territorial battalions, and sent them to Scotland to train and acclimatise themselves, not only on skis, but on snowshoes which would have been almost as valuable and much easier to use. Whilst it is easy to ridicule the embryo Guards mountain battalion; it is more sobering to note that the training of the other units destined for Norway almost totally failed to recognise at all that much of the country lay under a thick carpet of snow until well into May.

To return, however, to the interminable deliberations of the Allied Governments in February 1940. The continuing intransigence of the Scandinavians led to the suggestion that in addition to, or if necessary instead of the main operation, small bodies of unarmed volunteers could be filtered through Norway and into Finland. But it was estimated that 30 to 40 thousand ski-trained reinforcements would be needed by the Spring if the Finns were to have a realistic chance of holding the Russian offensive which had recommenced against the Mannerheim line on 2 February. Quite apart from the likely reaction of the Scandinavians, the fact that Britain only had a handful of skiers in the entire Army should have squashed this proposal immediately. In the fantasy atmosphere of early 1940, such practical difficulties in no way inhibited the endless debate.

Sweden was by now fully reconciled to Finland being sacrificed to bring peace to Scandinavia. The Government recognised quite clearly that the Allies' offer of support in the event of a German attack, even if well meant, was spurious. The German Army would always win a race for Scandinavia, and the Luftwaffe could devastate Swedish cities almost without hindrance. Unappealing though it might seem in London and Paris, the Swedish and Norwegian attitude in early 1940 was always more realistic than that of Britain and France. Their only hope was to dampen down the fires, not to feed the flames. Increasing recognition that her army might not be able to hold out beyond the Spring had even led to Finland toning down her pleas for assistance for fear of exciting the Germans.

When the Chiefs of Staff reiterated therefore on the 18 February that the mounting of the expedition was impracticable without Norwegian and Swedish compliance, one would have expected that any sensible and pragmatic government would have breathed a sigh of relief and decided to forget the whole risky operation. But fate, in the shape of the *Altmark*, was sufficient to stoke up the fires which the Scandinavian governments had been so anxious to contain.

Operation Wilfred – A Day Too Late

The Navy's Here

The *Altmark* incident on the 16 February provided a good example of the equivocal attitude adopted by Norway in a desperate attempt to cling to the tightrope of neutrality. In fact, Norway managed to antagonise both sides and the *Altmark* affair more than any other single event precipitated the disastrous chain of events which plunged the country into war.

Information had been received in London that the German auxiliary naval vessel the *Altmark* was returning to Germany carrying some 300 prisoners of war, victims of the German pocket battleship *Graf Spee's* raiding in the South Atlantic. The *Altmark* arrived off Trondheim on 14 February, and with her guns stowed below, was identified to the Norwegians as a tanker. Her master, Captain Dau, elected to proceed towards Germany through the Leads, and thus in international law the prisoners of war she carried were entitled to release whilst in neutral waters. The Norwegians were later to claim that they had inspected the *Altmark* and pronounced that she was unarmed and not carrying prisoners, but if they really believed she was as innocent as she seemed, it is difficult to understand why she was given an escort of two motor torpedo boats on her passage south to Germany.

Captain Philip Vian[1] leading the 4th Destroyer Flotilla in the *Cossack* was instructed to intercept the *Altmark*, if necessary, in neutral waters. Despite many false trails, the cruiser *Arethusa* eventually spotted the *Altmark* in company with the Norwegian torpedo boats *Kjell* and *Skarv*. Screened by the torpedo boats which maneouvred alongside to prevent boarding, the *Altmark* took refuge in the Jössing Fiord near Stavanger whilst the Norwegians took station in the entrance. By now the *Cossack* had arrived on the scene and Captain Vian demanded the right to search the *Altmark*. The senior Norwegian captain refused on the grounds that the ship had been searched three times and no prisoners found, and that she had been given permission to proceed within territorial waters.

Conscious of the sensitivity of acting within territorial waters, Vian withdrew his Flotilla to seek further guidance from the Admiralty. Mr Churchill now intervened directly, signalling Vian:

Unless Norwegian torpedo boat undertakes to convoy *Altmark* to Bergen with a joint Anglo-Norwegian guard on board and a joint escort, you should board *Altmark*, liberate the prisoners and take possession of ship pending further instructions. If Norwegian torpedo boat interferes, you should warn her to stand off. If she fires upon you, you should not reply unless attack is serious, in which case you should defend yourself using no more force than is necessary and cease fire when she desists. Suggest to Norwegian destroyer that honour is satisfied by submitting to superior force.[2]

Nothing could have been clearer, and Vian re-entered the Jössing Fiord to complete the task. After a token show of obduracy, the Norwegians withdrew and the *Cossack* approached the *Altmark* at the head of the fiord. The latter had meanwhile got under way and attempted to ram the *Cossack*, but in so doing merely ran herself aground: a fate which was to befall the *Cossack* as well less than two months later at Narvik. Boarding the *Altmark*, a brief fight ensued in which six Germans were killed, the rest escaping across the ice to the shore. Lieutenant Turner, leading the boarding party, searched the ship, shouting down into the holds 'Any British down there?' A unanimous response led to the oft repeated rejoinder: 'Come on up then, the Navy's here'.[3]

The 299 prisoners were soon on board the *Cossack* and heading for Leith, much to the relief of the Admiralty who would have been acutely embarrassed if the original report had been wrong. The day was completed in fine style when two destroyers of the 4th Flotilla intercepted a German iron ore carrier which promptly scuttled herself. The British public was delighted when they heard of the *Cossack*'s feat: good news was rather scarce in the early months of 1940. Neutral opinion was generally sympathetic.

Predictably, the Norwegian Government delivered a strong diplomatic protest regarding the violation of their territorial waters. But they could not make too much of the incident: in truth, they had been made to look rather foolish, and for them the war had moved one step nearer. In Germany, it proved decisive in deciding Hitler to proceed with the invasion of Norway. The *Altmark* incident clearly indicated either gross ineptitude by the Norwegian authorities, or more probably was another example of their overriding fear of upsetting the German dictator.

Whatever the reason, the Admiralty did not miss the opportunity of raising once again the question of mining the Leads. Mr Churchill strongly pressed this course of action at the War Cabinet on 18 February, arguing that the force of minelayers could be despatched in five days and that it would not prejudice the larger operation which was being planned. But the latter point was clearly untrue, and the Cabinet still prevaricated, the fear of antagonising neutral opinion, particularly in America, was now very much to the fore. And although they recognised that the transhipment of iron ore from Narvik had recommenced, there were only two more months before the re-opening of Lulea would remove the main reason for the operation. Nevertheless, on the following day, the Cabinet gave Mr Churchill the authority to make the necessary preparations to lay a minefield. At the First Lord's suggestion, the action was to be codenamed 'Wilfred' because it was 'minor' and 'innocent'.[4]

The Expeditionary Force Assembles

By the end of February, the Expeditionary Force, codenamed 'Stratford', assembled to occupy the southern Norwegian ports of Bergen, Trondheim and Stavanger was ready. But the earliest that troops could be landed in Narvik was 20 March, and it was desirable, although not perhaps essential, that the two landings were co-ordinated. Some material assistance was sent to Finland, but it was well recognised that this in itself could not stave off their capitulation indefinitely, and even though both the French and the British Governments agreed that this would be yet another major political setback for the Allies, the War Cabinet would still not authorise the launching of the land expedition without the agreement of both Norway and Sweden, and the likelihood of that was further away than ever.

The French, who had consistently shown a more aggressive approach than the British to the Scandinavian 'problem', still wanted to mount a land expedition to Narvik, and a reluctant Cabinet authorised preparations to continue. Admiral Sir Edward Evans and Major General P. J. Mackesy were appointed as the commanders of the Narvik expedition and given their objectives. These were somewhat vague: to give aid to Finland and to restrain the export of iron ore to Germany and Russia for as long as possible. But the directive went on to say that the Force should not proceed in the face of serious opposition from Norway or Sweden, although they were not to be deterred by a minor show of resistance. As if this was not sufficiently ambivalent, the directive continued that the expedition was only to use force 'as an ultimate measure of self defence should their forces be in jeopardy'.[5] Fortunately, perhaps, they were not required to walk along this tightrope as the pretext of providing aid to Finland was soon to disappear.

The Finns, who had listened to vague promises since December, were now becoming desperate and on 1 March expressed to Lord Halifax their disappointment at the lack of assistance. They required 50,000 troops and 100 bombers immediately to turn back the tide of increasing Russian pressure. Once again the War Cabinet returned to their interminable discussion of the best course of action. Lord Halifax suggested four options. Firstly, an ultimatum to Norway and Sweden that if permission was withheld the Allies would force their way through; secondly, a strong request for passage backed by the arrival of the expedition in Norwegian waters; thirdly, the passage of unarmed volunteers followed by their arms and ammunition; and finally, just sending the war material to Finland. Churchill, uncharacteristically subdued, favoured the second option, but the Chiefs of Staff warned that the Expeditionary Force had not been prepared for an opposed landing, and that even mild opposition would delay the advance and require additional men. The Chiefs of Staff were not exactly brimming over with enthusiasm for this Scandinavian adventure. It the event, none of Lord Halifax's proposed courses of action was taken up and instead the Norwegian and Swedish Governments were advised that an expedition was being prepared with a request for their active co-operation in its success. Thin words indeed, hardly likely to coerce the Scandinavians or to stir the Finns to renewed endeavour.

Even this mild message to Norway and Sweden was unequivocally rejected by both countries on 4 March, and Finland could not be persuaded to make an open appeal for Allied help unless such passage was assured. The Chiefs of Staff quickly concluded that the Scandinavian operation was impracticable.

By the second week of March, all parties were seeking to set themselves in the best possible light for the inevitable end of the Finnish resistance. On 8 March a Finnish delegation was on its way to Moscow to discuss peace terms. Although at the same time they had made another urgent request for the despatch of 100 bombers to Finland, it was thought in London, probably correctly, that this was intended more to improve their negotiating position in Moscow than a genuine attempt to continue the struggle. The Swedes, seeking to deflect any criticism for their lack of support for Finland, spread the word that the Allies interest in Finland was not altruistic, but was merely a ploy to involve the whole of Scandinavia in the war with Germany for their own economic reasons. This of course was more or less correct. There were even indications that the French were trying to shift the blame to the British for the lack of action by stating that they had 50,000 troops waiting for British ships to transport them to Finland. It is nevertheless true that in the last two weeks M. Daladier had been pressing the British to launch the expedition even without the agreement of Norway and Sweden.

In this second week of March, probably as a result of Churchill's incessant prodding, the Chiefs of Staff revived a limited amount of enthusiasm for gaining a foothold in Norway and proposed landings at Narvik, Trondheim, Bergen and Stavanger. On 12 March, the War Cabinet actually authorised a landing at Narvik which, if successful, would be followed by one at Trondheim. But the Cabinet was well aware of the talks in progress in Moscow between the Finns and the Russians, and it is difficult not to adopt the cynical view that they really expected this decision would be overtaken by events. In the light of so much prevarication, the decision to launch an expedition at this stage appeared to be more of a political gesture than a real operational initiative.

Within the War Cabinet, only Churchill had consistently advocated action in Scandinavia over the six months of the war, and even he would have been content with simply mining the Leads. Although varying degrees of enthusiasm for action had appeared in all quarters from time to time; after all, no member of the Cabinet wanted to be accused of wearing the appeaser's mantle, collectively they manoeuvred successfully to avoid any irreversible commitment. Their suspicion of being drawn into a futile and possibly disastrous adventure was probably well founded, but they tended to conceal such feelings behind a mélange of double speak and indecision.

The Collapse of Finland

Mercifully this whole unhappy saga was brought to a halt, albeit short lived, on 13 March when the Finns signed an armistice agreement with the Russians. Resistance had been heroic and skilful, but their army was at last exhausted and woefully short of officers. Even if assistance had been forthcoming within the final desperate weeks, it is extremely unlikely that the Finns could have held out until it had been effectively deployed. The decision to launch the Expeditionary Force was promptly cancelled, only Mr Churchill resolutely remaining in support of keeping together a force which could intervene in Scandinavia if another opportunity presented itself.

The Allies had spent over three months deliberating their policy towards Scandinavia and achieved nothing. They had made public avowals of support for

Finland which they had not been able to implement, and thus their loss of face when the resistance collapsed was that much greater. They had announced their intentions of stopping the flow of iron ore from Narvik to Germany, but had done nothing about that either for fear of upsetting the Scandinavians whilst there was a possibility of mounting the wider plan. The impression created on other neutrals could not therefore have been worse. It would have been far more logical to have said from the outset that for geographical reasons the Allies could not provide direct assistance to Finland, thus leaving themselves a free hand to stop the Narvik traffic by naval action if they considered it expedient to do so.

It is interesting nevertheless to reflect how close the French and British Governments came in these months to embroiling themselves in a disastrous war with Russia at a time when they could scarcely view with confidence their defences against Germany alone.

Following the Ribbentrop-Molotov agreement of August 1939, the Allies could hardly have maintained a harmonious relationship with the Russians, but there were compelling reasons for not provoking an outright conflict. There were useful trade connections between the countries: Russian timber was important to Britain, and the economic blockade of Germany would become that much more difficult to enforce if Russia and Germany acted more energetically together to circumvent it.

But the main arguments for avoiding war with Russia were political and strategic. The Russo-German agreement was a marriage of convenience which, if left to its own devices, would eventually germinate the seeds of disagreement between allies whose basic ideologies were so vastly divergent. After all, Hitler had made his intentions towards Russia plain enough in the mid twenties when, languishing in jail, he had composed his testament for the future. Speaking of the need for Germany to acquire more territory to house its burgeoning population, he wrote of the need to 'secure for the German people the land and soil to which they are entitled';[6] and later, 'if we speak of soil in Europe today, we can primarily have in mind only Russia and her vassal border states'.[7] Furthermore, Germany could hardly view with equanimity a major Russian intervention in Scandinavia, and Russia's designs on the Baltic states was a direct strategic threat. Russia's primary aim was still seen as world revolution which would be best fostered by allowing Germany, Britain and France to batter each other into military and economic insensibility. In such circumstances, Russia would hardly provide decisive assistance to the Germans which would militate against this objective in the long term.

In the shorter term, however, it would have been madness for the Allies to go to war against the overwhelming might of Russia and Germany combined. Not only would it focus the war on the Western Front, but it would have left the British Empire hopelessly isolated against Russian expansionism in Persia, Iraq and Afghanistan. Apart from taking the high moral ground against unprovoked aggression, there were few advantages for the Allies in 1940 in seeking direct confrontation with Russia. It is therefore not surprising that on 31 October 1939 a report compiled by the Chiefs of Staff Committee in association with the Foreign Office concluded that from a political and military point of view we should avoid war with the USSR.

Nevertheless, anti-Russian feeling ran high, particularly in France. A few pragmatists simply saw intervention in Finland as a means of deflecting German attention from France itself. But the majority of Frenchmen, blissfully blind to their own military weakness, brandished a sword of anti-bolshevik feeling with a fervour that eventually led to the fall of the Government. In Britain the War Cabinet, despite agreeing with the Chiefs of Staff appreciation of 31 October, pressed ahead, if less impetuously, with the planning of operations which could lead only to direct confrontation with Russia. In the end, the Allies were saved from their foolhardy adventures only by the collapse of Finland. Josiah Wedgwood echoed the relief in a speech to the House of Commons:

> It would have been the maddest military adventure upon which this country had ever embarked.[8]

On 19 March, the Prime Minister gave a rather vapid explanation to the House of the Allies failure to act decisively in support of Finland. But in France, where righteous indignation was more spontaneous, M. Daladier and his Cabinet were forced to resign, although Daladier himself retained a powerful voice in M. Reynaud's new Goverment as Minister of Defence.

The Allies were now at a very low ebb. There seemed to be no way they could get to grips with the enemy other than by fighting a defensive war at sea, and the feeling grew that they seemed powerless to prevent the steady collapse of the democracies they had pledged to help. There was talk in France of seeking a compromise peace. The American public was also becoming increasingly isolationist, and following a meeting with Hitler on 18 March, Mussolini was showing ominous signs of joining his fellow dictator in the war before all the spoils had been gobbled up.

In Britain the War Cabinet, so acutely sensitive to public opinion both abroad and at home, had contributed to this general feeling of unease with its continual dithering over what to do in Scandinavia. Reading accounts of the Cabinet deliberations over this period leaves an inescapable impression that the majority were only too relieved to postpone action whenever a suitable excuse presented itself. The Prime Minister who had said at the time of Munich 'I am myself a man of peace to the very depths of my soul' was still having difficulty persuading himself to wage the war in earnest in March 1940.[9]

Action at Last – Operation Wilfred

Both the Foreign Office and the Chiefs of Staff conducted a review of the overall war situation following the Finnish collapse. The general view appeared to be that no significant action on any front was either feasible or desirable. Lord Halifax suggested that it was important for British prestige to 'show the flag' and suggested he visit Turkey, Italy and the Balkans, but that was about the limit of his aggressive intent.

The Chiefs of Staff were also content for Britain to keep a low profile and concentrate on the economic blockade. Their memorandum suggested that, the invasion of Poland apart, Germany had not so far conducted the war very well, and it was in the Allied interest to continue to build up its forces prior to taking the offensive as soon after 1940 as possible. It tended to ignore the fact that Germany was actually enlarging her military strength at a faster rate than the Allies, and concluded, somewhat optimistically as it turned out, that the Allied forces in the field ought to be capable of stopping a German offensive against France.[10]

The advent of a new President of the Council in France, Paul Reynaud, led to a review of the war so far at the sixth meeting of the Supreme War Council on 28 March. The new French Government adopted a more belligerent approach than its predecessor and the frustration apparent in Britain was even reflected in a more positive attitude by Mr Chamberlain. The restriction of iron ore and oil supplies to Germany were still regarded as of paramount importance, and although measures to interrupt the flow of oil do not concern us here, the proposal to stop the flow of Swedish ore became linked to a plan which had been gestating for some time to float fluvial mines down the Rhine in an operation codenamed 'Royal Marine'. French enthusiasm for this project had always been muted because it was feared that Germany would retaliate by bombing French aircraft and munitions factories which were vulnerable to air attack. The British on the other hand were anxious to be seen to be taking some form of direct action against Germany to offset adverse international reaction against measures being proposed which only appeared to harm the interests of neutral countries. Nevertheless, the Supreme War Council agreed that, after a warning to Norway and Sweden to be delivered on the 1 April, minefields would be laid in Norwegian territorial waters on 5 April. Furthermore, plans would be prepared for interrupting the Lulea traffic once that port re-opened. In return, Reynaud accepted 'Royal Marine' subject to agreement by the French Conseil de Guerre.

The War Cabinet endorsed this decision on 29 March, recognising at the same time that German reaction might still provide the opportunity for a landing in Norway itself. Indeed, as the importance to Germany of the Narvik route would shortly disappear as the Baltic ports re-opened, it must be concluded that, in some minds at least, the provoking of Germany to invade Norway was the mainspring of plans to mind the Leads at this stage. That such provocation was not in fact necessary we shall see in the next chapter: German plans to invade Norway were already almost complete at this time. Furthermore, it was about this time that more precise information on the German intentions was reaching Whitehall although this was largely disregarded.

If the Germans invaded Norway or appeared to be on the brink of doing so in retaliation for the mining, an Allied expeditionary force would be ordered to sail on the assumption that in these circumstances their intervention would be welcome. However, the plan contained other assumptions which in the event proved unjustified. The Chiefs of Staff still believed that a prompt reaction could forestall German action against Bergen and Trondheim although the Germans might win the race to Stavanger. The possibility of German action against Narvik was not even countenanced. But the forces prepared under 'Stratford' for the intervention in Scandinavia had been dispersed after the decision of 14 March, and only one brigade for Narvik and a force for Stavanger was now immediately available.

A new plan was therefore hurriedly prepared codenamed 'R4', which was similar in some respects to the January plan, but involving smaller forces as it was now envisaged that the troops would be mainly employed to garrison the major Norwegian ports and airfields. One brigade with one light anti-aircraft battery in support was assigned to Narvik and five battalions with specialist troops earmarked for Bergen and Trondheim and to destroy the airfield at Stavanger. No air support was planned in 'R4' for the troops in Central Norway, an omission which is almost incredible in the light of the previous planning for 'Stratford' and the Chief of the Air Staff's comments at that time on the frailty of the air support. The troops for Narvik were positioned on the Clyde from whence they would be moved forward in transports whilst those for Central Norway were sent to Rosyth for embarkation on cruisers. The expedition to Stavanger could depart on 5 April with the balance of the force leaving as soon thereafter as possible. We shall examine later how, unbelievably, the Home Fleet came to leave port without the troops assigned to it.

The plan to mine the Leads, codenamed 'Operation Wilfred', had been ready for some time, but French reluctance to go through with the plan to lay fluvial mines in the Rhine caused further difficulties. Under the influence of the late President, Daladier, now Minister for National Defence, the French War Committee proposed delaying 'Royal Marine' for three months. Although by now determined on more positive action, Mr Chamberlain directly linked 'Wilfred' to 'Royal Marine' and informed the French that the British would proceed with the former only if the French adhered to the full package. Mr Churchill was despatched to Paris on 4 April to try to remove the deadlock. But as a result of this last minute hitch, warning of the impending action had not been sent to the Scandinavian governments on 1 April as previously agreed. After meeting both Reynaud and Daladier, Churchill quickly realised that the French could not be persuaded and with Cabinet approval, he informed them that as a concession to their wishes the British would nevertheless proceed with the mining of the Leads on 8 April. Predictably, the delayed Allied note was not well received by the Scandinavian governments, indeed the immediate reaction of Christian Gunther, Swedish Foreign Minister, was that 'This brings our countries very close to war'.[11]

As we have seen, the mining of the Leads had now of course become more a political than a practical measure because iron ore traffic from Narvik could be expected to cease within weeks. It was to a certain extent just a reaction to seven months of frustrating inactivity and could have little positive influence on the course of the war, at least until the following winter. Whether it would provoke a German invasion of Norway, as some people hoped, and whether such an event was strategically desirable for the Allied cause as Churchill believed, should have been a matter for serious debate. In fact, very little discussion appears to have taken place within the War Cabinet as to whether a German invasion of Norway was really in the Allied interest, perhaps mainly because the extent of its eventual success was simply not envisaged by the Chiefs of Staff or the War Cabinet at that time.

With the benefit of hindsight of course, such discussion was irrelevant as Hitler had already made a firm decision to invade Norway anyway. Also, as we now know, he was doing this independently of his plan to invade the Low Countries: the French expectation that action in Scandinavia might restrain a German advance in the West was a forlorn hope. In reality, therefore, although not known at the time, the Allied manoeuvring throughout those frenzied months of debate in 1940 was quite meaningless, action by Hitler was to prove the real arbiter of subsequent events. Nevertheless, whether the decision to lay mines in Norwegian territorial waters was a sound strategic move in April 1940 as opposed to September 1939 when its economic effects might have been more significant is at best every doubtful.

'Operation Wilfred' envisaged laying two minefields, one in the Vestfiord to the south west of Narvik and a second off Stadtland north of Bergen where the coastline swings round towards the south. As a deception, it was also planned to simulate the laying of a third field near Molde. The mines in the Vestfiord were to be laid by four heavily modified destroyers of the 20th Flotilla[12] escorted by four more destroyers.[13] Two destroyers were instructed to warn shipping of the non-existent minefield off Molde and the minelayer *Teviot Bank* with an escort of four destroyers of the 3rd Flotilla[14] was entrusted with the Stadtland field. But it could not be expected that the Norwegians would placidly standby and watch the minefields being laid, and it was known that two old but heavily armed coastal defence vessels were at Narvik. Accordingly, the *Renown* with four more destroyers[15] was ordered to support the Vestfiord operation.

The *Renown* sailed from Scapa Flow on 5 April and under her watchful eye the minefield in the Vestfiord was successfully laid by 0530 on the 8th. As expected, the Norwegians immediately started clearing them and also protested vehemently at this violation of their territorial waters. The force deputed to lay the Stadtland field was recalled before it could carry out its task when it was recognised that the German Navy was at sea. The delay from the 5th to the 8th had not proved critical – the main elements of the German fleet for the invasion of Norway had already left for their destinations on the 7th.

The Intelligence War – Another Mistake?

The mining of the Leads had not, as expected in some quarters, provoked the German invasion of Norway, the latter in the end had frustrated the completion of the laying of the minefield! Furthermore, as we shall see, the second part of the plan to forestall a German invasion by landing troops at selected locations in Norway was circumvented by unilateral Admiralty action. We know now that it would not have been successful because the Germans managed to conceal their invasion plan remarkably successfully. As a conclusion therefore to this unhappy saga in the months leading up to the invasion, it is worthwhile examining why the Allies knew so little at this stage of the war of their opponent's intentions.

Papers produced by both the Chiefs of Staff and the Foregin Office had considered the possibility of a German invasion of Scandinavia from the beginning of the war. But a belief persisted in many quarters, particularly in the Foreign Office, that the best interests of Germany would be served by Norway remaining neutral, and that any signs of a build-up of forces in northern Germany could be attributed to other reasons. The German landings on 9th April thus still came as a considerable surprise to many members of the War Cabinet and the senior military planners. Was this lack of awareness of the German intentions excusable, or had the nation's intelligence network blundered?

It is true that the Germans took special care to conceal their plans. No reference was made to the plan in German cypher communications, and Signals Intelligence (Sigint) which became such a vital source of information later in the war played no part in the lead-up to the Norwegian campaign. Photographic reconnaissance had also not been developed sufficiently by this stage to be of any real benefit in intelligence gathering. But there were sources of information, military and diplomatic, which should have provided clues. As early as December 1939 and again in January 1940, Secret Intelligence Service (SIS) reports indicated that a German expeditionary force was assembling in North Germany and conducting exercises in combined operations, and that merchant vessels had been modified to carry troops and vehicles. But Military Intelligence, the War Office's intelligence department, had concluded in December 1939 that twenty-five to thirty German divisions would be required to invade Norway and Sweden, and as intelligence sources indicated that no more than five or six were present in the area, they discounted any serious invasion plan. This proved to be a fatal assumption, for the invasion was in the event carried out by a force of just this size.

There was no shortage of invasion warnings from diplomatic sources either. Naval, Air and Military Attachés in both Stockholm and Copenhagen gave general warnings of German intentions and preparations from February onwards, and from late March, definitive reports of troop concentrations were being transmitted regularly. But like Military Intelligence, the Foreign Office was not convinced, one highly placed official annotating a report:

I wish I could believe this story. German intervention in Scandinavia is just what we want.[16]

The failure to co-ordinate individual intelligence reports also diluted their overall force. Not only did the three independent Service intelligence organisations and the Foreign Office not fully co-operate with each other, but there were communications failings between sections even within individual Services. But it was not so much the shortage of information, but the failure to correlate and interpret it correctly which proved to be the major mistake. Related occurences such as a Luftwaffe raid on 16 March on Hatston, a Fleet Air Arm airfield in the Orkneys, was interpreted as a prelude to an invasion of Britain rather than a pre-emptive measure against British interference in a German invasion of Norway. The significance of reports of the 28 March that all German leave had been stopped and that mine laying by destroyers in the sea approaches to Norway had ceased was totally missed.

Preconceived opinions also dulled intelligence perceptions. Military Intelligence was pre-occupied by thoughts of an invasion on the Western Front and the Naval Intelligence Department obsessed by the expectation of a break-out into the North Atlantic by the German Battle Fleet. This misconception continued to bedevil naval planning even after the Home Fleet had sailed on 7 April. British operations and planning staffs were also so absorbed in planning their own intervention in Norway that the thought that they could be pre-empted hardly crossed their minds. It was considered inconceivable that a German force could be landed at Narvik in the face of the vastly superior power of the Royal Navy.

Even in the last few days, firm evidence of German activity did not register at the highest level. Mr Victor Mallet, Ambassador in Stockholm had reported on 2 April that he had heard from Swedish sources that a concentration of about 200,000 tons of shipping, with troops on board, had been observed at Stettin and Swinemünde. On 6 April, the Ambassador in Copenhagen, Mr Charles Howard-Smith, telegraphed that Hitler had ordered a division to be moved unostentatiously in ten ships to Narvik and that Jutland would be occupied on the same day; Sweden would not be invaded. This message proved to be remarkably accurate.[17] Other reports of increased rail, air and naval activity failed to reverse the Military Intelligence view, repeated as late as 8 April, that intelligence did not support a probability of a Scandinavian invasion. A report that German soldiers rescued from a transport ship sunk by the submarine *Orzel* on 8 April were on their way to Bergen did not convince the Admiralty until the following day that an invasion was actually in progress.

It must be concluded therefore that sufficient evidence of the German intentions was available, if not to give a complete picture of the invasion plan, at least to prevent the sense of surprise which greeted the actual event. In intelligence, as in so many aspects of the Norwegian campaign, vital lessons were there to be learned, and fortunately for the eventual outcome of the war, many were.

A Day Too Late

Seven months of agonised discussion and planning therefore came to nothing. There can be no doubt that the Allies were far too concerned with the action that they might initiate in Scandinavia, and gave too little attention to what the Germans might do, and how effective such action would be. It is by no means uncommon for political and military planning to be conducted in a vacuum, as though the capabilities and intentions of the enemy were secondary to the aspirations of the planners. But the first seven months of the war provide a particularly good example of this self indulgent approach. It should have been more evident to the politicians and military alike that Germany (and Russia to a lesser extent) had very real interests in securing Scandinavia for their own purposes, and such indications as there were that this was under consideration should have been taken far more seriously.

This failure to recognise that the interests of other nations did not necessarily attune with Allied interests was also equally evident in their approach to the Scandinavian countries. There persisted a belief in many quarters, at least until the end of the Russo-Finnish war, that Norway and Sweden would eventually be persuaded or coerced to fall into line with the Allied wishes, whereas all the evidence indicated that they were far more afraid of Germany and Russia than they were of the liberal, but indecisive democracies of Britain and France.

There were of course some in positions of authority who recognised more clearly the German threat to Scandinavia. The Ironside Diaries show quite clearly that as early as January 1940 the CIGS was aware of the concentration of German shipping in the Baltic ports and was alive to the probability of a German intervention, although he thought it more likely to be an attack on Sweden through the Gulf of Bothnia in May to secure the Gällivare orefields. These diaries also make very apparent his frustration at the inability of the War Cabinet to reach a decision on positive action in Norway.[18]

Only Mr Churchill and a few of his supporters squarely faced the moral dilemma as to whether it was acceptable for short term expediency to violate the rights of neutrals in the cause of overcoming a greater evil. It was of course a respectable principle, if not perhaps a practical one, that the Allies should not resort to the barbarous strategies of their opponents. But it was a dilemma that had to be faced and resolved.

The politicians in both Allied countries, but particularly in Britain, stand condemned in 1940 not so much for the actions they authorised, for these amounted to little enough, and not even for failing to take action at all, for in truth opposition to the Russians in Finland would have been an operation fraught with danger, but for their endless indecision and prevarication which alienated their potential allies around the world and led to a feeling of helplessness and frustration at home.

This mood of indecision inevitably had an unfortunate impact on military planning and training. The planners never quite knew what the politicians intended and were themselves never totally enthusiastic regarding what was proposed. The Air Staff particularly were not keen to fritter away precious resources in Scandinavia, and in any case in 1940 did not regard army co-operation as other than a secondary task. It remained a blind spot for the RAF until Tedder, Coningham, Auchinlek and Montgomery forged the Desert Air Force in 1942. The Navy were naturally mainly interested only in action in the Leads, and so it fell upon the Army to prepare itself for the various schemes proposed for it in Scandinavia. Their preparation was ill considered and inadequate as we shall see more clearly in later chapters.

It is always easier to decide what should have been done with the luxury of hindsight. There was a good case for taking no action at all. After all, there is little profit in engaging in an arena of conflict in which the prospects of success are remote. The preservation of resources for the decisive battle which would inevitably have to be fought sooner or later on the mainland of Europe had a compelling ring of logic. Mr Churchill, often alone, constantly prodded the Cabinet to take action in Scandinavia, and had it not been for his incessant pressure, it is probable that no action would have been taken. On the other hand, if it was considered politically desirable to adopt a more positive course, a firm decision to instigate naval action in the Leads to curtail the flow of iron ore, perhaps as early as September 1939, and the assembly and training of a force to react to a German invasion of Norway should have been the limit of British action in the Scandinavian theatre in the first six months of the war.

It is therefore ironic that when after seven months of indecision, 'Operation Wilfred' was belatedly mounted to mine the Vestfiord, the German invasion force had already sailed. It was a day too late.

4

Weseruebung – A Plan For Action

'The prerequisite for the success of the operation are surprise and rapid action.'[1]

Admiral Raeder

Access to the Open Sea

In 1939, the Germany Navy was by far the weakest and least prepared for war of the three Services comprising the Wehrmacht, but it was the arm which to a large extent instigated and subsequently played the leading role in the invasion of Norway and Denmark. It was destined to be an operation which, although brilliantly executed, was to so weaken the German surface fleet that it never again played a really significant role in the conduct of the war. But 'Operation Weseruebung' (Weser Exercise) was far more than a naval swansong, it was the first occasion in the history of warfare that the three Services had participated in a tightly controlled and co-ordinated joint exercise in which failure of any one of the component parts would have irrevocably damaged the whole operation. Whilst the blitzkreig in Poland had been a brilliant exhibition of air and ground forces acting in unison, there was little participation by the Navy. But the campaign in Norway was to set a pattern which has dominated the structure of warfare ever since and, however haltingly, led inexorably to ever closer integration of the planning and execution of combined operations. It was a process which reached its apogee in the Normandy landings of June 1944, and was so vividly illustrated again in the Falkland Islands in 1982.

The genesis of Germany's interest in Norway as a forward operating base for the Grand Fleet lay in the First World War. The short German North Sea coastline containing the main naval bases of Wilhelmshaven, Bremerhaven and Cuxhaven was defensively very strong: screened by a string of offshore islands, its estuaries protected by sandbanks and tortuous channels, and with a formidable outlying fortress, the impregnable rock of Heligoland. The Baltic Sea was almost as impenetrable, its narrow entrance channels between the Danish islands an obvious lair for submarines and destroyers lying in wait for any intrepid intruder. Furthermore, the two stretches of the German coastline, the North Sea and the Baltic which were separated by the protruberance of neutral Denmark, were connected by the Kiel Canal, facilitating rapid movement and reinforcement from one to the other.

But whilst providing a formidable defensive haven for their inferior fleet, the German naval bases suffered from one decisive weakness. The bulk of the British landmass to the west, which Liddell-Hart likened to 'a vast breakwater',[2] and the

36

Norwegian peninsular to the north narrowed the exit to the outer oceans of the world. British maritime strategy was therefore simple and obvious: a strong naval barrier between the Orkneys and southern Norway would both prevent German surface raiders escaping into the open seas and equally cut off Germany from her lifeline of vital imports. From the outbreak of the First World War until the Armistice on 11 November 1918, the Royal Navy never relaxed its pressure on these northern waters, gradually but relentlessly soaking up the resources of the Kaiser and limiting his ability to continue the struggle. Whilst the economic blockade of Germany between 1914 and 1918 did not by itself achieve the ultimate victory any more than did the strategic bombing offensive between 1940 and 1945, it played a major role in weakening the economic strength and resolve of the enemy.

The German naval planners in the interwar years were very alive to this weakness, and the 1000 mile long Norwegian coastline, facing the Atlantic Ocean and opening up the seas of the world generated visions of a naval strategy that had been out of reach in the earlier conflict. Protected by the off-shore islands, German submarines could slip in and out of Norwegian ports with impunity and surface raiders could return to refuel and rearm without having to brave the submarine blockade of the North German ports. Finding expression in a book by Vice Admiral Wolfgang Wegener in 1929, Die Strategie des Weltkrieges, the advantages of controlling the Norwegian coast were well to the fore in German naval thinking as the prospect of international conflict again appeared on the horizon. Although the Scandinavian countries had even more strongly pronounced their commitment to neutrality after 1918, there were strategic advantages for Germany in seeking more positive co-operation from their northern neighbours. In any case, it was well recognised within Germany that they could not even depend upon the Scandinavians strict adherence to the fragile plank of neutrality. It had already been overturned once by the Allies in 1918 when they forced the Norwegians to support the completion of a mine barrier between Scotland and Norway. The Americans had laid a chain of 70,000 mines between the Orkneys and Norwegian territorial waters and the British had then brought political pressure to bear on Norway to complete the barrier by laying mines in her own waters. Whilst this chain had not been as successful as had been hoped because some of the mines proved defective, there was no justification for believing that it would not be technically possible to complete a very formidable barrier in 1940.

There was also the iron ore. Whilst the iron ore carriers were secure within the protection of the territorial waters inside the Leads, at least as long as the Allies respected this legal restraint, they would become easy prey for submarines and surface raiders if forced by mining into the open Norwegian sea. Other valuable imports also came into Germany from Sweden's industrial base, and Scandinavia was economically more important to Germany than to the Allies. So even though a strict interpretation of neutrality by the Scandinavian countries might have suited the German interests, at least in the early phase of the war when their forces were stretched, the British interest lay in interfering with Norwegian neutrality to the detriment of German trade and long term naval strategy. We have seen of course that such thoughts were being voiced within the Admiralty and elsewhere even before the war started.

Of even greater concern than a nominally neutral Norway under the influence of

Great Britain would be one actually occupied by the Allies. If the RAF could operate from airfields in Norway and the Royal Navy from ports in the Skagerrak, the Baltic Sea would become a British lake and the inferior German Navy would be systematically destroyed. Furthermore, British bombers would also dominate the industrial areas of northern Germany. A British occupied Norway would be a strategic disaster for Germany and must be avoided at all costs. The German Navy at least was well aware of this threat, although Hitler himself was rather taken aback when Admiral Raeder first drew his attention to this Achilles heel.

But Hitler had seen ample evidence in the pre-war years of British hesitance and weakness, and despite the resurgence of the German Army in the last years of peace, the Royal Navy was still indubitably the stronger of the two navies. The continuance of Scandinavian neutrality in so far as it profited Germany appeared the most sensible and pragmatic policy. Accordingly on 1 September 1939, the German Ministers in Norway, Sweden and Finland were instructed to notify their respective host governments in unambiguous but friendly terms that Germany intended to respect their integrity so long as they maintained strict neutrality, but that Germany would not tolerate breaches of neturality by third parties. In particular, they were warned against accepting any restrictions imposed from outside upon their trade with Germany. There is no doubt that at this stage this was a genuine reflection of German policy and not a subterfuge to lure the hapless Scandinavian governments into complacency. The Fuehrer had other fish to fry before he could turn his attention to Norway.

It was unlikely however, that this happy situation could last. The Scandinavians would need to tread a very fine line indeed if they were not to antagonise either Britain or Germany. As we have already seen, there were influential voices in Britain and France looking for any opportunity or excuse to interfere in Norway, either by mining the Leads or establishing a presence ashore to thwart the export of iron ore to Germany. Equally, there were those in Germany who wished to exploit Norwegian waters and safe harbours to break out of the straight-jacket that would inevitably be imposed on Germany's only access to the oceans of the world. Some of these arguments were reflected in discussions within the military structure in Germany. However, it would be helpful to a better understanding of the initiative and manoeuvres which led to the invasion of Norway on 9 April to first of all have a brief look at the political and military organisation in Germany in 1939/40. In some respects, it was just as conducive to muddle and mismanagement as the system in Britain and France that we have already examined. But there was one essential difference – a supreme and all powerful dictator to beat a way through the petty rivalries and mistrust within the organisation and structure of the armed services.

Disarray at the Top

It is not unusual for government and military hierarchies to construct complex and clumsy organisational structures for the creation and control of defence policy during periods of peace. It allows individual military factions a share of the power and the glory (and the money), and permits governments to rest more easily in the knowledge that it can divide and rule whenever it is expedient to do so. Although superficially logical, the military organisation in Germany in 1939 was no exception.

On 4 February 1938 Hitler unexpectedly announced on the wireless that 'From now on I have taken over personally the command of the whole armed forces'.[3] Until then he had remained on surprisingly equable terms with the military grandees who were so different in upbringing and temperament to the acolytes who had attached themselves to his political tail. But the German High Command was racked by two sex scandals in 1937 in which the War Minister, General Werner von Blomberg, had married his secretary who was later exposed as a prostitute, and the Commander-in-Chief of the Army, General Freiherr von Fritsch was framed by Goering on a trumped-up charge of homosexuality. Hitler had quickly seized the opportunity when the generals were in some disarray to make his move to subordinate their high Prussian principles to his more nefarious intentions. He abolished the War Ministry and sacked or down-graded most of the senior generals. In its place he created the Oberkommando des Wehrmacht (OKW) – the Armed Forces High Command. In theory, the three fighting services were subordinate to the OKW, in practice they worked assiduously to circumvent or dilute its control.

As Chief of Staff of the OKW, but with the high sounding title of Chief of the High Command of the Armed Forces, Hitler appointed Generaloberst Wilhelm Keitel, a third rate sycophant, but just the man Hitler needed for his purposes: he had little intention of devolving real authority to the generals. Keitel had enjoyed a steady but undistinguished career until the Blomberg-Fritsch crisis thrust him into prominence. He had been responsible for running Blomberg's private office and his loyal but subservient manner was exactly attuned to Hitler's intention to direct events himself after the putsch of the military heirarchy. As Albert Speer remarked 'Hitler said that he could not do without Keitel because the man was loyal as a dog to him'.[4] He managed to survive throughout the war but in the end proved a good servant to neither Hitler nor to the Army.

The Army High Command – Oberkommando des Heeres (OKH), went to General Walther von Brauchitsch, a respected and courageous soldier, but weak and compliant in the higher echelons of power. Brauchitsch's Chief of Staff was Generaloberst Franz Halder, shrewd and intelligent, but also cautious and negative and with little following within the Army. Halder was prominent among those who before the rape of Czechoslovakia were plotting to overthrow Hitler. But it was indicative of his conservative, hesitant personality that in the end he was unable to grasp the nettle. Hitler had very little regard for the leaders of the OKH and discounted their views at the slightest excuse. It was their resentment of Hitler's attitude towards them which led to many of the niggling little obstacles which marked the planning and conduct of the Norwegian campaign.

The Navy High Command – Oberkommando des Kriegsmarine (OKM) was led by Grossadmiral Erich Raeder who filled both the Commander-in-Chief and Chief of Naval Staff functions. The unchallenged doyen of the German Navy, he was probably the most capable of the German senior commanders. A veteran of Jutland and a man of irreproachable integrity, he established a high moral tone within the Navy which was quite apart from the sordid intrigues of the Nazi ideologies. He had laboured unwaveringly to rebuild the German Navy in the interwar years, but even so he was more aware than most in 1940 that it was still far from ready to challenge the superior power of the Home Fleet.

The most flamboyant Commander-in-Chief was undoubtedly General-feldmarshall Hermann Goering, Head of the Air Force High Command – Oberkommando des Luftwaffe (OKL): fat, egocentric, ambitious and cunning, even Hitler had to buy him off with a field marshal's baton during the putsch in February 1938.

One more name needs to be mentioned, for he increasingly became the guru of the high command structure. Generalmajor Alfred Jodl, head of the Armed Forces Operations Staff in the OKW, became Hitler's closest military adviser, and given his predilection for close control of all policy and operational decisions, a key figure in the military heirarchy. Jodl was an astute and intelligent man and a very capable staff officer. But he had little operational experience having been wounded in the early days of the First World War. Although not an outgoing personality, unlike Keitel he was by no means overawed by Hitler's overbearing attitude, and as the war progressed he became increasingly critical of Hitler's war aims. The detailed planning of the invasion of Norway was to provide his great opportunity to establish himself as Hitler's mentor and he grasped the opportunity with both hands.

The major constraint on the smooth running of the German war machine was the fractious relationship between Hitler, the OKW and the High Commands of the three Services. The OKW was intended to function as a co-ordinating agency and a personal military staff for Hitler. But because of his distrust of his generals in the OKH, it was increasingly given absolute authority, subject only to Hitler himself, for both the planning and in some cases the conduct of operations. This inevitably proved a catalyst of friction and misunderstanding.

The climate of disarray in the military high command structure had implications for the strategic conduct of the war which were as far reaching as that other major political consequence of the Norwegian campaign on the Allied side of the fence, the fall of Chamberlain and his replacement by the supreme war lord, Winston Churchill. As General Walter Warlimont recorded:

> This had been the first attempt on the part of the dictator to subordinate the organisation for command and leadership of an operation in war to his own personal ambition and thirst for political prestige.[5]

The Army commanders resented this assumption of control by Hitler, but they did little to oppose it. The presence of compliant and sycophantic generals in the OKW allowed Hitler the freedom to intervene on even the smallest points of detail and to make irrational judgements which went unopposed. In Hitler's eyes, the success of the invasion of Norway was to amply justify his personal and direct control and the Army generals were never to regain the initiative they had so weakly abdicated. But even in success, Hitler was effacing from his memory those bleak periods during the campaign when he almost succumbed to despair, and paradoxically it was the strength of his generals, particularly Jodl, who sustained his spirit when it seemed that Narvik had been lost. In the end, Hitler's intuitive approach was found wanting, and increasingly his judgement and control of events evaporated as the fortunes of war turned against him. How fortunate was Great Britain to have an Alanbrooke and Portal whose firm and usually tactful guidance tempered with sober realism the similar impulsive initiatives which from time to time sprang from Churchill's fertile imagination. But all this was in the future. In the Spring of 1940, on the crest of the victory in Poland, Hitler was able to dominate his senior commanders to an extent which assured a fixity of purpose which was quite lacking on the other side of the North Sea.

Opening Moves

At the end of the successful blitzkrieg against Poland, it was by no means clear within Germany what should be the next step. There was the possibility of negotiating peace with Britain and France, at least as a temporary measure while the military build-up continued, or alternatively a strategy of driving a wedge between the Allies. But reports were already being received in Berlin that Britain intended to obtain a foothold in Norway. Encouraged by Admiral Rolf Carls, Commander-in-Chief of Naval Group Command East and Germany's third ranking naval officer, Admiral Raeder on the 3 October directed the Naval War Staff to study the feasibility of gaining bases in Norway, either by political or military methods. Foreign Minister Joachim von Ribbentrop was also consulted on the probable reaction of Russia to such a move. At this stage Trondheim was considered the most suitable location for a main naval port with Narvik as an auxiliary base.

On balance, Raeder still believed that Scandinavian neutrality was the most beneficial policy for Germany to pursue, although he nevertheless brought the question to Hitler's attention in a long memorandum on naval operations on 10 October. But it was on this same day that Hitler had crystallised his views on the need for an immediate attack on the Western Front, and although he expressed some interest in the acquisition of bases in Norway, no further action was taken. In any case, many of the staff within the OKM were even less responsive to the idea than Admiral Raeder himself as was General Halder, the Chief of Staff Army (OKH). But the role of the Navy in the planned offensive in the West was minimal compared with that of the Army and the Air Force, and naval operations against Allied shipping were still restrained by Hitler. A natural hankering remained therefore to obtain a greater share of the action and this continually refocussed the Navy's thoughts on the Norwegian coast.

As it had in Britain, the subject came to the forefront again on 30 November when Russia invaded Finland. This blatantly aggressive act by his new ally brought little joy to Hitler, for in addition to bringing the prospect of Bolshevism into a country which he believed lay within his own sphere of interest, it provided the ideal excuse for the Allies to interfere in Scandinavia. And in going to the defence of Finland, how easy it would be to stifle the flow of iron ore from Sweden to Germany. This was of course a fair appreciation of Allied thinking, but as we have seen the vacillation of the Governments, particularly the British, prevented any significant action being put in hand. Even so, it is not surprising that Hitler was unsure what Britain and France would do – they hardly knew themselves. The opportunity of bringing Hitler's attention back to Norway was not missed by Admiral Raeder, and following reports from the naval attaché in Oslo that Allied landings in Norway were imminent, he advised Hitler directly of the importance of securing German interests by occupying the country. The appearance on the scene of Major Vidkun Quisling was also seized upon as another way of bringing influence to bear.

Vidkun Quisling was 52 years old when the war started and a political opportunist. Born of peasant stock, he had nevertheless prospered in Norway's egalitarian society, attended the Military Academy, and in his twenties had become military attaché in Petrograd. Ironically, the British Government had awarded him the CBE during this period for looking after British interests at a time when she did not maintain formal relations with the Bolshevik regime. The young Quisling was at first impressed by the Bolshevik system, and on his return to Norway offered his services to the Labour Party, at that time a member of the Comintern. He even served as Minister of Defence between 1931 and 1933. Eventually, rebuffed by the socialists, he veered in a totally opposite direction and formed a fascist party, the National Union, reflecting the Nazi Party which had just come to power in Germany. But fascism did not thrive in an inherently liberal Norway, and rejected at the polls, Quisling turned increasingly to Germany, establishing contact with Alfred Rosenberg, head of the Foreign Political Office of the Nazi Party.

Quisling appears in our story at the end of 1939 when Rosenberg arranged a meeting for him with Admiral Raeder on 11 December. Quisling professed to be capable of influencing important sections of the Army to accept a German occupation of Norwegian bases, and indicated that he had the support of men in such vital areas as the railways and communications. Although he had some support, Quisling undoubtedly grossly exaggerated his real influence in Norway. Even so, Raeder was sufficiently impressed to raise the matter with Hitler on the following day, proposing that the OKW should formulate plans in collaboration with Quisling for the peaceful occupation of Norway for consideration alongside the alternative option of an invasion by force. Hitler himself saw Quisling on 14 December, but was less convinced of the range of support he professed to command. Although going along to a certain extent with Quisling's proposals, he also ordered the OKW to prepare a draft plan for the occupation of Norway by force. But the loss of the *Graf Spee* had again concentrated Hitler's mind on the fundamental weakness of his Navy compared with that of Britain, and his thoughts had returned to maintaining Norwegian neutrality. Quisling therefore had to be content simply with an offer of money to strengthen his pro-German movement and to combat British propaganda.

The planning for a forcible occupation of Norway nevertheless continued to move slowly ahead. Jodl's first inclination had been to give the planning of the invasion to the Air Staff, for he saw the main burden of the operation falling on the Luftwaffe. But Hitler was unimpressed by this argument and insisted that planning should continue within the OKW. He already had strong reservations about the ability of the vainglorious Goering to plan a joint operation. In any case, he saw at this stage more clearly than Jodl that the Navy rather than the Air Force would play the key role in the invasion plan.

The responsibility clearly lying in their court, the naval officers in OKW pressed on with their plan, now given the title 'Study North'. Opinion regarding the efficacy of such a plan still wavered. The Operations Department of Naval Operations Command suggested on 13 January that they did not believe that a British occupation of Norway was imminent, and that a German invasion would be a dangerous diversion. Others, including Raeder himself, were less sure, he was by now more committed to an intervention in Norway. Unpredictable as ever, by the end of the month Hitler had once again swung in favour of a Norwegian move. Displeased with the vacillation of the naval staff and the progress of 'Study North' which had been presented to him in mid January, he now ordered that the plan should be reconsidered under his own personal and immediate supervision and three senior officers, one from each Service within the OKW, were detailed to undertake the necessary work. The plan was at this stage given its eventual codename – 'Weseruebung'.

'Weseruebung' – The Plan Takes Shape

The staff for the formulation of 'Weseruebung' assembled in the OKW on 5 February under the direction of Captain Theodor Krancke, who had previously been in command of the cruiser *Scheer*. Suffering from a fit of picque at not being given sole responsibility for the invasion planning, Goering initially withheld the Air Force member of the triumvirate. But Krancke and his Army colleague pressed on regardless and Goering soon recognised that his intransigent attitude could quickly become counter-productive.

Krancke ran into the same difficulties which had beset the British planners during these same months. Knowledge of Norway, its topography, military dispositions and the likely reaction of the population were surprisingly sparse, giving the lie to subsequent allegations that Norway was riddled with spies and fifth columnists. Sellers of tourist guides, maps and sea charts were doing good business in both London and Berlin in the early months of 1940. The influence of Quisling was now on the wane, and the planners were far more concerned with a military plan to achieve military objectives. As with most military organisations, the planners in the OKW had little confidence in political plots, although they had greater faith in the effectiveness of political pressure being brought to bear successfully on Denmark.

Despite the enthusiasm for action in Norway by individual officers within the German Navy, the balance of opinion still favoured retaining a neutral Norway as late as February 1940. But the Norwegian interpretation of neutrality was always suspect in German eyes and two incidents in that month seemed to confirm their fears. The *City of Flint* was an American merchantman which had been captured by the *Deutschland* and was returning to Germany with a prize crew on board. When she entered territorial waters, she was intercepted by Norwegian warships, the ship set free and the crew interned.

The *Altmark* incident on the night of the 16/17 February proved to be the decisive link in the chain.[6] Although the Norwegian Government made a vehement protest to Britain regarding the intrusion of the *Cossack* into territorial waters, their case, was quickly rebuffed by Mr Chamberlain in the House of Commons. There were even accusations in Berlin that it was an Anglo-Norwegian conspiracy. Whilst it appeared to Germany that Norway was discriminating against them in her interpretation of neutrality, in reality the presence of the *Cossack*, which was clearly perpetrating an illegal act in usurping Norwegian rights within her own waters, simply overwhelmed the courage and resolution of the Norwegian officers on the spot. In any event, it was sufficient to persuade Hitler that the Norwegians would not really oppose any determined display of force by the Royal Navy in their territorial waters. It was one of the more spectacular examples of the difficulty Norway was experiencing in treading the narrow path of neutrality, her weakness decried by both sides for wholly opposite reasons.

Hitler was by now convinced that the Allies intended to intervene in Norway and in his mind it became a race to see who could make the first decisive move. Outwardly, his perception was of course correct, the British Government had instigated the formulation of a military plan on 5 February. Bellicose speeches by Reynaud and Churchill added to his fears as did intercepted messages between legations in Scandinavia and their home governments. He was not to know that the War Cabinet in Britain was in fact quietly talking itself out of positive action in Scandinavia over this same period. Hitler now pressed the OKW to complete the planning of 'Weseruebung' as quickly as possible – 'Equip ships, put units in readiness' he raged at Jodl.[7] The placid Jodl, in turn, reminded him that no officer had as yet been appointed to lead the expedition.

On the advice of Keitel, the choice fell upon General der Infanterie Nicolaus von Falkenhorst, currently commander of the XXIst Corps at Coblenz. The General was descended from an old Silesian military family called Jastrzembski, but changed his name to Falkenhorst (Falcon's eyre),[8] presumably regarding this as more romantic and elegant for an aspiring military commander. Fifty-five years of age, he was a veteran of the war in Finland in 1918 which in Hitler's mind established his credentials for a further expedition to the north. He proved to be a good choice. He reported to Hitler, who had not met him before, on the morning of the 21 February. He had no idea of the reason why he had been summoned, but unlike many German generals he was not intimidated either by Hitler's reputation or presence. After being invited by Hitler to describe his exploits in Finland, Falkenhorst was led to a map table and told of the intention to occupy Norway to forestall a British invasion. Hitler clearly took to Falkenhorst and before the day was over confirmed his appointment as commander-in-chief, and sent him away to prepare a plan.

His preliminary plan, which was compiled with the help of a Baedecker travel guide, was approved by Hitler on the following day. The objectives were simple: to secure the ports and impose such firm control on the country that resistance or collaboration with the British would prove impossible. The occupation of Norway was now intended to be an entirely military operation. Quisling's plan to seize power was discounted, and he was told merely to stand-by for the eventuality that the British might force Germany to intervene. A selected staff from his own XXI Corps Headquarters led by Oberst Buschenhagen began work in Berlin on 26 February. It was an extraordinary break with precedent that a Corps Headquarters, the lowest level of the command structure, should have been entrusted with the planning of an operation that would normally have been given to an Army or Army Group Headquarters. But it is indicative of Hitler's increasing desire to keep everything under his immediate control and act only through individual officers he could trust. The General Staff of the OKH did not fall into that category.

First of all Falkenhorst reviewed the Krancke plan and made adjustments of his own, in particular to occupy Denmark by force rather than simply rely upon political pressure. Although there was no good political or strategic reason for invading Denmark, the Luftwaffe insisted that they needed forward airfields in Jutland to carry out the offensive and support operations in their part of the plan. This commitment would require an additional three divisions over and above those already earmarked for the invasion of Norway.

On 28 February, another important decision was made within OKW. It was decided that 'Weseruebung' would have to be planned to enable it to operate independently of 'Operation Gelb', the offensive in the West. This had the important consequence that the airborne forces available for Norway would be severely limited, only four companies of parachute troops and one airborne regiment in reserve. As all the planning so far had been concentrated in the OKW, the OKH were largely unaware at this stage of what was going on, and Falkenhorst received a frosty reception from General Halder, Chief of Army Staff when he visited him on 26 February to ask for mountain troops to carry out the operation.

Nevertheless, by 29 February, despite these niggling setbacks, the preliminary planning was complete and on 1 March Hitler issued the formal direction for 'Operation Weseruebung'. The directive stipulated that the invasion force would be kept as small as possible, as was inevitable given the concurrent planning for operations in the West, but this would be 'balanced by daring actions and surprise executions'.[9] If considered necessary, demonstrations by the Navy and Air Force would reinforce the formal demands that would be submitted to the respective governments in Oslo and Copenhagen immediately before the landings commenced, which would be timed to occur simultaneously. Falkenhorst was confirmed as the overall commander directly subordinate to Hitler, and forces from the three services would be requisitioned as necessary for the operation.

This was all too much for the complex and fragile nature of the German high command. The OKW had planned the operation with scant regard for the resources or sensibilities of either the OKH or the OKL. The former objected to the OKW making troop dispositions without its agreement, and in any case, Halder had not changed his opposition to the plan which he had expressed in October 1939. Goering, Commander of the OKL, was beside himself with rage, and went to see Hitler after venting his anger on Keitel. He was furious that he had not been consulted by the OKW, and even more enraged that units of his air force had been placed under Falkenhorst's command. More predictably the OKM endorsed the Fuehrer directive despite its previous misgivings – it was after all going to play a major role in 'Weseruebung' which would be denied to it in 'Gelb'.

On 3 March, Hitler decided to mount 'Weseruebung' before 'Gelb' and indicated 17 March as a probable date for the landings in Norway. But he still had to mollify his recalcitrant commanders-in-chief. On 5 March he called a meeting, ostensibly to review progress, but more probably to soothe Goering's still ruffled feelings. A compromise was reached by which all the air units to take part in 'Weseruebung' would be formed into X Air Corps, which would receive its orders 'based on the requirements of Group XXI'. Even so Falkenhorst had to make a further presentation to Goering on 7 March before final agreement on the complement of the Air Corps could be reached. Goering never really forgave this perceived insult and took several opportunities during the campaign to subtly obstruct its military direction and execution.

Nevertheless, concrete planning had forged ahead and on 7 March, Hitler signed a directive formally assigning forces to 'Weseruebung'. Four Infantry Divisions, the 69th, 163rd, 181st and 196th were assigned to Norway along with the 3rd Mountain Division and the 11th Motorised Rifle Brigade. To Denmark was allocated the 170th, 198th and 214th Infantry Divisions under General Kaupisch, a retired officer who had returned to play a distinguished role in the blitzkrieg in Poland. The 7th Air Division, which had been one of the major sources of dissension with Goering, was released for 'Gelb'. Even so, the remaining four parachute companies, far less than originally envisaged by Falkenhorst, were to play small but significant roles in the operation.

During this first week of March 1940, there was an atmosphere of frenetic haste and nervous tension in both Berlin and London. On 7 March, General Ironside had informed Marshal Mannerheim that an expeditionary force of 57,000 men was ready to come to the aid of the Finns. Although Hitler would have been aware that the Norwegians and the Swedes had rejected the Allied request for transit clearance, he could not be sure that the Allies would not go anyway. He could not advance his own plans because pack ice in the Baltic would prevent the earlier departure of his transports. But the following day the crisis began to dissipate, for it was apparent that the Finns were negotiating with the Russians and five days later their heroic struggle was over.

In many respects the conclusion of the Russo/Finnish war was welcomed in Germany. There were no international kudos in supporting their aggressive partner against tiny, helpless Finland, and Germany was very wary of the Russian intentions regarding the Baltic Sea. But most important of all, it removed the best excuse the Allies had for intervening in Norway before the German planning was complete. On the other hand, the peace treaty had its drawbacks, for it also removed at a stroke the main excuse that Hitler had for launching an invasion. Without the excuse of a British intervention in Norway 'Weseruebung' could only be regarded internationally as naked aggression.

In two separate entries in his diary for the 10 and 13 March, Jodl commented:

> The military situation is disquieting for if peace is concluded rapidly it will be difficult to find a good reason for undertaking this operation.

> Now that peace has been concluded between Finland and Russia, England has no political reasons to go into Norway but neither have we.[10]

On the following day, he continued that the Fuehrer was 'still looking for some justification' and on 14 March 'Fuehrer has not yet decided how to justify the Weser

Exercise.'[11] It was not the sort of problem that worried the Fuehrer for very long, and he ordered that planning should continue 'without excessive haste and without endangering secrecy.'[12]

But some doubts were arising. It had been established that 'Weseruebung' would take place shortly before 'Gelb', but inevitably planning and force requirements for the far more important invasion of the Low Countries were now exercising the OKW and the service commands to a far greater extent than this northern sideshow. Cold feet were also emerging even within Falkenhorst's own staff. On 28 March, Jodl commented in his diary:

> Certain naval officers seem to be lukewarm about Exercise Weser and want a shot in the arm. Even von Falkenhorst's three immediate subordinates keep on bringing up points which are none of their business.[13]

Admiral Raeder had again succumbed to doubts, and after the *Altmark* incident had suggested again that Germany's best interest lay in keeping Norway neutral. But by 26 March he had regained his resolve and advised Hitler that although he foresaw no immediate danger of an Allied intervention in Norway, 'Weseruebung' would have to be implemented sooner or later and that it would be better to do so as soon as possible.

In fact time was pressing, for as the shorter nights approached, the cover of darkness that was needed to ensure the fleet safely reached the open sea would disappear. Hitler and Jodl now had no reservations and were pressing on strongly, for both saw 'Weseruebung' as a way of enhancing their prestige – Hitler to consolidate the reputation he believed he had gained in Poland as a great military leader, and Jodl who recognised it as a means of establishing himself in a special niche as Hitler's right hand man – a man who could be trusted.

On 1 April, Hitler was given a comprehensive brief on the plan by General Falkenhorst and the senior naval and air officers. He was satisfied with what he heard, but even within this audience could not resist a harangue of self justification. He concluded that it was high time Germany provided itself with secure routes out into the world and did not allow every new generation to be subjected to British pressure. That was the fated struggle of the German people, and he was not the man to evade necessary decisions or battles.

On the following day, 2 April, Hitler announced that 'Weser Day' was to be Tuesday, 9 April, and 'Weser Time' 0515.

Blueprint for Invasion

The plan for 'Weseruebung' was bold, very bold. In the light of limitations of German naval strength relative to the Royal Navy, it might even have been considered reckless: if it had not proved such a resounding success, it undoubtedly would have been. The safe, conservative plan of invasion would have concentrated the assault on Oslo. Not only did this approach lie within the shelter of the Danish peninsular and was thus virtually immune to interference from the Royal Navy, but Oslo was also the seat of power, the hub of the communications system and the centre of agriculture and industry. Having established themselves in the south east of the country and consolidated their lines of communication through Jutland, the rest of the country could have been brought under control at leisure. Or could it?

Whilst a safe and secure means of establishing a foothold in Norway, the geography of the country exposed the limitations of such a plan. Norway is a very long, narrow country, its population concentrated in a comparatively small number of isolated communities, separated from each other by difficult, intractable country. Unlike many other small nations of Europe, to control its hub by no means controlled the whole. In any case, Germany's interest did not simply reside in the overall political control of the country; it specifically wanted to occupy the west coast ports and to control the sheltered waters which lay between the coast and the offshore islands. An assault on Oslo alone would undoubtedly generate an Allied reaction, which would inevitably include the landing of troops at Narvik and Trondheim and possibly Bergen as well. Furthermore, the Norwegian Army, small and ill trained as it was, could regroup in the north and together with the Allies resist any attempt to dislodge them in country which should have been well suited to defence. Having gained suzerainty over the heartland, a major offensive would still be needed before Germany could expect to establish control over the areas that it really needed. Tactically therefore it was necessary for Germany to seize the whole country in one step, to capture as many as possible of the centres of population, the ports and the airfields in the first assault, and to establish contact between these footholds at a later stage. It was a plan that offended one of the main principles of warfare, concentration of effort, but it was the only plan that could achieve the strategic aim. It depended upon surprise, speed of execution, precise timing and exemplary organisation. With Teutonic thoroughness, all these exacting requirements were to be met by Falkenhorst's planning team.

Potentially, the most vulnerable part of the operation was the transport of the troops to their various destinations. The German Navy could not expect to overcome the Royal Navy in a pitched battle, it therefore had to use guile and speed as its primary weapons; secrecy and surprise were the key to this first phase. It was decided therefore that all the troops required for the initial assault should be moved by warship, only follow-up forces and re-supply would be entrusted to transports. Eleven warship echelons were planned, six for Norway and five to Denmark. All the available major ships were devoted to the Norwegian echelons, designated Groups 1 to 6, which were destined for Narvik, Trondheim, Bergen, Kristiansand/Arendal, Oslo and Egersund respectively. The only capital ship with Groups 7 to 11 earmarked for Denmark was the First World War battleship, *Schleswig-Holstein*.

It was quickly recognised however that some support ships would need to arrive at the invasion ports at more or less the same time as the warships. The destroyers which were earmarked for Narvik and Tronheim would require refuelling before they could return to Germany, and whilst the warships could carry the soldiers and their personal kit, they did not have the capacity to carry much else. But the transports were slower than the warships, and if they sailed in convoy with them, it would increase the risk of interception and could compromise the essential elements of secrecy and surprise. A scheme was derived therefore by which tankers and transports disguised as ordinary merchant ships would make their own way independently to various Norwegian ports to arrive just before the warships. The Tanker Echelon consisted of four ships, and the transports carrying military equipment and supplies, known as the Ausfuhrstaffel, was made-up of seven ships. This was one element of the plan which proved to be less than successful and led to major difficulties later on. Even so, it was a bold and innovatory scheme which would be essential if the destroyers and the troops were not to be left high and dry on their arrival. The main reinforcement and re-supply ships, which were to arrive between W-Day and W+12, were divided into eight transport echelons (Seetransportstaffel).

Admiral Raeder recognised that the greatest danger for the warships lay in their return voyage to Germany. He was reasonably confident that he could achieve surprise and evade the Royal Navy on the outward journey; but on the way back, when the cat was out of the bag, they could expect to face a hornet's nest of Allied ships in the North Sea. Raeder, quite naturally, wished to get his ships back as quickly as possible, but just about everybody else opposed this. Their remaining in port or nearby would provide a welcome pyschological boost for the troops they had put ashore, as well as some measure of defence against air or sea attack. The matter was left undecided, but Raeder won his point after a direct clash with Hitler on 29 March.

The final element of the naval plan was the employment of submarines. None of the major warships were to engage the enemy unless they ran into them accidentally. Instead twenty eight U-boats were deployed along the coast south from Narvik and in the vicinity of the Shetlands and Orkneys to deal with any enemy ships making towards the points of landing.

The ground force element in the final plan for the capture of Norway remained similar to that authorised by Hitler on 7 March except that one more Infantry Division, the 214th, was transferred to the Norwegian force in exchange for the 11th Motorised Rifle Brigade now assigned to Denmark. Only the 3rd Mountain Division had seen previous active service in Poland, all the others were newly formed. Four batteries of 4-inch and two of 6-inch guns were provided in support with one tank company equipped with Mk 1 and 11 tanks. Just under 9,000 reinforcements were to be transported to Oslo within the first week in addition to 8,000 moved by air. An additional 40,000 would be provided thereafter as the availability of transport allowed. In total, nearly 75,000 troops were earmarked for the Norwegian campaign – rather less than the Norwegians could put in the field if their mobilisation plan could be put into effect. The three parachute companies which the Air Force in the event grudgingly provided were to be used to capture key targets – the airfields at Sola (Stavanger) and Fornebu (Oslo). After W-Day, except for the equipment contained within the Ausfuhrstaffel, the bulk of reinforcement and supply was to be routed through Oslo. It was therefore essential to the success of the plan that communications and lines of supply should quickly be established within Norway between the various elements of the original invasion force.

No X Air Corps was responsible for all air operations, in support of but not under the command of General Falkenhorst. A variety of aircraft were assigned for the operation totalling approximately 1,000, of which half were transports. The 290 bombers had two main roles. Demonstration flights were to be staged over Norway and Denmark to provide a less than subtle reminder to the population of the consequences of resistance, as well as to drop leaflets to help those with less imagination. The remainder of the bombers were to be held in readiness to attack any Royal Navy ship which ventured within range, and which had been spotted by the two long range reconnaissance squadrons. Twin engine fighters would escort the bombers and transports over Norway and both twin and single engine fighters would support the landings in Denmark. Some of the bombers and the twin engine fighters would land in Norway as soon as the airfields were captured. They would be quickly joined by further bomber, fighter and reconnaissance aircraft. The transport aircraft, mainly the ubiquitous Ju 52s, but including a few four engine Ju 90s, would provide transport from W-Day onwards.

The command organisation to support the operation was in many ways similar to that employed by the Allies, although this was essentially a combined operation directed by Hitler through the OKW, to whom General Falkenhorst was now responsible. The naval forces were directed by the OKM through Naval Group Command West (North Sea) and Naval Group Command East (Baltic and Kattegat), and the Luftwaffe by OKL through X Air Corps. General Falkenhorst, who set up his Headquarters in Hamburg, was to take over only when the troops were ashore, and a naval port commander was appointed to control sea defences. Neither side at this stage of the war had come to terms with the concept of a supreme commander and a joint operations staff. This had been proposed at any early stage in the planning process, but the suggestion was too radical for the individual Service chiefs, who in Germany as in the Allied camp were still prone to inter-service rivalry and faction. The unit of the command structure was therefore very dependant on personalities at all levels. It worked surprisingly well, largely because at middle rank level the three Services were able to achieve a remarkable coherence and unity of purpose. This is not unusual, there were to be many examples throughout the war on both sides of close and effective co-operation at working level when the commanders were totally at odds.

The plan for the occupation of Denmark may be quickly covered. It had three main facets. Firstly, the capture of Aalborg, the main airfield at the northern tip of Jutland, by a parachute platoon and an air-landed battalion. Once in German hands, the airfield would be quickly pressed into use. Secondly, the main body of the infantry, one division and the motor rifle brigade would cross the border and roll-up Jutland from the south. Finally, a division was to land on the west coast of Sjaelland and advance overland to Copenhagen. No XXXI Corps was given the task, comprising as we have seen of two infantry divisions, the 170th and 198th, and the 11th Motorised Rifle Brigade, supported by tanks. In addition, there were three motorised machine gun battalions, two batteries of heavy artillery and two more companies of tanks. The much easier terrain in Denmark allowed the commitment of far more mobile forces than those allocated to Norway, and the use of tanks was much more prominent. In the event, Denmark capitulated quietly.

In spite of this meticulous military planning, Hitler still hoped that it would not be necessary to actually fight in either Norway or Denmark. By a careful combination of stick and carrot, to be delivered simultaneously and unexpectedly, he hoped to throw the respective governments into such confusion that the assumption of control could be achieved without significant bloodshed. Secrecy was essential, for the outcome could prove disastrous if the Governments had sufficient time to steel themselves to resist, and more importantly, time to request the assistance of the only too eager Britain and France who had been seeking a reason to intervene for months. Furthermore, warships carrying the invasion troops could hardly be expected to evade successfuly an alerted Royal Navy, ready and waiting in the vulnerable approaches to the Norwegian ports, particularly those exposed to the North Sea from Bergen northwards. The political, diplomatic and economic planning was therefore conducted within the inner portals of the OKW by the National Defence Branch of the Operations Staff rather than within the Foreign Office as might have been expected. Foreign Minister Ribbentrop was not even informed of the invasion plan until 3 April, and even then brusquely told that the necessary diplomatic planning had already been undertaken by the OKW.

The political objective of the plan was to persuade the respective governments not to resist, and to tolerate a German occupation to prevent their country becoming a battlefield beween the combatant powers. The carrot would be the offer of a substantial retention of their internal sovereignty and a generous promise of economic aid. Their freedom of action in foreign affairs would however be severely curtailed. The intention was to build upon the known sympathetic elements within the country, and only to tighten the screw as necessary once the government and population had succumbed to the Wehrmacht occupation. The stick, on the other hand, was to be the display of force presented not only by the arrival of German troops at all the major centres of population, but also the threat of massive aerial bombardment by the formations of German bombers that would demonstrate over Oslo and other major centres of population within reach of the Luftwaffe.

The stage had been well prepared. The German minister in Oslo had ostentatiously shown to an influential audience a film of the blitzkrieg in Poland. Captured by cameramen crouched in the confined spaces of He 111s and Do 17s, the film recorded in stark detail the destruction of anonymous villages, reaching a climax in the systematic devastation of Warsaw itself. Aptly entitled Baptism of Fire, it was a blatant propaganda vehicle specifically designed to instil terror and defeatism in those capitals of the world which might in future become the victims of the Fuehrer's ambition. The force commanders on arrival at the invasion ports were also to seek to persuade the local officials to accept their presence as a *fait accompli* before bringing force to bear as a final resort. An intensive campaign of radio and leaflet propaganda was to be simultaneously directed at the mass of the population.

It was widely believed at the time, and to a more limited extent subsequently, that Norway had been led like a lamb to the slaughter by the treachery of its own subjects. It was thought that conspiracy, sabotage, espionage and the activities of fifth columnists had contrived the surrender of the ports which were so critical to the success of the German invasion. One newspaper columnist at the time wrote:

> Norway's capital and great seaports were not captured by armed forces. They were seized with unparalleled speed by means of a gigantic conspiracy . . . By bribery and extraordinary infiltration on the part of Norwegian civilians and defence officials, the German dictatorship built its Trojan Horse inside Norway.[14]

It is now known that such traitorous activities were greatly exaggerated. After his early appearance on the scence, Quisling was largely abandoned by both Hitler and the military planners and it is believed that he was unaware of the impending invasion. On the contrary, the key to success was to be laid entirely at the door of the military, whilst Hitler hoped that Norway and Denmark could be occupied without bloodshed, the plan did not depend on the support of local activists to ensure its fulfilment. It was to be the pusillanimity and incompetence of the Norwegian political and military leaders rather than their treachery which enabled the invasion to proceed so closely in accordance with the plan.

It was of course highly desirable that Sweden should remain neutral at least at the outset, although plans were made to restrict her external communications and to make use of her railways to transport troops and supplies into Norway subsequent to the invasion. The presence of Russian troops within Scandinavia following the invasion of Finland was also a complicating factor. Despite the Russo/German agreement, the intentions of the Russians in these northern territories were unpredictable, and Admiral Raeder suggested at one stage that they might be offered Tromso and the area north to the Cape as a sweetener to dissaude any thoughts they might have entertained of 'assisting' the Germans. But Hitler was unimpressed, he wanted to keep the Russians as far away from Norway as possible.

Generalmajor Kurt Himer and Lieutenant Colonel Hartwig Pohlman travelled to Copenhagen and Oslo respectively in civilian clothes two days before the invasion with two objectives. Firstly to brief the resident German ministers in the two capitals of their role in the political and diplomatic moves, and secondly to send a last minute intelligence report to the OKW. They carried with them secret radio codes which would advise Group XXI and the individual commanders at the invasion ports of the Governments' decision whether to capitulate or resist. The diplomatic ultimatum was to be handed to the respective Governments at 0500 – fifteen minutes before the invading troops were to reveal their own intentions.

The stage was now set. The planning was bold, innovative, precise, well concealed, and every aspect carefully considered down to the very last detail. The dangers and risks were recognised and accepted, the jealousies of the individual Services temporarily forgotten or overriden. Once the planning was firmly under way, the almost obsessive attention to minutia so typical of the German psyche had ensured that every plank in the plan had been neatly fitted into place, every event meticulously co-ordinated, all foreseeable loopholes fastidiously closed.

How different is this story to the series of events in London and Paris during the same two months of 1940 after the Altmark affair. The German military leaders were by no means all wholeheartedly in favour of invading Norway, and in the early stages Hitler could no more decide what to do in Scandinavia than could the Allied leaders. But following this early hesitancy, from mid February onwards, Hitler and Jodl brooked no more opposition and rode roughshod over waverers and procrastinators alike. By contrast, unsure of what they wanted to achieve and why, the Allies vacillated throughout the same period that Falkenhorst and his staff were methodically planning with clinical precision the dismemberment of two neutral countries whose military strength in no way threatened the security of the Third

Reich. The moral imperatives which repeatedly restrained the War Cabinet, despite occasional posturing, from actually taking any action in Scandinavia meant nothing to Hitler. Once his mind was made up, he looked at it from the perspective of his own strategic benefit. Even when the neutrality of Norway appeared to be in Germany's main interest, he still allowed the detailed planning to proceed. The collapse of Finland, which removed his main excuse for intervention, did nothing to restrain what had by now become a naked strategy of aggression. Norway had to be occupied to provide the outlet to the Atlantic that Admiral Wegener had identified some 10 years before. Denmark was marked as another victim merely for tactical expediency. The march of dictatorship was poised to take another step forward.

Ships That Pass in the Night[1]

The Opposing Fleets

In the early hours of the morning of 7 April, Admiral Lütjens gave the order for the *Gneisenau* to slip her moorings in the Schillig Roads off Wilhelmshaven and 'Weseruebung' was underway. The Germans had seized the initiative and they were to relinquish it only rarely during the succeeding two months. In fact, the ships of Groups 1 and 2 were not the first to depart as elements of the transport and tanker echelons had already left between 3 and 6 April. Group 1, in addition to the flagship, comprised another battle-cruiser, the *Scharnhorst*, and ten destroyers carrying 2000 troops for Narvik; and Group 2 the heavy cruiser *Admiral Hipper* and four destroyers with 1700 troops for Trondheim.

Admiral Günther Lütjens was a dedicated professional sailor, typical of many who, in the strong traditions of the German Navy, placed allegiance to Service ahead of that to the Nazi Party. Fifty years old, a man of few words but shrewd and perceptive, he was regarded as one of the ablest officers of his rank in the Navy. Although only the deputy commander of the Fleet, he was flying his flag because the Commander-in-Chief, Admiral Wilhelm Marschall, was temporarily sick.

As he crept quietly out of the secure haven of the Schillig Roads into the wide open spaces of the North Sea, Lütjens was only too well aware of the risks and dangers he faced. The invasion plan was totally dependent upon surprise and deception; if these had been lost, there was little he could do to escape the clutches of the far superior fire power available to the Commander-in-Chief Home Fleet.

Despite its growth in capability after the renunciation in 1932 of the provisions of the Treaty of Versailles, the Kreigsmarine was still significantly outnumbered in the Autumn of 1939 in all categories of warship by the combined strength of Britain and France. As late as 1938 Hitler had specifically promised Admiral Raeder that he would not require the Navy to support his political objectives until 1944 at the earliest. But this was perhaps more a realistic reflection on the capacity of the naval construction industry in Germany than an exposition of political strategy. In any event, that promise was severely eroded when he gambled on intervening in Czechoslovakia only months later.

The Allies between them had 22 battleships to Germany's 2, 22 heavy cruisers against 5 (including the pocket battleships), 61 light cruisers against 6, 255 destroyers and torpedo boats against 34, and 135 submarines against 57. Furthermore, the Germans had no aircraft carriers compared with the 6 British and one French.[2] The German sailor was generally well trained, as were most of the professional military men in the Wehrmacht, and they were led by seasoned and intelligent senior officers.

But lacking the world-wide commitments of Empire, the crews usually had less seakeeping experience than their British counterparts. The naval air arm was almost entirely controlled by Goering who had given scant recognition of the need for maritime operations until shortly before the war broke out. Admiral Raeder, recognising that the relative weakness in surface ships could not be readily redressed, had concentrated on the production of submarines as the cheapest and quickest way of forging an effective force. For 'Weseruebung' therefore, in addition to exploiting the element of surprise, he looked towards his U-boat screen to disrupt any intervention by the Home Fleet.

Despite its numerical superiority over the German Navy, the Home Fleet in 1940 was but a pale shadow of that which had left Scapa Flow in similar circumstances on 30 May 1916 as a prelude to meeting the High Seas Fleet under Admiral Scheer at the Battle of Jutland. Of that occasion, Sir Basil Liddell Hart in inimitable style wrote:

> They hailed each other in passing – with a hail that was awe inspiring but leaving an impression that was merely pen inspiring.[3]

It was prophetic that the Home Fleet was once again chasing the shadow of *Admiral Hipper* who had led the German battle-cruisers at Jutland, this time in the shape of the ship commemorating the name of the adversary who had proved so elusive in 1916.

Commander-in-Chief Home Fleet, Admiral Sir Charles Forbes, flew his flag at Scapa Flow in the *Rodney*, the largest battleship available to the Fleet in 1940. Constructed in 1927, the *Rodney* displaced 33,900 tons, had a main armament of nine 16 inch guns and was capable of 23 knots. The only other battleship immediately available at Scapa was the *Valiant*, built in 1915 but modernised shortly before the war. The *Repulse*, nominally a battle-cruiser, but of similar size and armament to the *Valiant* was built in 1916. The *Sheffield* was a modern heavy cruiser and the *Penelope* a light cruiser of only 5,220 tons. The screening force consisted of ten destroyers and the Home Fleet was supplemented by a French cruiser, the *Emile Bertin*, and two destroyers.

The 2nd Cruiser Squadron under Vice-Admiral Sir G. F. Edward-Collins was at Rosyth with two light cruisers, *Galatea* and *Arethusa*, of the same class as the *Penelope*, and eight destroyers, four already at sea on escort duty. Also at sea supporting the minelaying operation in North Norway was the battle-cruiser *Renown* with fourteen destroyers, and the heavy cruiser *Birmingham* with two destroyers, operating close to the Lofoten Islands on another task and with orders to join the *Renown*. The 18th Cruiser Squadron under Vice-Admiral G. Layton was at sea with the heavy cruisers *Manchester* and *Southampton* and five destroyers escorting a convoy bound for Norway. The 1st Cruiser Squadron (Vice-Admiral J. H. D. Cunningham) was meanwhile embarking troops into four heavy cruisers at Rosyth – *Devonshire*, *Berwick*, *York* and *Glasgow*, and the light cruiser *Aurora*, in which Admiral Sir Edward Evans had hoisted his flag, with six destroyers was waiting to escort transports from the Clyde carrying the troops bound for Narvik and Trondheim. In circumstances which we shall consider later, these ships also sailed to join the Home Fleet on the afternoon of 8 April, but without their troops. Finally, at the same time, the venerable battleship *Warspite* and the aircraft carrier *Furious*, also in the Clyde, were ordered to join the Fleet. However, the *Furious* left in such a hurry that she did not even have time to embark her squadron of Blackburn Skua fighters which, on the Admiralty's orders were left sitting impotently on the airfield at Evanton.

The total force available to the Commander-in-Chief consisted therefore of three battleships and two battle-cruisers, thirteen cruisers, one aircraft carrier and forty-seven destroyers: it was immensely stronger than the opposing German fleet, but the absence of a fully operational aircraft carrier was to prove crucial in a number of ways during the next few days. The lack of any form of search radar to warn of the approach of enemy aircraft was also a severe handicap.

Indeed, the Navy's whole approach to an air war at sea was sadly inadequate, not entirely of their own making as we shall see later. Like so many senior officers who had learnt their profession in the earlier war, Admiral Forbes had no strong conviction of the importance of aircraft on the operation of the Fleet despite the Luftwaffe's attack on the Ark Royal in the first month of the war. Indeed, it was an Admiralty initiative rather than that of Forbes himself which instructed the Furious to join the Fleet. The Commander-in-Chief's blind spot was to be quickly uncovered within the succeeding few days.

Where is the Enemy and What is he About?

The Home Fleet had not stirred when Admiral Lütjens was slipping quietly out of Wilhelmshaven on the morning of 7 April and any chance of forestalling the invasion of Norway was already fast disappearing. A patrolling Hudson of Coastal Command reported seeing one cruiser and six destroyers at 0850 as Groups 1 and 2 were crossing the Heligoland Bight, and reacting with commendable speed, twelve Blenheims of 107 Squadron engaged the force at 1330 but without success. The force was by now, rather more accurately, estimated as one battleship, two cruisers and ten destroyers, but unfortunately this was not reported until after the aircraft landed. A second foray by Wellingtons failed to locate the German ships.

Despite the many clues to the contrary, the Admiralty still did not believe the convoy was headed for Norway. The lack of any transports in the group was probably the deciding factor. Despite the fact that the Royal Navy intended to transport troops to Norway in warships, albeit only to disembark them in a friendly port, it was not apparently considered within the Admiralty that the German Navy might employ the same expedient against almost certain Norwegian opposition. Churchill later wrote:

> We found it hard at the Admiralty to believe this force was going to Narvik. In spite of a report from Copenhagen that Hitler meant to seize that port, it was thought by the naval staff that the German ships would probably turn back into the Skaggerak.[4]

Nevertheless, the information belatedly provided by the Blenheims was sufficient to move Admiral Forbes to action and at 1727 the Home Fleet was ordered to sail. By 2015, the last ship had cleared Scapa Flow and the Fleet headed north eastwards at high speed in pursuit of what proved to be a very elusive enemy. Vice Admiral

Edward-Collin's 2nd Cruiser Squadron was also ordered to sea from Rosyth to patrol the area 80 miles off the coast of Norway to the north of Stavanger. But by this time, Groups 1 and 2 were 50 miles south-west of Bergen, already to the north of the pursuing ships: the opportunity of catching the force destined for Narvik had disappeared. The only chance of intercepting Group 1 now lay with Admiral Whitworth in the battle-cruiser *Renown*, apparently well placed to achieve this cruising just to the south-west of the Lofoten Islands.

Mr Churchill reported the events of 7 April to the War Cabinet on the following morning. He said that the Vestfiord had been mined, but that a German naval force 'was undoubtedly making towards Narvik'.[5] This was an interesting statement at this time as the Commander-in-Chief at sea still thought he was trying to forestall a break-out into the Atlantic. Even so, as the Admiralty decision to unload the embarked troops had shown, the emphasis was now firmly geared towards intercepting and defeating the German fleet whatever task it was engaged in rather than to landing occupation troops in the Norwegian ports. As usual Mr Churchill was optimistic and thought that the clash which 'might take place very shortly . . . should not be on terms unfavourable to us'.[6] The fact that the plan to land troops in Norway in the event of a German invasion had been thrown away for no very good reason did not appear to worry the other members of the War Cabinet.

Although still not aware of the enemy's intentions and with no chance of catching Group 1, Admiral Forbes would still at this stage have been in time to oppose Group 2 as it prepared to enter Trondheim and Group 3 for Bergen which had not as yet even left port. That the latter would have drawn the Fleet within range of German bombers operating from airfields in northern Germany would probably not have worried him as he had still to learn the lesson of the vulnerability of surface ships to air attack.

As we have already seen, there was sufficient evidence to suggest that an invasion of Norway was at least a strong possibility. But despite the lessons of the First World War, Admiral Forbes' thinking, along with most senior Naval officers between the wars, had always been obsessed by the prospect of the clash of the Titans: the decisive confrontation of the Grand Fleets in the open sea. This attitude was unsurprising and indeed sensible. Defeating an enemy by sea blockade alone is a long and wearisome task, wasteful in resources and sometimes dangerous in that it dilutes the concentration of force over a wide area. On the other hand, the destruction of the enemy fleet is a single decisive act which would take years to make good: as Churchill had once said of the earlier war 'Jellicoe was the only man on either side who could lose the war in an afternoon'.[7] Even if this remark was to overstate the case, the destruction of the German fleet would have provided an immense moral uplift. Compared with this prospect, the harrassment of an invasion force hugging the coast was very small beer indeed. As a result Admiral Forbes never managed to get the Home Fleet into position to challenge any part of the invasion force, and contact with the enemy was largely fortuitous in the first few days of the campaign.

First Encounters

Meanwhile Groups 1 and 2 steamed single-mindedly northwards through the night.

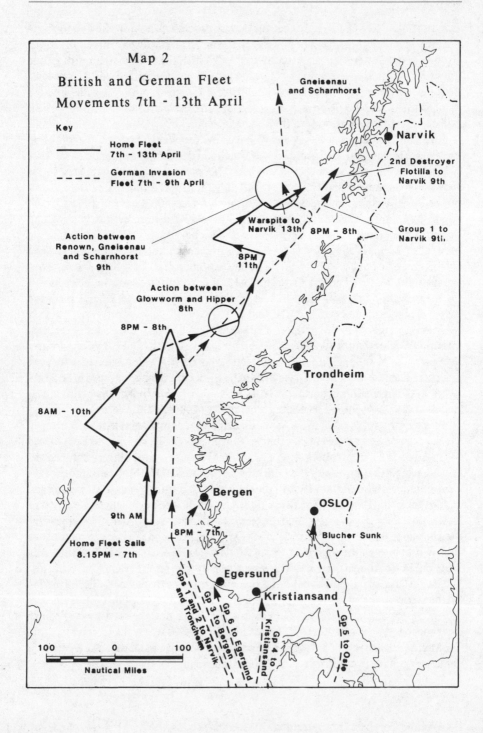

Map 2

British and German Fleet
Movements 7th – 13th April

Key

——— Home Fleet
7th – 13th April

– – – German Invasion
Fleet 7th – 9th April

Gneisenau
and Scharnhorst

Narvik

2nd Destroyer
Flotilla to
Narvik 9th

Action between
Renown, Gneisenau
and Scharnhorst
9th

Warspite to
Narvik 13th

8PM – 8th

Group 1 to
Narvik 9th.

8PM
11th

Action between
Glowworm and Hipper
8th

8PM – 8th

Trondheim

8AM – 10th

9th AM

Bergen

OSLO

Blucher Sunk

Home Fleet Sails
8.15PM – 7th

8PM – 7th

Egersund

Kristiansand

Gps 1 and 2 to Narvik
and Trondheim

Gp 3 to Bergen

Gp 6 to Egersund

Gp 4 to
Kristiansand

Gp 5 to Oslo

100   0   100

Nautical Miles

Not everything was going their way, the weather steadily deteriorated and a westerly gale battered the ships as they fought their way past Stadtlandet where their track turned north-eastwards to parallel the Norwegian coastline towards Narvik. The destroyers in particular were having difficulty maintaining the 26 knots set by the flagship *Gneisenau* and by the morning of 8 April had become scattered. The *Wilhelm Heidkamp* and the *Anton Schmitt* almost collided and two others suffered partial steering failures. The conditions were almost unbearable for the 200 men cooped up below decks in each destroyer. Thrown bodily across the ship from one bulkhead to another and overcome with nausea, some could stand it no longer and against strict orders found their way onto the open decks to gain a draught of fresh air. No less than ten were swept overboard, but there was no stopping to search for them: in such foul weather it would have been a fruitless task anyway. As dawn broke, the *Erich Giese*, the *Bernd von Arnim* and the *Hans Lüdemann* had all become separated from the convoy.

But despite the weather, the first chance encounter of the campaign at sea was imminent. The *Glowworm* (Lieutenant Commander G. Broadmead-Roope) was one of the destoyer screen escorting the *Renown* on the minelaying expedition in the Vestfiord, but had become separated from the rest of the force on 6 April when she stopped to search for a man swept overboard in the heavy seas. Shortly after dawn on 8 April, about 100 miles to the north-west of Trondheim, a look-out on the *Glowworm* saw a destroyer looming out of the mist to the east. Roope signalled a challenge and received the reply that it was the Swedish destroyer *Gothenburg*, but her true identity was quickly revealed when she opened fire. It was the *Hans Lüdemann*, out of contact with the rest of the convoy, but still pressing on northwards as fast as possible.

Roope immediately loosed two salvoes, which from such an unstable platform in the heaving seas, not surprisingly missed their target. The *Lüdemann* was now joined by the *Bernd von Arnim* which had accidently stumbled into the fray, but the two German destroyers did not stay to fight, Captain Friederichs in the *Lüdemann* quite correctly determining that their priority was to deliver their passengers to Narvik rather than to account for this unfortunate intruder which had blundered into their path. But with her heavier superstructure, the *Arnim* in particular was struggling desperately in the conditions and finding increasing difficulty in shaking off the *Glowworm* which had set off in pursuit. Desultory fire was exchanged for almost an hour, but no hits were achieved by either side. The *Glowworm* was herself in difficulty having lost two more men overboard and with her gun direction control position flooded. However, in danger of getting the worst of this chance encounter, Captain Rechel signalled for assistance and, fortunately for the *Arnim*, the *Hipper* which was just to the north-west of the two destroyers responded immediately.

The *Glowworm*, only 1,345 tons and armed with four 4.7 inch guns, was no match for the *Hipper* of 10,000 tons with eight 8 inch and twelve 4.1 inch guns, but she still managed to release a vital radio message giving the rest of the Fleet the information they so badly needed: the position of the German fleet. Trapped in heavy seas, too slow to make good her escape, the *Glowworm*'s demise was inevitable. But how gloriously she died. The *Hipper*'s first salvo was remarkably accurate and the second devastatingly effective, bringing down the foremast and the radio aerials which fouled the siren controls and led to the *Glowworm* completing the brief engagement with her siren wailing eerily at full blast. Recognising the futility of trying to escape, the *Glowworm* closed in on the *Hipper* and launched five torpedoes, all of which missed, but receiving in return further hits forward and in the engine room. The *Glowworm* tried to hide in a cloud of oily black smoke and manoeuvred for another torpedo attack, but Captain Heye, afraid of losing his quarry, pressed on himself into the murk. It was a mistake which could have proved disastrous, for the *Glowworm* suddenly appeared out of the smoke heading back towards the *Hipper* and launched five more torpedoes, one of which missed by only yards.

Roope, with few options left, now made up his mind to ram his adversary and turned sharply to starboard. Captain Heye, recognising the intent of this last desperate maneouvre and by now regretting his over-confidence, also turned rapidly starboard, whether to escape or ram the *Glowworm* himself is not clear. But it was too late, the more manoeuvrable *Glowworm*, still making 20 knots, struck the *Hipper* amidships on her starboard side, ripping away some 130 feet of armour plating and her torpedo tubes. The *Glowworm*, the end now near, fell away and was immediately swept by fire from the *Hipper*'s close range guns. But even now Roope was not yet ready to strike his flag, loosing one more accurate salvo from a range of about 400 yards.

The *Glowworm* was by now burning furiously amidships with her engines stopped and at last Roope, casually smoking a cigarette on the bridge, gave the order to abandon ship. Minutes later she blew up and sank. One officer and thirty men escaped to be rescued by the *Hipper* which gallantly stayed behind to pick up survivors, a mark of respect for her small but tenacious opponent. Roope himself was almost saved, but he could not cling onto the rope thrown from the *Hipper* and slipped back into the sea and drowned. No doubt Captain Heye would have been curious to meet the man who had been known for years before the war as 'Rammer' Roope. He was indeed fortunate that his damaged ship was still sufficiently seaworthy to carry on with his assigned task.

The whole story did not emerge until the end of the war when the *Glowworm*'s survivors were released from captivity. Lieutenant Commander Roope was gazetted for the Victoria Cross on 10 July 1945: Lieutenant R. A. Ramsay, the only officer to survive received the DSO and three seamen the GCM.

Admiral Forbes, 300 miles to the south-west, responded immediately to the *Glowworm*'s last message and detached the *Repulse*, *Penelope* and four destroyers[8] to go to her aid, and Admiral Whitworth in the *Renown* set course to intercept the force which the Admiralty had now signalled could be heading for Narvik.

Whitworth was a strict disciplinarian of no great charm, but he was possessed of a formidable fighting spirit: if his tactical acumen had matched his aggressive instinct, the course of events over the coming months might have been dramatically different. But it was not a misjudgement by Whitworth, but one of the many direct interventions by the Admiralty during the campaign which opened the door to Narvik for Group 1. At 1045 on the 8th, the Admiralty ordered the eight destroyers of the mining force to rejoin the *Renown*, thus removing them from their patrol line in the entrance to the Vestfiord.

Direct Admiralty intervention in naval tactics which might have been better left to the commander on the spot had marched hand in hand over the years with the development of W/T. In the First World War, misleading Admiralty directions facilitated the escape of the battle-cruiser *Goeben* into the Dardanelles leading directly to Turkey joining the war on the side of Germany. Even more blatantly, a whole string of confused and ambiguous signals left Admiral Cradock facing a vastly superior force at the Battle of Coronel off Chile on 1 November 1914, resulting in a defeat which shattered the image of the invincibility of the Royal Navy for the first time in over 100 years. It is not merely coincidental that Mr Churchill was also First Lord of the Admiralty in 1914, it was entirely alien to his temperament to allow the Admirals on the spot to decide how best to fight the tactical war. Thus the mistakes of the First World War were carried forward unrecognised into the new conflict.

Although Admiral Whitworth continued for a while towards the south in the hope of sighting the German fleet, he eventually turned back towards the north-east to join the destroyers, passaging south from the Vestfiord under the command of Captain Warburton-Lee. During the evening of the 8th, therefore, the *Renown* accompanied only by the destroyer *Greyhound* was steaming north-east on a similar track to Group 1 and about 50 miles ahead of them. Whitworth continued to receive a barrage of signals from the Admiralty and others, but none either clarified the situation or gave him direct instructions as to what to do next.

At this stage, he still half believed that the Germans were making towards the Atlantic, and so after he had collected the destroyers at the Stromvaer Light at 1715 he set course towards the west. His belief was reinforced by a report from a patrolling aircraft that the *Hipper* had been seen heading west, but as the latter was destined for Trondheim, this information was in fact irrelevant and misleading. At 1850 on the 8th, the Admiralty sent a direct order to Whitworth instructing him to concentrate on preventing any German force proceeding to Narvik and authorising him to enter territorial waters if necessary. But Whitworth disregarded this order and continued towards the west, reasoning that the Germans would not enter the Vestfiord in the darkness and continuing heavy weather. He misjudged his opponent, for with considerable determination, skill, and not a little luck, Commodore Bonte led his Destroyer Flotilla into the dangerous waters of the Vestfiord in the depths of darkness.

Their task completed, the *Gneisenau* and the *Scharnhorst* left the ten destroyers for Narvik at the entrance to the Vestfiord at 2000 on 8th and proceeded north-westwards to hold in the Atlantic until their services would be required to escort the ships back to Germany. Admiral Lütjens also hoped that he might lure away from the Vestfiord any Royal Navy ships which might be lurking in the path of the destroyers. For the second time that day therefore, the two German battle-cruisers were trailing astern of the *Renown*, now with her destroyers in tow. Throughout the night, the westerly gale raged on, reaching Force Eleven at one stage; but despite the weather the stage was being set for the second naval encounter of the opening days of the campaign.

At 0240 on the 9th Admiral Whitworth at last turned about to proceed back towards the Vestfiord at about the same time as Bonte was rounding Baroy Island into the Ofotfiord and beginning his final dash for Narvik. The Admiralty's order to remove the minelaying destroyers and their escort from the Vestfiord combined with Admiral Whitworth's decision to head for the open sea once he had concentrated his force on the evening of the 8th had laid the way open to Narvik for Group 1. Whitworth's judgement that the Germans would not attempt to enter the Vestfiord in the prevailing weather had proved wrong. We can of course only speculate on the outcome if the *Renown* and her nine destroyers had managed to intercept Group 1. Four destroyers[9] had their fighting potential much reduced on conversion to minelayers when two of their main guns and both torpedo tubes had been removed to compensate for the extra topweight of the mines. Much would have depended upon whether the engagement had occurred before or after the *Gneisenau* and the *Scharnhorst* had left the convoy.

There can be no doubt, however, that the key to the events of the next two months stemmed directly from Whitworth's fateful decision to turn west towards the open sea at 1715 on the 8th. It has been argued that the gale was so strong that patrolling the Vestfiord was simply not feasible that night, but it is irrefutable that Bonte's destroyers, with rather less seakeeping experience under their belt than the Royal Navy, successfully entered the fiord where they gained some relief from the weather in the lee of the Lofoten Islands. It is arguable that in the prevailing weather conditions, Whitworth's force would in any case have been better served by seeking the same protection. It must be concluded therefore that Admiral Whitworth was not really convinced during the early evening of the 8th that the German convoy was in fact heading for Narvik despite the unequivocal tone of the Admiralty message of 1850. But even if he had turned about as soon as he received that message, he would probably still have been behind the Germans as they entered the fiord at about 2000.

The second naval action of the campaign also came about by chance, for it was shortly before 0400 that the *Renown* stumbled upon the two German battle-cruisers steaming north-west on a reciprocal course about 50 miles to the west of the Stromvaer Light. The initial advantage lay with the *Renown* which obtained the first sighting in a temporary break in the wild, stormy weather, and still unrecognised by the enemy, turned onto a parallel course. In the heavy seas, even this manoeuvre took nearly half an hour, but the first indication the *Gneisenau* had of the impending action was shells bursting all round.

The protagonists were by no means evenly matched. The *Renown* had been the brainchild of Admiral Fisher, the First Sea Lord in 1914, and reflected his axiom 'speed is armour'. Fast, well gunned, but incredibly lightly armoured, the *Renown* never saw action in the First World War. Some attention was given to her armour protection between the wars, but she retained her main armament of six 15 inch guns. In the process, although still possessing many of the attributes of the 'greyhound' envisaged by Fisher, she had lost some of her dash and could now make only 29 knots. Her adversaries on the other hand had a top speed of 32 knots, better armour protection, nine 11 inch guns each, and were equipped with radar. Furthermore they were two heavy ships against one as the destroyers could not maintain position in the gale conditions.

Nevertheless, the honours went to the *Renown*. Two direct hits were scored on the *Renown*, neither of which caused significant damage; one armour-piercing shell passed through the deck and out of the side without exploding and the other hit the foremast damaging the transmitting aerials. But in return an accurate shell hit the foretop of the *Gneisenau* destroying her main fire control equipment. Admiral Lütjens hastened off towards the north-east assisted by the *Scharnhorst* steaming across his stern laying a smoke screen. He had been misled into thinking that he faced a larger force than was in fact the case by the shell flashes of the destroyers which had now dropped astern out of range, but still could not resist joining in the fun. The *Renown* transferred her attention to the *Scharnhorst* without success, although she delivered two more telling shots into the *Gneisenau* before both ships disappeared into a passing snow storm. Twenty minutes later, the duel was briefly renewed at greater range, but the fire from both sides was ineffective and the German battle-cruisers eventually disappeared from sight northwards at a full 30 knots. Unable to maintain position in the heavy seas, the *Renown* turned westward hoping to intercept the two battle-cruisers if they should turn back to the south, but Lütjens had seen enough action for one day and they did not make contact again. Whitworth had already ordered his destroyers to return independently to the Vestfiord and arranged a rendezvous for 1800 on the 9th. It was a day too late, Narvik was by then already securely in German hands.

The Royal Navy, albeit somewhat fortuitously, had gained most from the opening encounters. Including the *Hipper*, two out of the three capital ships of Groups 1 and 2 had been quite seriously damaged for the loss of the gallant *Glowworm*. The Germans on the other hand had missed a good chance of destroying the *Renown*, totally failing to capitalise on their numerical and firepower superiority once the destroyers escorting the *Renown* had lost position. This proved to be a major mistake by Admiral Lütjens; for although he had safely delivered the destroyers to Narvik, it was equally his responsibility to see them safely home again. If he had engaged and destroyed the *Renown*, with or without her escort, which with his superior firepower was quite feasible, he would have been able to dominate the Narvik area for at least the next 24 hours, which should have been sufficient time for Bonte's destroyers to unload and return to sea. The subsequent complete loss of the German destroyers in the two battles of Narvik might have thus been avoided. Lütjens was doubtless influenced, in the light of their overall inferiority, by the pervasive fear in the German Navy at this time of hazarding their capital ships, and of course he was not fully aware of the strength of the opposition. Even so, it was an opportunity missed. Both Admirals therefore made serious tactical errors in the first hours of the campaign which were to have far reaching repercussions.

Chasing Shadows – A Strategic Misconception

To return to the morning of 8 April, Admiral Forbes had at last begun to suspect that a German invasion of Norway was probably afoot. Even more hesitantly, the Admiralty came to the same conclusion and signalled the Commander-in-Chief accordingly. However, even now, he could not entirely banish his fixation with a German breakout into the Atlantic and consequently made a number of tactical errors at this crucial moment in the German operation. Clearly he could now do nothing to prevent the Germans landing at Narvik unless Whitworth's force could recover the situation, but he might have deduced that a simultaneous assault would be made on Trondheim and Bergen or Stavanger.

He continued north-east with his whole force towards Trondheim and at noon requested an aerial search. The RAF again responded promptly and at 1450 a Sunderland flying boat of 204 Squadron duly found the *Hipper* and four destroyers still lurking in the area of her encounter with the *Glowworm* some five hours earlier, 100 miles north-west of Trondheim. The *Hipper* and her escort at the time of the sighting were sailing west which was not in fact significant as they were merely passing time awaiting the appointed hour for the attack on Trondheim. Nevertheless, Admiral Forbes turned initially to the north and then north-west to intercept the last reported track of the *Hipper*. As a result he missed the Group by at least 100 miles as they turned back towards Trondheim. A second Sunderland and the *Rodney*'s Walrus carried out a further search for the *Hipper* but found nothing. Whilst Admiral Forbes' reaction was understandable, if he had really believed that an attack on Norway was now the Germans' prime objective, it would have been more sensible to position himself closer to land and to concentrate on the destruction of the invading force. He might have expected the troops to be carried in merchant ships, for he would have had no reason for knowing that they were actually in the warships. The Second Cruiser Squadron, which was patrolling only 100 miles off the coast could have even more readily been detached to watch the entrance to Trondheim fiord, a near certain objective if an invasion of Norway was indeed underway.

However, old habits die hard, and instead he succumbed to what developed into an abortive chase around the North Sea after a phantom enemy who was actually engaged in more positive work. At 2000 on the 8th he turned south and eventually met the 1st, 2nd and 18th Cruiser Squadrons on the morning of the 9th about 100 miles south-west of Bergen. Numerous reports of the enemy invasion were by now coming in and it quickly became apparent both on board the *Rodney* and in Whitehall that the Home Fleet had failed to make contact with the invasion force apart from the two accidental meetings already described.

This whole saga is an interesting reflection on the perceptions held in 1940 of the role of sea power. The Home Fleet saw as its objective the drawing into battle and the destruction of the German fleet. Other tasks were considered to be supplementary, to be dropped immediately when the opportunity arose of engaging in the grand strategy. The alacrity with which the Allied Expeditionary Force was disembarked as soon as it was known that the German fleet was at sea on 7 April is proof enough of the overriding priority given to this single-minded concept. The role of the German surface fleet was also seen in a crystal clear perspective as an ocean going raiding force; that it might be used simply to convey troops along the Norwegian coast was not considered a practical course of action. Throughout these two days therefore, both Admiral Forbes and Admiral Whitworth fell into the trap of looking for the German fleet much further from the coast than it actually was. Even if they had thought that the German fleet was acting only as a seaward screen for more conventional transports, they did not perceive that the key objective at this time was to frustrate a German invasion of Norway, of which there was ample evidence as we have seen from, at the latest, 7 April onwards. If the invasion troops had in fact been moved in transports, engaging the German fleet in the middle of the North Sea would still not have achieved the desired result of preventing the invasion. Even when the true intent of the German fleet began to be discerned during the 8th, the tactics adopted by both Admirals were subsconsciously directed to bringing it into battle rather than to prevent an invasion.

The Military Co-ordination Commitee and the Admiralty must also take a share of the blame. It was not until the early evening of the 8th that the Admiralty unequivocally spelt out, and then only in respect of Narvik, that the primary objective was to prevent an invasion of Norway. Even when Admiral Forbes directed the 1st and 2nd Cruiser Squadrons to patrol much closer to the coast from 0500 on the 9th, the order was countermanded by the Admiralty. In any case it would have been too late. The echoes of Jutland were still a pervasive influence on the Royal Navy in 1940.

Weser Hour – The Invasion Strikes

Let us return now to look at the progress of Group 1 which, as we have already seen, had a remarkable stroke of luck when the Admiralty and Admiral Whitworth between them had removed the *Renown* and her destroyers from the Vestfiord, thus throwing open the front door to Narvik. Commodore Bonte leading the Destroyer Flotilla in the *Wilhelm Heidkamp* arrived at the mouth of the Vestfiord around 2100, safely skirting to the west of the newly laid minefield, and immediately benefited from the much calmer waters in the lee of the Lofoten Islands. Only the *Erich Giese* was still adrift. General Dietl and his mountain troops particularly welcomed the smoother conditions: for most of them this had been the most uncomfortable two days of their lives.

At 0400, the Flotilla was well inside the more confined waters of the Ofotfiord and the *Diether von Roeder* had been left by the Baroy Light as a guard ship. Hidden by darkness and occasional snow showers, but assisted by the many navigation beacons which were still burning, the operation was unfolding exactly to plan. Two small patrol boats raised the alarm, but to singularly little effect. Before his departure, Bonte had been briefed by German Intelligence of the existence of two small fortresses at Ramnes and Hamnes close to the mouth of the Ofotfiord, and the *Hans Lüdemann* and the *Anton Schmitt* were detached with their troops to ensure they did not close the door behind them. In fact, it transpired that they were only half built block houses without guns, which was something of a setback for Bonte as he had intended to use them himself against a counter-attack by the Royal Navy which seemed inevitable. Approaching Narvik, three more ships were detached to proceed up the Herjangsfiord to capture the army depot at Elvegaardsmoen. It was taken completly by surprise and surrendered without opposition, yielding in the process many weapons, ammunition and useful stores which became invaluable when Dietl's expected supplies failed to materialise.

Still keeping to his tight time schedule, Bonte now proceeded directly to Narvik with his three remaining ships, the *Wilhelm Heidkamp, Bernd von Arnim* and the *Georg Thiele*. The harbour was crowded with ships, mostly ore carriers, but was protected only by two ancient coastal defence ships of 3,645 tons displacement; the *Eidsvold*

(Captain O. I. Wollock) and the *Norge* (Captain Per Askim). The Norwegian Navy had not been well provided with equipment during the years of neutrality despite the importance of the maritime trade to the economy. Even more significantly, its expertise and resolve had been eroded by years of neglect. The Ofoten Division (The Iron Clads), in addition to the *Eidsvold* and the *Norge*, consisted of two sumbarines of First World War vintage, the B1 and B3, which managed to evade the Germans and operate along the coast until the 8 June, a mothership, the SS *Lyngen*, two fishery protection vessels and a patrol boat. The fishery protection vessels were sunk by the Royal Navy in the harbour on the 12 April, but the patrol boat *Kelt* was captured and used by the Germans, but only until the following day when she too was sunk in the naval action.

The *Eidsvold* lay at the entrance to the harbour as Bonte's depleted convoy came into sight down the fiord. By now alerted to what was afoot, Captain Wollock ordered a single warning shot to be fired across the bows of the leading ship. But this proved the limit of his aggressive intent, for almost immediately he allowed an emissary dispatched by Bonte to board his ship. Although refusing the demand to allow the Germans to enter the harbour, he still signalled Captain Askim for further instructions. It was a fatal delay, for the emissary coolly left the ship, and when clear fired a red verey cartridge which was the pre-arranged signal for the *Eidsvold* to be sunk. Four torpedoes launched at very short range promptly sent the guardship to the bottom of the harbour with the loss of all but eight of her crew.

The *Eidsvold* should have achieved more. Although built in 1900, she had quite a formidable armament, two 8.2 inch, six 5.9 inch and eight 3 inch guns. Given that warning of the convoy approaching had been received from the patrol boats an hour or more previously and that an order to resist attack had been issued, the response of Captain Wollock was far from resolute. Although acting in accordance with his orders, Bonte had taken a considerable risk in first seeking to negotiate with the captain of the *Eidsvold*. The latter's armament at that range in the calm waters of the fiord could have proved lethal. The response of her sister ship, the *Norge*, still sheltering inside the harbour, was equally ineffective.

Leaving Bonte to deal with the *Eidsvold*, Captain Rechel in the *Bernd von Anim* proceeded directly to the Post Pier on the opposite side of the harbour to the ore depot, her troops already on deck, eager to face anything to escape the crowded malodorous hold that had been their home for the last two days. The *Norge* had by now slipped her anchor and was manoeuvring in the confined waters to engage the *Arnim* which was already tying up at the pier. Although the *Norge*'s first salvo fell short of the *Arnim*, Captain Rechel was faced with the unattractive task of fighting a naval action with the *Norge* on his port side at the same time as he disembarked the troops on the pier to starboard. But the *Norge* could still not get the range right and her next salvo landed in the town over the top of the destroyer. The *Arnim*'s gunfire was equally inaccurate, but eventually Rechel saw the chance to launch torpedoes as the *Norge* suddenly appeared in a clear line of sight between two merchantmen. Although the first five missed, the next two struck home and the old coastal defence ship, burning furiously, slowly rolled over and sank. This time 97 crewmen were saved, but between them, this ineffectual action cost the lives of 277 Norwegian sailors. Their memorial now stands in a secluded garden not far from the Post Pier. The British freighters *North Cornwall* and *Blythmoor* had watched the action, unable to escape, and not quite sure at this stage who was responsible for this carnage. The Master of the German *Bockenheim* had no such doubts. He was convinced that the attackers were British and promptly ran his ship aground at Ankenes and set fire to it.

The reaction of the Norwegian Army contingent at Narvik was even less resolute than that of their naval colleagues. Colonel Sundlo was the military commander in the town. Elderly and psychologically ill-equipped for drama on this scale, he surrendered unconditionally within an hour without firing a shot despite orders to resist. He was tried by court martial at the end of the war, and although found not guilty, was sentenced to life imprisonment for subsequently collaborating with Quisling. The only consolation for the Norwegians was that Major Spjeldnaes with about 250 troops managed to slip away to the east in the confusion of the landing.

Bonte's Flotilla of ten destroyers had completed its task immaculately, but none of them were to see the open seas again. At 0810, Dietl reported that Narvik was in German hands: he too was destined to face a long and arduous two months.

The landing at Trondheim was even less eventful. The *Hipper* and her four destroyers, having successfully evaded the Home Fleet entered at high speed the Krakvagfiord, some 40 miles west of Trondheim, at about 0300. Although there were coastal forts at Agdenes facing the open sea and at Hysnes and Brettingnes on the eastern shore of the Trondheimsfiord, they were taken completely by surprise and managed only to deliver a handful of despairing shells at the wake of the fast disappearing intruders. Three destroyers were detached from the Group to deal with the by now wideawake gun crews at the coastal forts, and the *Hipper* and one destroyer entered the harbour at Trondheim at 0525. The town authorities quickly capitulated: a second major objective was securely in German hands without loss, although it took a little more time to force the surrender of the coastal forts and the small airfield at Vaernes, 20 miles north-east of Trondheim. As well as the airfield, the coastal forts were subsequently put to good use by the German's coastal artillery.

Admiral Raeder had throughout believed that the assault at Narvik would be the most hazardous part of the operation, not only as a result of the long sea passage in the face of a potentially far stronger enemy fleet, but because of the risk that this early move would alert the Allies who could at least then react against operations in southern Norway. In the event, as so often happens in war, the expected pattern did not materialise, and it was in fact Groups 3 to 6 which encountered most difficulty in achieving their objectives, albeit with little interference from the British.

Group 3 was destined for Bergen. Under the command of Rear Admiral Hubert Schmundt, this force consisted of the cruisers *Köln* and *Könisberg*, a very old cruiser, the *Bremse*, and a transport, the *Karl Peters*. The capital ships were supported by eight small torpedo boats. The assault force consisted of 1900 troops under Generalmajor Tittel. The capture of *Bergen* was always a potentially vulnerable operation as the port on the south-eastern bulge of Norway is only eight sailing hours distant from Scapa Flow. Group 3 left Wilhelmshaven 24 hours after Groups 1 and 2 and some five hours after the Home Fleet had already departed Scapa Flow. Off Stavanger they narrowly missed being intercepted by the 2nd Cruiser Squadron, but nevertheless reached the

Korsfiord on schedule at about 0200 on the 9th. A small force of troops was dropped off to overpower the fort at Kvarven at the entrance to the Byfiord, but Schmundt pressed on regardless in his haste to make the appointed assault time. As a result, the Kvarven battery managed to score minor hits on the *Bremse* and the *Karl Peters* and more significantly inflicted serious damage on the *Königsberg*. But despite this damage, Group 3 broke through the coastal screen and Bergen was quickly taken against only minor resistance. Cleaning-up operations on the batteries at Kvarven and Sandviken were completed by 0930 with the help of the Luftwaffe who dispatched bombers to soften up the defenders.

One interesting feature of the assault on Bergen was that the *Köln* twice used deception measures in an attempt to confuse the opposition by signalling that she was the British cruiser *Cairo*. Despite the warning that had been given to the coastal forts of the German ships approaching, this appears still to have created some confusion in troops who were clearly psychologically unprepared for war.

The important airfield at Sola (Stavanger) was also captured in the early hours of 9 April by one company of parachute troops who cleared the runway and secured the airfield to enable two battalions of infantry to be airlanded in Ju 52 transports.[10] This classically executed air assault set the pattern for several more ambitious operations of a similar type later in the war, notably at Maleme in Crete in 1941. Sola provided the Luftwaffe with a first-class airfield both to harrass Allied shipping and to support ground operations to the north.

Less satisfactory however was the fate of one of the Ausfuhrstaffel destined to arrive at Stavanger that same morning. The transport *Roda* carrying anti-aircraft guns for the airfield was sunk by the Norwegian destroyer *Sleipner*, an enterprising step before hostilities had really commenced against a ship which had declared she was headed for Murmansk. Retribution however soon followed when the *Sleipner* herself was sunk by German dive bombers.

Group 4 also left in the early hours of 8 April for Kristiansand and Arendal. 1100 troops were carried in the cruiser *Karlsruhe*, the depot ship *Tsintau* and ten torpedo boats. Arendal was taken without resistance under cover of fog. At Kristiansand, Captian Rieve's first attempt to penetrate the narrow fiord was repulsed by accurate fire from the fort on the off-shore island of Odderöy and he was forced to call for air support before making his second effort which was equally unsuccessful. Fog then defeated his third attempt to send troops ashore in the torpedo boats, and in his impatience to force an entrance in unsuitable weather conditions, he all but ran the *Karlsruhe* onto the rocks. As at Bergen, he eventually found subterfuge to be the most useful expedient and successfully confused the commander of the obstinate battery by signalling in Norwegian code that British and French destroyers were coming to their assistance. Under cover of this deception, Group 4 slipped into the habour and quickly occupied the town without further resistance, twelve hours later than planned. Captain Rieve was doubtless greatly relieved after a hard and frustrating day.

Group 6 was a minor operation by four minesweepers and 150 troops against Egersund, a cable station in the south-west corner of the country: it was accomplished without difficulty.

The most difficult and costly operation of the six mounted against Norway proved to be that against Oslo. The early capture of the capital was an essential feature of the German plan for both political and strategic reasons, and the largest force, Group 5 under Rear Admiral Oscar Kummetz, was entrusted with this task. Although ultimately and inevitably successful given the unpreparedness of its defenders, the assault did not proceed according to plan and was not achieved without serious loss. Group 5 consisted of three cruisers, *Blücher*, *Lützow*[11] and *Emden*, three torpedo boats[12], two armed whalers and eight minesweepers: 2000 troops were on board.

Group 5 had left Swinemuende for Oslo at 2200 on 8 April: they did not proceed unnoticed. The Naval Attaché in Copenhagen, Captain Henry Denham, passed to the Admiralty that the *Gneisenau* or *Blücher* with two cruisers and three destroyers had been observed passing into the Kattegat. Later in the night, the submarines *Triton* and *Sunfish* observed Group 5 near Skaw, the former mounting an unsuccessful attack. Just after midnight they encountered a Norwegian patrol boat, the tiny armed whaler *Pol III*. Receiving no response to his challenge, Weilding Olsen, *Pol III*'s naval reserve captain, raised the alarm and with considerable courage and bravado tackled the force with his single gun. Inevitably he was quickly overcome, but as a last gesture, rammed one of his adversaries, the torpedo boat *Albatross*. Like the captain of the *Glowworm*, Olsen also gave his life in this last desperate act, killed by machine gun fire from the *Albatross* shortly after the collision.

Pressing on, aided by fog and an irresolute response, Group 5 slipped by the island forts at Rauoy and Bolaerne. The task of the torpedo boats and minesweepers was to subdue and occupy the strong points in the outer fiord and they dropped off troops to capture those two batteries from the rear. Another detachment was deployed to the naval base at Horten which eventually succumbed, but not before Captain Briseid in the minelayer *Olav Tryggvason* had accounted for one of the minesweepers with her four 4.7 inch guns. She also forced the *Albatross*, which had already suffered at the hands of the *Pol III*, to withdraw from the invasion force.

But the worst was yet to come, for disaster struck the *Blücher* as dawn was breaking and the visibility improving just before 0500. The Oslofiord at Dröbak narrows to 600 yards and was protected by the eighty-year-old fort at Oscarsborg on the island of Kaholmen and gun batteries on the mainland at Kopas. The 11 inch Krupp guns at Oscarsborg, installed in 1905, struck the first blow, hitting the Blücher with devastating effect with two shots at point blank range. At the same time, three 6 inch and two smaller guns on Kopas fired some 70 rounds at the *Blücher* and the *Lützow*. Her steering gear out of action, the stricken flagship, the newest of her class in the German fleet, drifted into the field of fire of fixed torpedo tubes, also on Kaholmen, which struck two decisive blows. Just before 0730 an explosion in the magazine of the 4 inch guns sealed her fate and she capsized and sank with the loss of more than a thousand men including most of the headquarters staff of the 163rd Infantry Division. The Norwegians still look back proudly at this dramatic blow and there is a very good diorama of the action in the Defence Museum in Oslo.

Captain Thiele of the *Lützow* now assumed command and withdrew in haste with the rest of the force, but not before the *Lützow* herself had suffered three hits. He quickly decided to adopt a more prudent and cautious approach and disembarked troops on the eastern shore of the fiord at Sonsbukten both to subdue the forts and to advance the twenty remaining miles to Oslo by road. But, elated by their success, some of the forts continued to put up a stout resistance despite concentrated air attack and it was not until nearly mid-day on the following day that the Oslofiord was deemed safe for the passage of German ships.

The simultaneous assault on the airfield at Fornebu also ran into trouble: this time with the weather. The first wave of paratroops in Ju 52s were forced to turn back to Aalborg in Denmark when the formation ran into fog. Bombers and fighters arrived over the airfield at dawn, but eight Bf 110s which were intended to land after the para-troops had secured the airfield were forced to land first when they ran short of fuel.

The second wave of fifty-three Ju 52s, which had already disregarded a recall message, now landed under the cover of the machine guns of the Bf 110s on the ground and the disembarked troops soon secured the airfield. The Norwegian Air Force Gladiators had already achieved a minor success by shooting down four of the bombers, but had either been damaged on the ground or dispersed before the airfield was taken. The first wave of Ju 52s was now called forward from Aalborg and by mid-afternoon the full complement of infantry was on the ground. Improvised methods, a large measure of luck and the inexplicable absence of any ground defence on the airfield had enabled the operation to succeed.[13]

The airfield secure, the capture of Oslo was now a formality. The King and his Government had already abandoned the city for Hamar and in the late afternoon the troops which had landed at Fornebu marched in orderly fashion accompanied by a band to take control of the city.

> They were trying to look cheerful; some were brazen enough to try waving to us, but they got an icy welcome. People stood staring at this procession with hard looks, full of hate. Others turned away with tears in their eyes and disappeared into the side streets . . . Nobody wanted to look anyone else in the face.[14]

Quisling seized his opporunity to declare himself the head of a national government, but his relations with the invader quickly deteriorated and his reign was short.

Unexpectedly, the capture of Oslo had proved the most difficult undertaking of XXI Corps. Allied with the mishaps which had befallen the seaborne invasion force, General Falkenhorst and Admiral Raeder could consider themselves fortunate that the assault on Oslo had not ended in debacle.

The Fall of Denmark

The invasion of Denmark, by contrast with that of Norway, was completed almost without a hitch. As previously related, General Kurt Himer, Chief of Staff of XXXI Corps, the formation entrusted with the occupation of Denmark, had arrived on 7 April to brief the Minister, von Renthe-Fink, and to review the situation immediately before the invasion was launched. The commander of the battalion which was to land alongside the quay at Copenhagen had also visited the capital in civilian clothes a few days before and was actually shown round the Citadel, his intended objective, by a Danish sergeant.

Meanwhile, the 170th Division with the 11th Motorised Rifle Brigade quietly moved towards the Jutland border at Flensburg on the night of 8 April while the 198th Division assembled at the ports of Kiel, Travemünde and Warnemünde to embark in Groups 7 to 11 of the naval invasion force. The invasion of the Jutland peninsula was quite straightforward. The land is flat and borders directly onto north Germany, the roads and railways are good, and unlike Norway movement was not constricted by snow. The occupation of the three largest islands which make up most of the rest of Denmark apart from Jutland was more complicated, but posed no great threat.

The invasion troops were all set to occupy Denmark at the precise time that their colleagues were moving into the Norwegian ports. The battleship *Schleswig Holstein*, the only substantial naval vessel committed to the invasion of Denmark, albeit of first world war vintage, led Group 7 comprising two transports to Korsör with nearly 2000 troops. Unfortunately, the venerable battleship ran aground and had to be left behind, but nevertheless the landing was completed without opposition and a beachhead established, as was also achieved at Nyborg on the island of Fuenen to the west. By 1300 on the 9th elements of Group 7 were in Copenhagen.

Group 8 carried an infantry battalion on the transport *Hansestadt Danzig* which was to berth in the heart of Copenhagen at the Langelinie Pier. This was a bold move, and as so often happens, totally successful. They slipped past the fort at the entrance to the harbour which could have devastated the merchantship at such close range, but did not do so because of grease in the gun barrels – or so it was subsequently claimed. By 0735, the Citadel and the Amalienborg Palace, the King's official residence, had been occupied without resistance. Group 9, with 400 troops had the task of securing the bridge across the Little Belt between Jutland and Fuenen, which again was accomplished without difficulty, while another battalion crossed from Warnemünde on two train ferries to Gedser. Groups 10 and 11 consisting mostly of minesweepers, but no troops, occupied the west coast ports of Esbjerg and Thyborön. Apart from the unfortunate *Schleswig Holstein*, all of these actions were completed without mishap or opposition.

The German forces approaching Jutland crossed the almost undefended border precisely on time at 0515, and tanks soon broke up the few minor pockets of resistance which developed. The bridges had already been secured by special forces before 'W' hour. Meanwhile, a parachute platoon, followed by an air landed battalion took possession of the most important airfield at Aalborg. In concept similar to the operation at Stavanger, it was accomplished with even greater ease.

The result was really a foregone conclusion. The Danish Commander-in-Chief, General Pryor, despite the refusal of his plea on 8 April for mobilisation to be ordered, was the only senior adviser to the King to recommend resistance, but this futile gesture was quickly overruled by Prime Minister Thorvald Stauning. One eyewitness stated later that the King plaintively asked the Commander-in-Chief 'whether our soldiers had fought long enough' to which he brusquely retorted that they had not.[15] Even so, General Himer was soon fretting at the delay of the Danish Government in registering their capitulation and summoned bombers to demonstrate over Copenhagen: the Danes had even omitted to cut the telepone links with Germany. Himer's message was at first misunderstood, and it was only by a last minute correction that the bombers were stopped from bombing Copenhagen.

This final show of force was sufficient to persuade the Government to dally no longer. The King rejected the suggestion of General Pryor that he should leave the capital and join the Army, and at 0720 the Government capitulated and ordered all opposition, such as it was, to cease. Thirteen Danish soldiers had been killed and twenty-three wounded – the Germans suffered twenty casualties. General Himer, with typical German forethought, provided the radio transmitter to enable news of the capitulation to be broadcast – it was too early for the Danish news service to be on the air.

It was almost a bloodless operation, but criticism of the Danish Government for its hasty surrender is perhaps far less justified than it would have been in the case of Norway. There was no prospect of Allied support, and indeed it is interesting that the British and French Governments which adopted such a strong moral stance in respect of the threatened violation of Norway and the actual invasion by the Russians of Finland hardly gave a passing thought to the equally threatened sovreignty of Denmark. The attraction of strangling the flow of iron ore to Germany had proved a compelling incentive for the display of moral principles in Norway and Finland.

Despite the various mishaps, by dusk on the 9th it was apparent that the invasions of both Norway and Denmark had been completely successful and all the major objectives secured. The ill-directed Norwegian response had achieved a few isolated successes to redeem their inevitable capitulation, notably the sinking of the *Blücher* and the disabling of the *Könisberg*, but on the whole the 9 April 1940 is not a day the Norwegians remember with pride. The Danes have even less reason to recall the day.

Equally, the Admiralty could not look back on the opening days of the campaign with satisfaction. The Home Fleet had sailed too late and with the wrong objective, as a result it spent the first two days chasing shadows and singularly failed even to impede, let alone forestall the invasion force.

Round one had been clearly won by the Germans. Their next task was to consolidate their gains whilst the Allies could only ponder how best to retaliate.

6

Consolidation and Retaliation

'The German forces which had been landed were commitments for them but potential prizes for us.'

Winston Churchill[1]

Taking Stock

The first formal indication of the German invasion of Norway reached the Foreign Office at 0325 on the morning of 9 April with a telephone call from Sir Cecil Dormer, the Minister in Oslo. The War Cabinet Office, the War Office, Admiralty and Air Ministry were informed at once and the War Cabinet met at 0830 and again at midday. The Cabinet was surprised but not dismayed by the news, after all, it was for some of them the news for which they had been waiting. Mr Churchill optimistically declared that we could liquidate the landings in a week or so,[2] an estimate that proved to be in error by some five years.

Shortly after the second Cabinet meeting of the morning, Sir Clive Dormer was instructed to assure the Norwegian Government of total British support and that steps were being taken immediately to deal with the invasion of Bergen and Trondheim. Contact was established with the French and a meeting of the Supreme War Council convened for that same afternoon in London. The Council reiterated their support for Norway and decided that the first objective should be the recapture of the ports. It was by now known that Narvik had also fallen and the French in particular were still concerned to resolve the iron ore problem.

But ominous signs of dissension within the Cabinet as to the strategic aim were appearing already. Mr Churchill wanted the initial retaliation to be directed against Narvik whilst the Secretary of State for War, Oliver Stanley, stressed the political advantages of regaining Trondheim and Bergen. As the week progressed more and more influential members of the Cabinet swung towards the latter view. Another source of disagreement was the attitude to be taken towards Sweden. Churchill, supporting the French view, was all for inveigling her into the war, but Chamberlain and Halifax were not to be persuaded. They were beginning already to recognise that it might be more difficult than had at first been thought to dislodge the Germans, and that the Allies should not commit themselves to any rash promises to come to the aid of Sweden as well.

In fact it was quickly ascertained that, true to form, Sweden intended to do nothing to aid Norway and would maintain a watchful neutrality – the fence upon which Sweden had been sitting for seven months must by now have felt uncomfortably narrow. Nevertheless, against most expectations, Sweden was able to maintain the perch for the remainder of the war, but had increasingly to accommodate German interests to do so.

By 11 April, much of the earlier optimism was waning, for it was by now clear that the German invasion had been completely successful. Mr Churchill faced a hostile House of Commons to explain the situation so far. His speech, not one of his best, was not universally well received. Harold Nicholson reported in his diary 'It is a feeble, tired speech and it leaves the House in a mood of grave anxiety'.[3]

On the same day, the Military Co-ordination Committee began to echo some members of the War Cabinet in thinking that not all of the effort should be directed towards Narvik. Mr Churchll remained totally unconvinced, but it was nevertheless agreed that the military staffs should study in detail how best to retake Trondheim. Operation 'Maurice' was thus conceived. By the following day, the 12th, Churchill had conceded at the War Cabinet meeting that a limited operation could be mounted in the Trondheim area without detriment to the main thrust against Narvik. The deliberations of these first few days after the invasion illustrate quite clearly that while some planning had been directed towards forestalling a German invasion, almost no thought whatsoever had been given to counteracting a successful occupation of Norway.

Although by the end of the first day the Gemans had gained control of all the major ports in Norway as well as the capital Oslo, in one respect they had failed to achieve their most fundamental objective. It had been hoped that the surprise and speed of execution of the invasion would lead to the complete collapse and unconditional surrender of the Norwegian Government. In this respect, Oslo as the seat of the King and the political and financial centre of the country was the key objective. But as we have seen, this was the target which caused the Germans the most difficulty and the vital hours which elapsed before they could occupy the city gave sufficient time for the Government to react, however hesitantly, to the events which earlier in the morning had threatened to engulf them.

The Storting (Norwegian Government), like its counter-part in Britain, had been receiving diplomatic warnings of a possible invasion for several days. During 8 April these warnings intensified from a variety of sources, but far from heeding them, the Government was more concerned with framing a diplomatic protest against the British for laying mines in their territorial waters. About midday, the Polish submarine *Orzel* in the Skagerrak had challenged and sunk a German merchantman, the *Rio de Janeiro*. Some of the survivors rescued by Norwegian fishing boats volunteered that they were German soldiers proceeding with guns and transport to protect Bergern. This information was available to the Storting by 1715, but they still failed to react positively. They discussed but did not implement mobilisation, they warned the coastal forts but did not authorise the laying of mines in pre-prepared fields, and north of Bergen they did not even order the extinguishing of navigation beacons. Most importantly, they took no action to order the protection of the airfields against attack by paratroops.

By midnight, the reality that invasion was imminent could no longer be evaded, but it was not until 0330 that a partial mobilisation was ordered, and even then they elected to send out the notices by post for activation on 11 April. It was more by accident than design that the Foreign Minister, Dr Halvdan Koht, indicated in a radio broadcast that general mobilisation had been ordered. Many reservists therefore reported unexpectedly early at their assembly points only to find the doors barred against them. Shortly before 0500 the German Minister, Dr Brauer, a diplomat of the old school who did not relish his task, arrived to deliver his ultimatum, but was brusquely seen off by Dr Koht, one of the more stalwart members of the Government. Perhaps heartened by the destruction of the *Blücher*, Dr Koht even suggested in the early morning that Oslo could be defended, but such confidence was not sustained for long, and by 0730 the Royal family, the Storting and several parliamentarians and civil servants left Oslo by special train and road for the north. They also managed to take with them the greater part of the nation's gold reserves. Rarely can there have been a Government which stumbled more ineffectively into war.

The Storting proceeded initially to Hamar and then to Elverum only 50 miles from the Swedish border. The Storting was at first disposed to negotiate with the Germans and the King himself, with Dr Koht, listened to the German demands. But once in control of Oslo, the German terms had hardened, and the establishment of an unconstitutional government under Quisling was too much for the Government to swallow and the King threatened to abdicate. At last the Storting made the decision to resist: it was the first courageous and decisive move they had made for some days. Even so, it was inevitable that a period of recuperation and consolidation was needed before the Norwegian Army could be regarded as a viable force.

The Grip Tightens

Consolidation was now the foremost requirement of General von Falkenhorst and Group XXI as well. Depending as it did on speed and precision and the consequential decision to transport the troops to their destination in warships, the invasion force had only been able to carry with it the minimum of equipment essential to the initial assault. Adequate reinforcement and re-supply were, therefore, an even more essential condition for the overall success of the operation than operations planners would normally consider prudent.

As we have seen, the Germans had ingeniously decided therefore to plant some of their most needed supplies in the invasion ports shortly in advance of 'W' day by concealing them in merchant ships ostensibly going about their normal day-to-day business. Officially known as the Ausfuhrstaffel, but subsequently more aptly described as 'Trojan Horses', this proved to be one of the least successful aspects of 'Weseruebung', and was to have serious consequences for both the survival of the fleet and the support of the ground forces. Of the four tankers, only the large *Jan Wellum* (12,000 tons) sailing from Murmansk by arrangement with the Russians reached her destination on schedule. The *Kattegat* scuttled herself off Narvik after sighting the Norwegian auxiliary *Nordkap*, and the *Skagerrak*, still at sea on the 14th, was also scuttled when challenged by a British cruiser. Of the three freighters for Narvik, the *Rauenfels* was sunk in the Vestfiord, the *Alster* captured, and the *Baerenfels* eventually put into Bergen where she was sunk by aircraft on 14 April. Only one of the three freighters destined for Trondheim survived, the *Levante*, which arrived four days late: the *Sao Paolo* hit a mine and the *Main* was sunk by a Norwegian torpedo boat. A Norwegian destroyer also sank the *Roda*, the last of the Trojan Horses making for Stavanger.

Their support arrangements now in disarray, the most pressing need for re-supply was at Narvik and Trondheim where the provision of fuel was essential for the destoyers which could not make the round trip without refuelling. Fortunately, the main support element (the Seetransportstaffel) of freighters and tankers had also left early to arrive at their destinations after the initial landing by the invasion force was complete. It was one of these, the *Rio de Janeiro* which had been sunk by the *Orzel* on the 8th and which had so nearly given the game away. But it was recognised that the passage of merchantmen along the Norwegian coast would become completely untenable soon after 'W' hour, and so it was intended that most of the follow-up troops would be channelled through Oslo as the shortest and safest route. From Oslo, they would fan out to link up with the assault forces and complete the occupation of the whole country.

Submariner's Revenge

At first, the main logistic chain also ran into serious trouble. Vice Admiral Max Horton commanding the British Submarine Service was very familiar with the shallow waters between Germany and Norway. In the First World War he had led a flotilla of submarines through the Skagerrak and the Kattegat into the Baltic where he had created such havoc with enemy shipping that it became known as 'Horton's Sea'. Unlike most of his colleagues he had long believed that Norway was too tempting a target for the Germans to ignore, and in the first week of April his submarines quietly slipped into place to wait for the invaders. Three each were positioned off the west coast of Denmark and in the Skagerrak and the Kattegat, to be joined on 8 April by six more.

But the War Cabinet, despite the toll of merchant shipping which had already fallen to the U-boats, still applied restrictive rules of engagement to the British submarine captains encountering transports or tankers. They were required to surface, order their quarry to stop and give the crew time to abandon ship before attacking with torpedoes. Whilst this generous code of chivalry may have been safe enough in the wider reaches of the Atlantic, it was far less healthy to linger on the surface in the restricted waters around Denmark. Even so, the *Orzel*, as we have already seen, had intercepted and sunk the *Rio de Janeiro*, and on the same day the *Trident* had sunk, by the approved method, the *Posidonia* carrying 8,000 tons of fuel to Stavanger.

It was not until 1330 on 9 April that the restrictions were lifted and the *Sunfish* immediately dispatched the German merchantman *Amasis* with a close range torpedo. Lieut Commander Slaughter was to claim three more victims before his patrol was complete.

On the following day it was the turn of the *Triton*. Lieut Commander E. F. Pizey lay in wait for a convoy heading for Oslo. Slipping through the screen of patrol boats, he sank the *Friedenau* and the *Wigbert*, between them carrying 900 troops, and for good measure accounted for one of the patrol boats as well. This was sufficient to persuade the German Navy to use only warships and small vessels making the short crossing from Jutland for the transfer of soldiers to Norway although equipment and supplies still had to be moved by merchantmen. On the 11th it was the *Triad* which sank the *Iona* at the entrance to the Oslofiord, and the *Sealion* which accounted for a supply ship in the Kattegat. The *Snapper* joined in the fun on the 12th, boldly surfacing in daylight to sink the tanker *Moonsund* by gunfire after missing with two torpedoes. The *Sunfish* completed her tally of four on the 14th.

But it became increasingly dangerous work and four submarines were eventually lost in return. Already on the 9th the *Thistle* had gone, sunk by the U-boat U4 after they had spent most of the day searching for each other. On the 14th the *Sterlet* was lost with all hands. Increased anti-submarine patrols both by aircraft and ships forced the submarines to lie low most of the day and success diminished as the hazards increased. Even so, Admiral Raeder was forced to resort to ordering the use of U-boats to carry essential supplies to Narvik and Trondheim, particularly aviation fuel and ammunition, although attempts to re-supply Narvik by submarine were soon abandoned.

In all, at least ten transports or tankers were destroyed and others damaged in the opening days of the campaign.

But the submarines alone could not stem the increasing flow of reinforcements and supplies to Norway. They were always likely to be observed if on the surface by the streams of aircraft which flowed regularly across the Skagerrak and Kattegat, and the shallow waters did not afford adequate protection against the anti-submarine ships which mounted regular patrols. Often they could only lie quiet and motionless during the day and hope both to recharge their batteries and air supplies as well as catch a passing ship during the hours of darkness. But they made a valuable, although not decisive, contribution to the Allied effort to disrupt the German lines of communication during the first weeks of the campaign.

On 22nd April, with typically Gallic bravado, three large French destroyers entered the Skagerrak where they were engaged by the German 7th Patrol Flotilla whilst still some way from the shipping lanes. After an indecisive action they withdrew before dawn when they would have provided more welcome target practice for the Luftwaffe. The exercise was not repeated.

The Luftwaffe also moved large numbers of troops in the early days in Ju 52 transport aircraft. It is estimated that over 13,000 missions were flown carrying a total of nearly 30,000 troops and large quantities of urgent supplies.[4] After a sticky start, the Germans steadily improved their logistic arrangements as the campaign progressed and as the submarine threat gradually diminished. By the beginning of May, the re-supply organisation was becoming remarkably efficient and was one of the main reasons why the Germans were able so successfully to secure a stranglehold on Southern and Central Norway. When the Allies eventually evacuated Norway completely in the middle of June, the 370 ships of the supply fleet had moved 108,000 troops, 16,000 horses, 20,000 vehicles and 110,000 tons of stores.[5] What had at first seemed an incipient disaster had been overcome by typically Teutonic thoroughness and tenacity.

The Home Fleet Attacked – The Lesson of Air Power

The Home Fleet, meanwhile, had joined up with its supporting Cruiser Squadrons by noon on 9 April and lay about 100 miles to the north-west of Stavanger. The Commander-in-Chief had been receiving reports throughout the morning of the German landings and it was now obvious that retaliation rather than prevention was the only positive response available to him. As a first step the Admiralty, at Admiral Forbes' suggestion, ordered an attack on Bergen by Admiral Layton's 18th Cruiser Squadron. Forbes, however, decided that only the supporting destroyers, seven in number led by Captain Vian of *Altmark* fame, but now flying his flag in the *Afridi*, would actually proceed up the fiord. But it would have been dark by the time they arrived, there was no information on the location of shore batteries or booms, and no time to prepare a proper plan. By mid-afternoon the operation had been cancelled.

It was all rather irresolute and negative, and despite the risks of operating large war ships in restricted waters, failed to make use of the overwhelming force which the Home Fleet could concentrate on individual targets. It contrasted unfavourably with the spirit and enterprise shown by Admiral Whitworth in the *Renown* earlier in the day, and shortly to be demonstrated even more forcefully by Captain Warburton-Lee at Narvik.

However, a new factor soon pervaded Admiral Forbes' thinking. The Home Fleet had been intermittently shadowed throughout the morning of 9 April by a German reconnaissance aircraft, and from 1430 onwards the Fleet was subjected to concentrated air attack by some 90 German bombers until approaching darknesss at last brought relief. It was not the first time the Home Fleet had been attacked from the air, for as early as the first month of the war, the aircraft carrier *Ark Royal* had been subjected to dive bomb attack as well as medium level precision bombing. That the former was the greater threat was already firmly implanted in Admiral Forbes' mind: 'control personnel were obviously unprepared for such high performance dive bombing'[6] he wrote in his dispatch of the action of 26 September 1939.

Since the First World War, the Royal Navy had maintained an uneasy relationship with the aeroplane – it introduced a new, and to many traditional sailors, an unwelcome element into the familiar arena of sea warfare. Nevertheless, it would not be correct to say they ignored the threat posed by aircraft in the inter-war years, but they made a number of critical misjudgements which in 1939 quickly exposed the vulnerability of surface ships to air attack. Firstly, they failed to recognise the value of the fighter aircraft as the most effective counter at that time to air attack; and secondly, they overestimated the killing power of the anti-aircraft gun. On small ship platforms in heavy seas, the guns fitted at the outbreak of war were clumsy and unreliable, and the destroyers traditional attributes of speed and agility generally negated their ability to provide a stable, accurate weapons platform. At the outbreak of war, the only Fleet Air Arm fighters were the Sea Gladiator, of which there were only twelve on the *Glorious*, and the dual roled Blackburn Skua which in 1939 was not really effective either as fighter or dive bomber despite its remarkable initial success to be recounted shortly. At the beginning of the war there were eight Skuas allocated to the *Furious* and eighteen on the *Ark Royal*. The *Furious* had subsequently been modified in 1940 to carry Swordfish only, although the possibility of embarking Skuas or a mixed force instead still existed. When the *Furious* departed the Clyde on the 8 April, it had been decided to sail without the Skuas. This was to prove a serious mistake.

The 18th Cruiser Squadron returning from the aborted sortie against Bergen was the first to attract attention. The cruisers *Southampton* and *Glasgow* suffered some damage from near misses and the destroyers were finding difficulty in aligning their guns in the heavy seas. It was too much for Commander Sir Anthony Buzzard in the destroyer *Gurkha* who turned his ship out of wind to establish a better gun platform. Unfortunately he quickly became separated from the rest of the Squadron and was immediately set upon by the bombers who relished the opportunity of escaping the concentrated fire of the whole escort. The *Gurkha* was quickly overwhelmed and left sinking, and Captain Vian regretted later not ordering the *Gurkha* to remain within the screen. But in these early days of air-sea warfare, there had been little time to work out the best tactics to confront the new threat from the sky. Fortunately the cruiser *Aurora* stumbled across the stricken ship by chance and saved most of the crew.

The anti-aircraft guns hammered away all afternoon, and whilst not achieving many direct hits, put up a sufficiently noisy barrage to deter the German pilots from coming too low or too close. The *Rodney* was the only other ship which received a direct hit, but her deck armour plating, on this occasion, proved sufficent protection against a 1100 lb bomb.

Several lessons were immediately clear for all who wished to see. Ships without fighter support were vulnerable against air attack and the anti-aircraft guns available were difficult to fire and inaccurate in other than relatively calm sea states. Armour plating, whilst providing some protection for the capital ships, was obviously no answer for those ships whose main characteristics were intended to be speed and manoeuvrability. All weather anti-aircraft guns were the only possible means of protection for the light cruisers and destroyers. Enormous quantities of ammunition were expended, in some cases nearly half the ship's total complement, but only four Ju 88s were destroyed. High level precision bombing against manoeuvring ships had proved almost totally ineffective and a direct hit could be claimed only as pure chance, but dive bombing was another matter entirely. It could be very accurate if pilots pressed home their attack, and as the ship's main armament could not be elevated above 40°, it was a comparatively safe form of attack as well. The same lessons were plain to see from British air attacks on German ships, with the essential difference that neither the RAF nor the Royal Navy possessed a dive bomber to match the Ju 87/Stuka.

Under cover of darkness, Admiral Fobres withdrew to the west and on the morning of 10 April met up with the aircraft carrier *Furious* and the battleship *Warspite*. But what to do next? Apart from the *Gurkha*, the Home Fleet was still intact after the air attacks of the previous afternoon, but the experience was sufficient to deter the Commander-in-Chief from risking his capital ships again within range of the Stuka which had made such an impression on his thinking. He decided to leave the area south of Bergen to the submarines and Bergen itself to the shore-based bombers, and concentrate himself on the more northerly objectives – Trondheim and Narvik. The Achilles' heel of the modern warship was already dreadfully apparent.

On the evening of 9 April, twelve Wellingtons and the same number of Hampdens attacked the harbour at Bergen without effect, and two hours later, the *Köln* departed to return to Germany. But the *Königsberg*, which had been badly damaged on the way in, was not so lucky.

The following morning, fifteen Skuas of 800 Squadron (Captain R. T. Partridge RM) and 308 Squadron (Lieutenant W. P. Lucy) based at Hatson in the Orkneys attacked the harbour which was at the limit of their radius of action. Flying above cloud most of the way and navigating by dead reckoning with remarkable accuracy, they made a perfect land fall. Captain Partridge was leading the formation and achieved complete surprise. All fifteen aircraft in line astern in a steep dive were able to complete their attacks, and the first seven had climbed away before the German gunners even awoke to the threat. Three direct hits with 500 lb bombs were scored on the *Königsberg* which quickly rolled over and sank. It was the first time that a capital ship had been destroyed by air attack, and it was ironic that this remarkable achievement should have fallen to the Fleet Air Arm which had been so sadly neglected in the run-up to the war. No aircraft were shot down in the attack although one failed to recover to Hatson. It was the first of many personal marks that Captain Partridge was to make on the air war in Norway.

Encouraged by this success, Admiral Forbes ordered Swordfish aircraft from the carrier *Furious* to be launched against Trondheim. Reconnaissance on the evening of the 10th had disclosed the *Hipper* anchored in the harbour and at dawn on the 11th, eighteen Swordfish trundled into the lightening sky, heavily laden with torpedoes. But their quarry had slipped away in the night and only two destroyers remained sheltering in the fiord. The much slower Swordfish did not achieve the surprise which had been so valuable to the Skuas the day before at Bergen and they encountered heavy flak as they approached the harbour. They pressed home their attack, but to no avail, the water near the destroyers was so shallow that the torpedoes hit the bottom and exploded before their depth keeping mechanism could achieve a stable platform for their run-in to the target. Unlike the first dive bombing operation which had accounted for the *Königsberg*, the first torpedo attack was a complete failure. The Swordfish had to wait for Taranto to achieve its moment of glory.

In the afternoon of the same day, the Luftwaffe retaliated and damaged the destroyer *Eclipse* which had to be towed back to Lerwick by the *Escort*.

Air power was quickly making its mark on the operations of both navies: it was soon to impose a similar burden on the land forces as well. Admirals and generals were being forced to look towards the sky in a way that had never been necessary in any preceding war.

Returning Home – The German Navy Suffers Again

It had been intended that having completed their tasks, the warships should return immediately to Germany. At Narvik, the arrival of only one tanker was a serious constraint as the *Jan Wellum* could only refuel two ships at a time, each pair taking about eight hours. Consequently, all the destroyers were still at Narvik when they were caught by the 2nd Destroyer Flotilla in the early hours of 10 April in the first major naval confrontation of the campaign. The *Gneisenau* and the *Scharnhorst*, after their encounter with the *Renown*, eventually followed a roundabout route to the west, joining up with the *Hipper* from Trondheim and entering Wilhelmshaven on the evening of 12 April. Neither the *Königsberg* or the *Bremse* was fit to return on the night of 9 April; but the *Köln*, despite being forced to hide in a fiord after being spotted by a British aircraft, also returned safely to Wilhelmshaven on 11 April.

The *Karlsruhe*, which had encountered so much difficulty getting in to Kristiansand, ran into even more trouble getting out, being torpedoed by the submarine *Truant* just outside the harbour. Lieut Commander C. H. Hutchinson had suffered a very frustrating day. He had been hounded by anti-submarine craft throughout the daylight hours and it was not until 1830 that he was able to bring *Truant* up to periscope depth. He was immediately rewarded however by the sight of the *Karlsruhe* zig-zagging across a smooth sea accompanied by three torpedo boats. He carefully manoeuvred into position and fired a full salvo of torpedoes. Captain Rieve saw the tracks approaching and turned violently to avoid. But he was not quite fast enough, one hit aft, putting both engines out of action and wrecking the steering gear. Drifting and taking in water, Rieve gave the order to abandon ship. Three hours later the *Karlsruhe* had to be sunk by her own escort of torpedo boats.

Lieut Commander J. H. James in the *Spearfish* was equally lucky. He too had had a harrowing day dodging the persistent anti-submarine ships which had held him submerged for 20 hours. At last the persistent throb of their propellors died away and at about 2330 James decided that it was safe to surface. He had few aggressive intentions, only seeking the relief of the cold fresh air and the opportunity to recharge the batteries. But an hour later he suddenly saw the wake of a large ship travelling at high speed. It was the *Lützow*, which had been the only ship able to leave Oslo after the devastating reception Group 5 had received on the previous day. There were no destroyers available to escort her, but it was believed that a high speed dash under the cover of darkness would be relatively safe, for she was badly needed to prepare for another Atlantic foray.

On hearing of the British submarine's successes in the Kattegat, Captain Thiele decided to make a wider detour to the west. It was an unlucky decision; for the new track led him straight into the path of the *Spearfish*. Hastily getting into position to fire, James loosed a salvo of six torpedoes at almost point blank range. One hit aft destroying both the *Lützow*'s screws and rudder. Drifting and taking on water, Thiele was very fortunate to be taken in tow by a Danish tug before running aground or sinking. It was to be 12 months before the *Lützow* left Kiel again.

The submarine captains had amply repaid Admiral Forbes' decision to leave the area south of Bergen to them. Although the loss of their transports did not prevent the Germans successfully establishing their lines of communication with Norway, the sinking of the *Karlsruhe* and the near destruction of the *Lützow* were both notable achievements even if abetted by a generous measure of good luck. They well deserved the Admiralty's message on 14 April 'You are all doing magnificent work'.[7]

Commodore Bonte's destroyer flotilla should have left Narvik on the night of 9 April, but because of the refuelling difficulties he now planned to leave overnight on the 10th: it was not to be. On the evening of the 9th, he dispersed his destroyers as a precaution against air attack; two to shelter in the Ballangenfiord and three in the Herjangsfiord, one to remain on patrol in the Ofotfiord and the remaining four to stay in the harbour refuelling.

The German Navy's intelligence at this stage of the war was far superior to that of the Royal Navy. Many of the Navy's signals were intercepted and Bonte had been notified by Group West of the presence of those elements of the Home Fleet which were in the vicinity of the Lofoten Islands. In the circumstances he took surprisingly few precautions against an attack from the sea and he was far more concerned by the risk of air attack. In such a distant location this could have been launched only from an aircraft carrier, the nearest of which was still far away at this stage. Perhaps like Admiral Whitworth on the night before, he considered that the weather was too bad for any attacking force to contemplate braving the hazardous waters of the Ofotfiord. He might also have had an exaggerated confidence in the ability of the three U-boats on patrol to sound the alarm if not deal themselves with any impending attack. He received a message from the U51 of the presence of five destroyers, but they were heading west at the time and he disregarded the information. It was, in fact, Warburton-Lee's destroyer flotilla passing time before making their assault up the fiord. Rather like the sighting of the *Hipper* by the Sunderland on the previous day which so misled Admiral Forbes, accurate information was misinterpreted. Perhaps, however, Commodore Bonte was exhausted by the traumas of the previous three days and simply failed to address the risk in sufficient depth. Whatever the reason, he retired to bed in his cabin, totally unaware of the nemesis approaching.

The First Battle of Narvik

Captain Warburton-Lee with his 2nd Destroyer Flotilla had by 0930 on the 9th already established a patrol across the entrance to the Vestfiord, but at this stage was still unaware that the Germans had actually landed at Narvik. At the same time, Captain Spooner in the *Repulse*, on his own initiative, signalled that he was proceeding to the Vestfiord with the light cruiser *Penelope* and four destroyers 'to prevent any German forces entering Narvik and to join Captain (D)'.[8] Shortly afterwards, Admiral Forbes sent a signal to Warburton-Lee ordering him to send destroyers to Narvik 'to make certain no enemy troops land there'.[9] Five minutes later, Admiral Whitworth signalled Warburton-Lee ordering him to join him 50 miles south-west of Skomvaer. At midday the Admiralty joined in, signalling Warburton-Lee:

> Press report states one German ship has arrived Narvik and landed a small force. Proceed Narvik and sink or harass enemy ship. It is at your discretion to land force and capture Narvik from enemy present. Try to get possession of battery if not already in enemy hands.[10]

Warburton-Lee might well have been forgiven for wondering who was running this show. Further comment on the command and control arrangements in force at this time is superfluous.

Warburton-Lee was initially cautious. His only source of intelligence was the press report passed by the Admiralty, which seemed hardly credible, that one ship had arrived at Narvik with a small force. His only other positive information, received from the Admiralty, was of the probable existence and strength of the batteries at Framnes on the peninsula immediately to the north of Narvik, and at Ramnes in the narrows at the head of the Ofotfiord. He decided therefore to consult the Norwegian pilot station at Tranöy in the Vestfiord. His fears were confirmed, he was told that six German warships larger than his own and a submarine were already in the fiord and that the entrance to the Ofotfiord was probably mined. In the Tranöy pilot's view, a much larger force than that available to Warburton-Lee would be needed to reach Narvik.

This posed a considerable dilemma for Warburton-Lee as he pondered what to do next. He had a clear direction from the Admiralty, but as he now knew, one which was based on inaccurate intelligence. He knew that stronger forces were on the way to assist him, both the *Renown* and the *Repulse* and her escort would arrive later in the day, but not, or so he believed, in time to mount an attack at dawn on the 10th. He retired to his cabin to consider his next step. Should he request further guidance or orders, should he simply wait for the reinforcements, or should he press on anyway even though his own small force was probably outnumbered? An attack at dawn had technical advantages in that he would be going in at high tide which might lift him over any mines that had been laid, and the longer he delayed, the more time the Germans would have available to organise their defences. But perhaps most influential of all, his training, background and above all temperament inclined him towards pressing on, and he knew he would have the full support of his Flotilla captains and their crews. He reasoned that speed and surprise were his strongest cards, if he waited for reinforcements the attack would have to be delayed beyond dawn. He decided therefore to press ahead, advised the Admiralty of the latest known enemy strength, and ended his signal with the now famous peroration 'intend attacking at dawn, high water.'[11]

The 20th Destroyer Flotilla was left to guard the Vestfiord and Warburton-Lee in the *Hardy*, accompanied by the *Hotspur* (Commander Herbert Layman), *Havock* (Lieutenant Commander Rafe Courage) and *Hunter* (Lieutenant Commander Lindsay de Villers) proceeded up the fiord. He was joined on the way in by the *Hostile* (Commander J. P. 'Willy' Wright) who had been escorting the *Birmingham*, but had turned back on his own initiative to join the action. Although the Admiralty began to get cold feet during the night and watered down their original directive, it was too late as the small force felt its way slowly up the fiord in mist and almost continuous snow. Admiral Whitworth, who had heard the exchange of signals between the Admiralty and Warburton-Lee was also debating whether to join in, for he knew that he could still make Narvik by dawn and believed that the *Repulse* or the *Penelope* could do the same. But the Admiralty appeared to have taken command and he decided not to intervene, although not before he had issued and then cancelled an order to the *Penelope* to support Warburton-Lee with four destroyers. This turned out to be unfortunate as in the later stages of the operation, the presence of a cruiser in the fiord would have proved extremely useful. Admiral Forbes did nothing, probably somewhat miffed by the way the Admiralty had taken matters out of his hands.

The entrance to Narvik is narrow and difficult and normally requires a pilot beyond Tranöy. The Vestfiord narrows abruptly at Baroy, turns towards the east and becomes the Ofotfiord for the final thirty mile run into Narvik. At the narrows, the position which both the Germans and the British mistakenly believed contained coastal batteries, the mountains fall sheer into the sea on both sides of the fiord. The Ofotfiord opens out again towards Narvik with wide inlets providing good shelter on both sides. At this time of the year all was shrouded in snow. Feeling his way gingerly up the fiord, Warburton-Lee at one stage all but led the whole force on to the rocks when a white, eerie, hillside suddenly appeared out of the blizzard. On another occasion, the line was again thrown into disarray by an unsuspecting merchantman which steamed straight through the formation, probably without seeing any of them. However, they had one stroke of luck, for due to an uncharacteristic misunderstanding, the *Diether von Roeder*, the destroyer detailed to patrol the Ofotfiord was absent at the crucial moment when the Flotilla was creeping up in the snow. Even so, it was fortunate that the Germans were incapable within the confined waters of the fiord of intercepting morse code messages, for the destroyers frequently had to transmit their position to each other in order to remain in contact. As mentioned above, one of the U-boats warned Commodore Bonte of the presence of destroyers in the Vestfiord, but the other two saw nothing, including the one critically located in the Baroy narrows. The surprise factor which was so crucial to Warburton-Lee's plan was working well for him.

At 0420, as dawn was breaking, the snow began to abate and the visibility temporarily improved. The Flotilla crept quietly round the corner into the Beisfiord and were amazed by the vast array of merchant shipping spread out before them. The harbour at Narvik consists of a shallow bay facing west at the head of the Beisfiord. On the north-east side of the harbour was the ore depot on the little peninsula separating the Beisfiord from the narrow Rombaksfiord. Towards the north could be seen the Herjangsfiord, although unfortunately when they passed it had been too dark and misty to see the three German destroyers lurking therein. The *Hardy* went in first alone leaving the *Hunter* and *Havock* to take their turn. Meanwhile, Commodore Bonte slept soundly in his cabin in the *Wilhelm Heidkamp*.

Indeed, there was little sign of life in the harbour at all as the *Hardy* gently nosed her way in amongst the mass of merchant shipping. At first there was no indication of the whereabouts of the destroyers which were anchored in line only about 500 yards offshore. But suddenly the *Anton Schmitt* and the *Wilhelm Heidkamp* were revealed through a gap in the merchantmen – they were a sitting target. The *Hardy* fired three torpedoes, the first of which missed but hit instead a merchantman, producing a satisfying explosion. But this was nothing to the impact of the second which hit the *Heidkamp* near the aft magazine causing an enormous explosion which literally blew off the stern. The town slept no longer, and Commodore Bonte and 80 of his men died instantly: nobody noticed where the third torpedo had gone. Warburton-Lee now swung his ship through 180 degrees and made his escape, launching two more torpedoes and firing at two other destroyers, but neither appeared to suffer any damage.

As soon as the *Hardy* had left the harbour, the *Hunter* replaced her and created absolute mayhem in the confined space. There was none of the clinical precision of the

Hardy, she blazed away indiscriminately at everything within sight with both guns and torpedoes, hitting several merchant ships and the *Anton Schmitt*. Meanwhile, Commander Wright in the *Hostile* who had been somewhat disappointed that he was missing all the action manoeuvred to a position from which he could engage the *Diether von Roeder* and scored two damaging hits. So far none of the British ships had been hit, although fire was now being returned from some of the destroyers and by light weapons from the battery at Framnes.

So surprised were the German crews at this unexpected awakening that for some time they believed they were under air attack. The *Havock* replaced the *Hunter* and quickly finished off the *Anton Schmitt* in even more spectacular fashion: the ship was blown into two pieces and sank immediately. Several merchant ships were attacked by torpedoes and the *Hans Lüdemann* by shell fire causing some damage and making her immobile. Well satisfied with his work, Courage now withdrew under the covering fire and smoke of *Hotspur* and *Hostile* who had been left on guard outside the harbour.

The information Warburton-Lee had been given by the Tranöy pilot now proved critically misleading. He had been told that six German warships had passed into the fiord and he had already counted at least five inside the harbour. It is difficult to comprehend why the British intelligence was so poor, after all one battleship, two cruisers and ten destroyers had been identified heading north as early as the afternoon of 7 April, at least part of the force was known to be north of Trondheim on the morning of the 8th, and it might have been surmised on the morning of the 9th that the *Gneisenau* and *Scharnhorst* who had now been observed without the destroyers, might have left them at the entrance to the Vestfiord. In fact, neither Admiral Forbes nor the Admiralty seem to have given much consideration to where the destroyers might have gone during the 9th, even though from midday at the latest, the scale of the invasion was known. It was a major mistake not to call for aerial reconnaissance on 9 April off the Norwegian coastline from Trondheim southwards which would have enabled a deduction to be made of the probable size of the residual force at Narvik. For had Warburton-Lee suspected that there were other destroyers lurking in the side fiords, he would surely have made his escape after the first successful attack.

But based on the information from Tranöy Warburton-Lee reasoned that there was little danger in returning to the attack to capitalise on their good work so far, and he quickly established that between them they had sixteen remaining torpedoes. Once more, the destroyers returned into the harbour mouth in an anti-clockwise circling manoeuvre to launch torpedoes and to rake the harbour with shell fire. This time they received a more hostile reaction and were lucky to escape a salvo of eight torpedoes launched by the *Diether von Roeder*, which although immobile after the hits from the *Hostile* proved the most wideawake and aggressive of the German destroyers. Nevertheless, considerably more havoc was caused within the harbour, and this time one of the British merchantmen, the *Blythmoor*, was sunk. The *Jan Wellum*, sitting right in the middle of the harbour miraculously escaped, and the *von Roeder* was eventually beached. Even now Warburton-Lee was not finished. The *Hostile* in which Wright had been carefully conserving his torpedoes in the hope of finishing off the *von Roeder* which he had selected as his own personal target, ran in again with the other ships, suffering the first hit the Flotilla received in over an hour's fighting – a remarkable result fully justifying their leader's faith in the value of surprise.

The three destroyers in the Herjangsfiord under Captain Bey, the *Wolfgang Zenker*, *Erich Köellner* and the *Erich Giese* had at last been alerted to the action taking place in the harbour and weighed anchor. They were sighted leaving the fiord as Warburton-Lee marshalled his ships into line for the return up the Ofotfiord. Signalling for 30 knots, he raced away to the west, firing as he went. Fortunately, these three German destroyers had not yet been refuelled and they soon dropped astern: it appeared as though the Flotilla would still escape unscathed. But the *Georg Thiele* and *Bernd von Arnim*, which had been sheltering in the Ballangenfiord, suddenly appeared out of the clearing mist: the *Arnim* rather happier in the sheltered waters of the fiord than when she had encountered the *Glowworm* in the open sea. Warburton-Lee thought at first that the oncoming ships were British reinforcements, but his challenge was answered by an accurately placed salvo of 5 inch shells. Unfortunately, the Flotilla was now in line astern and not well disposed to face a new threat. Furthermore, the vision of the succeeding ships was obscured by smoke and the last three in the line were concentrating their attention to the rear, not knowing that Captain Bey was in fact engaged in his own little action with the destroyers in the harbour still blazing away at everything in sight. The *Hardy* was thus left initially to face this new threat alone. Accurate shells continued to pound the Hardy, one destroying the bridge and killing or mortally wounding the captain and most of the other occupants. The *Hardy* turned away as her remaining crew sought to beach the crippled ship which Paymaster Lieutenant Geoffrey Stanning, the only officer left alive on the bridge eventually achieved.

The *Havock* was next in line and initially followed the *Hardy*, not realising that the latter was now only desperately heading for the beach. Eventually adjusting themselves to the rapidly reducing range, both sides began to take desultory hits. As they swung past each other, the two German destroyers reversed course to pursue the British line, but Courage in the *Havock*, also made a 180° turn towards the east, unwisely, as the sensible course of action would have been to head for the Vestfiord as fast as possible. As a result the *Havock* was straddled for no return and eventually rejoined the end of the line. The *Hunter* was the next to be hit, badly, her engines stopped and burning furiously, she swung out of control towards the enemy. The *Hotspur* immediately behind, her vision obscured by smoke and her bridge controls severed, had no chance – she drove straight into the side of the *Hunter* with a nerve rending roar of tearing steel and escaping steam. The *Hostile* only narrowly avoided joining the pile up – it was all rather like a 1940 version of a motorway shunt. At last the *Hotspur* withdrew painfully to the rear and the *Hunter* slowly righted herself, but burning furiously continued to roll slowly to starboard and settled lower in the water. Even so her aft gun continued to fire at the *Georg Thiele*, now very close.

The *Hotspur*, underway again, made her way slowly towards the west continuing to engage the *Arnim*, but receiving even more hits in return. The *Georg Thiele* also suffered in the exchange, burning fore and aft and with no fire control for her remaining guns, she withdrew from the battle. Captain Bey, having at last disentangled himself from his unfortunate encounter with his own destroyers in the harbour, now rejoined the action, although with nothing of the zeal and determination shown by Captains Wolff and Rechel in the *Thiele* and the *Arnim*. Indeed, the *Arnim* also having withdrawn to lick her wounds, it was Bey's lassitude which allowed the *Hotspur* to escape.

The operation that had been going so well was now a shambles, only the *Havock* and the *Hostile* had avoided serious damage although they had exchanged fire at point blank range with the German ships as they passed each other in opposite directions. The two remaining ships at first gave up the *Hotspur* for lost, but when they saw her emerge from the smoke two miles astern, both Wright and Courage instinctively turned back to offer assistance. Heading once again towards the east, all forward guns firing, it proved enough to deter the timid Bey, and the *Zenker*, *Köellner* and the *Giese* turned away to finish off the *Hunter*. But it was too late, the *Hunter* had already sunk. To their credit however, the Germans spent a long time looking for survivors and forty-eight were saved. As with the *Hipper* and the *Glowworm*, following even the fiercest encounters, the German Navy's humanity towards the survivors was in the highest traditions of the war at sea.

Having extricated the *Hotspur* from the very jaws of the enemy, the depleted flotilla limped away to sea. But their day was not yet quite finished. The *Rauenfels* was one of the missing supply ships which was already causing General Dietl increasing concern. Nevertheless, better late than never, she was now entering the Ofotfiord oblivious of the events of the last three hours. The Germans almost scored a home goal. The U25 patrolling near the Baroy Light fired a torpedo against the *Rauenfels* which fortunately missed. But her good luck was not to hold, for rounding the corner, she came face to face with the three departing British destroyers. Commander Wright ordered the *Rauenfels* to stop which was ignored, but quickly recognising her as an enemy merchantman, fired two shells which helped to concentrate the captain's attention. Wright, pressing on with the limping *Hotspur*, now ordered the *Havock* to sink the merchantman after giving the crew time to escape. Seeing the *Raunfels* had now stopped, Courage launched a whaler to investigate, but the boat's crew were surprised to see one of the *Rauenfels* lifeboats sailing towards them, the crew having apparently abandoned their ship with unseemly haste. Lieutenant Burfield cautiously boarded the *Rauenfels* which was burning and which had obviously been abandoned in a hurry with only the slightest attempt to destroy the ships secret papers. His unease growing he quickly reboarded the whaler to return to the *Havock*. After recovering the whaler, two more rounds were fired into the *Rauenfels* with spectacular results, leaving no doubt as to the ship's cargo and the reason why she had been abandoned with such alacrity. Commander Wright, well away round the corner in the Vestfiord, was convinced that he saw the *Rauenfel's* funnel gyrating above the top of a 500 foot hill![12]

The first battle of Narvik was over: it was now time to reflect on the balance sheet. Warburton-Lee's gamble on speed and surprise had been an outstanding success. In the first phase of the battle the honours lay entirely with the British. The *Wilhelm Heidkamp* and the *Anton Schmitt* were totally destroyed and the *Diether von Roeder* so damaged that she never sailed again. The *Hans Lüdemann* was also seriously damaged, all of this in return for a few inconsequential hits on the *Hostile*. If Warburton-Lees had departed at this stage, the operation would have been regarded as an astounding success, for in the absence of repair facilities, a seriously damaged ship was almost useless.

The honours in the second phase undoubtedly went to the Germans, in particular the *Bernd von Arnim* and the *Georg Thiele*. The *Hardy* was disabled and the *Hunter* sunk, and the *Hotspur* lucky to escape with severe damage. In return the two German destroyers were damaged, but still useable. Of the ten German destroyers, only the *Hermann Künne*, and the *Wolfgang Zenker*, *Erich Köellner* and the *Erich Giese* of the smaller and less heavily armed Leberecht Maas Class were undamaged. It was unfortunate that the *Jan Wellum* had escaped unscathed, for without fuel the remaining destroyers would have been helpless, and the second battle of Narvik would have been unnecessary. On the other hand, the sinking of the *Rauenfels* was a significant bonus. On balance, the advantage definitely lay with the 2nd Flotilla and Captain Warburton-Lee's agonising decision of the previous night had been vindicated.

However, none of the others in a position to influence the action – the Admiralty, Admiral Forbes or Admiral Whitworth emerge with quite so much credit. They all knew that Warburton-Lee's small force should have really been supported with heavier ships which were in fact available. Whilst it is dangerous to speculate on the outcome of a hypothetical action, the presence of the *Renown* or the *Penelope* in the Ofotfiord, as the *Warspite* was in the second battle, would almost certainly have tipped what was a worthwhile success into an overwhelming and conclusive victory. Captain Warburton-Lee was awarded the Victoria Cross for leading this daring and gallant action, the first to be awarded in the Second World War.[13] He lies buried today in the neat little churchyard at Ballangen along with other members of his crew and six soldiers of the South Wales Borderers.

Intermission

The two days after the Warburton-Lee operation reflected little credit on either side. After meeting the *Penelope* and briefly considering whether they should together return to the Ofotfiord, Commander Wright in the *Hostile* escorted the crippled *Hotspur* to Skjeldfiord in the Lofoten Islands where the extent of her damage could be assessed. Meanwhile a patrol was set up at the entrance to the Vestfiord both to preclude the escape of the ships incarcerated in the harbour and to prevent reinforcements getting in. On the evening of the 10th, doubtless on the arrival of Mr Churchill in the War Room, the Admiralty again intervened directly over the heads of the commanders on the spot, inviting the *Penelope*:

> If in light of experience this morning you consider it a justifiable operation, take available destroyers in Narvik area and attack enemy in Narvik tonight or tomorrow morning.[14]

Captain Yates responded positively, but claimed he would not be ready to attack until dawn on the 12th because of the time it would take to marshal together his supporting destroyers which were out on patrol and to issue the necessary orders.

Two other considerations were causing Yates some concern. The possible presence of a German cruiser in the Ofotfiord had been raised by Warburton-Lee in a hurried signal on the previous day when he first saw the German destroyers appearing out of the Herjangsfiord. Although not corroborated by any subsequent reports, the presence of this 'phantom' cruiser tended to dominate Yates' thinking. His other worry was the presence of German mines, of which in fact there were none. Surprisingly, little thought seems to have been given to the threat posed by enemy submarines, probably because none had apparently tried to interfere with the previous night's operation. In fact there were now five U-boats in the Vestfiord – a formidable obstacle in these restricted waters.

Nevertheless, another day had been granted to Bey to put his house in order and for General Dietl to consolidate his position ashore. Indeed, the longer the delay in renewing the naval battle, the stronger became the argument for waiting until a combined naval/land action could be mounted, for the loss of ships in a purely naval action might eventually preclude an assault on the town itself.

Admiral Whitworth, picqued by the way the Admiralty was sending orders direct to his subordinate commanders, was at last provoked into joining in the discussion of the next step. He complained to the Admiralty that he had been given three partly incompatible tasks: to prevent ships leaving Narvik, to prevent reinforcements arriving, and to attack Narvik itself. He believed that the situation needed some clarification, but the Admiralty ignored this intervention, and Admiral Forbes maintained a diplomatic silence. In fact the Admiralty's objective was now clear: they regarded the capture of Narvik as the main priority and the Military Co-ordination Committee was already that night briefing Admiral of the Fleet Lord Cork and Orrery, the newly appointed commander of the Narvik expedition.

The fear of mines was enhanced on the night of 10 April when Commander McCoy in the destroyer *Bedouin* mistakenly reported the presence of an electrically controlled minefield at the entrance of the Vestfiord. What he had taken to be mines were in fact torpedoes fired by a German submarine, the U25, which had exploded harmlessly nearby. It was, however, sufficient to deter Captain Yates, and more reluctantly the Admiralty, and the attack promised for dawn on the 12th was cancelled. The Germans were actually having considerable problems with their torpedoes. Not only was the depth keeping mechanism faulty, but the magnetic detonator which had been calibrated for German waters was proving ineffective in these northern latitudes. This was a considerable bonus for the Royal Navy, for an efficient submarine force in these waters could have proved quite lethal during the first few days of the campaign at Narvik. In practice, they achieved virtually nothing.

Reports were now received from a Norwegian source of a tanker lying in a fiord some 50 miles to the south and of a transport and possibly a warship in the Bodo area. Although there had been some substance in this report, the transport *Alster* had already been captured by the destroyer *Icarus* and the tanker *Kattegat* sunk by the Norwegians. The warship was a figment of the imagination. Nevertheless, the *Penelope* with two destroyers was dispatched to deal with these potential threats and headed off to the south looking for a pilot. It was as well that Captain Bey was unaware of this development or he might have been tempted to try to break out of Narvik on the night of the 11th. To complete an unhappy two days, the *Penelope* now hit a rock on the difficult approach to Bodo and was so badly damaged she was lucky to reach safety under tow by the destroyer *Eskimo*. She joined the *Hotspur* in the Skjelfiord which was now beginning to resemble a breaker's yard.

Admiral Forbes had meanwhile pressed on northwards towards Narvik although he had detached a part of the Home Fleet to escort the convoy containing the first element of the Allied Expeditionary Force on its way from Scapa Flow to Harstad. As well as his flagship, the *Rodney*, he still had the battleships *Valiant* and *Warspite* and the aircraft carrier *Furious*.

Despite the complete failure of the torpedo attack on Trondheim that morning, the Admiralty ordered a further air attack on shipping at Narvik to be synchronised with an attack by surface ships. This time the medium was to be dive bombing, for which the obsolete Swordfish was not designed and was totally unsuitable, but obviously the recent success of the Stuka in this type of attack had struck a chord. As they approached the Lofotens on 12 April, nine Swordfish of 818 Squadron under Lieut Commander P. G. Sydney-Jones were launched in the late afternoon in deteriorating weather conditions with 150 miles to run to Narvik. They reached their objective and attempted a dive bombing attack on the ships in the harbour. But the pilots, most of whom had practiced torpedo attacks incessantly before the war, were totally inexperienced in dive bombing techniques, and the slow and cumbersome Swordfish seemed to hang in the air while the ship's automatic weapons carefully lined-up the aircraft in their sights. The attacks were bravely pressed home and the bombs released as low as 400 feet, but no hits were achieved on the destroyers. Only a few sailors were killed and one of the Norwegian patrol boats which had been commandeered by the Germans sunk. The pilots were surprised and impressed by the intensity of the anti-aircraft fire and two aircraft were shot down. Nine Swordfish of 816 Squadron, which were launched just after 818, ran into a snowstorm and had to turn back before reaching their target.

The Germans were equally cautious and indecisive over the same two day period. Captain Bey had already shown a lack of dash and tenacity in not following up the good work which Captains Woolf and Rechel had achieved on the morning of the 10th, and his timidity came to the fore again as he considered what to do next. First of all he reviewed his surviving assets. He had four destroyers undamaged, the *Hermann Künne, Wolfgang Zenker, Erich Giese* and *Erich Köellner*. But the last three had used half their ammunition and still needed refuelling – it was a rare stroke of good fortune that the *Jan Wellum* had remained undamaged in the carnage all around her and could still dispense fuel. Three destroyers were either sunk or immobilised, the *Anton Schmitt, Wilhelm Heidkamp* and the *Diether von Roeder*, although the latter could still use her forward guns and had been relegated to the task of harbour defence. The remaining three destroyers were severely damaged, but useable in a very limited way.

Group West still wanted the serviceable destroyers to be evacuated as soon as possible, but only the *Zenker* and the *Giese* could be prepared to leave on the night of 10 April. In any case, knowing that the Royal Navy would almost certainly be lying in wait outside the Vestfiord did not encourage a hasty or ill prepared move. General Dietl at this stage was also quite content to see the ships remain in Narvik, he needed their gunfire support and could make use of the 2,500 sailors, many of whom were now surplus to the Navy's requirements. Bey began to think that of two undeniably unattractive options, remaining in Narvik was preferable to making a hazardous dash for safety. Nevertheless, on the evening of the 10th, Group West in no uncertain terms ordered the *Zenker* and the *Giese* to depart at nightfall. Captain Bey embarked on the *Zenker* and the two ships left at 2040, but as they rounded the Baroy Light, the sight of the still smoking hulk of the *Rauenfels* hardly fortified their confidence. Into the Vestfiord, they soon ran into further difficulties as the dark shadow of the *Penelope* and two other ships, probaly the *Eskimo* and *Bedouin*, loomed out of the night. It was too much for Captain Bey, he immediately went about and under cover of smoke raced back to Narvik. Neither the *Penelope* nor the destroyers noticed anything. Captain Bey's nerve had broken, for hugging the dark shadow of the shore and maintaining full speed, there was a good chance that they might have slipped away unnoticed, or at worst had to engage in a running battle under cover of darkness.

The following day, the 11th, Bey resisted all the exhortations of Group West to escape, and that night fate stepped in to reinforce his argument. As if in silent retribution for his timidity, two of the destroyers, the *Zenker* and the *Köellner*, ran aground while moving to their night dispersal anchorage. The *Köellner* in particular was badly damaged, and like the *Roeder*, became for all practical purposes an immobile gun platform. The abandoned German destroyers at least partially resolved one problem; some of their guns were mounted ashore as improvised, but by no means negligible, anti-aircraft defences.

The Second Battle of Narvik

At last on 12 April, Admiral Forbes broke the deadlock by issuing orders for the *Warspite*, to which Admiral Whitworth transferred his flag, supported by nine destroyers to make a second assault on Narvik. The objective of the second attack is not immediately obvious. It is true that the recapture of Narvik was now the strategic objective of the Allied Governments, but there was no mention of this aim in the detailed orders issued by Admiral Forbes on the 12th. The objective in those orders was stated to be 'destruction of German warships, merchant ships and defences in the Narvik area'. Whilst this may have been a prerequisite of a successful assault on the town, the remaining German destroyers could have been bottled-up in the Ofotfiord with rather less risk than that entailed in launching the *Warspite* into these restricted waters, at least until a landing force had arrived which could take over the town when it had been softened-up by naval gunfire. Furthermore, Forbes knew by the 12th that the advance party of the military expedition would arrive in the Narvik area on the 14th. The conclusion is that the second attack was seen as primarily a naval operation in its own right, a continuance of the policy of engaging and destroying the German fleet as an end in itself. The absence of a clear strategy embracing all three Services was particularly evident at this juncture, but even if such a strategy had existed, the lack of a Joint Force Commander to control and co-ordinate a combined operation would probably have negated its achievement. This was to be a recurring theme in Norway.

This was altogether a more balanced force than that available to Captain Warburton-Lee four days earlier. It had the benefit of the ten remaining Swordfish aircraft on the *Furious* now cruising off the Lofoten Islands, providing both reconnaissance and offensive support. Most important of all, it had the very substantial fire power of a battleship to give physical and moral backing. It was a brave decision to use the *Warspite* in the restricted waters of the fiord, although whether it would have been taken so readily had it been known that five U-boats lurked in the Vestfiord is a moot point.

The poor intelligence available to the British force was again a notable factor. It was still believed that there was a minefield in the Baröy area, that Baröy Island itself was fortified with the possible presence of magnetic torpedoes, and that there were three 12 or 18 pounder guns at Framnes facing north-west and 4 inch guns on either side of the fiord at Hamnes.[15] None of this was correct. The war in Norway was now four days old and it seems incredible that it had not been possible to establish from the Norwegians exactly what guns they had in position when the invasion occurred on 9 April: the Germans could hardly have made any notable additions in the short time available. Intelligence gained during the first battle of Narvik also seems to have been inadequately collated and analysed, for this too would have thrown doubt on the existence of the coastal defences. On the other hand, the lack of firm intelligence on the presence of submarines in the fiords proved to be an unexpected blessing: for the warning signal merely stated 'U-boat reported in Vestfiord'. The technical deficiencies in the performance of the torpedoes which in fact made the German submarine a negligible threat would not have been known to the British, indeed it was not recognised by the Germans themselves at this stage. The inadequacy of operational intelligence throughout the Norwegian campaign is a recurring feature, but although local commanders were only too aware of this limitation and the effect it had on their immediate operations, the higher commanders seemed singularly unperturbed by this weakness and took few urgent steps to rectify the situation.

The orders issued by Commander Hughes-Hallett on behalf of Admiral Forbes were surprisingly detailed, but Admiral Whitworth did not seem to object to this encroachment upon his authority; he was by now only too aware that his decision to leave the Vestfiord unguarded on the evening of the 8th had been a mistake and was relieved to be given another chance to recover the situation, at least in part. The force assembled in the Vestfiord at 0730 on 13 April. The day was overcast and heavy with snow clouds, but the wind was light and the visibility outside of the rain and snow storms was as much as ten miles. Whereas the first attack on Narvik depended on stealth, speed and surprise, the second was intended to be a *tour de force* in the full light of day. Captain Bey was aware of the British intentions from an intelligence summary which had been forwarded by Group West at 0838 that morning. The only mistake in their summary was a belief that the *Repulse* as well as the *Warspite* would be supporting the nine destroyers.

Captain Bey did not have much faith in the U-boat screen which had achieved nothing during the first battle of Narvik, and he now had only one fully serviceable and armed destroyer, the Hermann Künne, which was patrolling the Ofotfiord. The other destroyers had been rearmed as far as possible with weapons recovered from the sunk or immobile ships, but none were totally operational. The *Erich Köellner*, which should have been fully operational until its unfortunate grounding was dispatched to Taarstad, three miles east of Ramnes, to act as a static battery, the closest the Germans could get to replacing the missing fortress at the narrows. The *Wolfgang Zenker* and the *Erich Giese* had mechanical faults, but the *Bernd von Arnim* had been repaired and rearmed, as had the *Georg Thiele* and the *Hans Lüdemann* to a lesser extent. Despite his own caution and the only too apparent weakness of his resources, Captain Bey knew he had to give battle whatever the odds – the honour of the German Navy was at stake. Even so he was lethargic in disposing his forces and not all were under steam until after 1300.

The British ships proceeded sedately up the Vestfiord. They were fully armed and fuelled, a tanker, the *British Lady*, having arrived in time to relieve worries regarding the refuelling of the destroyers. In addition to the 1913 vintage *Warspite*, (Captain V. A. C. Crutchley VC, DSO), there were four modern Tribal Class destroyers of nearly 2,000 tons, *Bedouin* (Commander J. A. McCoy), *Punjabi* (Commander J. T. Lean), *Eskimo* (Commander St J. A. Micklethwait) and *Cossack* (Commander R. St V. Sherbrooke). Completing the force were five smaller destroyers, *Hero* (Commander H. W. Biggs), *Forester* (Lieut Commander E. B. Tancock), *Foxhound* (Lieut Commander G. H. Peters), *Kimberley* (Lieut Commander R. G. K. Knowling) and *Icarus* (Lieut Commander C. D. Maud).

One invaluable asset on this occasion which had not been available to Warburton-Lee was the presence of aircraft on the *Warspite*. Up to three Swordfish aircraft could be carried, although at this time the viability of the force was limited by only one pilot being available. Lieut Commander W. L. M. 'Bruno' Brown, the captain and observer, was tasked with his pilot, Petty Officer Ben Rice and Telegraphist/Gunner, Leading Airman Maurice Pacey, to carry out reconnaissance for the fleet and to bomb targets of opportunity. Both tasks were to be carried out admirably.

The Swordfish was lowered by crane into the sea and took off at 1152, quickly climbing to the cloud base of about 1,000 feet. The first contact Brown established was the *Künne* on patrol in the Ofotfiord, and then the *Köellner* lumbering at a steady seven knots to her last resting place. The only other destroyer observed at sea was the *Lüdemann* in the harbour entrance. But whilst Brown, aware of the importance of his reconnaissance mission was not prepared to get too close to the destroyers, his next sighting was too tempting to ignore. The U64, the most modern of the German submarines, was sitting only fifty yards from the head of the Herjangsfiord. Rice initiated an immediate dive bombing attack, pulling out at 200 feet and releasing two 100 lb anti-submarine bombs. One just missed, but the other hit the decking right behind the conning tower with stunning effect. The U64's machine gun had responded quickly, and a courageous gunner continued firing even after the submarine was sinking beneath him, but he only caused superficial damage to the Swordfish's tail surfaces. The U64 sank in less than a minute, but 36 of the crew of 48 were saved. Flushed with their success, Brown and his crew were now ordered to scout ahead of the advancing fleet.

The force now had a remarkable stroke of good fortune. The U46 patrolling a few miles to the east of Baroy spotted the convoy approaching along the Ofotfiord. Captain Sohler inspected the intruders carefully through his periscope and judged that the *Warspite* would cross within less than a thousand yards of his position: if he could only penetrate the destroyer screen he would have a remarkable chance of turning around the fortunes of the outnumbered German forces. He carefully manoeuvred his boat into a firing position, but when within seconds of pressing the button, the U46 hit an uncharted pinnacle of rock and lurched to the surface. Unseen, Sohler quickly submerged, but the chance had passed. Given the frailty of their torpedoes, success may still have eluded the U-boat, but it was a very large target and luck for once might have been on their side.

At almost the same moment as the U46's chance was slipping away, the *Hermann Künne* was spotted approaching on a reciprocal heading. But after a desultory exchange of fire at long range, the *Künne* retired discreetly up the fiord. Captain Schulze-Hinricks in the *Köellner* recognised that he was never going to make Taarstad at his maximum speed of seven knots, so instead slipped into Djupvik Bay. Unfortunately for him this coincided with the Swordfish passing overhead which duly recorded the diversion.

The *Furious* had been given three tasks to coincide with the progression of the operations: to bomb the supposed batteries on Baröy Island, to bomb the forts in the narrows at Ramnes, and to attack the batteries at Framnes and ships in the vicinity of Narvik harbour. The first two operations were unsuccessful due to the low cloudbase and it is as well that the guns at Baröy and Ramnes did not exist, for on schedule at 1300 the *Warspite* and her entourage negotiated the narrows and entered the Ofotfiord. Almost immediately, *Warspite* brought her 15 inch guns into play, the first occasion on which they had been used in anger since the Battle of Jutland. But the *Künne* was an elusive target and no damage was done. The *Warspite*'s slow rate of fire was better suited to heavy, more static targets than a manoeuvring destroyer. Nevertheless, whatever the limitations of her shelling, her presence made a compelling impact on Captain Kothe who saw the *Warspite* for the first time. Aware of the frailty of the defences behind him, he knew at that moment that there was little he or his fellow captains could do to stave off the inevitable defeat. The 30,000 ton *Warspite* with her eight massive guns and high superstructure was a majestic and formidable sight as she made her stately way towards Narvik.

The value of the airborne reconnaissance now emerged, for the three destroyers in the starboard van, *Bedouin*, *Punjabi* and *Eskimo* had their torpedo tubes and guns trained to starboard as they rounded the promontary sheltering Djupvik Bay. The three Tribals pumped shells and torpedoes into the luckless *Köellner* which, although stricken, stubbornly continued to fire, and it took the 15 inch guns of the *Warspite* to complete the destruction which she accomplished in very short order. Retiring up the fiord, the *Künne* joined up with the *Lüdemann*, *Zenker* and *Arnim* and a long range action with guns and torpedoes was generally ineffective on both sides. But as they reached the head of the Ofotfiord, the German destroyers were forced eventually to turn and face the enemy, a substantial amount of their ammunition and torpedoes already exhausted. The *Bernd von Arnim*, as on the 10th, was most daring and caused a few moments of alarm in the *Warspite* with a determined torpedo attack.

A timely intervention by ten Swordfish from the *Furious* led by Captain Burch RM took the heat off, but like the German attacks on the Fleet of the previous three days, the British pilots found that hitting a moving ship even with their newly acquired technique of dive bombing was a very difficult task. About 100 bombs were dropped, but no hits were scored and two aircraft were shot down. It was another gallant effort, but achieved little.

The four German destroyers were now almost out of ammunition and the result of the battle a foregone conclusion. Even so, significant damage was to be sustained by the British ships before the *coup de grace* was finally administered. The Germans had committed a tactical error by seeking to engage the British ships in the more open waters of the Ofotfiord where they were inevitably kept at bay by the longer range striking power of the *Warspite*. They would have been better served to have adopted the tactics of the 10th when they suddenly emerged out of the side fiords and engaged the enemy at closer range, although in the presence of the all seeing Swordfish they could not have achieved the same degree of surprise on this occasion. But with their more accurate gun laying, they might have caused greater damage to the opposition before inevitably succumbing. On the other hand the British, who were not short of ammunition, could afford to allow their opponents to blaze away as they slowly but relentlessly drove them into a corner.

Captain Bey's only thought now was to save his crews and he ordered the remaining serviceable destroyers to head into the Rombaksfiord. The *Herman Künne* however failed to hear Bey's instruction and instead turned into the Herjangsfiord where Captain Kothe drove the destroyer firmly aground at Trollvik. Quite remarkably, the *Künne* had not received a single direct hit throughout the two days of fierce action and none of her crew were lost. Nevertheless, Micklethwait in the *Eskimo* who had failed to hit the *Künne* with gunfire as he pursued her into the fiord finished her off with a torpedo which produced a most spectacular explosion, probably detonating in unison with the ships own demolition depth charges.

The other three German destroyers, now joined by the *Georg Thiele* disappeared into the Rombaskfiord, a cul-de-sac to the east of Narvik from which there was no escape. The *Erich Giese*, at last underway, made a brief appearance from the harbour; but it was only a curtain call, for she was immediately set upon by the *Bedouin* and the *Punjabi* and soon abandoned and left drifting, although not before she had forced the *Punjabi* to retire temporarily from the battle. The *Roeder*, which had been so badly damaged in Warburton-Lee's attack four days before was still tied up to the quay, immovable, but able to use her forward guns effectively and she soon hit the *Cossack* which was rather incautiously picking her way through the wreckage in the harbour, and now had to be run aground after being hit seven times in two minutes. The *Roeder's* crew eventually abandoned ship, but not before setting delayed action charges which almost accounted for the *Foxhound* which had gone to assist the *Cossack* and to attempt to board the *Roeder*. The U51 which had been refuelling in the harbour when the excitement began had immediately dived and remained firmly on the bottom. In a considerable feat of seamanship, although it did little for the German cause, Captain Knorr manoeuvred his way unseen out of the harbour and took shelter in Ballangen Bay.

Whilst accounting for the *Künne*, Micklethwait also noticed the remaining German destroyers disappearing up the Rombaksfiord and was the first to give chase, followed by the *Forester, Hero, Bedouin* and *Icarus*. Reconnaissance by the *Warspite*'s Swordfish was again proving invaluable as Brown advised Micklethwait that whilst two of the destroyers had proceeded to the head of the fiord, the other two had stopped at Straumen, about eight miles from Narvik, hidden behind two promontories projecting into the fiord where the waters narrow to about 500 yards. It was a good position, and the *Lüdemann* and the *Thiele*, although very short of ammunition, were determined to sell themselves dearly. The *Lüdemman* had four torpedoes as well as four guns trained on the narrows from her aft starboard quarter, and she was facing in the right direction to run for the shore as soon as the ammunition had been expended. The *Thiele* lay on the opposite side facing athwart the channel, she had four guns and two torpedoes. The *Warspite* followed the destroyers into the Rombaksfiord, but did not proceed through this narrow gap, prudently leaving the clearing-up exercise to the more nimble destroyers. The two at the head of the fiord, the *Zenker* and the *Arnim*, which had enjoyed a short but adventurous war, were being abandoned and scuttled.

The intrepid Micklethwait was first through the gap, hotly pursued by Tancock in the *Forester*. It was an act of considerable daring to proceed blind through the narrows, for the two ships on the other side would undoubtedly have their gun ranges worked out in advance whereas the *Eskimo*'s gunnery officer, Lieutenant Duncan Ritchie, had to make the calculation when he rounded the corner. Fortunately, the fire control systems of both the *Lüdemann* and the *Thiele* had been damaged, and in the event, the advantage lay with the *Eskimo*. With commendable coolness and speed Ritchie laid the guns unerringly on the *Lüdemann* causing Captain Friedrichs to make off up the fiord, launching his four torpedoes almost as an afterthought as he disappeared out of the action.

Both the *Eskimo* and the *Forester*, which was now through the gap, turned their attention to the *Thiele* which was hit constantly. Even so, she seemed to be a long time submitting and becoming impatient, Micklethwait manoeuvred the *Eskimo* to launch a torpedo. It proved a near fatal step, for no sooner had he steadied on his new heading than he saw one of the *Lüdemman*'s torpedoes homing straight towards him. Frenetically avoiding the *Lüdemann*'s parting shot – which he did successfully – the *Eskimo* now came broadside-on to the *Thiele*, almost stopped. Captain Wolff did not miss with his torpedo which only had to run straight and on the surface to score. It hit the *Eskimo* forward, almost severing the bow and putting out of action her two forward guns: fifteen seamen died instantly. The *Hero* now joined the fight and the end was near, although the *Thiele* kept firing until the last round had gone. There was nothing more Captain Wolff could do and he drove the *Thiele* ashore at Sildvik at such high speed that her bow was lifted high over the narrow rock beach where it still rests today. The battle had been running without respite for two hours, but the last desperate shot had now been fired.

With considerable sangfroid, Micklethwait carefully manoeuvred the *Eskimo* stern first out of the Rombaksfiord until unfortunately grounding in ninety fathoms due to the wreckage hanging down from his forecastle. The only remaining task was to ensure that the three destroyers aground at the head of the Rombaksfiord would be unable to return and fight another day. This task was at first enthusiastically accepted by the crew of the *Swordfish*, but after taking a look Brown declined, somewhat reluctantly, on the advice of his pilot because the mountains at the head of the fiord encroached so closely to the shoreline that escape from such a constricted area in the prevailing weather conditions would have been extremely hazardous. Instead they attacked, and missed, the *Georg Thiele* and then landed alongside their parent ship in the Rombaksfiord. The *Swordfish*'s contribution throughout the afternoon had been invaluable, not only in sinking the U64, but in providing essential reconnaissance of the enemy's whereabouts, and even on the track of individual torpedoes. A grateful Admiral in his official dispatch wrote: 'I doubt if a ship-borne aircraft had ever been used to such good purpose'.

The final destruction of the three grounded destroyers still apparently posed problems, particularly as the torpedo tubes of one of them were pointing down the fiord. In fact, there were no torpedoes left and Captain Bey had already elected to scuttle the ships himself. Eventually the *Hero*, *Icarus* and *Kimberley* ventured into the inner fiord and completed the demolition for him with shells and torpedoes. At last silence descended on this enclosed and forbidding fiord, now liberally littered with the debris of Bonte's once proud flotilla.

The German destroyers had generally fought well, particularly the *Georg Thiele*, *Erich Giese* and *Bernd von Arnim*. They had received less support than they might reasonably have expected from the five U-boats and their shortage of torpedoes and shells in the second battle was a handicap which would inevitably lead to their demise unless they achieved an early success. The failure of the depth keeping device in their torpedoes had been a major limitation, but an unquestioning confidence in the ability of their guns to score at long range had been profoundly misplaced, as indeed it had on the British side as well. The British destroyer captains had also used their seamanship, experience and initiative to good advantage and displayed a spirit and zeal which approached, but rarely crossed the boundary between calculated risk and recklessness. Behind them, of course, was the *Warspite* which had taken little direct part in the action, but whose ominous presence provided immense moral support. From his flagship Admiral Whitworth had controlled the battle on a loose rein, and the efforts of his destroyer captains had well vindicated his faith in their judgement.

The *Warspite* moored off Narvik to count the cost. The *Eskimo*, *Cossack* and *Punjabi* had all been seriously damaged and most other ships had suffered some hits. Forty-one British sailors had been killed bringing the overall total in the two actions to 188 compared with about 300 German casualties. In the end, the action had been a complete success, the destroyer force of Group 1 had been totally annihilated even though it had perhaps not been quite as straight forward as Captain Crutchley's reported comment 'Just like shelling peas'.[16]

Elated by his success and encouraged by the Admiralty, Whitworth toyed with the idea of landing a force to capture Narvik itself. It would have been the icing on the cake. Eventually he elected not to do so and departed the Ofotfiord in the early evening. The decision was probably wise in the light of the information he had at the time: his available force was very limited and he had no accurate information on the number of German troops ashore. We now know that General Dietl had dispersed his troops forward from Narvik and that the action may well have succeeded, but we cannot criticise Whitworth, as many subsequently did, with the benefit of knowledge which was not available to him at the time.

He should, however, have been more concerned by the possible presence of German submarines, but this does not appear to have entered his reckoning as after Trannöy he suddenly turned about and retraced his course. The U25 which had been lying in wait in the Vestfiord made two attempts to attack the *Warspite*, once on her way out and again on her return. The first was driven off by the *Foxhound* and the second failed, probably because of a faulty torpedo. The reasons for Whitworth's return into the Ofotfiord are not recorded, and in retrospect it would undoubtedly have been considered reckless if the U25's attack had succeeded, or if the other U-boat captains had shown a little more spirit. It may be thought even more foolhardy in the light of the air attack, ineffective though it had been, which had appeared that evening and which could with some confidence be predicted to reappear at first light. Having collected the casualties and survivors from the *Hardy*, who had survived an adventurous time ashore at Ballangen, the *Warspite* finally left the fiord early the following morning. Captain Schütze in the U25 again managed to penetrate the destroyer screen and fire a single torpedo at the *Warspite*. Once again it missed. In the latter stages of the action the aged battleship was leading a charmed life.

The failure of the U-boats to make a more telling contribution to the two battles of Narvik was one of the more fortunate aspects of the action for the Royal Navy. On a number of occasions they managed to infiltrate into good firing positions only to see their torpedoes run astray or not explode. The problems lay in the impact pistol and the depth keeping mechanism which had been inadequately tested due to a shortage of funds. The consequences were so serious that Admiral Raeder convened a court of inquiry to investigate. Several senior heads rolled, and Raeder dispatched a memorandum which itself had many consequential ramifications:

> The requirements for weapons or naval warfare must be submitted by naval officers, who alone are responsible for their development and operational effectiveness. The designers and constructors are merely an agency for fulfilling the military requirements.[17]

The *Cossack* and the *Eskimo* were eventually refloated and both sailed slowly, sedately and stern first all the way to the Lofoten Islands – safety rather than dignity was their order of the day.

Interim Balance Sheet

The second battle of Narvik marked the end of the opening phase of the Norwegian campaign, Admiral Forbes departing with the major part of the Home Fleet for Scapa Flow on 15 April.

The opening round had clearly been won by the invaders. They had established themselves in all their objectives throughout the length of Norway, although their occupation of Narvik was tenuous to say the least. They had established lines of communication with their home base, although not without difficulty thanks to the activities of the Allied submarines in the Skagerrak. They had also achieved complete air superiority over the eastern North Sea and the Skagerrak and established forward operating airfields at Oslo, Vaernes and most importantly at Stavanger. In so doing they also obtained a psychological advantage over the Commander-in-Chief Home Fleet in persuading him that the area south of Bergen was unsafe for surface ships. On the other hand, they had not achieved the outright victory for which they had hoped and had paid a high price in naval losses: one heavy cruiser, two light cruisers, ten modern destroyers and a submarine destroyed, as well as sustaining serious damage to other capital ships which kept them out of action for some time. Admiral Raeder's forecast that this operation could not be achieved without serious losses had proved only too correct.

The Norwegians had clearly lost the first round. But although the army was forced to withdraw from all the major ports and centres of population, the Government was still in being and the bulk of the army, unprepared as it was, intact. They were alive to fight another day.

There had been mixed fortunes for the Allies. The Navy had clearly failed to achieve either its main aim of engaging the German fleet in a decisive action, or that of the War Cabinet which was to frustrate a German invasion of Norway. The *Gneisenau*, *Scharnhorst* and *Hipper* were still afloat if not unscathed. But considerable success had been achieved elsewhere, notably Narvik, but also at Bergen and in the Skagerrak, and Royal Navy losses were considerably less serious than those of the Germans. No capital ships had been seriously damaged and only four destroyers totally lost, although several, as well as the light cruiser *Penelope*, required extensive repair.

The strengths and weaknesses of air power were also much in evidence during this early phase. The ability of air power, even when weakly applied, to impose limitations on the strategic thinking and flexibility of naval forces had been demonstrated, although the ability to mount effective attacks against manoeuvring warships was by no means proven. The inadequacy of conventional level bombing techniques against ships was evident, but the potential of the dive bomber was clearly signposted for the future. There should have been no need for a reminder of the importance of aerial reconnaissance, for that was a lesson learnt by 1918, nevertheless the lack of adequate intelligence on German shipping movements was the primary reason for the Navy's inability to locate and destroy the German fleet. The value of tactical air reconnaissance was clearly demonstrated at Narvik and also by the German shadowing of the British fleet on the 9 and 10 April. Finally, the tactical benefits of surprise and flexibility of assault from the air by paratroops and air landed forces had been demonstrated by the Luftwaffe even though the concept could hardly be said to be proved in the light of the almost non-existent defences encountered at Sola, Fornebu and Aalborg.

The initial period of consolidation and retaliation was over. The initiative lay clearly with the Germans, the only option now available to the Allies was counter-invasion. But the Allies were still in some disarray and could not yet decide how best to respond. Mr Churchill at this stage was convinced that the greatest effort should be directed to the recapture of Narvik – not only did it offer the best chance of chalking-up a badly needed success, but it would resolve the iron ore problem in the longer term. But Cabinet opinion was swinging in favour of attacking Trondheim. The advantages were mainly political in that it would stiffen Norwegian resolve and be more acceptable to Sweden who saw concentration on Narvik as simply threatening the iron ore mines at Gallivare.

We shall pick up events at Narvik later, but in line with the way thoughts were moving in London, it is appropriate to consider first developments in Central Norway.

Counter Invasion – 'Mauriceforce'

'I got a signal from the War Office saying I was to be Acting Lieut-General, but as I felt in my bones that the campaign was unlikely to be either long or successful, I did not bother to put up the badges of my rank.'[1]

General Carton de Wiart

But Should it be Narvik or Trondheim?

It had been expected in many quarters that the Germans might well react by invading Norway when Operation 'Wilfred' was implemented. We have seen how Plan R4 was conceived therefore to forestall this contingency and troops embarked at Rosyth and on the Clyde. In the event the Admiralty, strongly influenced by the prospect of bringing the High Seas Fleet into battle in the North Sea, ignored the indications of the impending German intervention in Norway and on the afternoon of 7 April directed that the troops at Rosyth should be disembarked and that the 2nd Cruiser Squadron and the ships designated to act as escorts for the transports from the Clyde should sail in support of the Home Fleet. There is no evidence that this decision was discussed with the other Chiefs of Staff, the Commander-in-Chief Home Fleet or the War Cabinet. The best chance of putting troops ashore in Norway was therefore lost before the campaign even started despite the evidence that the very contingency they were intended to forestall was in fact underway. The land campaign in Central Norway was to suffer severely from the disruption caused by the hasty disembarkation, although it is unlikely that it influenced the end result.

When the Chiefs of Staff were drawn from their beds in the early hours of 9 April, it was already apparent that the opportunity of forestalling the invasion of Central and Southern Norway had been overtaken by events, and by midday any lingering hope of getting into Narvik before the Germans arrived had also vanished. Counter invasion was now the reality. The following morning the War Cabinet endorsed the Chief's view that the recapture of Narvik was the first priority and that the possibility of getting a foothold at Namsos and Aandalsnes should also be explored. These latter two operations, codenamed 'Mauriceforce' and 'Sickleforce' respectively, were mounted, but not before a more ambitious plan was first envisaged as the key to Trondheim. In the far north, the Narvik expedition, Operation 'Rupert', was ordered to depart at 1300 on 12 April.[2]

After Oslo, the most important political and strategic centres of Central Norway were Trondheim and Bergen. Although the Admiralty had indicated an intention to capture Bergen in a signal to Admiral Forbes on the 10 April, the latter was by now firmly convinced that to take the Home Fleet so far south within easy range of major German airfields was to invite disaster. The Norwegians and the French both pressed strongly for a counter invasion to be centred on Trondhiem and accordingly were assembling their thoughts for an assault in that area. Uncertainty was already rife therefore on the very morning after the invasion even though the Allies had been planning and thinking about action in Norway for seven long months.

Trondheim was the medieval capital of Norway, the third largest city and an important agricultural and industrial area. It was a nodal point for both road and rail routes to the north and had a large deep water anchorage with extensive quays and dock facilities. The recapture of Trondheim would provide a secure political and strategic base for any future operations towards the south whilst at the same time isolating the German forces in the north.

By 12 April, the Foreign Office was convinced that Trondheim rather than Narvik should be the key objective. Lord Halifax pointed out that whilst an attack on Narvik was militarily sound, its capture would have much less impact on Norwegian resistance and neutral opinion than the repossession of Trondheim. The Admiralty and the War Office on the other hand had reservations about mounting a seaborne landing at Trondheim without the most careful preparation. The need for a secure airfield in the area played little part in the debate at this stage although later it was to become, albeit still largely unrecognised, the key to maintaining a foothold in Central Norway. For the time being, however, the Cabinet was persuaded by the Admiralty's arguments and agreed that Narvik should remain the first objective.

The following morning Lord Halifax returned to the theme and now had some support from the Prime Minister although Churchill still preferred to gain control of Narvik first. But information regarding the German strength and disposition was very sparse and so the Cabinet readily approved a proposal from the First Lord to put an exploratory party of three hundred sailors and marines ashore at Namsos and a small party at Aalesund. Unable to reach a firm decision, the Cabinet notified the Norwegian Government that the Allies intended to recapture both Narvik and Trondheim.

By 14 April, the wheel had turned full circle. Accounts of Admiral Whitworth's annihilation of the destroyer flotilla at Narvik on the previous day had reached London, and in the ensuing euphoria it was now thought that the capture of Narvik should not prove too difficult. Mr Churchill even ventured that a landing at Trondheim as well might be feasible and justified the risks involved. In fact, detailed planning had already commenced the night before.

Operation 'Hammer' – The Thrust for Trondheim

Operation 'Hammer' was conceived at the Military Co-ordination Committee Meeting on the evening of 13 April. Encouraged by the news that the *Warspite* had safely penetrated the narrow Ofotfiord at Narvik, the Committee considered that it would be feasible to mount a direct assault on Trondheim in conjunction with the plan to launch a pincer operation from Namsos and Aandalsnes. The approach from the sea to Trondheim is no more difficult than at Narvik and the operation could be supported

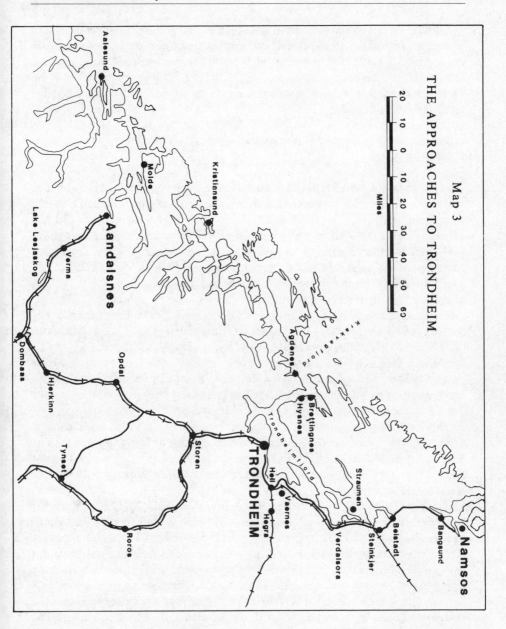

Map 3

THE APPROACHES TO TRONDHEIM

by RAF bombers and two aircraft carriers, the *Ark Royal* and the *Glorious*, carrying between them one hundred aircraft. The Navy was reasonably confident that it could deal with the shore batteries at the entrance to the fiord which it was known were now in German hands. Mr Churchill's hand in this turnover of events is transparent, his predilection for Narvik had, temporarily, been overtaken by an impetuous enthusiasm for any avenue of progressing the war.

Admiral Forbes on the other hand was much less sanguine about other aspects of 'Hammer'. In addition to the aircraft carriers, the task force would need to include two supporting battleships as well as the *Warspite* for bombardment purposes, four anti-aircraft cruisers and twenty destroyers. All of these in the restricted waters of the Trondheimfiord would be at enormous risk from air attack. He concluded his appreciation by recording:

> I do not consider Operation feasible unless you are prepared to face very heavy losses in troops and transports.[3]

Mr Churchill, ever ready as usual to interfere in other Minister's responsibilities, was with some justification concerned at the quality of the troops available for the Trondheim operation. He recognised, almost alone at this early stage, that the Territorials were raw, half trained soldiers who needed a stiffening of regular units to hold them together. Churchill himself was however warming to the Trondheim operation, largely because he thought the early capture of Narvik was now certain. He hoped therefore to be able to use the Guards Brigade which had been sent to Harstad to provide the stiffening of regular infantry that he believed so necessary. With his usual exuberance and energy for any project that appealed to his imagination, it was not long before Churchill was running ahead of the Chiefs of Staff in his enthusiasm for 'Hammer'. He outlined the plans to the War Cabinet on 13 April, and gave 22 April as the provisional date for the operation. The Home Fleet had meanwhile been ordered to Rosyth to prepare for the expedition. The landing itself would be carried out by two infantry brigades and two Canadian battalions although it was by now clear that the Guards Brigade could not be released from Narvik.

The operation was dogged with bad luck right from the start. The first commander, Major General F. E. Hotblack, had a stroke on the day he was appointed and his deputy, Acting Major General H. P. M. Berney-Ficklin was injured in an air crash at Kirkwall two days later. But as the day approached for the expedition to set sail, the early confidence began to seep away.

The implications of the Luftwaffe attack against the cruiser *Suffolk* (Captain J. W. Durnford) on 17 April gave much food for thought. *Suffolk* with her eight 8 inch guns had been tasked with bombarding the airfield at Stavanger.[4] The shelling was not particularly accurate, although some damage was caused to the airfield and casualties inflicted. But her troubles really began on the way home. First of all she missed her fighter escort because of a mixed up rendezvous and was unescorted when the first German attack started shortly after 0800. From then on at regular intervals over the next seven hours she was attacked by thirty three aircraft. About mid morning, a Stuka scored a direct hit knocking both turrets out of action and causing extensive flooding. Damage extended into the engine room and the fuel tanks were holed. In all thirty three officers and men were killed and thirty eight wounded from this single bomb. Several near misses shook the ship and added to the flooding and by early afternoon her steering was temporarily out of action. It was not until 1415 that escort aircraft put in an appearance, a mix of Hudsons, Blenheims and Skuas, but even these could not prevent the ship being attacked again over the next hour. The *Renown* and the *Repulse* arrived shortly afterwards to provide further protection. The *Suffolk* limped into Scapa Flow the following day, her quarter deck awash and her steering out of action: she had to be beached to prevent her sinking.

The vulnerability of surface ships to air attack weighed very heavily on the Admiralty's thinking and Admiral Forbes remained unenthusiastic about 'Hammer' throughout. The War Office as well was becoming increasingly concerned at the prospect of making an opposed landing under heavy air attack. Almost totally disregarded by an unenthusiastic Air Ministry during the run-up to the invasion, the air environment was already proving the crucial factor. As confidence waned, the date was first postponed to 24 April and then the 25th. The First Sea Lord, Admiral Pound, was the first to actually voice the view that 'Hammer' should be cancelled, but he had little difficulty persuading his fellow Chiefs of Staff. Mr Churchill, by now firmly wedded to the operation was furious, but even though he subjected the Chiefs to close interrogation, he could not persuade them to change their collective view.

On the morning of 20 April, Churchill reluctantly reported to the War Cabinet that the Chiefs of Staff were recommending the abandonment of 'Hammer' in favour of the enveloping movements from Namsos and Aandalsnes already under way. Although other reasons were given at the time, there is no doubt that the fear of exposing a major part of the Fleet to air attack was the predominant reason for abandoning the operation.

The decision was hotly debated at the time, provoking Admiral of the Fleet Sir Roger Keyes, a Conservative MP, to make a dramatic appearance in full dress uniform in the House of Commons to attack the Government and to beg to be given the opportunity of leading the expedition himself. One Admiral of the Fleet, Lord Cork, had already been recalled to the colours, and Keyes, a belligerent and forceful officer himself, was not going to be left out of the action if he could help it.

But, on balance, cancellation was probably the correct decision. Although we now know that the German strength in Trondheim was initially only two battalions which were very short of almost all essential supplies, by 25 April, the latest date for mounting the operation, the air support available to the Germans would have increased rapidly as would the influx of reinforcements who were being steadily flown in by Ju 52s. In any event, even if it had been captured, it is doubtful whether Trondheim could have been held against a counter attack from the south by forces who could so much more easily be reinforced and logistically supported. The only hope of success would have arisen from the capture of the airfield at Vaernes and its occupation in strength by RAF fighters to nullify the advantage the Luftwaffe gained from the use of the airfields at Stavanger and Oslo.

It was not only in London, but in Berlin as well that the fate of Trondheim was causing consternation. Hitler, who had already suffered and overcome, with the help of Jodl, one crisis of confidence over the plight of General Dietl in Narvik, now became increasingly alarmed that the German force in Trondheim could not be sustained either. General Pellengahr appeared to be making only slow progress up the valleys from Oslo towards Trondheim and was about to confront the first brigade of 'Sickleforce' which had disembarked at Aandalsnes on the 19th. In desperation, Hitler suggested to Admiral Raeder that the large passenger liners *Bremen* and *Europa* should make a dash for Trondheim with reinforcements and supplies. Raeder was horrified, protesting that they would require the protection of the whole German fleet, already mauled by the losses and damage sustained so far. Hitler was eventually dissuaded from this rash venture, but he did order General Feuerstein's 2nd Mountain Division to be taken out of the Western Front and shipped to Oslo.

The abandonment of 'Hammer' certainly spelt the end for 'Mauriceforce' and 'Sickleforce'. Both could now be attacked at will and their bridgeheads decimated by German aircraft, in addition the former could be bombarded from the sea by destroyers moving up the fiord from Trondheim. Unfortunately, this conclusion, in retrospect so obvious, was not fully appreciated at the time and both were to suffer more agonies before their helpless plight was recognised.

The Indirect Approach

With the abandonment of Operation 'Hammer', we may now focus our attention again on the two landings which had already occurred at Namsos and Aandalsnes. 'Mauriceforce' and 'Sickleforce' were intended to converge on Trondheim in a pincer movement, isolating the garrison before it could link up with the Germans advancing from Oslo. The major role was assigned to 'Mauriceforce' striking down from the north, with 'Sickleforce' intended to act as a kind of base plate to prevent the garrison breaking out to safety or reinforcements arriving from the south. The enemy at Trondheim was to be cut off and destroyed. In fact, 'Mauriceforce' and 'Sickleforce' never joined up and it quickly became evident that neither had the weight or support to make the overall plan viable: it is therefore feasible to look at each arm of the pincer in turn from inception to evacuation.

Even though the intitial landings had been so successful, the German position in Trondheim in the days immediately following remained precarious. They encountered considerable technical difficulties in attempting to reactivate the captured Norwegian batteries guarding the entrance to the fiord and had only two destroyers in the harbour, both suffering from engine problems. The original 1,700 troops had been increased by air lift to about 4,000, but half of these had moved forward from Trondheim itself, mostly towards the Swedish border. They were also very short of equipment, particularly artillery, as only one of the 'Trojan Horses' had arrived, and that three days late. Such was the precariousness of their lines of communication that two weeks after the invasion the Germans still contemplated sending in vital supplies by submarine.

The concept of landings at Namsos and Aandalsnes, which in contrast to a direct assault on Trondheim would not be immediately opposed by ground troops, was soundly based provided both contingents could be given sufficient backing as soon as they were ashore. There was a reasonable chance that Trondheim could be fairly quickly captured and the position stabilised if German reinforcements from the south could be prevented from linking up with the Trondheim force by the Norwegian Army denying access through the Österdal and the Gudbrandsdal valleys. The other essential conditions for success were that the Navy would continue to blockade the sea approaches and that the RAF could neutralise the airfield at Vaernes to prevent the flow of troops and supplies coming in by air. The crucial factor in satisfying these conditions was control of the air: if the Germans maintained absolute air superiority, the troops on the ground could not hope to resist a German advance and the Navy could not expect to be able to protect the essential lifeline of reinforcements and supplies. As the plan involved minimal air support for the troops, it was doomed from the moment it was conceived.

Since the evening of 12 April, Captain Pegram in the cruiser *Glasgow* had been leading a small force consisting of another cruiser, the *Sheffield*, and six destroyers searching the Leads in the neighbourhood of Trondheim for enemy shipping. On the 13th, Pegram was ordered to land a party of sailors and marines to secure the quays at Namsos and the adjacent town and bridge at Bangsund as a preliminary step towards the arrival of a larger force. He could not comply immediately until he had gathered in his dispersed force, but at twilight on the 14th a small reconnaissance party was ferried ashore from the *Sheffield* led by Captain W. F. Edds, Royal Marines, with two seasoned explorers and travellers to assist him, Colonel Peter Fleming and Captain Martin Lindsay.

In 1940 Namsos was a small town of 3,600 inhabitants lying at the head of a long fiord. It had one stone quay and a wooden slip, mainly used in peacetime by ships calling to collect wood pulp. Although there were no Germans in Namsos, Captain Edds' report was gloomy. There was little cover for an assembling force and no chance of concealment against the daily German air reconnaissance flights. Travel across country other than on skis or snowshoes would be virtually impossible in the deep snow which still covered the ground in mid April. In fact Edds' report was too pesimistic as the early landings were totally hidden from the prying eyes of the Luftwaffe. Pegram's destroyers now withdrew to sea leaving just Captain Nicholson in the *Somali* to welcome 'Mauriceforce' which was now on its way. Nicholson also sent a signal drawing attention to the vulnerability of the docking facilities against air attack. He recommended that the troopships should be sent elsewhere and the troops brought to Namsos by destroyer under the cloak of darkness.

In command of 'Mauriceforce' was Lieut General Sir Adrian Carton de Wiart VC, DSO, a 60-year-old veteran of the Boer War and the Great War with a formidable reputation for imaginative leadership and fighting spirit. Retired and living in Poland, he had returned to England in the face of the Russian invasion and had been quickly recalled to the colours. He was short and wiry, completely impervious to personal danger, and not a man to complain unnecessarily in the face of adversity. But even his indomitable spirit was to be sorely tested by the inadequacy of the means at his disposal to force a way through to Trondheim.

It had been intended initially to use the 148th Brigade as the main invasion force at Namsos, but because of the favourable news from Narvik, it was decided instead to use the 148th for a landing at Aandalsnes and to divert to Namsos the 146th Brigade which was on route to Narvik.

Part of the 49th West Riding Infantry Division (Major General P. J. Mackesy), the 146th Brigade comprised three territorial battalions, the 4th Royal Lincolnshire Regt (Lieut Colonel H. W. Newton), the 1/4th York and Lancaster Regt (Hallamshires) (Lieut Colonel C. G. Robins) and the 1/4th King's Own Yorkshire Light Infantry

(K.O.Y.L.I.) (Lieut Colonel W. S. Hibbert). Their only supporting echelon was a section of the 55th Field Company Royal Engineers. The Brigade numbered just under 2,200 men, but it had temporarily lost its commander, Brigadier C. G. Phillips, who had been in a different ship and was carried on to Narvik: he rejoined the Brigade on 17 April.

The troops available were of variable quality and of course like most units of the British Army, untried in combat. It had been decided in the summer of 1939 to double the size of the Territorial Army and this was achieved by splitting each battalion into two, with each half forming the nucleus of a new battalion. Although hailed at the time as a master-stroke, the actual result in the short term was that in place of one keen and tolerably efficient unit, there materialised two untrained, badly equipped and generally inefficient battalions. These defects had by no means been rectified when the Lincolnshires, the K.O.Y.L.I. and the Hallamshires were summarily sent to war. But untrained and untested, they were hard and tough: brought up in the uncompromising environment of the Yorkshire coal mines, they had a patriotic fervour which belied the years of deprivation and depression immediately preceeding the war.

The Brigade had been standing by under first 'Stratford' and then Plan R4 since 25 February for duty in Scandinavia. Their task was to secure ports of entry into Norway through which other forces could pass to the aid of Finland, and at the same time act as a deterrent to a German retaliatory invasion. They may have proved adequate in this garrison task, but they were totally unprepared for the mobile offensive role for which they were now destined. They had no transport, inadequate signals equipment, poor maps and no artillery support. Intelligence was scarce, largely dependent on such *ad hoc* methods as that adopted by the Hallamshires of sending an officer in civilian guise to have a look at Norway during the month of March. Good quality winter clothing had been rushed on board the transports at the last minute; thick string vests, five pairs of socks per man, white sheepskin lined coats and hats, frost-proof rubber boots, fur gloves and Arctic sleeping bags of three thicknesses. At this stage it all looked very reassuring, but it was to prove more of a burden than a blessing when the men found they had no transport in which to carry it around. Carton de Wiart said that when fully dressed his force looked like 'paralysed bears'. Most of it eventually had to be abandoned, and was doubtless gratefully put to good use by the Norwegians or the Germans.

146th Brigade was embarked in two large transports, the *Chrobry* and the *Empress of Australia* escorted by three cruisers, *Manchester*, *Birmingham* and *Cairo*, and three destroyers. The Hallamshires at last boarded the *Chrobry* and set sail on 9 April from Glasgow up the west coast of Scotland to Scapa Flow. They rested there for two days while the rest of the Brigade and its escorts joined up and finally left for Norway on the 12th. Their destination at this stage was still of course Narvik in company with 24th Guards Brigade, but as already observed, confidence in the early capture of Narvik had now led to their diversion to Namsos.

General Carton de Wiart arrived at Namsos by Sunderland flying boat on the afternoon of 15 April expecting his main force to arrive at dusk. The spectre of air attack immediately placed its indelible mark on the expedition. The General could not disembark from his aircraft until a marauding German bomber broke off a machine gun attack which injured his Staff Officer who had to return to England. When at last he was able to get ashore he found that the Admiralty, acting on Nicholson's advice, had already decided to divert the transports to Lillesjona, a supposedly quiet fiord about 100 miles to the north, and move them onwards to Namsos in destroyers. The indefatigable General immediately set off to Lillesjona in the *Somali* to co-ordinate the landing arrangements. No time was lost in readying the force to move on to Namsos, the *Afridi*, *Sikh*, *Matabele*, *Mashona* and *Nubian* quickly refuelled and took on board the Hallamshires and half the Lincolnshires. Even at Lillesjona the troops experienced their first taste of air attack, and the K.O.Y.L.I who had not been lucky enough to get away on the first shuttle to Namsos spent a most uncomfortable day cooped-up in the transports while bombs fell all around them, fortunately without damage except to their nerves.

The Hallamshires and the first echelon of the Lincolnshires eventually arrived at Namsos after a high speed dash down the coast on the evening of 16 April. It was twenty-five years to the day since the Hallamshires had first set foot in France as part of the British Expeditionary Force. Despite Captain Edds' gloomy prognosis, the troops quickly dispersed so effectively that the regular early morning reconnaissance flight, soon christened 'Henry the Hun', failed to notice the intrusion. So far all was going well.

After a day of almost continuous, albeit ineffective, bombardment from the air, it was decided that the *Chrobry* might just as well proceed to Namsos as sit like a fairground target at Lillesjona, and she sailed with the K.O.Y.L.I and the rest of the Lincolnshires to arrive at the entrance to the Namsenfiord at dusk on the 17th, unloading the troops but not all their stores before dawn broke at around 0200. The following night, having stood off-shore during the day, she returned to unload the rest of the equipment. But even so one hundred and seventy tons of stores had been carried back home in the *Empress of Australia*, and a Brigade which had been badly equipped at the outset now had only two full days of essential supplies. However, quite remarkably in the face of the difficulties they had encountered, the 146th Brigade was ashore without loss.

The second echelon of troops to join 'Mauriceforce' was three battalions of the French 13th Chasseurs Alpins under General Audet. They were due to arrive on 18 April in four French troopships[5] escorted by the cruiser *Emile Bertin* and four French destroyers. In fact, they were a day late, which at least allowed the *Chrobry* to complete the unloading of her stores at the only tiny quay available at Namsos. Although the landing of 146th Brigade had been successfully concealed from the enemy, the French were not so lucky. As their troopships led by the anti-aircraft cruiser *Cairo* steamed in line astern up the long fiord they came under sustained bombing attack. Miraculously the troopships were not hit, but the *Emile Bertin* was forced to retire after receiving a direct hit. The troops were successfully disembarked overnight, but they did not disperse quickly as had the British and the morning reconnaissance flight was able to observe large quantities of stores scattered around the quayside which gave some indication of the scale of the landing.

The French troops made only a minor contribution to 'Mauriceforce' and it is well encapsulated in the words of the Force Commander:

> The French Chasseurs Alpins were a fine body of troops and would have been ideal for the job in hand, but ironically they lacked one or two essentials, which made them completely useless to us. I had wanted to move them forward but General Audet regretted they had no means of transport as their mules had not turned up. Then I suggested that his ski troops might move forward, but it was found that they were lacking some essential strap for their skis, without which they were unable to move. Their other equipment was excellent; each man carried some sixty pounds and managed his load with the utmost ease. They would have been invaluable to us if only I could have used them.[6]

It was a week since the calamitous invasion of their soil, but the Norwegians were at last collecting their wits and getting their forces together. They had three battalions in the area of Grong and Lake Snaasa and other isolated units to the south towards Trondheim. Thier commanding officer, Colonel Getz, was not however optimistic regarding their effectiveness: they were inexperienced militia with obsolete rifles and little ammunition. The local population, whilst generally friendly, were unable or unwilling to provide genuine assistance and there were reports, certainly exaggerated, that there were pro-fascist elements amongst them.

By the morning of 20 April, the Allies were ready to undertake the first stage in the recapture of Norway. Ostensibly they were in a strong position. With the help of the Norwegians, Carton de Wiart possessed more combat soldiers than the Germans in Trondheim, roughly nine battalions against three. But numbers alone meant little. The majority of his troops were under-trained or ill-prepared. Their supporting arms and equipment would have made a tolerably efficient army staff hide their head with shame or disbelief. Above all, they had no air support, and soon they were to have no lines of communication. The first disaster for the Allies on land in the new European war was inevitable and imminent.

Writing on the Wall

The Germans were now well aware that a sizeable force had landed at Namsos and the Luftwaffe responded promptly. Throughout 20 April waves of German bombers attacked Namsos at regular intervals. The town which was largely built of wood was almost totally destroyed as were the wooden wharves, the railway station and the rolling stock. Late in the day when the *Nubian* arrived with French stores, the captain graphically described the scene:

> (The area) was just a red flare in the sky which was realised to be a big fire. When the town came into view the sight was remarkable: the whole place was a mass of flames from end to end and the glare upon the snows of the surrounding mountains made an unforgettable spectacle.[7]

The fundamental weakness of 'Mauriceforce' was already only too apparent. The enemy had full command of the air and could control the lines of communication and thus limit the scale of attack. The problem was exacerbated after 22 April when the

Germans at last brought the airfield at Vearnes into full operational use and could wield their air power at will over the battle and support areas just a few miles to the north. Even if it had been possible to introduce reinforcements it would have been totally impossible to support them. General Carton de Wiart concluded in his report after the evacuation:

> The prospect for the landing at Namsos appears to have violated nearly all the conditions for the success of such an operation which have been thought out in staff exercises since the last war.[8]

As well as delivering stores, the *Nubian* remained at Namsos after 20 April to provide much needed anti-aircraft support. But the destroyer's anti-aircraft guns were largely ineffective; only 2 pounder pom-poms and 0.5 inch machine guns. Fighter aircraft rather than point defences were the sole hope of stemming the tide of the relentless air attack, and at Namsos this support could come only from an aircraft carrier of which none were available. There was nowhere ashore to sort and store equipment; such items as were landed had to be left out in the open where the Luftwaffe would surely see and destroy them. Carton de Wiart signalled to the War Office:

> I see little chance of carrying out decisive or, indeed, any operations unless enemy air activity is considerably reduced.[9]

The following day the sloop *Auckland* took over from the *Nubian*. Enemy air activity was so high that a ship's entire complement of shells could be exhausted within 24 hours. The *Auckland* was bombarded continuously as it progressed up the fiord, but even so escaped a direct hit. As we have already seen, the accuracy of the German bombers at this stage of the war was poor, otherwise it is probable that not a single warship could have survived in the restricted waters of the Namsemfiord. Indeed, the only consolation in an otherwise bleak prospect was that the Luftwaffe tended to concentrate on the ships in the fiord, thus giving the troops ashore a slightly easier time than they might otherwise have expected. But this was but a temporary benefit, for the ever shortening nights were inexorably reducing the hours of respite which darkness provided against air attack. Having controlled the logistics, the troops on the ground could now be picked off at leisure. The writing was already on the wall, and even at this stage the possibility of evacuation was beginning to figure in the Force Commander's thinking.

General Carton de Wiart's original objective was quite straightforward. In co-ordination with 'Sickleforce' and 'Hammer' he was to advance to the south and re-capture Trondheim. In practice, the co-ordinated operation did not materialise and he was not even told until a late stage that 'Hammer' had been cancelled. In fact, the paucity of information became so serious that he eventually sent Colonel Fleming to London in an endeavour to seek guidance on the way forward, but it was only to learn that plans regarding Norway were somewhat confused: Fleming reported 'You can really do what you like, for they don't know what they want done.[10]

There were two roads and a railway line to Trondheim. The shorter and better road ran south across the Bangsund bridge and met the coast again at Steinkjer, about forty miles from Namsos. The second road and the railway ran eastwards to Grong, turned south-west along Lake Snaasa and rejoined the main road at Asp Junction just to the north of Steinkjer. Steinkjer, an attractive wooden town of some 4,000 inhabitants, was therefore the key defensive position for the protection of the Namsos bridgehead. Beyond Steinkjer, the road continued south intermittently touching the Trondheimfiord until at Hell it turned westwards for the final fifteen miles into Trondheim. It was important to control both routes to Steinkjer because the road bridges at both Bangsund and Beitstad on the direct route were vulnerable to air attack. Cross country travel was extremely slow and difficult in the snow, four foot deep in places, which still covered the entire area. The roads at this time of the year were in particularly poor condition as the frost had broken up the surface, and the daytime thaw which had now set in made driving hazardous and marching tiresome.

Carton de Wiart intended to establish his Brigade Headquarters at Steinkjer and push troops as far forward as Verdalsora where a Norwegian detachment was guarding an important bridge across the River Inna. The Hallamshires, the first battalion ashore, were pushed forward immediately in requistioned civilian lorries on 17 April to establish companies at Steinkjer and at Malm and Follafoss on the opposite side of the Beitstadfiord. This was a bold move, fully justified by the total absence of German troops in the area. Some of the subsequent dispositions were to be less well judged. The Norwegians agreed to protect the mountain flanks of the alternative route through Grong and to provide skirmishing parties to push forward towards Trondheim. On the evening of 18 April, the Lincolnshires moved forward to Steinkjer by rail and established themselves in and around the town. The K.O.Y.L.I were also entrained to take up positions even further south between Steinkjer and Verdalsora, twenty miles on the road towards Trondheim. The Hallamshires now withdrew to the Beistad area to guard the important bridge on the route back to Namsos.

All of these movements were carried out at night with maximum concealment and the Germans were certainly not aware by the 19th of the extent and strength of the British advance. But the Brigade was now strung out in small packets along the fifty five miles of road which was vulnerable at several points to both direct attack as well as harassing fire from the fiords on their right flank. This disposition has been rightly subjected to criticism and it would have been more prudent to have consolidated the Steinkjer position before venturing further forward. The K.O.Y.L.I particularly were now dangerously exposed. It is nevertheless relevant to recall that at this stage Carton de Wiart was still expecting 'Hammer' to go ahead, thus distracting the Germans in Trondheim from looking towards the north. That he was well aware of the danger is evident from a signal he sent to the War Office on 20 April advising that the ice on the Trondheimfiord was breaking up and that any attack from the sea would be difficult to counter, particularly in view of the lack of artillery. As Operation 'Hammer' had been cancelled the day before, this potential threat was now very real as the Germans had complete control and freedom of operation in the Trondheimfiord.

On the morning of 21 April, the K.O.Y.L.I was ordered to withdraw from their forward positions near Verdalsora to concentrate around Lake Strommen about 10 miles to the south of Steinkjer and at Stiklestad close to the southern end of Lake Leksdal. The retreat which led inexorably to evacuation was already under way and the advance towards Trondheim was effectively abandoned even before a shot was fired. On the same morning, German sea movements had been observed at the entrance to the Beitstadfiord and a company of the Lincolnshires was detached to watch the beach at Egge to the north-west of Steinkjer.

Despite all the manoeuvring and the absence of any encounter with the unseen enemy, the troops were uneasy. German reconnaissance aircraft continually scoured the area at very low level and the men had to remain under cover in the woods during the day to avoid being seen. They could not dig in because of the frozen ground and were reluctant to construct other defensive works which would have been readily observed from the air. Of greater concern was their lack of offensive weapons. They had no artillery, no machine guns and only a handful of 3-inch mortars: they had to confront an unknown enemy with small arms and grenades. Most worrying of all, watching the German aircraft lazily roaming the open sky brought starkly home to them that they had no air support whatsoever and no anti-aircraft weapons.

As their bridgehead gradually became more secure, Group XXI gave two objectives to the Trondheim Group: to occupy Steinkjer and to secure the railway running eastwards to the Swedish border which they hoped to establish as a vital line of re-supply. By the 16th, the latter objective had been achieved, but it was not until 20 April that Generalmajor Kurt Woytasch ordered the 181st Division to advance towards Steinkjer. By this time the German strength in Trondheim was about 4,000 men. On the morning of 21 April, one infantry company was landed from a torpedo boat to the north of Verdalsora while another company with artillery support proceeded north by rail. After three hours of sporadic house-to-house fighting the Verdal road bridge was secured intact from the isolated Norwegian company. The Sappers had been rushed forward to complete the demolition, but arrived too late.

Meanwhile, a threat developed on the flank of the British positions between Vist and Verdalsora when a mountain battalion was landed from a destroyer at Kirknesvaag and Skjenstadaun about fifteen miles south-west of Steinkjer on the eastern shore of the Beitstadfiord. Brigadier Phillips redeployed his forces to meet this threat, moving a company of the Lincolnshires forward to Vist and a company of the K.O.Y.L.I to the west to hold the Strommen causeway. The Germans promptly swung their main line of advance north-eastwards towards Vist which, if successful, would cut off the retreat of the K.O.Y.L.I from the south. From noon onwards, the Germans began an intense action against the Lincolnshires with mortars and machine guns and by 1800 had forced the two leading companies to retreat to a position just to the west of Vist after the farm buildings in which they were sheltering were set on fire.

The K.O.Y.L.I, dangerously strung out along the road between Vist and Verdalsora were also soon in trouble. 'C' Company was sent to Strommen to help out 'A' Company which had already been detached to guard the causeway. But the latter had been unable to move forward from the village because of the deep snow.

Meanwhile, news arrived that 'B' Company was in difficulties at Stiklestad, and so 'C' Company once again clambered aboard their two ramshackle requisitioned buses and returned down the road towards Verdalsora. Despite a risky manoeuvre in crossing the enemy front at Fleskus the two companies eventually linked up.

Despite all the frantic scurrying back and forth, the Battalion had still not really come to grips with the enemy, and they were helpless to prevent the more mobile German troops on snow shoes infiltrating through their position at Strommen. In danger of being cut off, 'A' Company along with 'D' Company was ordered therefore to withdraw along the road northwards towards Vist. The K.O.Y.L.I was now split into two distinct groups and were paying the penalty for being strung out along a too deep and narrow salient. By faulty positioning, one of the three battalions had failed to make any worthwhile contribution to the defence of Steinkjer.

Coinciding with their advance towards Vist, the Germans mounted heavy air raids against Steinkjer which like Namsos was constructed of wood and suffered an identical fate. The town was almost entirely destroyed and the Brigade Headquarters had to be evacuated: the civilian population had already taken to the mountains. A large quantity of stores was destroyed, but Major A. S. T. Godfrey RE managed to rescue most of the rations by driving a train consisting of an engine and four trucks across the blazing railway bridge before it collapsed.

The Retreat Begins in Earnest

By nightfall on the 21st it was clear that holding on to Vist was no longer tenable and Carton de Wiart ordered a retreat along the main road back towards Namsos. The K.O.Y.L.I who had the furthest to travel were allocated the only available requisitioned lorries, just eighteen in number, and the Lincolnshires were ordered to remain in position to fight a delaying action on the 22nd. But the following morning the daily reconnaissance flight, 'Henry the Hun' to the Hallamshires, but now christened 'George' by the K.O.Y.L.I, was able to spot 'D' Company and directed German ski troops to their position just south of Sparbu. The K.O.Y.L.I thus came under pressure from both front and rear before they could withdraw and it was now clear to Colonel Hibbert that his only chance of saving the Battalion was to strike across country to the north east. Only a handful managed to retire to the north to join up with the Lincolnshires, and a rendezvous was arranged for the main body at Fisknes at the northern tip of Lake Leksdal. One platoon was actually caught on the road and its whole complement killed or captured: the rest melted away into the woods, fortunately undetected by the Germans.

'B' and 'C' Companies had, meanwhile, contrary to the orders received from Brigade HQ to remain in position overnight, had continued their retreat under the cover of darkness along the east shore of Lake Leksdal. The journey back for troops not equipped to travel across country was a daunting prospect, but the only other options were to surrender, stand and fight and inevitably suffer heavy casualties, or make across country to Sweden, 60 miles away. Given the alternatives, the K.O.Y.L.I set off determinedly to walk to rejoin the rest of 'Mauriceforce'.

The main fighting on the 22nd, as on the previous day, was to the west of Vist. Despite being shelled by destroyers from the fiord and machine gunned from the air, the Lincolnshires managed to hang on throughout the morning, but it was clear that they would not be able to hold Vist until darkness as planned. The withdrawal became disjointed as some of the troops did not receive the message until three hours after it had been issued at 1120; nevertheless, most of the battalion managed to struggle back through Steinkjer before the Germans arrived at 1900. Despite an abortive attempt to establish a line just to the south of the town, the Germans landed from ships on the waterfront after further shelling.

The main action for 'Mauriceforce' was already over, but many difficulties remained. Major Stokes commanding HQ Company of the Lincolnshires had received the order to withdraw very late, and to his dismay learned that the Germans had now occupied Vist blocking his retreat through Steinkjer. Joining up with 'C' Company, he therefore decided to bypass Steinkjer to the east and set of across country. Without snowshoes, the two hundred men had enormous difficulty fighting their way through snow four feet deep. The men were ordered to discard most of their equipment including their steel helmets, but even so only managed to cover a mile in the first three hours. Fortunately, the Germans had not detected their departure and they struggled on throughout the following day eventually reaching Five on Lake Snaasa about 0100 on the 24th. Here they joined up with a Norwegian outpost, but the following morning at dawn set off on their own again towards Beistad where, totally exhausted, they made contact with an advance party of the Hallamshires. They had covered 45 miles in 49 hours, much of it through trackless country under deep snow.

HQ Company and 'D' Company of the K.O.Y.L.I. had also set off across country at midday on the 22nd. Their maps showed no sign of a bridge crossing the River Ogna to the west of Steinkjier, but by an extraordinary chance Colonel Hibbert recalled a fishing visit to the area in 1910 when he was a boy of sixteen. He remembered a wooden bridge above a pool and he wracked his brain to try to remember where it was – he was not absolutely sure it was even on the Ogna. There was a road of sorts from Sparbu to Fiskness, but the lorries which had been allocated for their withdrawal along the main road to the north spent most of the time sliding into hidden ditches and overturning. To add to their difficulties, 'George' was clearly looking for the missing battalion and twice flew low overhead as they crouched in the shelter of the trees bordering the road, fortunately on both occasions failing to spot them.

At Fiskness, 'B' Company rejoined the Battalion and just before setting out towards Henning, news arrived that 'C' Company was struggling along the shore of the lake but hoped to catch up with the main body at Henning. One stroke of luck for the re-united Battalion was the attachment of a Norwegian interpreter, Private Matheison, who while at Fiskness had managed to discover the whereabouts of Colonel Hibbert's bridge. Although it was rumoured that it had already been destroyed by the Norwegians, it was the K.O.Y.L.I.'s only chance of rejoining the main force. Beitstad was still thirty two miles away and the Battalion was already exhausted. Travel by day would have risked observation from the air and so there was no alternative to marching at night. They set off at 2100 jettisoning most of their equipment except their rifles and Bren guns. Soon the battalion was strung out in single file over more than two miles like a long black snake winding its way across the hills and valleys, the wounded, wrapped in blankets, strapped to sledges drawn by horses. To their left they could see the glare of Steinkjer burning in the night sky, but it was at least some compensation to know that for the time being they were safe from air attack. To their enormous relief the leading party, shortly after dawn, came in sight of the bridge; it was intact, but had it already been taken by the Germans? A small patrol was sent forward to find out. The mountains and forest on the far side looked black and ominous, but as the rest of the Battalion watched with bated breath, the patrol crossed the flimsy bridge and disappeared into the silent forest on the far side. All was quiet and they pressed on, another obstacle overcome.

Shortly after 0600, the leading party reached Stod where they had an anxious few minutes persuading a Norwegian outpost that they were indeed British and not Germans. Across the Sunnan bridge and on towards Beitstad, there was little time for rest, for Colonel Hibbert was not to know that the Germans had not pressed on beyond Steinkjer and he decided to make straight for Namdalseidet, eighteen miles further on. At last, with the welcome relief for some of the party of covering the last few miles by lorry, the bulk of the battalion reached their destination on 25 April. It had been an epic march: they had covered 58 miles in 42 hours, and that immediately after withdrawing from a brisk action. The K.O.Y.L.I. may have been inexperienced and ill-trained, but they were undeniably tough.

The Cabinet Decides to Evacuate Central Norway

We have moved on to the 25 April with the K.O.Y.L.I., but it is now necessary to look back to the events which culminated in the decision to evacuate Central Norway. Lieut General H. R. S. Massey, the Deputy Chief of the Imperial General Staff, had been appointed on 21 April to be the overall commander of Allied troops in Central Norway and established his Headquarters temporarily in Nobel House close to Buckingham Palace, intending to transfer it to Aandalsnes as soon as a major base could be established. In the event, he and his staff never left London as the pincers had not closed, indeed did not look like closing, and the only means of reliable communication between the two arms was through London. Despite Carton de Wiart's reports of the destruction of Namsos and the loss of Steinkjer, there was still some confidence in London that the situation could be retrieved. But attention was again being transferred to Narvik where the earlier optimism of a quick victory had been shown to be misplaced. It was thus decided that a French demi-brigade of Chasseurs Alpins which had been earmarked for 'Mauriceforce' should proceed instead to Narvik.

The Supreme War Council met again in Paris on the 22 and 23 April. M. Reynaud was still keen to prosecute the war in Scandinavia and thought that severing the ore supplies should remain the primary objective. Merely closing Narvik at this stage of the year when the ports in the Gulf of Bothnia were reopening would not have achieved this end and thus, once again, intervention in Sweden was under discussion. The Foreign Office judged, almost certainly correctly, that any measure, no matter how improbable or whimsical, of diverting German interest from the Western Front was the primary French concern. Nevertheless, the Council reaffirmed their aim of capturing Trondheim and Narvik followed by rapid concentration of forces on the Swedish frontier.

On 23 April, further thought was given to reviving a modified Operation 'Hammer' by seizing the forts at the entrance to the Trondheimfiord, thereby gaining control of the waters on the flank of 'Mauriceforce' which had proved such a thorn in the side of the Lincolnshires defending Vist and Steinkjer. This would be a prelude to renewing the pressure from the north and the landing of two additional brigades close to Trondheim. But the uncertainty of being able to defend the landing against air attack was a constant worry, and concern over the increasing threat against France and the Low Countries led to reconsideration within the Military Co-ordination Committee of the advisability of remaining within Central Norway at all.

Mr Churchill, who had originally opposed serious intervention in Central Norway and then subsequently wholeheartedly backed 'Hammer' when others were losing faith, now turned full circle again. His summary of events at the Military Co-ordination Committee meeting on the evening of 24 April sowed the seed which led to the decision to withdraw. By the 26th, the Chiefs of Staff were recommending evacuation, and Mr Chamberlain, with supreme ingenuity, remarked that a withdrawal done well could be claimed as a 'strategic triumph',[11] all a part of the plan to concentrate on Narvik.

The Prime Minister passed on the unpalatable news to the War Cabinet. He said that even if fifty heavy and eighty light anti-aircraft guns were sent to Trondheim – on the unlikely assumption that it could be captured – it would still be difficult to use the port in the face of heavy air attack. Furthermore, most of the Home Fleet would be needed to support the force which was an unjustifiable risk, particularly if, as now looked likely, Italy might be on the point of joining the war.

The French were furious at this weakening resolve and General Gamelin was immediately despatched to London to present the French case. Another Supreme War Council was hastily convened which met in London on the afternoon of the 27th. Chamberlain now said bluntly that the Allies could not capture Trondheim and that sooner or later would have to withdraw completely from Central Norway. The prospect of Italy entering the war was discussed and again Chamberlain stated quite clearly that the Allies could not fight in the Mediterranean and in Scandinavia at the same time. Albeit under protest, Reynaud at last gave in and it was agreed to forget the projected attack on Trondheim and consider moving the Namsos force northwards towards Narvik: it was still intended to repossess Narvik although it was admitted that even that might not be accomplished as quickly as earlier expected.

The way was now clear to concentrate on the extrication of the Allied forces from Central Norway. Like most British retreats, it was planned and executed with enterprise and skill: if only Napoleon had thought to invite the British to organise his retreat from Moscow in 1812, he may well not have ended his days in a country retreat on St Helena!

The withdrawal, not unnaturally, had a most depressing if not embittering effect on the Norwegians. Speculation was rife that they would seek terms from the Germans and it was only as a result of a hastily contrived undertaking that the Allies would continue the fight for Narvik – a promise which at this stage must have had a distinctly hollow ring – that the Norwegians reluctantly agreed to continue the struggle. After all they now had very little more to lose except pride.

The indirect effect in Britain was even more dramatic. Mr Chamberlain announced the withdrawal from Central Norway to an angry House of Commons on 2 May. A debate of the House followed on 7/8 May in which the Government was severely battered from all sides. In the subsequent division, thirty three Conservatives voted with the opposition and sixty abstained. Although the Government comfortably survived, Chamberlain knew that he no longer had the confidence of either the Party or the House. On the following day he tried to form a National Coalition Government under his own leadership, but he could not gain the support of the Labour Party. On the 10th he resigned – a new era was about to begin.

'Impossible' – The Word the Navy did not Recognise

General Carton de Wiart was told of the decision in principle to evacuate on 26 April. By now most of his forces had withdrawn to the area north of Hjelle, 15 miles north-west of Steinkjer. The Hallamshires who had not been involved in any of the action so far now occupied the leading positions on the main road to Namsos, with the exhausted K.O.Y.L.I. north of Namdalseid and the Lincolnshires, who had borne the brunt of the fighting, withdrawn to the rear just south of Bangsund. There had been a lull in air attacks for three full days from 23 April, mainly due to a welcome spell of bad weather and a relatively successful Fleet Air Arm attack against the airfield at Vaernes.

The French and the Norwegians, emboldened perhaps by the fact that they had seen little of the action so far were keen to mount a counter-offensive and the Norwegians, more comfortable in guerilla type activities than set piece actions, gave a good account of themselves. A final British fling was a patrol of the Hallamshires led by Captain R. O. S. Dimmock on 28 April which in broad daylight raided a German post and escaped without loss – an action perhaps more gallant than prudent, but nonetheless good for morale at this stage of the retreat.

A final diversion for General Carton de Wiart was a proposal, first mooted by General Gamelin, that elements of 'Mauriceforce' should withdraw to the north towards Mosjöen with the intention of delaying a possible German advance on Narvik. It was also suggested that a part of the force should be transhipped to Mosjöen in case the Germans should attempt to take the town with paratroops. Carton de Wiart believed that the road to the north was still blocked by snow and impassable for infantry and strongly resisted the proposal. To prove his point he sent Colonel Fleming and Captain Lindsay to reconnoitre the route who needed twelve hours to cover forty miles. The proposal was dropped, as we shall see, prematurely. The French, in conjunction with the Norwegians who had not yet been told of the evacuation, briefly considered a counter-attack on Steinkjer and the 13th Chasseurs Alpins actually exchanged positions with the Hallamshires which placed them about halfway between Namsos and Steinkjer, but nothing came of the plan.

On 26 April air raids were resumed on Namsos resulting in further damage to the stone quays and the warehouses. A Royal Marines Bofors anti-aircraft battery arrived on the 27th but never came into action due to lack of ammunition, and two sloops, *Bittern* and *Janus*, were left in the harbour to provide a measure of air defence. It was becoming increasingly difficult to sustain Namsos as a viable bridgehead. Ships could only be safely unloaded during the brief hours of darkness, and any vessels remaining in the fiord during daylight hours did so at their peril.

The difficulties of operating a ship-to-shore link at Namsos are vividly illustrated by the story of Lieut R. B. Stannard RNR in command of the trawler *Arab* which arrived at Namsos during the night of 28 April. The trawlers had been intended to undertake anti-submarine patrols in the entrance to the fiords, but when it was found that their asdic equipment was useless in the shallow waters, they were often pressed into more general duties. Stannard was ordered on his arrival to ferry stores and equipment from the cruiser *Carlisle* to the shore, but when the first air raid commenced at dawn, was directed to secure alongside a jetty astern of a French ammunition ship, the *Saumur*, not the healthiest berth during an air raid. A bomb hit the wooden jetty which contained crates of ammunition, but Stannard immediately ran his bows into the jetty and spent two hours trying to fight the fire, saving a part of the jetty which proved invaluable later.

The night passed busily but uneventfully as the *Arab* ferried troops from shore to ship – the first part of the evacuation of the Chasseurs Alpins. The following day the air attacks resumed in earnest, the *Arab* suffering sixteen near misses which caused damage to the engines, rudder and screw. She took cover in the lee of cliffs to await the following day's attack which duly arrived. Stannard decided the time had come to fight back, and with the help of the crew of the trawler *Gaul*, set up and manned a machine gun post on the cliff top. In the course of a bitterly cold night Stannard, wounded by a stray bullet, and his colleagues had frost bite to contend with as well. The *Arab* then continued with the evacuation of troops until on 2 May they were ordered to return home. Their troubles were still not over, they had barely cleared the fiord moving cautiously on the damaged engines when they were approached by an He 115. The strafing attacks were wild, but the aircraft approached too close to the *Arab* and was immediately assailed by every gun on board. The action was successful and the crew had the satisfaction, and some compensation for all their difficulties, of seeing the aircraft crash into the sea. The *Arab* eventually arrived safely home: Lieut Stannard was rewarded with the Victoria Cross on 16 August 1940.

Many of the trawlers, mostly manned by RNR officers and men, had similar adventures and in all, between Aandalsnes and Namsos, eleven were lost. Equipped only with Lewis machine guns and a single 20mm Oerlikon, they were always fighting a losing battle against air attack. But as so often in the naval war, the little ships played just as valiant a role as their more renowned larger sisters.

The withdrawal began on 29 April when the 53rd Chasseurs embarked on two French transports. But the main evacuation was planned for two nights, 1/2 May. The anti-aircraft guardships, despite the constant attempts of the Luftwaffe to destroy them, had managed to keep parts of the quay intact. Quite remarkably, despite the battering they had received, only one anti-aircraft guardship was sunk at either Aandalsnes or Namsos although many were damaged. On 30 April, the *Bittern* was still on station at Namsos. She had survived repeated air attacks throughout the day, but at about 1700 she was once more assailed by three Ju 87 Stukas, two over the bow and one from astern. It was the latter which struck, placing a bomb neatly against a locker containing demolition charges. The stern was completely removed in the subsequent explosion and the ship engulfed by fire. Her fellow guardship, the *Janus* bravely came alongside the burning hulk to rescue the crew and then sank the *Bittern* by torpedo. Fortunately, the cruiser *Carlisle* had already arrived to take over the *Bittern*'s duties to cover the remainder of the evacuation.

It was intended to move out the French first, who after their brief interest in a counter-offensive now appeared only too ready to leave.

> General Audet came to see me and begged me not to leave his troops until the last when the hour came to embark. He seemed much moved, and by answering him that not a single British soldier would be embarked until every Frenchman was on board ship, I had a narrow escape from being embraced and was told that I was un vrai gentlemen.[12]

The evacuation from Namsos was planned to take place after that from Aandalsnes and it could be expected that the Germans would do all within their power to distrupt the proceedings. After all, there could now be no doubt that the Allies were leaving Central Norway. The intended plan was for half the force to be removed on the first night in three large French transports[13] and the rest the following night in the cruisers *Devonshire* and *York* and the French cruiser *Montcalm*. Fog caused the evacuation planned for the first night to be cancelled although it did not prevent some of the destroyers being attacked in the fiord. Despite the fog, the *Maori* had established contact with the Kya Light at the mouth of the fiord and was joined by the *Kelly* (Captain Lord Louis Mountbatten) and two other destroyers. They received permission to proceed to Namsos to lift troops, but as soon as they broke out of the fog bank they were pounced upon by waiting German bombers and had to retreat hurriedly back into the welcoming cover of the sea mist. Even so the *Maori*, whose superstructure was still showing over the shallow bank of fog, received a near miss so close that over twenty of her crew were injured by flying fragments.

The troops assembled on the quay were hastily dispersed under cover to sit out a tense twenty-four hours waiting for the ships to appear. Exacerbating the threat to their security, the Prime Minister announced to the House of Commons on the afternoon of 2 May that the evacuation from Aandalsnes was complete, which was tantamount to an open invitation to the Germans to turn their full attention towards Namsos. Admiral Cunningham decided therefore to implement a contingency plan he had prepared some days before to evacuate the whole fore on the night of 2 May.

The *Carlisle*, the anti-aircraft guardship, had retired to sea for safety during the day but was back on station at 1930. Admiral Vivian, who was flying his flag in the *Carlisle*, went ashore to confer with Audet and Carton de Wiart, who remained very sceptical of the Navy's ability to evacuate the whole force in one night. Meanwhile five hundred French troops were embarked in Commander Sherwood's trawlers ready to be taken out to the *York*.

The fog cleared and the three French transports and the cruiser *York*, escorted by six destroyers, arrived off Namsos about 2230. Two transports embarked troops at the stone quay and the remainder of the force was ferried out to the two other ships in destroyers and trawlers. The *El Kantara* quickly embarked a full complement of 1,700 men and returned to sea with the *Kelly*. The *York* and the *Nubian* soon followed. But the Hallamshires had still not arrived and every available means of transport was commandeered to expedite their progress. The desperate race against the dawn was gathering momentum. By 0220 they were embarked and only the *Afridi* was left behind to bring off the rearguard, Colonel Robins and thirty-three men whose final task had been to demolish the Bangsund bridge. It was touch and go, but the last elements arrived on the quay as the first light of dawn was breaking over the mountains. As a departing gesture, the remaining vehicles on the quay were shelled by the *Afridi* as she hurriedly cast off and made her way down the fiord. Carton de Wiart had thought it impossible to complete the evacuation in one night, but as he later remarked, 'he learned a few hours later that the Navy do not know the word.[14]

The morning was again clear of fog and German reconnaissance aircraft quickly found the departing ships. The convoy was subjected to regular bombing attacks throughout the day until they passed out of range of the aircraft from Vaernes. The Stukas and the Ju 88s used steep dive bombing attacks which were increasingly recognised by both sides as the only effective way of hitting moving ships. All went well for a while despite near misses, but then the French destroyer *Bison* received a direct hit in the forward magazine which spectacularly blew up, taking with it the bridge and many of the ship's officers. Some of the survivors had to leap for safety from the listing hulk into the oily waters which were intermittently bursting into flame, but most were rescued by the destroyers which stopped to help. More unfortunately, the destroyer *Afridi* which had stayed behind to help the *Bison* was herself hit by two bombs just after she rejoined the main force at 1400, one of which exploded between decks causing heavy casualties. An effort was made to take her in tow, but it was soon recognised that she was sinking and had to be abandoned. She went down twenty minutes later with the loss of nearly one hundred men, including thirteen of the Hallamshires who sustained their only losses in action during the campaign and thirty Frenchmen from the *Bison* who had been rescued from their own stricken ship only hours before.

The cruellest blow was suffered by the Norwegians who were not told of the evacuation until the very end, indeed subterfuge was employed to keep the information from them. But resistance had already effectively ended south of Trondheim and at 1400 on the 4 May Colonel Getz surrendered. Even then, the more spirited who could not face the prospect of surrender formed small groups and took to the mountains to create the nucleus of an increasingly active and courageous Norwegian resistance movement.

A more general evaluation of the campaign in Central Norway must await the survey of the other arm of the pincer movement – 'Sickleforce'. The operations based on Namsos had not been disastrous in terms of casualties, only four officers and one-hundred and fifty-three other ranks, some of whom had been taken prisoner. The one significant action was that in the vicinity of Vist on two successive days and the Lincolnshires, who had been mainly involved, emerged with credit from this encounter. The two other territorial battalions, particularly the K.O.Y.L.I., had gained useful experience, if not in the actual fighting, at least in terms of the mental and physical toughness required in war which stood them in good stead in later campaigns.

'Mauriceforce' was not outnumbered by the Germans in Trondheim during the early stages of the operation and it is conceivable that a rapid thrust south in strength might have put the Germans under some pressure. But the airfield at Vaernes had to be put out of action, and neither the RAF nor the Fleet Air Arm could do this for long. Once the Germas had shown that they could bomb the bridgehead at will, the danger and difficulty of keeping the force supplied became overwhelming. Surprisingly few soldiers were killed directly by air attack, the Germans preferring to blanket bomb the occupied towns, particularly Namsos and Steinkjer. Although this caused major disruption to the civil population, its impact on the troops was not quite so serious. Although men out in the open were often machine gunned, there was plenty of cover close to the roads along which most of the fighting occurred, and neither side had developed the ground attack fighters armed with cannon and rockets which proved so effective later in the war.

The main burden borne by 'Mauriceforce' was the lack of the right kind of support, no artillery, no aircraft and no anti-aircraft guns except belatedly at Namsos. Furthermore, the administrative chain was totally inadequate even for such a small force as was subsequently reported by Carton de Wiart:

> The Administrative Staff which was to implement the plan had no opportunity to study the problem beforehand and was gravely handicapped by no arrangements being made for a reconnaissance party in advance and for sound administrative arrangements to be made from the start.[15]

Despite the epic retreats of the K.O.Y.L.I. and a part of the Lincolnshires, the inability to operate off the roads was a major handicap, and the silly mistakes which prevented the Chasseurs Alpins getting into an offensive situation at all were most damaging. 'Mauriceforce' had in the end achieved nothing, it was fortunate that it had not proved more costly.

'Sickleforce' – Diversion to Disaster

'The Regiment had what I think might be described as an unlucky war.'[1]
Major General R. N. White
Colonel of the Sherwood Foresters

The Germans Fan Out

Although the stirring deeds of the Royal Navy in the two battles of Narvik raised the spirits of the nation, the euphoria could not disguise the fact that the first round of the battle for Norway had been convincingly won by Germany. Areas of Norway from Kristiansand in the south to Narvik in the north were under German control even if in places their grip was still precarious. Whereas the German aim was now to consolidate their hold on the major ports and centres of population and to extend their control to the whole of the country, the Allies had the far more difficult task of establishing a foothold and maintaining it over long and tenuous lines of communication. It was to prove a task beyond their capability at this stage of the war.

It had been intended that as soon as they were established in Oslo, Group XXI would link up by rail with the invasion forces in Bergen and Trondheim. But the delay in imposing political and military control in the capital had allowed Norwegian mobilisation to be set in motion, and however uncontrolled and unco-ordinated, some resistance to the German advance could now be expected. General von Falkenhorst quickly decided therefore that it was imperative to establish a secure base in Oslo before advancing along the main interior lines of communication.

The Storting quickly dispensed with the military old guard. The Commander-in-Chief was retired on the grounds of age and was replaced by Colonel Otto Ruge, the Inspector General of Infantry, a younger and more vigorous officer and an energetic proponent of continued resistance. He had already been responsible for thwarting an ambitious attempt by the German Air Attaché, Captain Spiller, and a small group from the 1st Parachute Regiment air landed at Fornebu to seize the King near Elverum on the evening of the 9 April. Ruge established his headquarters at Öyer in the Gudbransdal valley on the main route north to Trondheim. His strategy was to keep the resistance alive for a period of up to ten days whilst the Allies could fulfil their assurances of prompt and powerful support. But he also saw only too clearly the fragility of his hastily mobilised force, short of ammunition and other vital supplies, poorly trained, and most important of all, demoralised by the catastrophe which had so dramatically overtaken their country. It was vital therefore that his troops should not become involved in a set piece battle with a superior German force which would inevitably overwhelm and further weaken the spirit of resistance which it was so important to nurture at this early stage. His tactics were to mount a carefully thought-out series of delaying actions, to withdraw and regroup when the pressure increased, and to hinder the German advance by selective demolitions.

The early signs were not promising. In many parts of the country the assembly points for the reservists in the main towns had been overrun and much of their equipment was already in German hands: of the 120,000 eligible for mobilisation, only about 50,000 eventually managed to report for duty. One of the more successful mobilisations was General Steffen's division based in the mountains at Voss, fifty miles to the east of Bergen, which was later destined to play a vital role in delaying a German breakout towards the north. Mobilisation in the south of the country had been patchy, but the 2nd Division to the north of Oslo had been more successful and had four groups prepared to make a fighting withdrawal through the Oslo plains to the relative security of the mountains to the north.

After their early difficulties, the Germans firmly established their authority in the capital. Generalmajor Englebrecht, fresh from his ducking in the Oslofiord after the sinking of the Blücher set up his Divisional Headquarters in the Hotel Continental. On the evening of the 10th, Falkenhorst himself flew into Oslo. On the 12 and 13 April Falkenhorst issued the orders to initiate the breakout from Oslo. The 196th Division was to operate to the south and east of Oslo and the 163rd Division to the north and west. The 196th Division was immediately successful and within three days organised Norwegian resistance to the east of Olso had been destroyed with nearly 1,000 troops taken prisoner and 3,000 forced to flee across the Swedish border into internment. The Norwegian 1st Division had already ceased to exist. The 163rd Division was equally successful, greatly assisted by irresolute Norwegian leadership, and the key railway junctions at Kongsberg and Honefoss on the lines to Kristiansand and Bergen respectively were captured by the 14 April with the loss of the Norwegian 3rd Infantry Regiment.

Having secured the immediate hinterland of Oslo, the main German objective was to establish control of the area north to Trondheim. The rich agricultural lands surrounding Olso soon give way to a rugged mountainous area containing only two passable valleys, the Österdal in the east and the more important Gudbransdal to the west containing the main road and railway routes. The Germans pushed cautiously but skilfully north in four battle groups. General Englebrecht struck out towards Bergen with part of 163rd Division and along the east bank of the Randsfiord to join up with General Tittel and to confront General Steffen whose mobilisation in the rugged country to the north-east of Bergen had been accomplished more successfully than elsewhere in Norway. The main thrust however was entrusted to General Pellengahr's 196th Division which was to advance along the two main valleys towards Trondheim.

Once clear of the plain, however, their advance was hindered by the Norwegian rearguard which destroyed the bridges and blocked the tunnels as they retreated northwards. Even so Elverum in the Österdal was occupied on the 18th as was Hamar on the eastern shore of Lake Mjösa in the Gudbrandsal. Such was the situation when the first British troops landed at Aandalsnes in the early morning of 19 April.

But Where are we Going?

The 148th Brigade under the command of Brigadier H. de R. Morgan was composed of two territorial battalions, the 1/5th Royal Leicestershire Regiment (Lieut Colonel G. T. German) and the 8th Battalion Sherwood Foresters (Lieut Colonel T. A. Ford). Both battalions, in common with the rest of the Territorial Army, had been divided into two in 1939 in the general expansion of the reserve volunteer forces. They had therefore very little time to train their raw recruits after mobilisation on the outbreak of war, and the problem was exacerbated by the need to familiarise themselves with the new weapons which were issued at that time. Only three members of the Brigade had seen previous active service. Neither battalion had the benefit of any winter warfare training and were only partially equipped to operate in the extreme winter climate they were to meet in Norway.

The Brigade had at first been earmarked as part of the force designed to bring succour to the Finns. Their role, as befitted a newly formed and only partly trained unit, was considered quite straightforward – to occupy the town and airfield at Stavanger in south-west Norway to deter any possible German riposte to this breach of Scandinavian neutrality. It was not expected that they would remain ashore longer than was necessary to render the airfield un-usable, not such a simple task as might sometimes be thought. Stavanger remained their objective even after the Finns capitulated, but now in support of 'Operation Wilfred'. After destroying the airfield, they were to link up with other groups landed at Bergen and Trondheim if the Germans should retaliate with superior forces. A glance at a relief map will quickly disclose that this was a formidable objective. The Brigade was equipped to a light scale, for they were not expected to make an opposed landing, only to restrain misguided Norwegians who did not immediately appreciate that the Brigade was actually there to protect them.

They travelled north only on 6 April and immediately embarked on ships of the 2nd Cruiser Squadron at Rosyth; the Leicestershires on the cruiser *Devonshire* and the Foresters on the *Glasgow*. At this stage their equipment was carefully loaded in the order in which they expected to need it. This well ordered arrangement was soon to be drastically upset. The following day they were ashore again: summarily disembarked as the Squadron hurriedly departed to oppose the High Seas Fleet – wrongly thought to be making a break-out into the Atlantic, but in fact on the very mission that 148th Brigade was intended to deter.

Despite its long period of gestation, the final few days before the Brigade eventually departed for Norway witnessed scenes of almost unbelievable confusion and a succession of conflicting orders. At last on 13 April, Colonel Dudley Clarke was dispatched from the War Office on the night train to Edinburgh clutching secret orders in his breast pocket as well as two car loads of mailbags containing maps, pamphlets and £10,000 in cash. He was accompanied by a somewhat eccentric Norwegian businessman who introduced himself as Krefting, wearing skiboots and trousers surmounted by the top half of a city suit and a standard pattern Army steel helmet. He had been commissioned into the Army that very afternoon as a Norwegian Liaison Officer.[2]

Brigadier Morgan studied these latest orders in the Port Office and then conferred with Vice-Admiral Edward-Collins who was responsible for transporting the force to Namsos. The orders were vague, but in essence 148th Brigade was to establish itself ashore in the vicinity of Namsos and to act in an independent role. The troops were now to travel in greater style in the Orient liner *Orion* with a strong escort to leave as soon as possible. Morgan and his Brigade Headquarters would sail with the Admiral in his flagship *Galatea* together with an assault company from the Sherwood Foresters. Another Forester's Company was to travel on the *Arethusa*.

It was a grey, foreboding day with a gale ominously brewing in the west as the Leicestershires and the Foresters boarded local paddle steamers to be ferried out to the *Orion* moored some way downstream from Rosyth. Many were seasick and all were cold, wet and thoroughly miserable by the time they struggled up the gangplank onto their luxury liner, now garbed in sombre battleship grey in place of her more customary sparkling white. It was not until the morning of the 15th that the final company straggled aboard.

It had by now been revealed that a Royal Navy party had already made an unopposed landing at Namsos and that 146th Brigade, which was on its way to Narvik, was being diverted to Namsos instead. General Carton de Wiart, who was to command 'Mauriceforce', was flying there direct. 148th Brigade had been due to leave early on the 15th, but it was learnt that morning that the order brought up by Dudley Clarke had been cancelled and a new set of orders were on their way to Rosyth by courier.

By midday on the 16th, it had been decided that the *Orion* was too large to get alongside the jetties at Namsos and that it would be too risky to disembark in the fiords. Instead, the whole force would transfer to the cruisers *Galatea*, *Arethusa*, *Carlisle* and *Curacoa*, supplemented by the destroyers *Acheron* and *Arrow*. This transhipment, plan four, threw the distribution of equipment, which was already pretty confused, into complete chaos. As each warship came alongside, layers of stores were skimmed off the top of the *Orion*'s hold and loaded aboard – they now bore no direct relationship to the troops on any individual ship. Inevitably some things were lost, there was no HE ammunition for the 3 inch mortars and the Brigade wireless transmitter disappeared. It had already been discovered on the previous day that the four Bofors guns belonging to the 168th Light Anti-Aircraft Battery lacked their predictor sites. Two were hastily acquired and two more rigged from wood and wire by the *Orion*'s ships carpenter. The Brigade's motor transport was to travel separately, but was destined never to arrive: the transport ship was torpedoed and the Brigade eventually landed in Norway with one lorry and three motor cycles. Two companies of Leicestershires, the Sappers and the Field Ambulance could not be fitted into the warships and were reluctantly left ashore.

At last in the early hours of the 17 April, 148th Brigade belatedly got underway. The two companies of the Leicestershires for which there had been no space meanwhile travelled north to Aberdeen to await alternative transport. It was an unpleasant voyage for most of the troops huddled together wherever they could find space on the crowded ships. The day was fine, but a strong swell added to the discomfort. By late afternoon, a Focke-Wulf Condor found the convoy and shadowed it for the rest of the day: the Brigade now had the added worry that their arrival in Norway was not to go unnoticed.

The two day delay in sailing had enabled the Brigade staff to give some attention to their destination and to contemplate the task ahead of them despite the paucity of maps and intelligence. This also was now to prove to have been of no avail, for amongst the many signals which arrived on *Galatea* during the 17th was one changing their objective yet again. During the afternoon Brigadier Morgan briefed his staff that they were now proceeding, not as they had thought to Namsos, but to Aandalsnes, some one hundred and eighty miles to the south between Oslo and Trondheim. The new plan was that 'Sickleforce', as it was now desginated, would secure the important railway junction of Dombaas, sixty miles inland by road from Aandalsnes and one hundred and twenty south of Trondheim. They would then 'demonstrate' to the north whilst Carton de Wiart with 'Mauriceforce' would descend on Trondheim from Namsos. As we have already seen, this part of the plan was not to be achieved, and Trondheim was to play an even smaller role for 'Sickleforce' in the forthcoming two crowded weeks.

But the most important problem was that the maps that Dudley Clarke had carried so laboriously down from London did not cover Aandalsnes. They had some Shell tourist maps on a scale of sixteen miles to the inch and a little intelligence information which had also arrived from London. The muddle and prevarication which had characterised the lead-up to the campaign was continuing with a vengeance into its execution.

Aandalsnes was little more than a hamlet lying at the head of the Romdalsfiord: a pretty place sheltering under its mountain screen and a popular tourist centre in the summer. Its harbour was designed mainly for passenger traffic with a small quay and a sixty feet wide jetty. Its normal handling capacity amounted to about seven hundred tons daily and it could just accommodate one cruiser and two destroyers. At the entrance to the fiord lay the rather better equipped commercial port of Molde, but unfortunately there was apparently no good road from Molde round to Aandalsnes which was the terminus of both the road and the railway from Dombaas, the ultimate objective. Ferries provided a tenuous link between the two ports.

Nevertheless, it was quite clear that not all of the troops could be landed at Aandalsnes if the warships were to be safely clear of the fiords by daybreak. *Arethusa* and *Carlisle* were therefore diverted to Molde with two companies of the Sherwood Foresters to travel onwards to Aandalsnes by ferry. Nobody knew if the Germans were in either port, whether the road was blocked by snow and if the railway was still workable – or even if it ran by steam or electricity.

Dudley Clarke, who had talked himself into joining the expedition as a liaison officer described the scene as the *Galatea* deftly picked her way up the Romsdalfiord in the early evening of 18 April.

> The last quarter of an hour drew all ranks on deck. The troops stood silently around, awed by the grandeur of the scene and perhaps by the significance of the moment, for none could tell if the next few minutes might not see Briton and Boche in the first real clash of arms on land in the new World War. Whatever their subsequent experiences in the eventful years which were to follow, I doubt if any who were present then could easily forget the thrill of

that spring evening, while the ships slipped silently along, as though threading their way through a canyon, with the darkening glow of a starlit night overhead. We felt an icy chill on the deck from the snowclad slopes, closing in nearer and nearer, while the Norwegian pilot led a breathless convoy in line ahead up the fiord.[3]

The *Galatea* tied up at the small jetty at Aandalsnes just before 2200 on the 18th. There were no Germans to be seen, but to their great surprise a Lieut Colonel Royal Marines and the British Consul stepped forward to greet them. Although a signal had been received at sea mentioning the possibility of Marines being put ashore at Aandalsnes, nothing further had been heard.

The unlikely named 'Primrose Force' consisted of seven hundred Royal Marines and seamen under the command of Lieut Colonel A. W. Simpson RM. They had left Rosyth in a flotilla of four sloops[4] on the night of 14 April in gale conditions which soon proved too much for the Marines on board if not for the sailors, and they were forced to run for shelter into Invergordon during the night of the 15th. The following day was little better, but Captain Poland decided to attempt the crossing and by dusk on the 17th the first two ships were safely tied up alongside at Aandalsnes.

'Primrose Force', also not expecting to come to Aandalsnes, had no maps except sea charts and no clear idea of the task facing them. For the present however it was sufficient to have firm ground beneath their feet after a hideously uncomfortable voyage. Even they were not the first arrivals at Aandalsnes as a small group of sailors had been put ashore from the destroyer *Ashanti* earlier in the day. A small detachment with 4 inch guns was sent to Aalesund, the largest port between Bergen and Trondheim, but they lacked essential mountings for their guns which were never brought into use. Fortunately, no German ships came within range anyway.

The off-loading of 'Sickleforce' proceeded smoothly enough with the help of wooden ramps which had been specifically constructed by the ship's carpenters on the way across, and all the troops were ashore and dispersed by the time the first rays of daylight appeared over the mountains to the east. Leaving the *Black Swan* to provide a token gesture of anti-aircraft defence, the other warships were back at sea before dawn. The Royal Navy had brought the unopposed landing to a fine art, and having thrown off their escorting Condor overnight, the Germans were at first even unaware that a landing had taken place.

The Brigadier's Dilemma – To North or South?

The situation at Aandalsnes was not encouraging. Simpson had commandeered all the available transport but there was little petrol available. This was quickly rectified by running fuel lines ashore from the destroyer's tanks and every available receptacle was soon filled. Simpson had established contact with the colonel commanding a local Norwegian ski regiment who had all his men staked out along the railway to Dombaas as a precaution against a paratroop attack against this vital line of communication. But the railway was still open and the resourceful Simpson had a train already waiting in steam in the station for the Brigade's use.

At this stage the plan to make a direct assault on Trondheim, 'Operation Hammer', was still running and Brigadier Morgan's orders were simple and clear. He was to proceed along the Romsdal to Dombaas, secure this important railway junction, and then turn northwards as the subsidiary arm of the pincer movement on Trondheim. But he had also received instructions on board the *Galatea* to make contact with the Norwegians fighting in the valleys to the south of Dombaas and this was to increasingly influence his actions. The naval party had already pressed forward to Dombaas leaving platoons at key points along the road.

Dombaas was the key to the approach to Trondheim from the south. If this road and railway junction was lost, there was nothing to prevent the Germans reinforcing the garrison at Trondheim overland from Oslo, which itself had relatively secure lines of communication with Germany, either direct or through Denmark. Dombaas sits at 2,000 feet at the head of the Gudbransdal valley where the road and the railway fork, north-west to Aandalsnes and north to Trondheim. The road and the railway ran down the valley to Lillehammer, some eighty miles to the south. A mile or so below Dombaas the valley reaches its narrowest point with the road winding along the precipitous sides of the valley and across several streams before spilling out onto the plateau containing the town. Dombaas was a good defensive position, and given time and adequate strength might have held up a German advance for some time. The alternative approach to Trondheim through the Österdal was a much inferior route, but it nevertheless had also to be secured if the Dombaas position was not to be bypassed.

The Germans had also recognised the importance of this key juntion, and under Hitler's personal direction a company of parachute troops was dropped a few miles to the south of Dombaas to secure the road and railway. The landing was not very successful and several men were killed when they were dropped from too low a height. The Norwegians reacted quickly and rounded up some of the survivors, but a party of about sixty had nevertheless effectively severed communications with the Norwegian Army operating to the south. The British Consul who met the arriving 148th Brigade at Aandalsnes had been the last traveller to get through although he had to run the gauntlet of a German patrol in which his driver was killed.

By the morning of 19 April the paratroops were cornered with a group of Norwegian hostages in a farmhouse about five miles south of Dombaas. A small party consisting of the newly arrived naval attaché, a captain RN, and his lieutenant RNVR assistant had by now arrived on the scene with a 3.7 inch howitzer with which they were threatening the farmhouse. They were on their way south to join up with General Ruge and had taken the gun with the intention of shooting their way through. Because of the hostages, the Norwegians were reluctant to see the howitzer used directly against the farmhouse, which was akin to taking a sledge-hammer to crack a nut, and so the improvised naval gun crew was liberally peppering the ground around to try to induce the Germans to surrender. This was duly achieved and the railway and road to the south were re-opened by mid morning. Whilst a spirited initiative, the paratroop landing was unlikely to have been successful unless it could be quickly supported by an infantry breakthrough in the Gudbransdal.

There was always the risk that further paratroops would be landed and Brigadier Morgan had already decided to push forward quickly to Dombaas. Two companies of Sherwood Foresters left by train at 0100 on the 19th arriving without mishap by dawn. But contrary to Hitler's intention, Goering, who thought the Luftwaffe was bearing too much of the weight of the Norwegian campaign, refused to release any more paratroops and this brief threat disappeared. The balance of 'Sickleforce' was billeted in Aandalsnes and set up the Bofors to protect the railway station and the jetties.

The orders which had originally been given to Brigadier Morgan soon became blurred. In accordance with his directive to make contact with the Norwegian Army GHQ, Morgan himself went forward to Dombaas and on the evening of the 19th met Lieut Colonel E. J. King-Salter, the British Military Attaché. King-Salter, who was accompanied by the French Military Attaché, brought a grim story. After ten days of fighting the Norwegian Army was all but spent, kept going only by the resolution and spirit of their commander General Ruge. They made a strong plea for 148th Brigade to turn south to assist the Norwegians and cited an exchange of telegrams between the War Office and General Ruge which purported to agree support for the hard-pressed Norwegians. In fact the British reply was ambiguous, no doubt intentionally, and whilst offering general support and accepting Norwegian assistance with transport made no actual commitment to proceed south of Dombaas. Nevertheless, King-Salter's arguments were persuasive and Morgan called forward the rest of his Brigade to Dombaas, signalled London for further instructions and himself proceeded to meet General Ruge.

They arrived at midnight to find General Ruge with his small staff in a secluded house at Öyer. He was forced to take extensive security precautions to avoid betrayal by the supporters of Quisling and frequently had to change his headquarters, preferring quiet farmhouses hidden deep in the forest. Dudley Clarke who had travelled south with Morgan described their first meeting:

> Inside the main house we were given coffee and food . . . The Commander-in-Chief appeared shortly afterwards, apologising for not being there to meet us and insisting that we should talk no business until we had finished supper . . . Morgan and I had an opportunity of studying this erect, spare figure, with keen blue eyes, lined features and close-cropped grey hair, whose dominating will and military reputation was keeping alive the resistance of Norway. We found a kindly, friendly man with something of the appearance of a Master of Foxhounds, who spoke good English when he took it slowly, in a soft inflexion which might have come from Wales, dressed in the blue-grey field uniform of King Haakon's Army with baggy breeches tucked into canvas gaiters over ski-boots. There was no sign of ceremony about him; and we found afterwards that he lived with the same austerity as his soldiers, served by a staff which must have been a record for economy in man-power.[5]

But despite its benign beginning, the meeting soon became more tense. Notwithstanding that it had been General Ruge himself who had called for the concentration of the Allied force against Trondheim, he now claimed that 148th Brigade should react to his strategic direction and reinforce the Norwegian 2nd Division below Lillehammer. This posed a difficult dilemma for Brigadier Morgan whose latest directive was still to move north rather than south from Dombaas. Ruge argued persuasively that Trondheim could wait – it could only be supported by a handful of Ju 52s and might well collapse anyway unless the Germans could establish a land bridge with Oslo. On the other hand, Trondheim might be lost forever if the Germans broke through the thin screen of Norwegian troops in the Gudbransdal.

General Pellengahr was now advancing steadily up the Gudbransdal with three infantry battalions with supporting engineers, motorised machine gun troops, artillery and a few light tanks which he had not yet brought into play. An artilleryman himself, Pellengahr was using his field guns with great skill and the accuracy of the German gunnery was a feature throughout the campaign. His tactics were to press gently upon the Norwegian rearguard who would obediently withdraw. He would then make good or bypass any bridges which had been demolished and continue the advance. The advance would only be halted if a good position could be defended in depth.

As Morgan listened to the anguished account of the German's relentless drive northwards, he became increasingly convinced of the need to change direction. Although it was totally contrary to his orders from London, these were now nearly a week old, and without further advice he felt he had to adapt to the changing situation. With some hesitation Morgan eventually agreed and ordered the Brigade to move south from Dombaas. He was doubtless greatly relieved the following morning to receive a telegram from the C.I.G.S. endorsing his decision. It was of course on the 19th that the Military Co-ordination Committee had decided to abandon 'Operation Hammer' which changed the whole course of events in Central Norway.

Taking the Strain

Another more stormy meeting took place on the following day at which General Ruge demanded that the British contingent should come under his direct command, but deft footwork and a degree of deception by King-Salter defused the situation. Nevertheless, for all practical purposes 148th Brigade henceforth came under Norwegian operational control: it was the only sensible decision once the direct attack on Trondheim had been abandoned. Brigadier Morgan however had considerable misgivings about the next proposal to divide his Brigade and distribute his troops across the whole front. Whilst indefensible in purely military terms, General Ruge considered it necessary to bolster the morale of his own troops and to give them the opporunity to rest and regroup. He later, with perhaps only a little over-statement, graphically described how his makeshift army had been forged:

> Remember what kind of an army this was. From Oslo for instance, came hundreds of men who could not mobilise because the Germans held the city. They gathered round some leader and became a 'Company'; they met other groups of the same kind and became 'battalions' under the command of some officer. Casually assembled infantrymen, artillerymen, sailors and aviators, with cars and chaffeurs collected from God knows where, became fighting units. A Commissary department was improvised, the women on the farms doing the cooking.[6]

The Norwegian 2nd Division under General Hvinden Haug was holding the Lundehögda ridge on the west bank of Lake Mjösa with some 1,500 troops, the main element of which was a Dragoon Regiment about 1,000 strong under Colonel Jensen. On the west side of the lake was another brigade of infantry with some supporting artillery under Colonel Dahl.

Brigadier Morgan went forward to the front to talk matters over with Jensen and Dahl. It appeared that the Germans were advancing along the east bank of Lake Mjösa with about 4,000 troops with artillery support. They had not been pressing their advance too hard, merely pushing the Norwegians back and then proceeding cautiously in their own time. The Norwegians had suffered very few casualties and lack of rest was their main complaint. Even as they surveyed the scene, a steady stream of Ju 52s passed undisturbed overhead carrying reinforcements and supplies to Trondheim. It was an early illustration of the complete mastery of the air which the Germans were to enjoy throughout the campaign in Central Norway.

The advance party of 148th Brigade moved rapidly forwards from Dombaas on the evening of the 19th and by the early hours of the following morning were settling into position astride Lake Mjösa. The lake was a vast sheet of grey ice reflecting gloomily in the moonlight. But even as they took up their assigned positions, the racing clouds obscured the moon and the snow began to fall: it already lay two to three feet deep in the birch and conifer woods bordering the roads and was freezing hard. The enemy was just to the south being held, it was claimed by the Norwegians, at Gjovik. It was all very bewildering for a Territorial Brigade formed only months before.

In accordance with General Ruge's wish to distribute the British troops over a wide front to stiffen Norwegian resistance, 'A' and 'D' Companies of the Sherwood Foresters were sent to Nykirke, a village in a side valley on the western side of the lake about thirty-five miles south of Lillehammer. The other two companies of the Foresters were directed to Bröttum, eight miles south of Lillehammer on the eastern shore. The HQ Company was divided between the two groups. 'A' and 'D' Companies of the Leicestershires, who arrived on the morning of the 20th, were sent along a side road south-east of Lillehammer towards Aasmarka in support of the Norwegian Dragoon regiment. Apart from isolated machine gun attacks from marauding aircraft, the deployment had been conducted quickly and safely. Except for two companies of the Leicestershires who were still on route from Scotland and a small group remaining in Dombaas, the Brigade had moved forward over one hundred and fifty miles from Aandalsnes in little over two days.

General Ruge called another meeting at his GHQ on the afternoon of 21 April. His earlier resilience had been replaced by a mood of despondency. He had heard that German tanks and reinforcements had been pouring into Oslo over the last few days and be believed that the situation would quickly become critical. He said that he was now withdrawing all the Norwegian troops to rest and regroup near Tretten some twenty-miles to the rear, leaving the one and a half newly arrived British battalions to face the Germans alone. Brigadier Morgan protested strongly, but there was little he could achieve as the move was already underway. He said he would do his best but 'begged the Commander-in-Chief to recognise the utter inadequacy of the force at his command to carry out the role which was now imposed upon it'.[7] General Ruge also asked that Clarke should return to London as a personal emissary from himself to the C.I.G.S. asking for the immediate despatch of strong British forces to the southern front. When he handed Clarke the letter, which was penned in his own hand, it was with gloomy foreboding that he reminded him 'You carry the fate of Norway in your hands, and I wish you a safe journey'.[8]

General Haug pressed the British troops forward to relieve the retreating and exhausted Norwegians on the afternoon of the 21st, too quickly as it transpired, for the latter stages of advance had been hampered by the shortage of suitable transport. 'B' and 'C' Companies of the Foresters on the east bank soon came under considerable pressure. Their mortar section was deployed on a hill on the Lundehögda Ridge, but was quickly forced to retire by the German artillery. The Foresters were then moved east towards Aasmarka to support the Dragoons and the Leicestershires whose front was rapidly crumbling under the relentlessly accurate fire of the German field guns.

The Leicestershires had taken over as planned the forward positions from the Dragoons which were located on a bleak wooded hillside 1,200 feet above sea level. The terrain was almost hopeless for troops without skis, the snow in the woods was soft like a bog during the day though frozen at night. Although they had no option but to stick to the compacted and frozen tracks, they nevertheless managed to bring their mortar section into action, but with their position rapidly being outflanked they were quickly forced to retreat to a new line behind Aasmarka.

Fortunately, with the arrival of nightfall, the Germans ceased to press their advance. It was a feature of the action in the Gudbransdal that the Germans restricted their operations to daylight hours and rarely commenced their advance until a comfortable hour in the morning. On more than one occasion this allowed the British to establish at least a semblance of a reasonably defensible position.

At 1700 on 21st April, General Haug decided to withdraw from Lillehammer to Faaberg about six miles to the north. The retreat was chaotic. Although the Dragoons had transport, the Norwegian civilian drivers refused to return for the Leicestershires who had to set out at midnight after a day under mortar and artillery fire to walk the fourteen miles to Lillehammer on snowbound hilly lanes: this did nothing to improve the already fragile relationship between the two Allies.

At one stage even the Brigade Headquarters only escaped in the nick of time as a German ski patrol swooped unexpectedly out of the mountains. In a hasty effort to destroy secret papers, even a part of the £10,000 in notes so carefully carried from London by Clarke was bundled onto the fire to stoke up the flames. 148th Brigade's efforts to shore-up the crumbling Norwegian defences was not only falling into disarray, but becoming expensive as well!

The retreat opened up the main road to Lillehammer for the Germans which not only threatened to cut-off Colonel Dahl's forces on the west bank, but hazarded the withdrawal of the Leicestershires and the Foresters who only just managed to escape through Lillehammer in time. Even so, the Germans managed to cut off thirty of the Leicestershires, including six officers, and seized the stores which had been accumulated at the railway station.

The Foresters first experience of battle on the west bank of Lake Mjösa had been rather less eventful. They soon discovered that Gjovik had fallen on the morning of the

20th and therefore retired along the lakeside road as far as Biri. Colonel Dahl now asked the British to take over the forward positions to allow the Norwegians to withdraw through the line: but as the retreating Norwegians passed through, the Foresters could not help but remark that they did not really look as though they had been engaged in serious fighting. Relations between the new found Allies were already crumbling rapidly as misunderstanding and mistrust set in.

But it was events fifteen hundred yards away on the other side of the lake that were soon claiming their attention. It was becoming increasingly obvious that their escape route though Lillehammer was coming under increasing threat as positions on the east bank crumbled. In the early hours of the 22nd their worst fears were confirmed as a series of dull thuds announced the demolition of their lifeline, the bridge at Lillehammer, by Norwegian sappers. Throughout the day they were forced to take cover in the dense pine woods lining the road as they were now within range of the artillery on the opposite shore. The Battalion suffered its first casualties of the war as a stray shell killed five men and wounded three more. Machine gunning aircraft added to their discomfort, but they claimed in return to have brought one down by small arms fire. Fortunately, the enemy was not pressing on their own front although it was obvious now that they would have to beat a hasty retreat through the mountains if they were not to be totally cut off. Fortunately they had some transport, and under the cloak of nightfall set out by a long detour over narrow hilly roads to the west through Gausdal to the next river crossing north of Lillehammer at Tretten. Their journey was not without incident. The cold and discomfort of open lorries, the surly lack of co-operation from some of the Norwegian drivers, and the ceaseless rumours as to how far behind were the pursuing Germans all added to the unease and confusion.

The threat in the Gudbransdal would have been greater if it had not been for the stout delaying action by General Steffen's division which with 3,000 well armed and disciplined troops had been ordered earlier in the campaign by General Ruge to cross the mountains from Voss to protect the Valdres valley which lies to the north-west and is an extension of the Randsfiord. They established themselves at Tonsaasen and for four days from the 23 April made a courageous stand against the German 163rd Division advancing up the Randsfiord. The possibility of the British and Norwegian forces in the Gudbransdal being outflanked from the west was thus avoided. They had, nevertheless, enough problems of their own.

It had not been an auspicious beginning for the British campaign in Central Norway, although no blame could be attached to the soldiers who were fighting in a totally unfamiliar and hostile environment. It was as though a local amateur dramatic society had been asked to perform on a national stage a play they hardly knew.

Action at Faaberg

The defence of the river bridge at Faaberg was left entirely to the British contingent as all the Norwegians had withdrawn to regroup further north. The valley narrows just south of Faaberg to no more than a few hundred yards wide and the village and river are dominated to the south-east by the Balbergkamp, 2,200 feet high, tree-lined and dotted with small farm buildings. Impressive though it appeared from the road, its slopes were not sufficiently steep to preclude an outflanking movement.

The forces available for the defence consisted of 'B' and 'C' Companies of Foresters who, although engaged at Bröttum, had been withdrawn before coming under prolonged pressure, and the remnants of the two companies of the Leicestershires who had not been cut off at Lillehammer or by mistake overshot the new position in their earlier withdrawal. The total was 650 officers and men, but many of these were support troops and the majority were totally exhausted having been on the move continuously for thirty-six hours with little to eat or drink. They had lost their wireless equipment and their entrenching tools in the retreat and did not have sufficient time to reconnoitre the ground. Unless they could be reinforced by fresh troops, their stand at Faaberg would be brief, and so it proved.

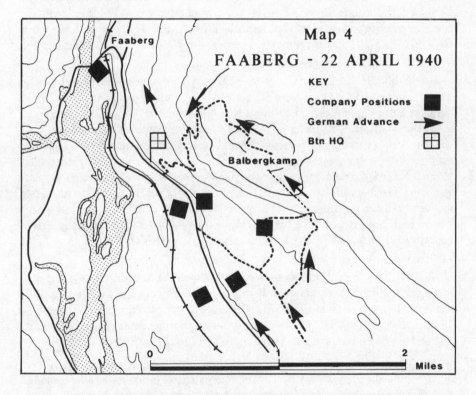

They took up positions on the morning of the 22nd about 1500 yards south of the village in isolated farm buildings with a good field of fire along the main road. However, the woods to their left were uncomfortably close providing excellent cover to troops infiltrating round their flank. They had no time, or indeed tools, to dig themselves in and at about noon came under air attack by incendary bombs followed by a mortar bombardment from the enemy on the hills above. A tentative attack along the road appeared to have been repulsed, but the main threat developed as was feared in the foothills on their left flank where the German ski troops with machine guns were working their way round to the rear of the village. Patrols were sent up the mountain, but their task was hopeless in the deep snow and German ski troops continued to encircle the British positions.

Close range skirmishing in the woods was always a difficult proposition in Norway. Quite apart from the fundamental difficulty of moving around in soft snow, the trees obscured the line of vision and fire and there was the constant risk of losing contact with the battalion on the road. Imprecise information on the location of friendly forces added to the problem. The German and Norwegian uniforms with their round caps and ear flaps were very similar and there was little time to decide as a shadowy figure loomed out of the forest whether he was friend or foe. Lieut Campbell's platoon, sent up into the woods of the Balbergkamp at about 1400, saw and heard nothing except the rattle of distant rifle fire. They might well have passed within a few yards of a German patrol without making contact. Some eight hours later as dusk fell, with the sound of gun-fire now dying away, Campbell decided to move cautiously back towards the road to find out what was going on. The Germans were now ten miles ahead of him up the valley.

By the middle of the afternoon the position was no longer tenable and a hasty retreat ordered. Rations and stores were jettisoned as the troops piled into the twelve available lorries and proceeded northwards as quickly as they could under occasional machine gun attack from the air. The two forward companies of the Foresters were late in receiving the order to disengage and only a small number managed to rejoin the main force by walking through the night across the mountains. Although Brigadier Morgan ordered forward one of the two remaining companies of the Leicestershires who had arrived at Aandalsnes two days after the rest of the Battalion, it was too late for them to make any difference. There was no support at all from the Norwegians who were by now a spent force. The retreating troops, bolstered by the newly arrived company of Leicestershires, took up another defensive position south of Öyer on the evening of the 22nd.

Second Lieut Jessop's platoon was entrusted with the forward position and they maintained this manfully for four hours. One enemy attack along the road was repulsed, but almost immediately the Germans started working round the flanks. Nevertheless, Jessop was able to withdraw skilfully despite casualties and eventually rejoined the Battalion some hours later. Jessop was awarded the Military Cross.

The delaying action at Faaberg had resulted in casualties quite out of proportion to the time gained and the withdrawal was now in danger of becoming a rout. It was the first major action of the campaign and it was already becoming apparent that there was little chance of retaining a foothold in Central Norway without a substantial injection of suitably trained and equipped reinforcements.

Although 15th Brigade was now on its way, 148th Brigade suffered another serious setback when the transport *Cedarbank*, which had been travelling with the Leicestershires, was torpedoed off Aalesund with the loss of the Brigade transport, ammunitions and rations. Nevertheless, a stand had to be made, if only to ensure an orderly withdrawal and to allow Group Dahl and the two companies of Foresters from the west bank of Lake Mjösa to rejoin the main force. And so on the morning of 23 April, St George's day, the weary troops once again took up defensive positions at Tretten, ten miles north of Faaberg and still some sixty miles south of Dombaas.

Demise of a Brigade – The Action at Tretten

The Gudbransdal at Tretten becomes a narrow gorge with the railway on the west bank of the River Laagen on a tiny ledge against a steep rock face and with the road hugging the eastern bank. The road from Gausdal along which the Foresters had retired from the west bank of Lake Mjösa runs into Tretten from the south-west. The village consisted of just a railway station, a few houses and a large grey stone cheese factory. About two miles south of the village, the river valley bends from a north/south direction towards the east with a 1,750 foot hill, Vardekampen, overlooking the elbow in the river. On the reverse side of the hill in a saddle lay a farm track running parallel to the road about 1,500 yards distant. It might have proved a reasonable defensive position providing sufficient troops could be found to guard the saddle and the farm track to prevent the Germans encircling the forward positions as at Balbergkamp. But the flanks were always vulnerable as the British could only function effectively on the roads or tracks which greatly restricted their manoeuvrability and field of fire.

General Ruge, with some difficulty, persuaded Brigadier Morgan that his by now depleted and exhausted Brigade should provide the main defensive force to hold this position as well, but he did make available three weak squadrons of Norwegian Dragoons with four machine guns and a mortar under Colonel Jensen which were placed under British command. Lieut Colonel German with the two companies of the Leicestershires who had arrived late were still four miles south of Tretten at Öyer, and as already described, Lieut Jessop's platoon had provided a brief but important delaying action which enabled the main defensive position at Tretten to be established.

'B' and 'C' Companies of the Foresters were placed on the road just beyond the elbow. Although they could not dig themseves in because they had lost their entrenching tools, some rudimentary sangars had been constructed by Norwegian civilians some days previously. One company of the Leicestershires was placed on a rise overlooking the elbow to guard the centre and a detachment of HQ troops deployed to watch the farm track. The Norwegian Dragoons took up positions on the hill behind the Leicestershires.

'A' and 'D' Companies of the Foresters arrived at Tretten early in the morning, cold and tired after their long roundabout journey from Lake Mjösa: the Norwegian component of Dahl force did not make the rendezvous at Tretten for reasons never satisfactorily explained. After a meal of hot stew and a brief rest in the cheese factory, 'A' Company was pushed forward to a position about halfway between Tretten and Vardekampen and 'D' Company ordered to secure the narrow western bank of the river near the bridge, which was a good defensive position and never under serious threat. Lieut Colonel King-Salter, the military attaché, also arrived in the early morning to help bring some order to an increasingly confused situation.

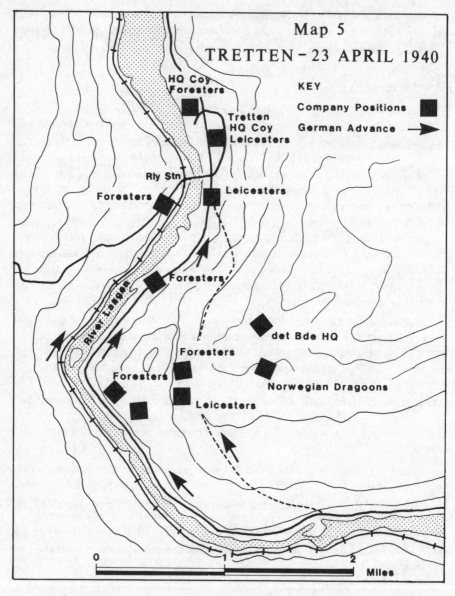

The noise of gunfire from Colonel German's Companies at Öyer could be heard as early as 0830, but the leading German patrol did not reach the forward positions at Tretten until after midday. It was just as well as the British were only finally in position just in time. The two forward companies of the Leicestershires, with serious losses, rejoined the main force during the late morning and were posted in reserve just south of the village.

However, the Germans were now able to introduce another trump card as six tanks of various Marks had joined the force, supported by armoured cars. Unlike at

Balbergkamp, the Germans could now more easily mount a major frontal attack, even though the close terrain was really unsuitable for armoured warfare, as well as adopting their normal tactic of sending ski troops round the flank. Three tanks led the assault with infantry following. Theoretically, the Boyes anti-tank rifle with which the British were equipped should have been able to penetrate the German armour, but many of these had been left behind in the retreat from Faaberg and, despite the theory, it soon became apparent that in practice they had no impact on the tanks at all. The leading tank took a run at the hastily constructed log road block, and although it ran off the road and nearly into the river, it was sufficient to enable the two following immediately behind to burst their way through. Even when one broke down inside the British positions it remained a very effective static gun post, almost annihilating a platoon which was sent to deal with it.

The German artillery and mortars had meanwhile maintained continuous fire on the forward platoons and forced them up the hillside away from the road, and the encircling troops now began to make their presence felt against the rear positions as well. Colonel German made a determined effort to keep open the road which was the only line of retreat from the forward positions, but as so often in this campaign, no clear orders to withdraw were received by many of the leading companies. As expected, the west bank proved secure, and a small German force probing along the railway was repulsed with a bloodied nose.

Firing continued throughout the afternoon, and although the forward companies' retreat had been cut off by the tanks, the rear echelons managed to hold up the main body of German infantry in and around the village. Nevertheless, by early evening many of the troops were out of ammunition and it was clear that the village could not be held until dusk to enable an orderly withdrawal under the cover of darkness. An improvised rearguard was established by the Leicestershires about one mile to the north of the village and some of the Foresters managed to straggle through. But a tank arrived at dusk to put an end to this last vestige of resistance at Tretten, few escaped and a number were killed. The Norwegian Dragoons, who had not been much involved in the action, were able to withdraw in more orderly fashion in commandeered buses, but the Leicestershires on the hill had to be abandoned.

The ordeal was not yet over even for those who managed to find their way through Tretten, for they were subjected to air atttack and pursued by armoured cars. Most took refuge in the forests on either side of the road until darkness. As a consequence of a misunderstanding between the British and the Norwegians, the river bridge at Tretten was not blown, although this would have done little to hinder the pursuit as the main road remains on the same side of the valley. Some of those encircled managed to find their way back to safety through the forest and deep snow with the help of local farmers and villagers. A few with considerable ingenuity and resourcefulness found their way either to the coast or the Swedish border, but most were rounded up by the Germans during the next few days, many of them far to the north of Tretten. Of those who reached the coast, some managed eventually to get back to the Shetlands or Faroes in fishing boats to rejoin their Regiments. Sixty-five who found their way into internment in Sweden were eventually repatriated through Finland.

Harassed by aircraft prowling up and down the road until nightfall at about 2130, a few managed to struggle towards Faavang. The lucky ones even managed to get a lift on buses provided by the Norwegian support position, but the rest had to continue on foot a further twenty-five miles to the Heidal valley where they at last gained some respite, billeted in houses and huts. Those who made it to Heidal had achieved a remarkable feat of endurance, for even before the action at Tretten they had already been moving and fighting for thirty-six hours with no rest and little food. As with 'Mauriceforce' many of the territorial soldiers had displayed remarkable stamina and resilience.

The action at Tretten completed the first phase of fighting in the Gudbransdal. Of the original Brigade strength, only thirty percent remained: nine officers and about three hundred men. Both Battalion Commanders were taken prisoner, and most of the Brigade equipment was captured or abandoned, 148th Brigade was clearly completely finished as a fighting unit. Losses at both Faaberg and Tretten had been high, and even the main objective of allowing Group Dahl to rejoin the force had not been totally achieved: the Norwegian element appeared to have vanished into thin air. The Brigade had received little or no assistance from the Norwegians who professed themselves exhausted even before the British arrived, and nowhere was 148th Brigade able to establish itself in a well prepared defensive position or have sufficient time to allow its troops to be fed and rested. They were undoubtedly pushed too far forward too quickly. If, for example, they had been allowed to assemble at Tretten on their arrival in the Gudbransdal on the 21st, they could have dug themselves in and converted a reasonable defensive position into a strongpoint. This may have delayed the Germans for several days while the Norwegians recovered and given time for British reinforcements to arrive. But the troops who were constantly on the move, often without transport, never had the time to recover and compose themselves, physically or mentally, before they were once again in action.

Brigadier Morgan was criticised in Lieut General Massy's official report[9] for allowing this situation to develop. Whilst the criticism is apparently valid, the unfortunate Morgan was in fact following the direction of General Ruge who had 'assumed' command of all the Allied forces in Central Norway in the absence of any clearly defined lines of command and control laid down by the War Office at this stage of the campaign. A typically British compromise, engineered on the spot mainly by the military attaché King-Salter, allowed the muddle to develop. It was in fact inevitable and correct that the senior officer, in this case General Ruge, should be responsible for operational control of the whole force and Morgan had to comply, however reluctantly, with his directions. The disaster which ensued must therefore be laid largely at the door of General Ruge, although in mitigation he was understandably reluctant to relinquish even an unnecessary inch of his native heartland. It is ironic to note that General Paget who pursued exactly the same tactics in fighting five more rearguard actions in the continued retreat up the Gudransdal received nothing but praise from Massy in the same report.

Even the weather did not help, for most of the time the country was bathed in bright sunshine which allowed the German bombers, totally without opposition, to range up and down the roads looking for targets of opportunity. Although not many casualties were sustained from air attack, the continued harassment was disruptive and demoralising. In the circumstances, the Brigade fought as well as could have reasonably been expected in very difficult conditions.

148th Brigate had met its 'Waterloo' at Tretten at sunset on St Georges Day 1940. It had been thrust into an arena for which it was totally unprepared after days of ever increasing confusion even before leaving Rosyth. Believing it was heading first for Stavanger and then Namsos, the Brigade eventually found itself, without maps or transport, artillery or anti-aircraft guns, deep in the Gudbransdal valley of Central Norway. It was undoubtedly a diversion to disaster.

'Sickleforce' – Defeat in The Gudbrandsdal

> 'We trained hard, but it seems that every time we were beginning to form up into teams we would be reorganised. I was to learn later in life that we tend to meet any new situation by reorganising, and a wonderful method it can be for creating the illusion of progress, while producing confusion, inefficiency and demoralisation.'
>
> Caius Pètronius AD66

Reinforcements – and Aberrations

Major General B. C. T. Paget[1] had originally been appointed on 19 April to follow the ill-fated Generals Hotblack and Berney-Ficklin as commander of the forces assigned to Operation 'Hammer'. However, 'Hammer' was cancelled before Paget could proceed north to take up his command and instead he was given command of the two brigades now assigned to 'Sickleforce'.

Bernard Paget had been a contemporary of Montgomery on the 1920 Course at the Staff College at Camberley and again as an instructor in 1927. Regarded as a leading military thinker in the inter-war years, he was later Chief Instructor at the Staff College at Quetta in India. However, he subsequently lost the confidence of both Churchill and Monty and was superseded as the commander of 21st Army Group before the invasion of Normandy.

Overall direction of military operations in Norway had by now been given to General Massy, but as we have seen, his intention to transfer his Headquarters to Aandalsnes never materialised. Although an advance element was deployed forward, it did not prove possible to transfer the main staffs to Norway and General Massy never in fact left London. Operational control at such long distance given the paucity of communications available at the time was of course quite impracticable and thus central direction of the fighting was always lacking. The lessons of command and control have to be relearned with every conflict, even with sophisticated satellite communications long distance tactical control is studded with pitfalls as was seen again in the South Atlantic in 1982.

The ill-fated 148th Brigade had landed at Aandalsnes on 18 April and the 15th Infantry Brigade was nominated to follow on the 23rd. 15th Brigade was a part of the 5th Division, distinguished by its 'Y' flash signifying Yorkshire and known as the 'Globetrotters' from its traditional role as a reserve division throughout the world since the days of General Picton's Division on the field of Waterloo. At one time, the 5th Division had been earmarked as one of the divisions to go to Finland, but in the event it was only 15th Brigade that saw service in Scandinavia. Under the command of Brigadier H. E. F. Smyth, MC, 15th Brigade comprised three regular battalions: 1st King's Own Yorkshire Light Infantry (K.O.Y.L.I.) (Major E. E. E. Cass),[2] 1st York and Lancaster Regiment (Lieut Colonel A. L. Kent-Lemon)[3] and the 1st Green Howards (Lieut Colonel A. E. Robinson).[4]

15th Brigade had spent the first part of the year in France where at least the severe winter had provided some experience of working in ice and snow. They also had four months of valuable training time to mould the Brigade into a fighting force even though the terrain they encountered in Norway was vastly different to the flat plains of Northern France. The Brigade travelled to England without their divisional complement of artillery, tanks, bren gun carriers and engineers, all of which were to be sorely missed in their operations in the Gudbrandsdal. But they did salvage their 25mm Hotchkiss anti-tank weapons which proved to be unexpectedly valuable even though Norway was not recognised as good tank country. Their sudden move was conducted in far more orderly fashion than that of their predecessors; equipment and arms were made up into one man loads, and during their two day stopover at Dunfermline they practiced route marches in full kit. They even had time to collect together Norwegian interpreters. They proceeded uneventfully onwards from Rosyth aboard cruisers and destroyers.

The first echelon disembarked at Aandalsnes and Molde on the night of 23 April and the whole Brigade was ashore by the evening of the 25th. Unfortunately the Navy was so anxious to be clear of the fiord before first light that they inadvertently departed with some of the rations and other stores.

Even before they left London, the Brigade had heard disturbing reports of the speed and precision with which the Germans were advancing along both the Österdal and Gudbrandsal, and General Paget's orders[5] issued on 22 April made no mention of the original plan to strike north towards Trondheim as the second arm of the pincer movement. The task now was:

to co-operate with the Norwegian Army in preventing the northward advance of the German Army based in Southern Norway.

In acknowledgement of the original aim, Paget was merely informed that it would be:

necessary for you to safeguard your left and rear against attack by the German forces in Trondheim.

It is now apparent that the British strategy in Central Norway became even more than usually incoherent in these few days either side of 15th Brigade's arrival. On 23 April, a revamped operation against Trondheim christened 'Hammer 2' was conceived by the Chiefs of Staff and planning put in hand. It envisaged the capture of the forts at the entrance to the Trondheimfiord by two battalions to be put ashore from landing craft and paddle steamers after naval bombardment. Subsequently, the force was to be increased in strength to two brigades, to be disembarked at as yet unspecified locations to complete the capture of Trondheim in co-ordination with 'Mauriceforce' and 'Sickleforce'. But the actions at Vist, Faaberg and Tretten, and the earlier bombing of Namsos and Aandalsnes had all occurred by 24 April, and it should by now have been obvious that 'Sickleforce' and to a lesser extent 'Mauriceforce' either needed to be immediately reinforced and provided with the logistic and air support they required – or alternatively evacuated as expeditiously as possible. Certainly by this date, neither force was in any condition to provide worthwhile support towards the capture of Trondheim, and in any case this contradicted Paget's orders issued only two days previously.

At this time more immediate pressure on our forces in Central Norway was not emanating from the Germans in Trondheim, but those advancing north from Oslo. Nevertheless, on 25 April the Prime Minister indicated through the First Sea Lord, who was strongly advocating the operation, that 'Hammer 2' should be implemented, although as with the original Operation 'Hammer' at least some of the Chiefs of Staff were now beginning to have second thoughts. This was hardly surprising, the naval reasons for abandoning 'Hammer' were even more relevant now that the Luftwaffe was operating in strength from Vaernes. It should have been abundantly clear by the evening of 25 April that if anything was to be salvaged in Central Norway, the pressing priority was to prevent the Germans from breaking out of the Gudbrandsdal and the Österdal valleys.

It was not in any event the town or harbour facilities of Trondheim which were now of such immediate importance, but the airfield at Vaernes fifteen miles to the east. Possession of a permanent all weather airfield, backed up of course with the will to put it to good use, had become vital to the sustainability of the Allied cause in Central Norway. Not only was it necessary to oppose the aircraft which were bombing and machine gunning troops in the Gudbrandsdal, but even more importantly it was essential to provide some protection for the bridgeheads at Namsos and Aandalsnes. Without a secure airhead, the campaign in Central Norway was always doomed.

It is quite clear that insufficient weight was given to this requirement in the Chiefs of Staff consideration of both 'Hammer' and its sequel. It had always been the Admiralty which had initiated and sustained the momentum for the intervention in Norway, but the Air Staff, who had never been overly enthusiastic about operations in Norway were strangely reticent about the need to secure an intact airfield. To them, it was seen as a potential drain of precious aircraft needed for the defence of the homeland and if they had appeared more forthright in support of Norway, pressure to send scarce fighters might have become difficult to resist.

Although communications between London and Norway were always a barrier to coherent appreciation and planning, the rapidly changing circumstances required a fundamental re-appraisal of the Allied aims and strategy in Central Norway rather than a despairing stab at an objective which had already been evaluated and rejected as unsound. 'Hammer 2' was fortunately soon forgotten as a far more profound decision had to be made – the total withdrawal from Central Norway.

In London it had been intended originally that the 15th Brigade would concentrate in the Österdal leaving the Gudbrandsdal to the 148th Brigade. 15th Brigade would advance along the Österdal until they were in line with 148th Brigade in the parallel valley and then the two would advance in unison until they joined up at the point north of Oslo where the two valleys converged. But events in Norway had moved much faster than the planners expected and this was no longer a practicable option. If 148th Brigade was not to be totally overrun, 15th Brigade had to be committed immediately to stop the rout. Whilst this was an inescapable decision to prevent complete disaster in the Gudbrandsdal, the German breakthrough in the Österdal would expose the British left flank and invite the risk of leaving two Brigades trapped in a valley with no escape route.

At a conference with General Ruge on the morning of 24 April, it was decided that Brigadier Smyth should make a stand at Kvam, thirty miles up the valley from Tretten and just short of the Heidal Valley where the remnants of 148th Brigade were recuperating. The Norwegians were ordered to hold their forward positions at Faavang and Ringebu until the following night, 25-26 April, to allow the British position to be properly established. But events were soon overtaking the plan and it was recognised later on the 24th that the British contingent would inevitably be brought into action the following day.

The K.O.Y.L.I. was sent forward to Otta by train, but Norwegian civilian drivers refused to carry them the last ten miles to Kvam because the road in its narrow valley was under almost continuous air attack. As they passed through Dombaas, the reality of war was vividly brought home when they saw the devastated town: hardly a building was left standing and it was fortunate that one railway line had miraculously remained intact. He 111s and Bf 110s ranged up and down the road and railway between Faavang and Aandalsnes paying particular attention to the railhead at Otta where three Bofors anti-aircraft guns were temporarily silenced. They machine-gunned and bombed anything moving on the road and travel to the forward areas became a most tiresome and hazardous process.

The Action at Kvam

The valley of the River Laagen at Kvam, rather like Tretten, bends through 90 degrees, this time from east to south in the direction of flow. The west bank is again steep and wooded and readily defended; but the east bank rises gently, divided by walls and fences into small fields and dotted with houses and farm buildings. At distances varying from half to three quarters of a mile from the river, the gradient suddenly increases and the hillsides are clothed with pine and birch up to 2,000 feet with the bare summits rising to over 3,000 feet. The road and railway at Kvam both follow the east bank. The village itself was just a cluster of some 50 wooden buildings sitting on a ledge some 250 feet above the river. In the middle of the river are four islands, two small and two rather larger. In April, most of the river was still frozen over and troops could easily cross to the islands on foot. The valley floor was generally clear of snow, but higher up the slope the hillsides were impassable except on skis or snowshoes. Kvam was a rather stronger defensive position than Tretten in that there were wider fields of fire and outflanking manoeuvres were more difficult because of the steepness of the slopes and the depth of snow.

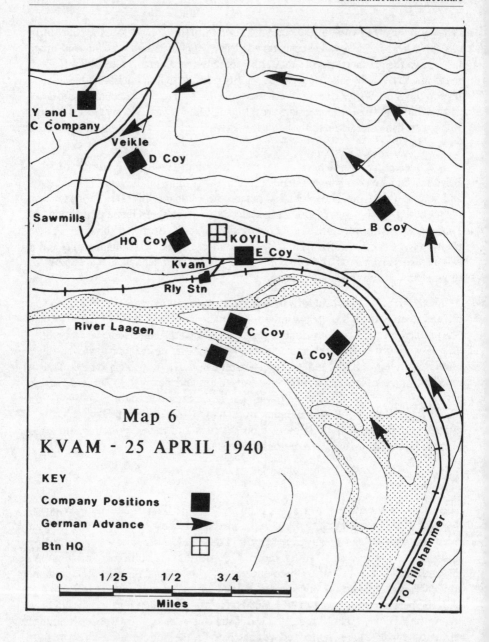

Map 6

KVAM - 25 APRIL 1940

KEY

Company Positions

German Advance

Btn HQ

0   1/25   1/2   3/4   1

Miles

'A' Company and 'C' Company, less one platoon which was located on the steep west bank of the river, were placed on the largest of the islands; a flat, open area with willow scrub overlooking the elbow in the river. 'B' Company was placed on the hillside directly to the north overlooking the road and the railway and 'D' Company held in reserve above the village near Veikle. An overborne group was gathered together as 'E' Company and located in the village itself with Battalion Headquarters.

Of the eight 25 mm French Hotchkiss anti-tank guns which were the sole support weapons brought from France, five were deployed forward and three held in reserve. Only two 3 inch mortars were available and there were no high explosive bombs for the 2 inch mortars.

The Battalions had no artillery support whatsoever. The German strength was growing all the time as the Groups which had been moving up both sides of Lake Mjösa now linked up under the command of General Pellengahr making an overall force of seven infantry battalions, including one mountain battalion, supported by a troop of tanks, two artillery batteries and a motorised machine gun battalion. The Germans therefore now possessed an overwhelming numerical superiority and a far more balanced force, although of course they could only deploy a comparatively small component forward at any one time in the narrow confines of the valley.

25 April dawned bright and clear and the sun soon made the day unusually hot for the time of year, melting the snow which ran down onto the road only to freeze again during the still bitterly cold nights. Rather surprisingly in view of the opportunity for unrestricted air reconnaissance and despite having captured in the early morning part of a reconnaissance patrol led by Lieut J. H. Oldman, the Germans did not seem to be fully aware of the British presence at Kvam. After the last of the retreating Norwegians, orderly but weary, had passed through their positions, 'A' Company waited expectantly for the first of the German troops to appear.

It was not until 1130 that the leading formation arrived, two tanks and an armoured car followed by infantry on foot and in lorries. The K.O.Y.L.I. carefully held their fire until the tanks closed to about 150 yards when the single anti-tank gun on the island managed to halt both tanks which took no further part in the action: the armoured car and the infantry quickly took cover. But the British did not have long to celebrate their opening success as the Germans quickly brought their artillery into play both against the troops on the island and the village itself which was soon ablaze. As always the German artillery was both economical and accurate and few buildings escaped destruction. 'A' Company suffered nearly one hundred casualties and had to retire to the western end of the island whereupon 'C' and 'E' Companies were brought forward to reinforce the position. An outflanking manoeuvre to the north-east was held with some difficulty by 'B' and 'D' Companies, supported from about 1730 by the newly arrived Company of the York and Lancasters which took up a position on the slopes to the north of Kvam. A determined advance along the river bed was thwarted by 'C' Company on the islands and another tank was knocked out on the road. Two more rather half-hearted attacks along the road were easily repulsed and then darkness came to the rescue before the Germans could consolidate their advance. The anti-tank guns had done particularly well and clearly deterred the Germans from pressing forward too determinedly along the road.

Brigadier Smyth had been injured in the shelling of the village quite early in the day and was relieved by Lieut Colonel Kent-Lemon, who in turn handed over the York and Lancasters to Major D. C. Tennent.[6]

The opportunity was taken overnight to redeploy the force and Kent-Lemon withdrew 'B' Company, who had had a very good day with only two casualties, from its now isolated forward position leaving behind two of the anti-tank guns which had been damaged during the day's shelling, and placed the York and Lancaster Company to their rear to cover the line of retreat. It was hoped with these dispositions to hold on at least one more day. But this had been the most successful day of the campaign so far and the K.O.Y.L.I., despite the almost total loss of 'A' Company, were in good spirits.

The Germans made an unusually early start on the following morning after a short but bitterly cold night. Occasional artillery shelling commenced at first light at 0230 and intensified about three hours later. Even so, the time had been used to good effect to strengthen the badly damaged buildings in and around the village which were being used as defensive positions. At 0630, ski and mountain troops began their familiar outflanking manoeuvre on the British left flank. The main thrust along the gentler slopes of the valley was held although heavy fire restricted movement. But the infiltration through the trees on the higher slopes could not be arrested and by 1100 German machine gun positions had been established above 'D' Company at Veikle and 'B' Company was threatened from the rear.

At one stage it was thought the Germans were using poisoned gas and masks were hastily donned; but it was a false alarm, it was only pollen from the scrub. Throughout another clear day the Luftwaffe gunned and bombed the troops in the valley preventing their redeployment to meet the new threat in the hills above the left flank. The York and Lancaster Company which had arrived just in time on the previous afternoon to stabilise the position on the hill was at one stage completely isolated, but a gallant counter-attack by Second Lieut French's platoon rushed the main German position in a sawmill by the river and forced their retreat with severe losses.

At midday a new frontal attack was launched, but two tanks and an armoured car which attempted to penetrate along the road towards the village were both halted minutes before the anti-tank gun was itself destroyed by a shell. Captain McC Riggs particularly distinguished himself in this action when he rushed forward under heavy fire to remove a road block which was screening the tanks from the line of sight of an anti-tank gun. He was wounded for his pains, but recovered to command the battalion later in the war in Sicily.

Despite these individual successes, German machine gun nests continued to be established on the left flank and pockets of troops became isolated from each other and unable to provide mutual support. Even so, the Germans for the first time in the campaign were showing a decided disinclination to press forward their attack. But casualties were mounting, and the Germans were now operating at around Brigade strength: an early withdrawal was becoming inevitable.

The order to withdraw at dusk through Kjörem, which was to be the next defended position up the valley, duly arrived at 1700. But in the early evening the Germans, trying a new tactic contrived to set fire to the forest which forced Major Cass to instigate an earlier retirement. 'D' Company and the York and Lancaster Company did not receive the instruction and only realised what was happening when a runner sent to Battalion HQ to ascertain what was going on found the village full of Germans. They had to make a long detour through the hills overnight, punctuated by intermittent skirmishes, to rejoin the main force. This too had become a familiar

1. The *Altmark* cornered in the Jossing Fiord by *HMS Cossack*. IWM

2. *HMS Glowworm* manoeuvring prior to ramming the German heavy cruiser *Admiral Hipper*. IWM

3. *HMS Hardy* (Captain Warburton-Lee VC) which led the 2nd Destroyer Flotilla in the First Battle of Narvik. *IWM*

4. *HMS Warspite* (Captain Crutchley VC, DSO), Admiral Whitworth's flagship at the Second Battle of Narvik. *IWM*

5A. Gladiators destroyed on the ground at Lake Lesjaskoz. *IWM*

5B. The German destroyer *Thiele* beached in the Rombaksfiord in April 1940 after the second battle of Narvik. *IWM*

6. Lieutenant General Sir Adrian Carton de Wiart VC with his ADC at Namsos. *IWM*

7. Into captivity – British prisoners in the Gudbrandsdal. *IWM*

8. Stavanger airfield after being bombed by Blenheims of No 107 Squadron on 17 April 1940. *IWM*

9. The last Gladiator of No 263 Squadron at Setnesmoen, destroyed to prevent it falling into enemy hands. *IWM*

10. Troops waiting to board the Polish liner *Sobieski* at Gourock. *IWM*

11. A planning conference on the liner *Oronsay* en route to Norway. *IWM*

12. General Auchinleck discusses tactics with Group Captain Moore on the *Chrobry* on the way to Harstad. *IWM*

13. Narvik. The iron ore terminal still dominates this little port north of the Arctic Circle. *Author's photograph*

14. The small town of Namsos after Luftwaffe bombing in May 1940. *IWM*

15. An oil storage dump on fire at Harstad. *IWM*

16. General Claude Auchinleck, Commander of the North Western Expeditionary Force. *IWM*

17. General de Brigade Bethouart, leader of the French contingent at Narvik. *IWM*

18. General Bohucz-Szysko (second from right) leader of the Polish Chasseurs du Nord at Narvik. *IWM*

19. A Hurricane of No 46 Squadron being winched aboard the aircraft carrier *Glorious* en route to Narvik. *RAF Museum*

20. A Gladiator of No 263 Squadron at Bardufoss. *RAF Museum*

21. Dalsklubben from the south. The Germans climbed the ridge to outflank the Scots Guards dug-in in the trees across the river. *Author's photograph*

22. The Randalsvolen Plateau. The Scots Guards had to cross this snowfield which lies on the Arctic Circle after their action at Krokstranden. *Author's photograph*

23.   A light anti-aircraft gun in position at Harstad. *IWM*

24.   A Norwegian farmer gives a helping hand to an anti-aircraft gun crew. *IWM*

SO DATER OG   ENN OM FA   AMPEN FOR
ANNEN VERDENSKR G DEN POLSKE FOLKEREP BLIK
IEMINN SMERKER NARVIK 1979

25. The memorial at Narvik to the 277 sailors of the Norwegian coastal defence ships *Norge* and *Eidsvold*, sunk in Narvik harbour on 9 April. *Author's photograph*

26. The memorial at Narvik to the 59 dead of the Polish cruiser *Grom* sunk in the Ofotfjord on 4 May. *Author's photograph*

27. A French Hotchkiss tank used in the attack on Narvik now on display at the Red Cross Museum in Narvik. *Author's photograph*

28. The beach at Bjerkvik, scene of the French amphibious landing on 13 May.
Author's photograph

29. British troops return home from Narvik aboard the liner *Lancastria*. IWM

30. The aircraft carrier *HMS Glorious*, sunk returning from Narvik with the two RAF squadrons on board. *IWM*

31. The battle cruisers *Scharnhorst* and *Gneisenau* in action against the *Glorious*. *IWM*

32. Blindfold German prisoners board a naval ship at Narvik bound for England. *IWM*

33. King Haakon and his family arriving in Oslo on their return to Norway aboard *HMS Norfolk* in 1945. *IWM*

occurrence in this difficult terrain. The Germans did not follow up the retreating troops and the withdrawal was completed without further serious loss.

The K.O.Y.L.I. had distinguished themselves at Kvam in their first action of the war. There were many individual acts of heroism, and the dogged determination to hang on against a larger and far better armed force promised well for more trying days ahead in other theatres of war. In particular, they had suffered almost continuous air attack and artillery bombardment which can be very wearing when there is no adequate shelter, or even the satisfaction of knowing that your own retaliation in kind is wreaking similar havoc on the enemy. The feeling of helplessness in these circumstances is one of the most demoralising features of warfare, and the morale of the troops stood up pretty well to several such periods in Norway. The village churchyard at Kvam nevertheless contains more British war graves than any other single location in Norway, many of them from the almost obliterated 'A' Company on the first morning.

The success of the Hotchkiss anti-tank guns was particularly rewarding, for even in the close terrain in Norway a tank could be an embarrassingly successful close range field gun as was discovered again in the bocage country of Normandy in 1944. The Brigade Anti-Tank Company was formed from all three battalions and commanded by Captain P. H. D. Dessain of the Green Howards. Dessain was awarded the Military Cross for his efforts on the 26th:

> Throughout the day Captain Dessain visited his detachments, and by his example and personal disregard for danger he encouraged his gun teams to hold on, and bar the way to any advance by hostile armoured fighting vehicles. In particular, in the afternoon, when the situation was becoming critical, the sight of this officer riding a lady's cycle up the road under heavy machine gun fire and some shelling encouraged all who saw him.[7]

The Campaign is Crumbling

In strict chronology we should now consider the brief and disastrous introduction of Allied air power on Norwegian territory which began on the 24th and had been totally destroyed two days later. 263 Squadron flew a single Gladiator reconnaissance sortie over Kvam on the 25th, but that was the sole RAF impact on the ground action in the Gudbrandsdal, and consideration of this less than weighty contribution can therefore be left to a later chapter.

General Paget arrived at Aandalsnes on the evening of 25 April and assumed direct control of 'Sickleforce'. He quickly recognised the rapidly deteriorating situation after a brief conference with Brigadier Morgan and signalled his conclusions to the War Office. The overwhelming need was for air support, but already the single fighter squadron sent to Norway had been all but destroyed. Anti-aircraft weapons, artillery, communications equipment, transport and base facilities were all woefully inadequate. Even more disturbing, without a secure port of entry there was little prospect of improving the situation. In his report after the evacuation, General Paget wrote in respect of the difficulties of the lines of communication:

> A fair estimate of the capacity of the port (Aandalsnes) is to say that it could be precariously worked for some 4 to 5 hours out of the 24 thus reducing the tonnage handled to about 100 tons per day (compared with the estimated 700 tons). This figure, however, assumes that

skilled labour is available to deal with the ships and that the tonnage, when unloaded, is not destroyed by enemy air action. The skilled labour was not available. The enemy could destroy what he liked, only having to press home his attack in the face of a weak AA defence.

But even if adequate supplies could have been brought into Norway through Aandalsnes, the difficulties of distributing them to the front line were immense. General Paget again:

There was only one single road with laterals opening from it which could be put to any useful purpose. Throughout its length it did not exceed 18 feet in width and was considerably narrower in many stretches. The surface was stone dust, water bound and the foundation, judged from a number of bomb craters in various parts, did not exceed 8 inches to 1 foot of natural unpacked stones set in earth which rapidly became thick mud when thawed out. On each side of the road was an open drainage cut about 18 inches wide by two feet deep packed, originally, with frozen snow. Whenever the thaw had started these ditches became vehicle traps of great efficiency. The melting snow gave way leaving the vehicle ditched to the axle. Over considerable stretches of the road abandoned Norwegian vehicles averaged 10 to 17 to the mile. The local view was that in peace the road had to be used with extreme care during the thaw . . . it could not survive the heavy and erratic traffic of war. In addition the road suffered from all the disabilities due to enemy air action which could have applied to the railway had the enemy so wished. Over considerable sectors road and railway lay within 50 yards of each other.

As far as the railway was concerned the position was even less satisfactory, for here, over by far the greater part of the line, the enemy was faced by no defences of any nature and could destroy as he pleased. The lower limit of the practical capacity of the railway was therefore what the enemy choose to make it. Fortunately instead of concentrating the efforts of his Air Force to destroy a few vital points of the railway system he was inclined to sprinkle several sections of the line and thereby did not achieve a complete destruction anywhere.[8]

148th Brigade was of no further practical value as a front line fighting unit and Norwegian support had almost completely died away. Although on paper the Norwegians had two brigades in the Gudbrandsdal and Romsdal, the only practical contribution they could make now was to provide ski troops for operations on the flanks of the British front line positions. Paget foresaw the need for more reinforcements but recognised that there was no means of supporting them without a secure bridgehead.

General Ruge, who had played such a stalwart role in organising and keeping the resistance going was now tired and prone to fits of despondency, and the Norwegian Government no longer played any effective role in controlling events or in rallying the army and the civilians to prolong the resistance. The Norwegian forces in the Österdal seemed close to collapse and this posed a further threat, for not only would it open up an alternative path to Trondheim, but it would enable the Germans to threaten Dombaas from the east and thus risk trapping the British troops in the Gudbrandsdal. Paget was already aware, and warned the War Office accordingly, that the possibility of evacuation must be considered. Although the Chiefs of Staff promised artillery and anti-tank guns, as well as fighter support from aircraft carriers based off Aandalsnes and Namsos, the situation was already critical. On his first night in Norway, Paget perceived only too clearly that he would be lucky to escape before disaster overtook his whole command. Perhaps surprisingly, his spirits and optimism actually improved in the succeeding days, for he was clearly affected by the plight of the Norwegians and increasingly anxious to render whatever support he could, even in a forlorn cause.

The following day brought more bad news; German troops were reported at Alvdal in the Österdal from whence there was a direct road to Dombaas. Although there were weak Norwegian units along this road, Paget was forced to deploy the remnants of 148th Brigade (now about 400 strong) supported by a bren and mortar section of the Green Howards to watch this vital route to his back door. It is surprising that the Germans did not make more of this opportunity to cut off completely the remaining resistance south of Trondheim. He also heard on the 26th that General Steffen's heroic action at Tonsaasen in the Valdes valley had at last ended which opened up another route towards Aandalsnes and Otta. Finally he heard that Aandalsnes had suffered its heaviest air raid so far, most of the town and the wooden quay were burning and a large quantity of ammunition stored by the quayside had been destroyed. The single anti-aircraft sloop in the fiord was the sole source of defence and she soon ran out of ammunition. Skuas from the *Ark Royal* arrived too late to intercept the raiding Heinkels but patrolled the burning town until dusk. General Paget decided to make his next major stand at Otta, but even before that there was further action at Kjörem (also known as Lien) as the K.O.Y.L.I. withdrew from Kvam to join 148th Brigade at Dombaas.

The River Laagen at Kjörem, a tiny hamlet of only a score or so houses, is wider than at Kvam, which lies two miles to the east. But the valley floor is narrower, although unlike Kvam, accessible on both banks; the river, road and railway line continue in company along the north bank of the river and a farm track parallels the river on the south bank. The area was heavily wooded giving restricted fields of fire and making detection of enemy movement difficult. It was not a good defensive location.

The defence of Kjörem was entrusted to the York and Lancasters supported by 'B' Company and the Carrier Platoon of the Green Howards. At dawn on 27 April the dispositions were as follows. The Headquarters Company was based on an island in the river with 'D' Company holding the forward position on the road with 'C' Company and half of 'B' Company in support in the foothills about one and a half miles to the rear. 'A' Company, the other half of 'B' Company and the Green Howards Company were deployed in the hills to the south of the river. The slopes were not steep enough to seriously impede troops trying to work their way round the flanks, but by now the British were alive to this tactic and had extended standing patrols some way up the hill.

As if the days were already not long enough, the fighting started in familiar fashion rather earlier than usual. Just after 0800 infantry appeared along the road, and when fired upon took to the hills to infiltrate the flanks. Once again the German reconnaissance left something to be desired. On a number of occasions German infantry pressed on along the road oblivious of the trap waiting for them: if the British had only possessed a minimum of artillery they could have made the enemy pay dearly for this lapse at least once. Tanks now followed along the road coinciding with the

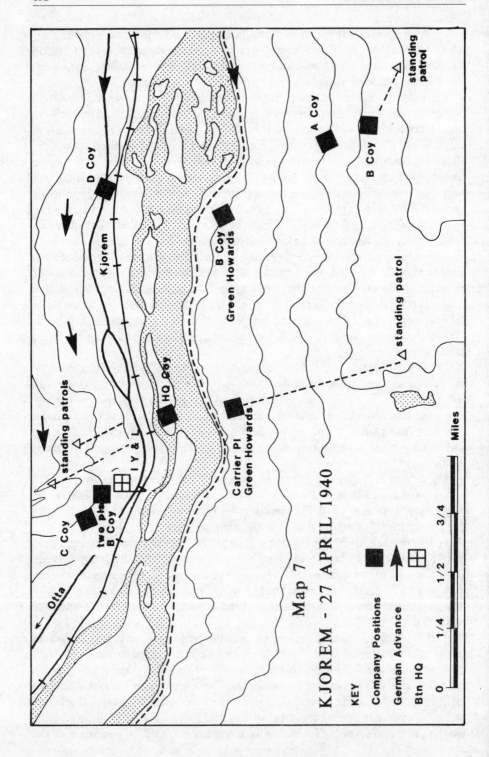

Map 7

KJOREM - 27 APRIL 1940

KEY

Company Positions

German Advance

Btn HQ

opening up of an artillery barrage. Mortar and machine gun positions were established on both banks of the river, providing the added distraction for the defenders of cross fire. Once again the forests were set on fire and 'D' Company had to retreat quickly to a position closer to the village where they clung on tenaciously for the rest of the day. Firing the woods was proving a very useful tactic as it not only confused the defenders but allowed machine gun positions to be established under the cover of the smoke. The forward British companies suffered the added discomfort of being accidentally shelled by their own mortar platoon in the rear.

'A' and 'B' Companies were withdrawn in the early evening as they came under intense fire across the river from the north. They took up a new position to the west of the village at Soja intending to cover a final withdrawal which was timed for 2300. But by midway through the long evening the situation was becoming desperate. A German patrol had worked its way round to the rear of the forward troops and established a road block in front of Soja totally cutting off the line of retreat. Fortunately, a hastily dispatched battle patrol managed to dislodge them before they could consolidate their advantage, otherwise up to three companies would probably have been surrounded and lost.

The troops on the north bank maintained their positions until after nightfall when they were ordered to withdraw. But the Germans had been so successful during the day in infiltrating the line of retreat that this was only accomplished with great difficulty. Many were killed, captured or had to take to the mountains to escape. A few straggled through to join up with 'A' and 'B' Companies at Soja who then retired to Otta. Unfortunately, one company took a wrong turning in their withdrawal and succeeded in getting themselves cut off in the Heidal Valley which had previously sheltered 148th Brigade after its retreat from Tretten. As there was no other way out of the valley, they eventually had to walk across country to Dombaas which they reached on 29 April. Although they saved most of their transport and bren gun carriers, only thirteen officers and 300 men managed to struggle back to Otta. Major Tennent, the acting commanding officer, was one of those cut off, but with sixteen men found his way over the one hundred miles to Sweden and was eventually repatriated.

Another battalion had been effectively destroyed as a front line fighting unit and 15th Brigade was suffering the same rhythmic fate as had 148th Brigade earlier in the week. The supporting Green Howard's Company, severely depleted, struggled back to Otta by 0700 the following morning.

Withdrawal – The Inevitable Step

It was on the evening of the day of the action at Kjörem that General Paget was informed of the decision in principle to evacuate the Allied forces from Central Norway. The decision had in fact been made by the Cabinet on the morning of the previous day, 26 April, after they had been advised of Paget's initial appreciation of the situation in Central Norway. It was the first logical and coherent decision that had been taken for some days and the first to recognise the reality of the situation. Once a decision had been made, quite correctly in the circumstances, to abandon the direct assault on Trondheim, both 'Mauriceforce' and 'Sickleforce' were fighting and, particularly in the case of the latter, suffering severe losses without any clear objective in view.

The Cabinet decision to evacuate was impelled by the now unavoidable recognition that our forces were being consistently forced to withdraw without the resources to halt let alone reverse the retreat. Although 'Mauriceforce' which had only been involved directly in the one action at Vist could hardly be said to have been defeated, it lacked the means to turn round the tide of retreat unless the Navy could relieve the threat to its seaward flank. 'Sickleforce' on the other hand was being systematically defeated in the Gudbrandsdal, battalion after battalion was being thrown piecemeal into the front line, and after one or at most two days in action had been so badly mauled that it could no longer be considered a front line unit. Reinforcement was essential to stem the tide, let alone reverse the flow. But even if the Cabinet had summoned the will to reinforce Central Norway, it did not have the means. The relentless destruction by air attack of the only two ports which could service the lifeline of support made defeat inevitable. Without air superiority, or at the very least parity in the air, the operation in Central Norway was never a practicable proposition: this essential principle was simply not recognised by those who conceived or acquiesced in the decision to re-invade Central Norway in 1940.

Wider ranging strategic factors also began to condition the Cabinet's thinking. The threat to the Low Countries and France appeared to be growing daily even though the French, perhaps with a hint of desperation, were keen to step up the action in Norway in an attempt to suck resources out of Germany which might otherwise have been available in the West. It was a forlorn hope. Although it was always difficult to convince the Cabinet and perhaps even more the RAF who adhered to the panacea of strategic bombing to the end of the war, it was inevitable that the destiny of Western Europe would sooner or later be settled in the fields of France, as indeed, with a four year interlude, it eventually was. There was also increasing unease regarding the situation in the Mediterranean. It appeared that a significant Allied reverse, particularly one that would force a reduction in Naval strength in the Mediterranean, might well be sufficient to persuade Italy to chance her arm in support of her fascist neighbour. In this context there seemed, quite rightly, little point in continuing to squander vital manpower and resources on a sideshow in Northern Europe.

However, withdrawal of 'Sickleforce' was no longer an entirely simple process. There was a real risk that 148th and 15th Brigade could be cut off in the Gudbrandsdal by the rapid German advance up the Österdal. There was an even greater risk that there would simply not be sufficient forces ashore to mount the delaying actions necessary to ensure that the troops could be withdrawn in orderly fashion. General Massy considered initially putting in further reinforcements to enable a more orderly evacuation to commence on 10 May. But in the light of the faster rate of build up of the German land forces and their overwhelming superiority in the air, this posed the risk of an even greater disaster than now seemed possible with those forces already in Norway. In the end, the War Office decided that no further troops or weapons should be unloaded at either Aandalsnes or Namsos and that all forces should be evacuated from Central Norway as soon as ships could be made available. It was calculated that this would be on the night of 1/2 May. This was undoubtedly the right decision. Communications with Norway were so bad that detailed instructions for the withdrawal had to be sent by courier. Colonel Clarke who had brought back General Ruge's impassioned plea for reinforcements was sent back to Aandalsnes and Major Ditton entrusted with a similar mission to Namsos. Both were delivered by separate Sunderland sorties on the night of 27 April.

General Paget took on the unpleasant task of informing General Ruge of the decision to withdraw the British troops on the morning of 28 April. Ruge was predictably disappointed, even angered by the decision, but he could hardly doubt its validity. He sent a strongly worded signal to the C.I.G.S. protesting that the sacrifice of his own soldiers in the early fighting had been in return for a promise of Allied support which had never in the event been forthcoming on the scale that was necessary to halt the German advance. In this he was undoubtedly correct, but by this time Whitehall had a clearer grasp on the strategic reality of the situation than the commanders in the field. General Paget gave some support to Ruge's argument; he had already signalled the War Office on the night before giving his view that the situation was not desperate provided that effective action could be taken to deal with enemy aircraft. On the morning of the 28th Paget was praising the high morale and staying power of his troops and asking only for a modicum of support weapons and air cover. But the logistics by this stage were becoming desperate. On the 28th the base troops at Aandalsnes were put on half rations and the prospect of the British force being starved into surrender was becoming a real possibility. It is not difficult to imagine the frustration felt by the British commander who in his three days in the country had seen his forces perform reasonably well against a greatly superior force. Nevertheless, it must be concluded at this stage that his spirit was beginning to overtake his logic. That afternoon, Paget was informed by General Massy that the decision was irrevocable, air support on the scale required simply could not be made available. General Ruge was assured of further, if unspecified assistance, but was promised that the Government would aim to embark his army as well to enable it to regroup and continue the resistance in more favourable circumstances. It was, of course, vital to retain the passive if not the active support of the Norwegian Army: a decision to change sides, however unlikely it may have seemed, would have made evacuation well nigh impossible. However, 15th Brigade had one more major action to fight before their brief sojourn in Norway came to a close.

Action at Otta

Otta was the best defensive position which the British troops had encountered in the Gudbrandsdal. It lies ten miles to the north of Kvam and twenty five miles south of Dombaas. The River Laagen turns abruptly from an easterly to a southerly direction at Otta and is joined at right angles by a tributary from the north. The town was rather larger than most of those which had seen the action downstream and sits snugly in the promontory between the main river and its tributary. The main road hugs the east bank of the river, but the railway has crossed to the west bank where it runs parallel with a farm track before crossing a combined road/rail bridge into Otta itself. Both banks of the river, but particularly the east bank, rise quite sharply to two pronounced spurs, that on the east bank about one and a half miles from the town rising to 2,000 feet and that on the west bank rather closer to the town rising to over 2,000 feet. These two spurs dominated the German approach. The whole area except in the immediate vicinity of the town was heavily wooded.

It was considered that two battalions would be necessary to provide the correct level of defence at Otta, but after the action at Kjörem the York and Lancasters had to be withdrawn to the rear to recuperate. The Green Howards therefore had to undertake the task alone, but even they did not have a full complement. 'B' Company

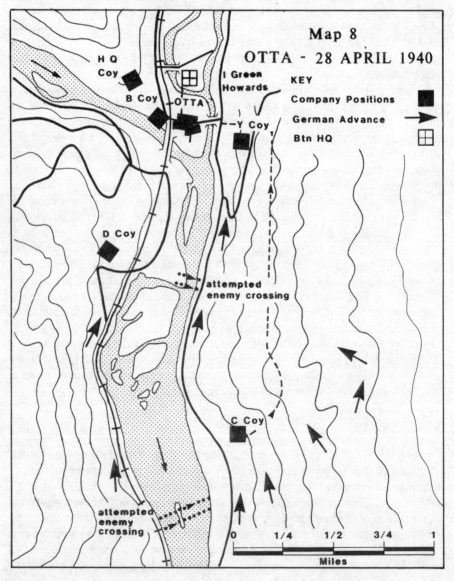

had been helping the York and Lancasters at Kjörem and had spent an adventurous night making their way back to rejoin the Battalion; their Carrier Platoon failing to make the rendezvous, being surprised by a German armoured car and destroyed with only a single survivor. Furthermore, 'A' Company had been left behind at Dombaas, so the Green Howards had only three fresh companies plus the remaining five Hotchkiss guns of the Brigade Anti-Tank Company to spread thinly over quite a wide area. 'C' and 'D' Companies were allocated the forward postions, the former dug-in to the slopes of the hill on the east bank and the latter rather closer to the town on the west bank. 'Y' Company, which was a scratch group of MT drivers, dispatch riders and other assorted support troops, and the weary 'B' Company were posted in the town with Battalion Headquarters. The troops had more time to prepare their positions than on other occasions in the Gudbrandsdal and were well protected in trenches and sangars. But there was still no artillery, a vital deficiency, and little expectation of any air support.

On 28 April, the early morning reconnaissance aircraft made its by now familiar appearance on cue at 0700, followed shortly thereafter by Heinkels which first carried out bombing runs and then machine gunned any defensive positions they could find or sprayed bullets hopefully into the woods. But the troops were well hidden and suffered little discomfort and once again the reconnaissance aircraft appeared not to locate the forward positions. At about 1030 the German front echelon at about company strength supported by armoured vehicles walked almost unconcernedly along the railway track on the west bank into a carefully laid trap. 'D' Company waited until the advance party of 150 infantry reached about four hundred yards from their position and then opened fire with everything they possessed with devastating effect. Those not killed either retreated or dispersed rapidly into the trees. 'D' Company remained in action throughout the day against armour, infantry and artillery attack. Air bombardment continued regularly throughout the day and one innovative tactic tried by the Germans at Otta was to drop bombs on the mountain peaks in an attempt to start avalanches. However, although adding a further worry to the troops on the slopes below, the force of the rolling snow was soon dissipated when it hit the tree line. Further attempts to dislodge them at 1130, 1500 and again at 1630 were also repulsed with many casualties. It was not until 1800 that a heavy attack against depleted numbers forced 'D' Company to give ground: it had been a skilfully executed and courageous stand and for once enemy losses far exceeded those of the British.

On the east bank, the first major attack developed about 1330 when light tanks were observed advancing down the road. But 'Y' Company brought this manoeuvre to a halt by knocking out the leading tank and blocking the road. Later, a rather ambitious, not to say rash, attempt by a German section to cross the river at its narrowest point in a collapsible boat was also summarily dispatched by 'Y' Company, leaving their craft drifting aimlessly downstream. For a scratch team 'Y' Company was doing pretty well and P. S. M. Askew well deserved his Distinguished Conduct Medal. In the early stages of the battle at Otta, the topography made the Germans less inclined to attempt to encircle the defenders and the British themselves were now more wary of infiltrating troops and covered a broader front than hitherto. Nevertheless by 1700 Captain E. R. P. Armitage, seconded from the Royal Scots to command 'C' Company, became increasingly concerned that he was in danger of being outflanked and he had already lost contact with one platoon which he had ordered higher up the spur. But 'C' Company was well dug in and continued to exact a severe toll on any German groups venturing too close. They also made the occasional sally forward, on one occasion to disrupt an attempt to erect a pontoon bridge on the river, and on another, led by Lieut Rawson, to surprise a conference of about thirty German officers.

At 1700 Lieut Colonel Robinson issued the order to initiate a withdrawal from the Otta position at 2100. 'D' Company was skilfully withdrawn under cover of mortar fire and only 'C' Company, who had not received the order to retreat, was still in position as dusk approached. Captain Armitage decided on his own initiative to withdraw just before 2200 after an unsuccessful attempt to regain contact with his missing platoon. However, the Germans made one last major frontal attack on 'C' Company about 2230 as darkness fell which was repulsed with considerable losses. Captain Armitage was reluctant to take his Company down to the road in the darkness and directed them instead to follow a line just below the crest of the ridge. The going was rocky and icy, the weather by now bitterly cold, and the troops had to traverse the more difficult stretches on hands and knees. It took seven hours to reach Otta where, predictably, they found the Germans already in possession. After a short exchange of sniper fire, Armitage divided his Company into four groups to make their own way the twenty five miles back to Dombaas: they all arrived safely during the following day, still carrying most of their equipment. 'C' Company had also performed exceptionally well throughout the day. Captain Armitage was awarded the Military Cross, Sergeant Roche the Military Medal and there were many other incidences of individual gallantry and ingenuity. Colonel Robinson was also awarded the Distinguished Service Order for his conduct of the action at Otta.

This had been the most successful action fought by British troops in Central Norway. It showed a regular infantry battalion, most of whom were under fire for the first time, operating as a cohesive, disciplined force. Well led at all levels down to platoon commander and NCO, making the most advantageous use of the terrain, fighting within the limitations of their strength and fire power; the 1st Battalion of the Green Howards had shown the British infantryman at his best. It certainly supported the contention that, given sufficient troops and time to prepare, there were good defensive positions in the Gudbrandsdal which could have been held for much longer than was achieved by dissipating the Brigade strength in individual battalion actions. Nevertheless, it did not and could not alter the irrevocable requirement to evacuate the British force at the first opportunity.

The Beleaguered Bridgehead

The only possible places of evacuation were Aandalsnes and its neighbouring port of Molde, so it is necessary to look briefly at what had been happening there since the Naval party first came ashore on 17 April, an unbelievably short two weeks ago. As has already been mentioned, the Corps Commander, Lieut General Massy, was never able to transfer his Headquarters in its entirety to Central Norway, but he sent Brigadier

D. Hogg and an advance party on 25 April to set up a base at Aandalsnes and to relieve Headquarters 'Sickleforce' of its administrative and logistic responsibilities. Among Hogg's other tasks was a requirement to organise the anti-aircraft defences of Aandalsnes and to reconnoitre subsidiary bases for resupply at Geiranger and Sunndalsfiord. For anti-aircraft defence he had the 21st (Royal Marines) Light Anti-Aircraft Battery armed with eight naval 2 pounders on improvised mountings and a single anti-aircraft sloop in the fiord. The Royal Marines provided base guards.

Communications between the Aandalsnes bridgehead and the front line were always tenuous. Indeed communications within the base area itself were often difficult enough. Brigadier Richards, the senior Gunner ashore in Central Norway commented:

> The exercise of any sort of effective command was rendered almost impossible by the complete absence of staff, transport, maps or communications of any sort. My first intention was to go forward after I had seen the base defences established to find out how matters were going at the front: but this was impossible. No cars were available and where one could be collected it was invariably required for sending some of the staff up to see General Paget on more important liaison duties. Even the warnings of the arrival of friendly aircraft had to be taken to the gun positions on foot either by an officer or a runner, often with very little time to spare.[9]

Unfortunately, there were not enough friendly aircraft at Aandalsnes to cause the Gunners undue concern!

Aandalsnes was subjected to sporadic air attack from the time of the first landings and a few small ships were sunk in the fiord. But on 26 April the Germans turned their full attention to the destruction of Aandalsnes as they had already achieved at Namsos on 20/21 April. Much of the town was destroyed and the wooden quay set on fire. Even when the anti-aircraft guns were available they were extremely difficult to site. The bombers usually ran in between 8,000 and 16,000 feet for which a minimum of two 4 gun or four 2 gun positions were required which could pick-up the target at between 12 and 13,000 yards. The mountains and fiords totally precluded this kind of disposition for the guns. The mountains also allowed the German bombers to approach unobserved, and in the absence of any other warning, the gun crews had to remain on immediate alert for eighteen hours or more a day. It was a very wearing and nerve wracking existence waiting for the scream of a Stuka to suddenly shatter the silence as it erupted over the mountain crests. Brigadier Richards commented of Aandalsnes 'No experienced AA officer would have recommended its adoption as a base'.[10]

In addition to the anti-aircraft guns ashore, there was always an anti-aircraft guardship in the fiord. Some First World War cruisers had been modified as anti-aircraft cruisers by the addition of eight 4 inch high angle guns. The sloops of the Black Swan class had also been fitted out as anti-aircraft ships with six 4 inch high angle guns. But these weapons were not really effective even against aircraft flying straight and level. It was not properly recognised before the war that the lethality of an anti-aircraft gun depended largely on its rate and velocity of fire rather than the size of the shell. If a single 4 inch shell hit an aircraft it was, not unexpectedly, very effective, but the chances of achieving a hit without an automatic gun were very small. The 2 pounder pom-poms and the 0.5 inch machine guns were equally useless. Of the only effective anti-aircraft weapons of the day, the 20 mm Oerlikon had been rejected by the Navy except for armed trawlers and the 40 mm Bofors had not yet arrived in any numbers.

Captain Poland's sloop *Black Swan* first took on the guardship duty and was quickly singled out by the Luftwaffe for special attention. The Stukas were her most dangerous opponents; often operating in tactical formations, they dived almost vertically out of the sun to very low level before flattening out and releasing their bombs. Fortunately their aim was usually poor and no hits were registered although many bombs landed too close for comfort. The pilots also gradually became more circumspect in pressing home their attacks.

On 21 April, the anti-aircraft cruiser *Curacoa* relieved the *Black Swan*. She was not to be so lucky. On the 24th, after surviving regular air attacks throughout the day, a bomb eventually hit below the bridge killing thirty and injuring many more. She struggled back to Scotland and was replaced by the sloop *Flamingo*. On the 26th the *Black Swan* was back in place and again she bore a charmed life. It was not until the ship was almost out of ammunition that at last a Stuka managed to plant a bomb astern which, although it did not explode, passed straight through the deck and out through the ship's bottom between the propeller shafts. Taking in water heavily, she too limped home for repairs.

The expenditure of ammunition for the high angle guns was now giving cause for concern. Admiral Forbes received a signal from the Admiralty that only 7,000 rounds remained in the armament depots. He decided to keep this unwelcome news to himself.

Molde was also subjected to its first significant air attack on 26 April. The following afternoon four more air raids on Aandalsnes destroyed substantial quantities of rations, ammunition and stores and damaged the railway yards. By now the shore parties had to take cover throughout the day, leaving only the few brief hours of darkness to keep the supplies moving. It was clearly apparent to Hogg and his senior Naval officer, Captain M. M. Denny, that the logistics chain could not be maintained. A convoy which entered the fiord on 27 April had to depart before it was possible to unload its heavy anti-aircraft battery: the first to be sent to Central Norway. On the afternoon of the 27th Hogg signalled the War Office that in the absence of communications with Headquarters 'Sickleforce', he was planning to evacuate Aandalsnes in the first ten days of May. There ensued a difference of opinion between Paget and Hogg because at this time, Paget, perhaps under the influence of General Ruge, had sent one of his more optimistic communications to the War Office. But Hogg was undoubtedly right – without a secure bridgehead 'Sickleforce' could not be maintained and reinforcement was totally out of the question.

All was settled by the following day. The evacuation was to commence on the night of 30 April and be completed on the following night. Men were to take priority over equipment and maximum use was to be made of Molde. The last decision was not really practicable: although closer to the open sea and therefore more congenial to the

Navy, Molde could only be reached overland from the Romsdal by a long detour, and the owners of most of the small boats which had been used to ferry men from Molde to Aandalsnes had by now been intimidated by the most recent air raids.

Fighting Withdrawal

General Paget's problems were by no means over even after the irrevocable decision had been made to evacuate. By 29 April most of the British force was concentrated in the area of Dombaas. The Green Howards had withdrawn through the K.O.Y.L.I. who now held the forward position about two miles south of the town. They had a quiet day from air attack as the Germans were still concentrating on Aandalsnes even though there was little enough remaining of value to attack. Although the first attempt by the Germans to land paratroops in the Romsdal had been unsuccessful, there was always the risk of further incursions and 148th Brigade was re-organised and pressed back into use again to protect the line of communication between Dombaas and Aandalsnes. Even the Norwegian forces in the Österdal had generated a new lease of life and were conducting a spirited fight for Röros which changed hands five times in all. However, there was nothing that could prevent their being encircled once the Germans had occupied Dombaas. The Norwegians would withdraw from the Romsdal by 1 May and General Ruge promised that they would undertake demolitions on the road and rail links between Trondheim and Dombaas.

A single line railway and a road connected Dombaas with Aandalsnes. The road had been damaged both by enemy air attacks and the pounding of heavy lorries, and the arriving thaw which was so welcome in other respects was rapidly making some stretches unusable. The road was littered with hundreds of abandoned vehicles, many bombed or shot up by the Luftwaffe, some just out of petrol. The road was patrolled regularly by German bombers which, without any form of opposition, carefully dropped their bomb loads on bridges and cross-roads and then methodically machine-gunned anything which appeared capable of moving.

Communications between Brigadier Hogg and General Paget remained difficult, leading to numerous misunderstandings and contradictory instructions. Seen from the ruins of Aandalsnes, the situation appeared hopeless to Hogg and he had signalled the War Office requesting ships be made available on the night of 29 April to enable base and support troops to be evacuated.

Paget met General Ruge for the last time on the afternoon of 29 April. Their meeting was friendly although Ruge still resented what he believed, not without justification, to be the failure of the Allied Governments to redeem their promises of support to the extent necessary to provide a reasonable chance of stemming the tide of the German advance. He was still willing to continue the struggle if there was any hope of a further Allied intervention in Norway, otherwise he believed that further resistance would be fruitless.

The York and Lancasters, consisting now of less than 300 men, was the first battalion to proceed to Aandalsnes and it was hoped that they might be evacuated on the night of the 29th. For the first time in Norway the Germans carried out a night raid on Aandalsnes, their navigation and target acquisition made easy by the glow from wooden houses and the surrounding woods which were all burning steadily. In the event only 340 were able to sail on the sloop *Fleetwood* including many of the wounded.

King Haakon and his ministers together with the British and French delegations also sailed that night in the cruiser *Glasgow* from Molde to Tromso, north of Narvik, which at this stage was still a safe haven from the German advance. The King had originally wanted to go only as far north as Mösjoen, midway between Trondheim and Bodo, but was persuaded that it could only be a matter of time before a German advance north of Trondheim would again place him in jeopardy. The King was downcast but dignified:

> His Majesty had undergone the severest ordeal and was feeling brokenhearted at the fate of his country . . . His quiet composure and dignity, his kindliness and thought to others, his confidence, even cheerful bearing when in public were an inspiration to all of us and unforgettable.[11]

This proud, courageous and sensitive man did much to sustain the spirits of his countrymen during the ensuing five difficult years.

The first night of the evacuation was entrusted to Admiral Edward-Collin's Second Cruiser Squadron, escorted by five destroyers, and the two troopships *Ulster Prince* and *Ulster Monarch*. The *Ulster Prince* and the destroyer *Tartar* were sent to Molde to collect the remainder of Captain Denny's Naval Base Party, many of whom had left on the previous night in the *Glasgow* with King Haakon. Captain Ruge and the remainder of his staff were also to be embarked, but there was a last minute hitch. Ruge had believed he was to be taken to Tromso and was indignant to discover that his intended destination was in fact Scotland. After a gangplank confrontation, he and his staff turned about and strode resolutely back into the burning town.

In the meantime the *Galatea* had tied up to the stone quay in Aandalsnes and quickly embarked nearly 600 men, to be followed by the *Arethusa* which lifted a similar number. The *Sheffield* at anchor in the fiord had troops ferried out to her in the destroyers *Walker* and *Westcott*. More men were picked up from the village of Alfarnes to the north of Aandalsnes and ferried out to the *Southampton*. The *Walker* and the *Westcott* were now detailed to pick up a party of 300 marines from Veblungsnes across the Romsdal River. It was already daylight and the usual early morning bombers had arrived before the *Walker* and *Westcott* could escape to sea, but they still managed to get away with the help of some friendly support fire from one of the cruisers.

The first night's evacuation had been very successful. 2,627 men had been evacuated although they had to leave behind almost all of their equipment. No ships had been lost or damaged so far and the voyage back to Scapa Flow was uneventful.

The K.O.Y.L.I. was the last battalion to see significant action in Central Norway. On the afternoon of 30 April, a German force of infantry approached their positions just to the south of Dombaas. Once again their advance guard was surprised by well-concealed and dug in troops and suffered heavily for their carelessness. Although the German forces were generally cautiously and skilfully led, one mistake they frequently made was to push a large body of infantry forward without first sending patrols to reconnoitre the ground. As a result they suffered quite unnecessary casualties when their leading troops were caught by surprise. On this occasion they did not have the support of tanks and artillery and quickly withdrew. For the first time the British had some artillery support, a battery of four old Norwegian field guns, although the K.O.Y.L.I. were less than appreciative when the first salvoes found their forward companies rather than the enemy. But once they found their range, the moral uplift of having artillery support at last far outweighed the physical damage they actually achieved. There was also a success against a lone dive bombing aircraft which was brought down by small arms fire. Although the Germans initiated their usual flanking manoeuvre, Major Cass skilfully withdrew each company before it became encircled. For some unexplained reason the Germans did not press too hard on this occasion, and as at Otta the British campaign was finishing on a relatively high note. That evening the K.O.Y.L.I. withdrew to Dombaas and entrained for Aandalsnes with one company of Green Howards. Exhausted, they soon fell asleep, huddled together for warmth in the cold, windowless carriages.

But their problems were not yet over. Despite having been bombed during the previous day the railway line to Aandalsnes was still thought to be open, but at about 0100 the train careered at some speed into a new crater near Lesjaskog, still more than thirty miles from their destination. Both engines were derailed and the first carriage telescoped: eight soldiers were killed with many more injured and a large quantity of mortar bombs and small arms ammunition in the leading truck caught fire and exploded. It was a spectacular sight on a pitch black night, but not one greatly appreciated by the troops who struggled to get away from the doomed train through snow waist deep. It was a considerable feat of organisation that within forty five minutes most of the uninjured had set out on foot with all their arms, equipment and anti-tank guns for the relative safety of the tunnel at Verma, some seventeen miles distant. Although they did not make it under cover of darkness and suffered more casualties from sporadic air attack the following morning, they nevertheless covered the distance in eight hours along badly pot-holed roads. They were still cheerful enough to sing when they gained the relative safety of the tunnel. Very few of the British troops in Central Norway were not well accustomed to walking by the end of their two week campaign.

The tunnel at Verma was chiselled out of solid rock, eight hundred yards long, soot lined, cold and damp. It was already occupied by two trains, one an abandoned ammunition train, the other a troop train which was to take them forward to Aandalsnes. In all there were some 1,700 men crammed into the tunnel including General Paget, and despite the discomfort most managed to resume their interrupted sleep. The Germans made several attempts to bomb and machine gun the tunnel entrances, but did not succeed in blocking this vital escape route or inflicting any casualties. However, their rest was interrupted in the late afternoon when it was learned that the pursuing Germans were only about three miles away and had broken through a Royal Marines rearguard. Companies from the Green Howards and the K.O.Y.L.I. were dispatched post haste up the road while the engine of the escape train was rapidly steamed up. Despite the risk of being caught out in the open by marauding aircraft, the troops had to vacate the tunnel to avoid being suffocated, but nevertheless were safely under way at 2030 notwithstanding a somewhat unresponsive train crew who had to be encouraged to co-operate by troops on the footplate.

But another hazard still remained to be faced. The railway made a complete 180° turn inside the tunnel and re-appeared adjacent to the entrance at a lower level. The train was therefore travelling back towards the Germans during the first part of its journey which had to be undertaken in daylight. Slowly but surely the train gathered speed and turned back towards the north-west without attracting German attention – a lucky escape. Having heard that the train had departed, the rearguard quickly disengaged and embarked on lorries and made their own way back to Aandalsnes. Once again, 15th Brigade had managed to withdraw in the nick of time.

The Evacuation is Completed

The following night it was the turn of Admiral Layton's Cruiser Squadron. Edward-Collins had signalled to Layton that he thought there were 1,500 more men to uplift; in fact there were over 2,000. May 1 dawned ominously bright and clear, but there were now two anti-aircraft cruisers in the fiord, *Calcutta* and *Auckland*, and despite ferocious dive bombing attacks by Stukas throughout the day, they remained unscathed even though they had to withdraw to sea late in the afternoon when they ran short of ammunition. Admiral Layton arrived at the entrance to the Romsdalfiord just before dusk. The *Somali* was sent to Aalesund to collect the detachment of 'Primrose Force' and the *Diana* to Molde to pick up the indefatigible General Ruge and to transport him and his staff in accordance with his wishes to Tromso. The *Manchester* and *Birmingham* were too large to use the quay and four destroyers were detailed as ferries. Unfortunately, the troops had not yet arrived.

At about 2300, the first of the K.O.Y.L.I. straggled into Aandalsnes and quickly transferred to the waiting ships. By midnight some 1,500 had already been embarked and thirty minutes later the cruisers were at sea. General Paget estimated that only 200 remained and so the *Calcutta* and the *Auckland* were detailed to pick up the rearguard. But as they waited patiently for the final party to assemble, company after company emerged from the battered streets onto the quay and soon the *Calcutta* had collected over 750, as many as she could squeeze on board. Leaving the *Auckland* to pick up the remainder, the *Calcutta* moved into the fiord to wait until the last man arrived. Fortunately only another 241 remained, the real rearguard of Green Howards and Royal Engineers who had been carrying out some last minute demolitions. At 0200 the ships were at last able to escape, just before the breaking rays of daylight would have subjected them to inevitable air attack. It is an indication of the troops' resilience that even at the last, after all they had undergone, there was still some banter as to whom should fall the privilege of being the last man off Norwegian soil.

In all, 5,084 troops were embarked on the three nights and the whole evacuation had been completed without the loss of a single ship or soldier. Despite the imprecise information on the numbers to be lifted, it was a remarkable feat of organisation and daring, reinforced by a little bit of well-deserved luck. It was helped also by the skilful way in which the troops had been disengaged from the enemy advance at Dombaas.

'Sickleforce' had been involved in much heavier and more sustained fighting than 'Mauriceforce' to the north of Trondheim and had predictably suffered far higher casualties. 101 officers and 1,301 other ranks were killed, wounded or missing. 148th Brigade had sustained the greater losses in their actions at Faaberg and Tretten, only thirteen officers and about 400 men were evacuated out of an original strength of sixty five officers and over 1,000 men. 15th Brigade had also sustained substantial losses, thirty two officers and 552 other ranks, but spread across three battalions compared with the two in 148th Brigade. Most of their equipment, including a high proportion of personal arms, had been lost. It was a happy irony however that the 15th Brigade, which had been so hounded from the mountain slopes by, among others, the Hermann Goering Regiment, was to chase that very same regiment down similar wooded valleys in Italy some three years later. Revenge was all the sweeter when the boot was on the other foot.

The Intelligence Gap

'Sickleforce' faced many difficulties ashore, to most of which we have already made reference. But another problem was the lack of effective intelligence both for the strategic direction of the force from London and for the execution of operations on the ground. This is an appropriate moment to consider how the intelligence war influenced events in Central Norway.

The defects in co-ordinating intelligence which had characterised the lead-up to the German invasion persisted throughout the campaign itself.[12] Although an increasing flow of material became available, a lack of trust and co-operation between the stubbornly independent intelligence departments prevented the operational staffs in both Whitehall and in the field operations turning it to good use. During the first week of the campaign, intelligence reports were received only through diplomatic channels and from SIS agents on the ground. But the material was confusing and conflicting, and the speed and precision of the German advance negated its significance.

However, there was a dramatic development in intelligence gathering as the campaign entered its second week. The Government Code and Cypher School (GC and CS) at Bletchley made a significant practical breakthrough in deciphering the Enigma code. Enigma was an electro-mechanical wired encyphering machine which had been adopted by the German Navy in 1926, the Army in 1929 and the Air Force in 1934. It was a formidable challenge to the cryptanalyst, but valuable work by the Poles and French and subsequently by GC and CS led to the first practical de-cryption of Enigma in January 1940.[13] On 10 April, the Germans introduced a new Enigma code (yellow) specifically for Air Force and Army operations in the Norwegian campaign. This was broken by GC and CS only five days later and comprehensive and up to date information of potentially great importance was available until 14 May. Not only did it contain valuable data on Army and Air Force operations and logistics, but regularly provided as a bonus useful information on Navy movements. Regrettably its potential was barely exploited. Sigint had never previously been a significant factor in intelligence gathering and neither GC and CS or the Service intelligence departments were organised to handle, evaluate and disseminate the flow of information which ensued.

Apart from the sheer volume of material which constrained the necessary sifting by the small staffs available, the main deterrent to its effective use was the existence of internal security measures designed to deny its source. Intelligence has always depended upon the compilation of the best picture from a variety of sources of varying integrity. In this weighting process, low credibility had traditionally been given to intelligence from agents in the field, but desk officers within both Military and Air Intelligence were led to believe that the Enigma reports had originated from espionage sources, and thus did not give it the immediacy or credence it deserved. Naval Intelligence (OIC) had insisted that the true identity of the reports was known and C-in-C Home Fleet received Sigint material prefixed by the code name 'Hydro'.[14] Even when its true source was known at the highest levels, difficulties of disseminating the information to operational staffs and forces at sea and in the field were never successfully resolved. This dilemma had long frustrated the effective use of intelligence, and it is difficult not to conclude that excessive secrecy to protect the source of the material is the fundamental reason why commanders in the field instinctively tended to rely on their own eyes and their own sources of information in preference to that received from external agencies.

But in terms of their own intelligence resources, British commanders in Norway were poorly served. Army commanders were deprived of the means of gathering local intelligence as most of the field Sigint units had been despatched to France or were left behind in the rapidly re-arranged shipping arrangements necessitated by the German pre-emption of the original plans. Even if field units had been available, it is doubtful if they would have been able to read the German Army field codes. Although better intelligence would almost certainly not have had a decisive influence on the outcome of the Norwegian campaign, its absence was undoubtedly recognised as a serious deficiency in a rapidly moving operational scenario.

The lack of topographic intelligence also proved a serious handicap, for although some attempt had been made to obtain accurate information on terrain, lines of communication, airfields and harbours, this effort was generally devoted to areas where British forces planned to operate rather than those areas where the German intervention of necessity forced them to operate. It is an illuminating reflection on the inadequacy of our planning that the pilots of the bomber squadrons prepared their target maps from the pages of Baedeker's Scandinavia, 1912 edition.

Naval intelligence was equally spasmodic and unreliable. Some useful information was gained on 14 April of U boat dispositions in the North Sea following the sinking of U-49 near Narvik. But knowledge of surface ship movements was largely dependent on sightings by friendly aircraft which were often unreliable as to numbers, imprecise as to type and inaccurate as to position. In contrast, German Naval Intelligence enjoyed a fair degree of success in intercepting and interpreting British naval transmissions as we have already seen in the naval operations at Narvik. During the spring and summer of 1940, it is estimated that the German Navy was able to decypher and make use of some 30 per cent of intercepted traffic in the North Sea and Norwegian theatre of operations.[15]

The limited information of Naval movements resulting from the Enigma Yellow decoding died out in mid May with the demise of that source of intelligence, but the

Naval Section at GC an CS could still make some deductions regarding the location of surface ships by analysing the geographical distribution of wireless transmissions even though they could not decode them. But Naval Intelligence (OIC) was sceptical of the value of such information and made little use of it. Again the perceived need for internal security of information created almost as many difficulties for the home side as its inadvertent release would have benefited their opponents. Those responsible for receiving and interpreting the mass of data could not recognise its significance because they were unaware of the Allied operations on which it might impact. The intelligence and operational staffs were acting in isolation almost totally oblivious of the need to co-ordinate their activities. Fortunately, it was an omission which was recognised and rectified at this early stage of the war and thereafter co-ordination and co-operation steadily improved. By the time that the campaign in North West Europe was underway, not only was intelligence information being distributed more freely in Whitehall, but it was being transmitted onwards to France. In future, the difficulties lay more in the field of correct interpretation rather than dissemination.

The Unrecognised Truth

The campaign in Central Norway had undoubtedly been a failure. In little more than two weeks, 12,500 men had been landed at Namsos and Aandalsnes, travelled considerable distances, fought several short but intensive actions, and retired from whence they came.

There were many reasons for the German success, some of them political and strategic, but in the campaign itself, although the Germans eventually achieved numerical superiority over the combined Norwegian and Allied forces, it was not this factor which decided the issue. Two fundamental factors stand out – logistics and air power. The British, French and Norwegian forces were inadequately equipped in almost every respect – no tanks or artillery, inadequate transport and rations, and no secure base. The retreat up the Gudbrandsdal never quite became a rout, but it came perilously close to it at times.

In his report after the evacuation, General Paget was scathing in his condemnation of the lack of preparedness for the support of the expeditionary force:

> It has become the habit of the British Army in recent years to assume that what the General Staff consider to be politically or operationally desirable is administratively possible. No greater or more dangerous fallacy could exist. In the case of the Aandalsnes expedition it appears to have been assumed that the port of Aandalsnes and the line of communication running forward therefrom was capable of maintaining the force which it was considered operationally desirable to disembark there. As far as can be ascertained no attempt to verify this assumption was made although opportunity to do so existed.[16]

One wonders what the military attachés and planners had been doing in the months preceeding the German invasion – certainly little attention seems to have been given to contingency thinking let alone planning.

But, of course, it was German air power which controlled and constrained the logistics and thereby prevented the introduction of reinforcements or even adequate support for those troops already ashore. General Paget again referred in his report on the campaign to this fundamental problem:

> My considered view in the light of experience remains that which I expressed to the D.Q.M.G. before I embarked. It is that the possibility of maintaining any force through the single port of Aandalsnes depended primarily upon whether or not local air superiority could be established and maintained. To that view I would add that, since the necessary degree of air superiority could scarcely be expected to exist throughout the whole length of the line of communication, and since that line was peculiarly vulnerable to both air action and to seasonal changes, the Aandalsnes project was not administratively practicable. Operationally, therefore, it was doomed to failure.[17]

For General Pellengahr, who was to retire again into the obscurity from which he had emerged, the campaign was an unqualified success. The join up with the Trondheim garrison was effected on 25 April. He had covered some three hundred miles from Oslo to Trondheim in two weeks against stiffening opposition in country which one would normally have expected to favour the defence. His troops were also inexperienced, but they had solid lines of communication and the inestimable benefit of close air support. Whenever a frontal advance looked as though it was running into resistance, Pellengahr had the priceless advantage of troops who could don skis or snowshoes and move round the flank. This tactic was invariably successful and precluded any defensive position being held for long. It could have been prevented only by greater concentration of force than the Allies adopted and a willingness, as well as the capability, to move up into the mountain slopes flanking the valley floor.

On 4 May, General Englebrecht at last made direct contact with Bergen and on the following day resistance in Central Norway ceased. The last to surrender was the fortress of Hegra, twenty five miles east of Trondheim, where 300 Norwegians had gallantly resisted a siege for nearly a month.

In the Name of God, Go

Unmitigated military disaster though it may have been, the campaign in Central Norway had a profound political impact on the future conduct of the war. Optimistic accounts in the press of military advantages had quickly given way to realisation that the whole expedition had in fact been a resounding military defeat. The Prime Minister's statement on 3 May that 'Germany has not attained her objective' was palpably false and the people and their elected representatives could see this only too clearly. Chamberlain's remark at the beginning of April that Hitler had 'missed the bus' was now to rebound upon him with all the ferocity that the House of Commons can summon on such occasions.

In the first week of May opposition to the Government within the House mounted, cabals fermented discontent and declined as rapidly as they had arisen. Only one common thread emerged, there must be a change at the top. But who was to assume the reins of leadership at this critical time with Norway apparently lost and the holocaust on the Western Front about to begin. Lord Halifax, Mr Churchill, Anthony Eden, even Lloyd George were mentioned, but first of all there was the debate in the House on the evacuation from Norway.

The debate opened on 7 May in response to an opposition motion for the Adjournment of the House, but this was in effect a euphemism for a vote of censure. Mr Chamberlain opened feebly, but the leader of the Liberals, Sir Archibald Sinclair, was more forthright. He recognised quite clearly the reason for the failure in Norway – there had been no foresight in the political direction of the war, it had been conducted extempore; improvisation followed by inevitable confusion. He added:

> The right hon Gentleman (Mr Chamberlain) today told us that south of Trondheim and north of Trondheim we had succeeded, by a masterly policy, in evacuation with no losses. Wars are not won on masterly evacuations.[18]

The debate continued with Admiral of the Fleet Sir Roger Keyes in full dress uniform again with six rows of medals, breathing fire and brimstone. His words were quickly forgotten, but the dramatic impact could hardly be exceeded. It is the words of Leo Amery that are best remembered:

> This is what Cromwell said to the long Parliament when he thought it was no longer fit to conduct the affairs of the nation 'You have sat too long for any good you have been doing. Depart I say, and let us have done with you. In the name of God, go'.[19]

Less dramatically, but adding to the fire, Lloyd George joined in on the following day:

> I say solemnly that the Prime Minister should give an example of sacrifice, because there is nothing which can contribute more to victory in this war than that he should sacrifice the seals of office.[20]

Mr Chamberlain had the unenviable task of winding up the debate on behalf of the Government. It was one of the most difficult speeches that he had ever been called upon to make. If he was to fulfil the hopes of his many supporters, he had to avoid or rise above the disasters of the policy for which he had been so largely responsible. Although, or perhaps because, his speech ended in uproar on the opposition benches, he did just enough to quieten his detractors in his own party, but it was not enough to sustain his administration.

Despite a three line whip, thirty three Conservatives voted against the Government and sixty abstained. Mr Chamberlain's halting, ineffectual government was clearly finished. Two momentous events crowned 10 May 1940 – Hitler invaded Holland and Belgium and the King summoned Mr Churchill to Buckingham Palace and asked him to form a government. At its hour of greatest need, the ill-conceived and maldirected Scandinavian adventure had, by a supreme irony, projected upon the country the man most responsible for its instigation, and now the leader most likely to save it from defeat.

Air Support – The Missing Link

'I do not believe that the essential elements of the war will be altered by the air arm.'[1]

Winston Churchill

An Untempered Sword

On 1 November 1911, Giulio Gavotti, an Italian Army lieutenant, dropped the first bombs in anger from an aeroplane in Libya during the Italo-Turkish war. They weighed only 4 lbs each and caused little damage, but Gavotti had set in motion a new concept of waging war which has remained paramount ever since.

Yet no less than forty years later, after one major war and several lesser engagements had amply demonstrated the significance of air power, the political and military heirarchy in Britain had still been prepared to launch a major campaign without taking proper cognizance of its impact on land and sea operations. That the RAF could not support the Army in the field in Norway in 1940 was recognised, but its significance was largely ignored. The Army was to pay the price, and regrettably had to relearn the lesson more than once before the war drew to a close.

It is already clear from our consideration of the plight of 'Sickleforce' and 'Mauriceforce' that the Allied forces in Central Norway were severely, even decisively, handicapped by their inability to impose any measure of control over the Luftwaffe or to exert any comparable restraint themselves on the German ground operations. We have already seen[2] that the RAF's inability to prevent air attack on Norway was recognised as early as September 1939, and again in February 1940 the Chief of Air Staff expressed concern over the potential strength that the German Air Force, even from bases in Northern Germany, could bring to bear over Norway as far north as Trondheim, and the even greater benefits that would accrue if they could operate from Norwegian airfields. But notwithstanding this clear warning, 'Sickleforce' and 'Mauriceforce' were launched with minimal air support, and in the event, the overwhelming degree of influence that the Luftwaffe was able to bring on the course of the campaign was even greater than had been envisaged when the operation was being planned. That the Chiefs of Staff underestimated the impact of the Luftwaffe's control of the air is incontrovertible, particularly their ability to bring such extreme pressure on the use of the two main bridgeheads at Namsos and Aandalsnes. But even if this had been foreseen, the RAF and the Fleet Air Arm's ability to counteract German air superiority was very limited. There were many reasons for this of which the physical location of the conflict, so distant from homebase airfields, was by some way the most important. But the real difficulty was more deep seated and it is necessary to look back to the policies, prejudices and perceptions of the use of air power in the pre-war years to understand why the cupboard was so bare in 1940.

Although the machinery for joint decision-making and the planning of combined operations maintained a tenuous existence in the early months of the war, the single Service Departments were all-powerful and always had an inclination and tendency to work independently of each other, the legacy of inter-Service rivalries and jealousies which had long existed, and to some extent probably always will. The creation of a third service did nothing to foster co-operation; the fledgling Royal Air Force which was formed in 1918 had to fight for its separate existence against the two established Services who by no means generally accepted the need for a separate air arm. The RAF had been created to provide an independent strategic bombing force, free of the demands of the British Expeditionary Force in France whose requirements were for tactical support of ground forces. Although the concept of strategic bombing and its effects on the industrial resources and the civilian morale of the enemy were by no means proven in the First World War, it so dominated Air Ministry thinking that some senior officers even believed that the other arms could become largely superfluous in future wars. General Smuts had sown the seed as early as 1917 when he reported to the War Cabinet:

> The day may not be far off when aerial operations with their devastation of enemy lands and destruction of industrial and populous centres on a vast scale may become the principle operations of war, to which the older forms of military and naval operations may become secondary and subordinate.[3]

As other countries produced their own long range bomber forces it became necessary to devote, belatedly, some resources to the provision of air defences and it was in these two roles that the RAF developed its ethos and expertise in the years before 1939. That the effectiveness of aerial bombardment as a war-winning force in isolation was exaggerated is now widely accepted, but its single minded pursual almost without interruption from 1918 had serious consequences upon the development of other elements of air power. Direct air support of naval and land operations were both badly neglected in the inter-war years and the Admiralty and the War Office constantly sought to bring these two elements back under their own control. One can hardly criticise them for their concern, and the inadequacies of both were glaringly apparent in the Norwegian campaign.

In July 1936 the RAF was reorganised to meet the coming challenge. The single Command, Air Defence of Great Britain, was abolished and four functional commands were established, Fighter, Coastal, Bomber and Training. Of these, Coastal and Bomber played a direct role in the Norwegian campaign, and Fighter Command squadrons were transferred to Norway in support of the land operations.

Allied air operations and their influence on the course of the campaign in Central Norway may be considered under four main headings: maritime reconnaissance, bomber operations from homebase airfields, the employment of fighter aircraft from

Norwegian airfields, and finally Fleet Air Arm operations from aircraft carriers. The air contribution to the fighting at Narvik will be examined in our consideration of that part of the campaign which was always totally independent of the action in Central Norway where at least some aircraft based in the United Kingdom were within range of the scene of events, except for the most northerly operations at Namsos.

The Cinderella Command

Coastal Command was the least well prepared of the RAF commands at the outbreak of the war. Co-operation with the Navy had taken a very low priority in Air Ministry thinking in the inter-war years, and its predecessor, Coastal Area, had been more concerned with leisurely long distance flights by flying boats and in organising the Schneider Trophy than in the more serious business of preparing for the war at sea. In September 1939, Coastal Command was equipped with a range of aircraft, only 230 in all, of which most were obsolete – of the six flying boat squadrons, only two had the relatively modern Sunderland, and of the eleven land-based reconnaissance squadrons, one only was equipped with the new Hudson. The American-built Hudson was eventually to establish itself as one of the legendary successful aircraft of World War II. A derivative of the Lockheed 14 civil airliner, it had two powerful radial engines and the endurance to range along the Norwegian coast, but it had one or two quirky flying characteristics and some were lost in accidents in the early days of the war. A cynic suggested that on sighting an enemy aircraft the Hudson would spontaneously burst into flames.[4] The other ten squadrons were equipped with the worthy but low performance Anson which did not have the range or defensive capability to operate off the Norwegian coast. Operational control and tactics were undeveloped, and navigation aids of doubtful accuracy and reliability. In recognition of its lack of preparedness and the inadequacy of its equipment, responsibility for attacking the German Fleet had been transferred to Bomber Command in January 1939: this task was to prove beyond the capability of the bombers as well.

Of the many tasks assumed by Coastal Command in the early days of the war, the main requirement of the Admiralty was air patrols to search for German surface ships. But the aircraft of the time were mainly dependent on visual means of search, and this was a very hit or miss affair in the unpredictable weather over the North Sea in winter. It was not until 1940 that the first of the early radars, ASV Mk I, was fitted to the Hudsons, by then steadily increasing in numbers after a slow start. Surface raiders from time to time slipped out of the North German ports, but on only one occasion during the period from the outbreak of war until March 1940 did Coastal Command aircraft locate and shadow German naval forces breaking out into the North Sea. This was on 8 October 1939 when Hudsons of 224 and 233 Squadrons located the *Gneisenau*, the cruiser *Köln* and nine destroyers. However, it was a Hudson of 220 Squadron which first sighted the *Altmark* in the North Sea in February 1940, and another Hudson of 233 Squadron which established her position in the Jössing Fiord later in the same day.

In April 1940 there were four Hudson squadrons in being, although 224 and 233 Squadrons saw most of the action in Norwegian waters. The Hudson was not only used as a maritime reconnaissance aircraft, but also as a bomber and even a long-range fighter. It was a Hudson of 223 Squadron captained by Flight Lieutenant Womersley which claimed the first enemy aircraft shot down by the RAF in the war, a Dornier 18 on 8 October 1939. Heinkel 115 float planes also regularly fell victim to the far more powerful Hudson. But the Hudson was no match for the new German fighters, the Bf 109 and 110, which were a good 100 knots faster, and a singleton aircraft could only operate safely in Norwegian waters if there was a handy bank of cloud to hide in if attacked by predatory fighters.

It was not only enemy fighters which were to prove a hazard in Norwegian waters. The Royal Navy's anti-aircraft cruiser *Curacoa* had been retained at Aandalsnes after the landings to provide some protection for the bridgehead against enemy air attack. But on 23 April, the *Curacoa* vigorously attacked three Hudsons of 224 Squadron despite their frenetic signalling of the recognition letter of the day by Aldis Lamp and firing the colour of the day from a Verey pistol. One was shot down and another badly damaged: aircraft recognition was never the Navy's strong suit.

Communication between ships and aircraft was a problem more often than not during this period. A Hudson of 233 Squadron was tasked on 17 April with co-operating with the cruiser *Suffolk* in the bombardment of the airfield at Stavanger. The Hudson was to mark the airfield with incendiary bombs and then spot for the gunners. In fact the *Suffolk* heard only one of the RT transmissions from either the Hudson or two Walrus seaplanes which were aloft on a similar mission.

On 29 April, another Hudson of 233 Squadron claimed the first anti-shipping success of the war when it damaged the merchant vessel *Theodor* in the Grimstad Fiord. Flying in the fiords could be a stimulating experience. The aircrew welcomed the protection of bad weather, but cloud also obscured the mountain tops and many a Hudson had a close encounter with the ground, and some failed to return. Flight Lieutenant Gron Edwards was a pilot on 233 Squadron:

> We did our recce of Bjorne Fiord. Hunting up and down the fiords could be quite pleasant flying. Some of the fiord systems such as Hardanger and Sogne Fiords were very extensive and you could fly for hours and still not cover them all. Sometimes, as we had a habit of flying as low as possible to avoid any radar, we would end up towards the top end of a very steep-sided fiord and have to do a really tight turn to get out of it, with the belly of the Hudson flitting around not many feet from the rocky sides.[5]

Even so, the Hudson made only a minor contribution to the campaign in Norway before June 1940, although as a final fling, twelve Hudsons of 269 Squadron attacked the *Scharnhorst* at Trondheim shortly after the final Allied withdrawal from Norway. No hits were scored – which is a fair summary of Coastal Command's contribution to the campaign in Norway in the spring of 1940 despite many hours of earnest endeavour and frequently tedious, and occasionally exciting flying. The Hudson's day was yet to come.

A Hollow Threat

If Coastal Command was the Cinderella of the Royal Air Force at the outbreak of war, Bomber Command could hardly be described as its Leviathan. In 1933 the bomber force consisted of a mix of Heyfords, Harts, Hinds, Wellesleys and Harrows, all already obsolescent, and whilst retaining some utility for colonial policing, were totally unfitted for a war in Europe. Thus the whole of the bomber force (as well as all the fighters) had to be replaced by new models when the expansion schemes began in July 1934 in contemplation of a war with Germany. A bewildering succession of plans emerged in the ensuing years with the emphasis gradually changing from the production of bombers to that of fighters, fortunately so as events turned out or the Battle of Britain would have been lost and Bomber Command would never have had the chance to prove its worth. The planned ratio of light to heavy bombers also fluctuated, but the Air Staff never lost their ultimate faith in the philosophy of the strategic offensive even though for reasons of expediency the introduction of the four engined and heavy bombers slipped inexorably backwards.

At the outbreak of war Bomber Command consisted of thirty three operational squadrons, sixteen of light bombers (ten Battles and six Blenheims) and seventeen medium or heavy (six each of Wellingtons and Hampdens and five of Whitleys). The Battles were sent to France and took no part in the Norwegian campaign, but all the others performed various roles in the North Sea and over Norway in 1940. One has to be very cautious when defining the capability of individual aircraft; performance figures vary widely for different marks of the same aircraft as, it must be said, do the so-called official figures published by different sources. The quoted ranges of individual types must be treated particularly carefully as they are usually consideraby more optimistic than what might be regarded as a reasonable operational range when account is taken of wind, weather, manoeuvring over the target or when attacked by fighters and the need to carry sufficient fuel to proceed to a diversion if the home airfield is not available on return. The effective operational radius of action of an aircraft is thus often surprisingly small when compared with the manufacturer's published range in ideal conditions. This goes some way to explaining the almost complete failure of Bomber Command, despite a significant effort, to impose any real influence on the campaign in Norway.

The Blenheim Mk IV, which was normally confined to daylight operations, had a top speed of 266 mph and a nominal range of 1460 miles. But its bombload was small, only 1000 lbs, and by 1940 it was no match for the faster and better armed German fighters. Its effective radius of operation was never more than 500 miles from base. Of the medium bombers, the most effective and eventually the most numerous was the Wellington. Its ingenious geodettic lattice work construction made it strong and durable and it could withstand a lot of punishment. Its range was only 1200 miles with a 4500 lb payload, but its radius of action could be increased slightly by reducing the bombload, as could that of all the other medium bombers. The Hampden had a similar range with 4000 lbs of bombs and was slightly faster than the Wellington with a top speed of 254 mph. But the Hampden had no armour and a poor defensive capability despite forward, dorsal and ventral guns: it was largely used in the minelaying role during the Norwegian campaign. The biggest of the 'heavies' was the Whitley, but it was slow and cumbersome and had poor defensive armament: it could carry 5000 lbs of bombs over about 1250 miles. The potential capability of Bomber Command to act in Norway was thus severely limited from the outset and only the

Whitley had a sufficient radius of action to reach the farthest of the airfields in Central Norway. None could penetrate to the Narvik area.

It was hoped to use all the bombers in daylight, but provision had been made to operate at night if necessary. However, early experience soon showed that, for different reasons, both expectations were over-optimistic. Bomber Command entered the war under a very restrictive policy of confining attacks to the German fleet and the dropping of propaganda leaflets on the mainland. This was necessitated not only by the incapacity of Bomber Command itself to carry out offensive missions, but also from a desire not to provoke Germany into unrestricted bombing of Britain until Fighter Command could be built up to face such a threat. Shipping searches were conducted over the North Sea throughout the months of September to mid-December without conspicuous success, and after a bad start in September, without significant loss.

But in the dying days of the year there were far-reaching developments. On 14 December, the largest shipping search of the war so far was mounted involving twenty three Hampdens, seven Whitleys and twelve Wellingtons. The Hampdens and Whitleys saw no action, but the Wellingtons of 99 Squadron were engaged by flak and German fighters at low level north of Wilhelmshaven and five were shot down. Worse was to follow. On 18 December twenty four Wellingtons of 9, 37 and 149 Squadrons were tasked with a similar mission. Approaching from the north, they were attacked south of Heligoland by a mixed force of Bf 109s and 110s which, benefiting from experience, made their approach from above and abeam rather than from astern. The Wellington proved defenceless against this form of attack as the front and rear turrets could not traverse to the side. Furthermore, as the Commander-in-Chief of Bomber Command, Air Chief Marshal Sir Edgar Ludlow-Hewitt, had regularly pointed out, the practice of air gunnery had been woefully neglected in the run up to the war. The aircrew category of air gunner was not even formally recognised until January 1939, before which the task had fallen to volunteer ground crew. Twelve aircraft were shot down, nine falling to the guns of the twin engine Bf 110s of ZG 76, and three more badly damaged. Apart from one more isolated effort on 12 April 1940, this virtually marked the end of daylight operations by the Wellingtons, Hampdens and Whitleys, and henceforth, except for the Blenheims, Bomber Command aircraft were generally restricted to operations at night.

This shattering experience for Bomber Command was to have an overriding importance for air operations in the Norwegian campaign. For the inescapable conclusion that daylight operations were not tenable was accompanied by the recognition that night operations had proved to be almost valueless. Deficiencies in navigation equipment and techniques made it quite likely that the bomber would not even find the target area let alone identify an individual target: the need for a specialist navigation course had not even been recognised until 1938. In the improbable event that the target was found, the inadequacies of bombsights and the problem of illuminating the target made precision bombing at night an impossible task. Even the bombs themselves were suspect, frequently not exploding or causing little damage if they did so. Although Bomber Command was nominally capable of operating at night, very little attention had been given to training or the development of tactics: in 1938 only ten per cent of Command training had been conducted in the dark. These deficiencies had been masked to a certain extent by the Whitley leaflet raids, which although reported as successful, left no firm evidence on the ground as to whether individual targets could be located and destroyed. The tasks assigned to Bomber Command in the Norwegian campaign were therefore largely incapable of being attained: given that for the twenty two years of its existence, the stated priority of the RAF had been the prosecution of strategic bombing, it was painfully apparent in 1940 that it had lamentably little to show for it.

The early months of 1940 were comparatively quiet in the North Sea and may be quickly passed over. Nearly 400 North Sea shipping searches were conducted by Bomber Command up to 1 April of which 337 were by Blenheims of No. 2 Group. Most were uneventful, but surface ships were bombed on six occasions without success: only five Blenheims were lost. The highlight of this period was the sinking of a U-boat on 11 March by a Blenheim of 82 Squadron captained by Squadron Leader M. V. Delap.

Early April produced the first indication of the forthcoming invasion of Norway although the intelligence significance was not recognised. On the 4th Blenheims on a reconnaissance sortie in dreadful weather with a cloudbase of two hundred feet spotted two German warships in the Wilhelmshaven Roads, identified as the *Scharnhorst* and the *Gneisenau*. These were attacked by two of the force of six Blenheims without scoring any hits, but photographs taken on the raid disclosed two large ships at anchor, another alongside the quay, five destroyers, many minesweepers and sixty merchant vessels. A follow up raid on the following day was thwarted by weather, but on the night of the 6th a night reconnaissance by eight Wellingtons, six Whitleys and fourteen Hampdens disclosed further intense shipping activity at Eckerndorf and a battleship steaming north twenty miles north of Heligoland. A Hampden spotted about fifty ships moving west one hundred miles from Borkum. The main invasion fleet had actually sailed in the early hours of 7 April and this was confirmed at 0800 when a patrolling Hudson identified a cruiser and six destroyers, escorted by eight fighters steaming north at eighteen knots, twenty eight miles west of the Horns Reef. This proved to be Groups 1 and 2 of the invasion force on their way to Narvik and Trondheim.

A force of sixteen Blenheims led by Wing Commander Basil Embry,[6] four from 21 Squadron and twelve from 107 Squadron, was tasked to attack the convoy. They estimated the probable new position of the German ships and by careful dead reckoning navigation located them as expected. They attacked at 6,000 feet under intense fire from the ships, but no hits were achieved even though conditions for precision bombing were good: the difficulties of hitting a moving target at sea were once again clearly demonstrated. Although details of the enemy fleet were immediately passed on W/T, they were received at only one station at Drem in Scotland where the airman receiving the message failed to appreciate its significance and took no action. But photographs taken on the raid disclosed a fairly accurate estimate of the composition of the force as one pocket battleship, two cruisers and ten destroyers. This was the sighting which set in train the sailing of the Home Fleet that evening, but several valuable hours were lost because of the communications failure and the Royal Navy never had a chance of catching the German force. In any case, as we have seen, even this intelligence did not alert the Admiralty to the real intention of the enemy ships.

A follow-up raid by twenty three Wellingtons failed to locate the ships. The difficulties of daylight operations were only too apparent. The aircraft needed cloud cover in daylight to avoid enemy fighters, but if the cloud cover was too extensive, the chances of finding a target at sea (or overland for that matter) were greatly reduced. The ideal conditions were thus rarely encountered. A large scale raid planned for 8 April was thwarted for this very reason, and again on the 11th six Hampdens on a shipping search off Kristiansand had to abandon their task because the weather was too clear. It proved to be a constantly recurring problem in the North Sea during the next few months and it was a dilemma which was never resolved by Bomber Command until 1944 when the Allies at last achieved air superiority by day.

When it was recognised that the German invasion force had reached its destinations unscathed, the task of Bomber Command became to try to catch the German ships as they returned to their home ports and to slow down the German expansion in Southern Norway. Coastal Command reconnaissance flights had supplied some information on the whereabouts of the German ships. The presence of two cruisers (*Köln* and *Könisberg*) at Bergen had been reported on 9 April and twelve Wellingtons of 9 and 15 Squadrons were immediately dispatched. But precision bombing even against ships at anchor was not easy and no hits were scored. The *Köln* escaped the same night, but the *Königsberg* was sunk on the following day by Fleet Air Arm Skuas from Hatston as has already been recounted. The lessons learned regarding daylight bombing on 18 December were reinforced on the 12 April when eighty-three aircraft, a mix of Wellingtons, Hampdens and Blenheims were tasked to attack the *Scharnhorst, Gneisenau* and the *Hipper* which had been sighted by the Hudsons off south-west Norway on their return to Germany. This raid was thwarted by the weather and the German ships were not located, but as an alternative twelve Hampdens attacked a warship in Kristiansand and were intercepted by German fighters: six were destroyed by beam attacks against which there was no defence. Three Wellingtons were also lost on this raid which was the last occasion that Wellingtons and Hampdens were used in any major daylight operation.

A more worthwhile policy than looking for ships at sea which were difficult targets both to find and attack would have been to attack Northern Germany from which the lifeline to Norway had to be sustained, for there were critical shortages of supplies for at least the first two weeks of the campaign as we have already seen. But the restriction on bombing land targets in Germany was still in force and so the ports and their hinterland of roads and railways were left untouched throughout the whole period of the Norwegian campaign. Even so, although night bombing could have been conducted with relative safety, the chances of securing a significant success would have been relatively slim.

The British landings in Central Norway began on the 16 April and thereafter Bomber Command concentrated on night attacks on Norwegian airfields. The formulation of this policy is laconically explained by Air Chief Marshal Sir Edgar Ludlow-Hewitt who had left Bomber Command on 3 April 1940:

> The main fighting on land took place in the neighbourhood of Trondheim which is 800 miles from the principle bases of our heavy bombers in England and 600 miles from our nearest bases in Scotland. The principle German air bases are at Stavanger and in the neighbourhood of Oslo. Stavanger is 350 miles across the North Sea from our nearest northern aerodrome and 500 miles from our English air bases. Oslo is 500 miles from our most northerly aerodromes and 600 from our main bases. In order, therefore, to get to these German air bases, or to attack their sea communications across the Skagerrak our bombers have to fly as much as 1200 miles there and back across the North Sea; or at the very least 700 miles to the nearest aerodrome at Stavanger and back to Scotland. On the other hand the Germans have aerodromes in Norway at a distance of 250 to 300 miles from Trondheim. If, however, we could prevent the Germans from using these bases in Norway they would have to fly from Denmark which is 100 miles further; and if we could knock-out the bases in Denmark they would have to fly from their main bases in Germany which could make the distance 500 miles, or 1000 miles return. This begins to compare more favourably with the distance we have to fly from England.[7]

It would certainly have proved an inestimable bonus if the Luftwaffe could have been precluded from using the Norwegian and Danish airfields. The maximum range of the German bombers was scarcely more than 1000 miles, and from the nearest German bases only the Ju 88 could have reached Aandalsnes, and Trondheim and Namsos would have been out of reach. It would have been quite impossible for the Luftwaffe to harass troops on the ground in the Gudbrandsdal, and the Allied bridgeheads, and consequently the supply chain, would have been far more secure. The selection of the airfields as the main targets for Bomber Command was undoubtedly the correct decision – if only effective means of hitting them could be found.

But, in fact, the task of attacking the airfields in Norway was fraught with difficulties. Vaernes, which it was essential to neutralise if counter-invasion through Trondheim was to have any chance of success, and Oslo (Fornebu) were out of range of the Blenheims, by now the only aircraft considered capable of daylight bombing, and could only be attacked with reasonable safety by Whitleys at night. It is notoriously difficult, even today, to close an airfield for any length of time by air bombardment as we were reminded in the Falklands War in 1982 by the Vulcan raid on Stanley. But at least in 1982, the attack was facilitated by good navigation aids and a precision bomb sight. In 1940, as we have already noted, the chances of achieving a significant success at night with the aids available were very slim – and so it proved.

Two hundred and seventy-four night sorties were flown against Norwegian airfields between 15 April and the 9 May, mostly by Whitleys and Wellingtons, which were occasionally joined by Hampdens.[8] Discounting a few which crashed in England on return from their mission, only four Wellingtons and five Whitleys were lost on these operations, proving that night bombing at this stage of the war was a relatively safe occupation. But many aircraft did not reach their target areas because of weather and even those which bombed their targets achieved little success. A Blenheim reconnaissance of Stavanger on 30 April estimated that there were still one hundred and fifty useable German aircraft on the airfield, and as the troops on the ground would be only too ready to vouch, the bombing appeared to have little effect on the German air effort. After 10 May night bomber operations were directed towards the Ruhr.

The Blenheims were used only against Stavanger airfield during the day as they did not have the range to reach either Vaernes or Fornebu. 107 Squadron led by Wing Commander Basil Embry was moved to Lossiemouth for this task: he has graphically described the difficulties of their task in his autobiography.[9] His plan was ambitious: to mount two attacks daily of twelve aircraft each. But even though he was later assisted by 110 Squadron, on no single day did it prove possible to launch a total of more than twelve aircraft. In all, one hundred and nine sorties were targetted against Stavanger between 15 April and 2 May when the Blenheims were totally withdrawn from Norwegian operations because of the increasing threat against the Low Countries. Comparatively slow and unmanoeuvrable, they needed the ideal conditions of cloud and visibility both to locate the target and to hide from enemy fighters. Many of the crews did not reach their targets: fifty-six at least, more than half the total, are known to have abandoned their task. Losses were not unduly heavy, only six succumbing to enemy fighters or flak. Some German aircraft were destroyed on the ground, but not many.

One further aspect of Bomber Command operations deserves mention. In the face of air attack the Royal Navy had quicky concluded that it could not safely use surface ships south of Bergen and therefore entrusted submarines with the task of disrupting the German reinforcement routes to Oslo. But Hampdens of Bomber Command were given the task of laying magnetic mines in the coastal waters of northern Germany and in the Oslo Fiord. The mines were dropped by parachute from 500 feet which could be hazardous work, particularly in a heavily defended area such as the Kiel Canal. Operations commenced on the night of 13 April when fifteen Hampdens laid mines in the sea-lanes off Denmark: one aircraft was lost. In all, two hundred and eighty-four minelaying sorties were mounted for a loss of only seven aircraft: a very fair return even though not all aircraft managed to complete their tasking. However, the results were by no means decisive as between mid-April and mid-June, the Germans lost only nine per cent of their shipping in these waters to all forms of attack including submarines. On 25 April, a minelaying Hampden of 49 Squadron had the dubious distinction of being the first Bomber Command aircraft to be shot down by a fighter at night; it was claimed by a Bf 109 near Sylt.

Bomber Command also flew a number of reconnaissance and shipping searches, but more often than not without success. In all, Bomber Command flew 931 operations in support of the Norwegian campaign for the loss of thirty-six aircraft (3.9 per cent). The losses were not especially high, but the rewards were poor and overall it could not be claimed by even the most optimistic supporter of air bombardment that Bomber Command had any positive influence on the battle for Norway. Some experience was gained and lessons learned, the most notable being that the heavy bombers were too vulnerable to operate in daylight. It was to be nearly three years before Bomber Command could develop its equipment and tactics to operate effectively at night. In 1940 it was still a hollow threat.

The Demise of an Air Force . . .

The contribution of the Norwegian Air Force in the battle for Norway can be quickly told. Twelve Gloster Gladiators, a fighter already obsolescent in the RAF, had been acquired by 1940 of which seven, based at Oslo Fornebu, were serviceable on the evening of 8 April. Five aircraft led by Lieutenant Rolf Tradin, the Wing's deputy commander, scrambled at 0700 on the following morning on reports of a large formation of aircraft approaching Oslo. It was Goering's 'demonstration' against the city. The enemy force, judged to be about seventy bombers and transports, was intercepted at 5000 feet and two He 111s and two Dornier Do 17s were reported shot down.[10] But the Gladiators were heavily outnumbered and were themselves attacked by both Bf 110s and He 111s and only one aircraft was able to return to Fornebu. One crashed, and of the other three which landed on frozen lakes, one sank through the ice and had to be abandoned. One other Gladiator had taken off from Fornebu that morning and although engaging German bombers, none were destroyed and the aircraft eventually landed on a thinly frozen lake and also had to be abandoned. The two Gladiators on the ground at Fornebu when the airfield was attacked were both destroyed. The remnants of the Norwegian Air Force, one Gladiator, two Tiger Moths and a few Fokker C Vs were gathered together at Lake Vangsmjösa. The remaining Gladiator made one more reconnaissance sortie on 21 April, but the aircraft hit some trees after suffering an engine failure and had to be written off. The Norwegian Air Force made no further contribution to the defence of Central Norway.

. . . And of a Squadron

The Air Minstry had never been enthusiastic regarding the dispatch of valuable fighter aircraft to Scandinavia, and in any case the absence of suitable airfields in Central Norway precluded the use of the higher performance modern fighters, the Spitfire or the Hurricane. However, following the representations made by General Paget to General Massy on 21 April of the urgent requirement for air support, it was decided to allocate at least one RAF squadron of Gloster Gladiators to Norway. The Gladiator was a single engine, single seat, biplane fighter first introduced into service in 1937. Armed with four Browning 0.303 machine guns, its maximum speed was 249 mph at 10,000 feet.[11] Although the last biplane fighter to enter production and intended only as a stop-gap measure until the faster, better armed monoplane fighters could be introduced in sufficient numbers, the Gladiator was by no means hopelessly out-classed by the German aircraft it encounterd in the Norwegian campaign. There were only two Gladiator squadrons in Britain in April 1940, 247 and 263, and the choice fell upon the latter. 263 Squadron was based at Filton for the night defence of Bristol and South Wales, a role which was totally unsuited to the Gladiator and whose loss to the air defence of Great Britain could hardly be considered too serious.

Squadron Leader Whitney Straight had been sent as the RAF Liaison Officer to the Norwegian High Command on 17 April charged with locating a suitable landing ground to the south of Trondheim. There were just two possible sites situated on frozen lakes, Lesjaskog which lies on the watershed between the Romsdal and the Gudbrandsdal, and Vangsmjösa, a high site in the Valdres about sixy miles south-west of Kvam. Whitney Straight strongly recommended Vangsmjösa: it was clear of snow, large enough for two squadrons, and had good road connections with the Sognefiord which could be used as a port of entry for supplies independently of the other lines of communication. The remnants of the Norwegian Air Force were already in situ at Vangsmjösa.

The Air Staff nevertheless preferred Lesjaskog because it was closer to the British area of operations in the Gudbrandsdal and to the bridgehead at Aandalsnes and less vulnerable to a rapid German advance. Although Straight continued to believe the decision mistaken, Lesjaskog was certainly the better geographical choice and it is unlikely to have affected the end result. Lake Lesjaskog is about eight miles long and one thousand yards across at its widest point, surrounded by trees and bordered by the railway and road from Aandalsnes to Dombaas. It had been used in peacetime as an emergency landing strip by the Norwegian Air Force.

The advance party of the air contingent arrived at Aandalsnes on 23 April on the cruiser *Arethusa*, accompanied by fifty tons of aviation fuel which to the disgust of the crew was strapped onto the deck. They immediately ran into difficulties. There was no military transport available and even though the party was able to requisition two lorries, this proved totally inadequate to move everything forward to Lesjaskog. Their stores, hastily collected, had been loaded into boxes without labels and each had to be opened to ascertain its contents. All of this was done under spasmodic air attack, although fortunately the ships in the harbour rather than the quaysides were attracting the major share of the Luftwaffe's attention.

When they arrived at Lesjaskog, the prospect was no more encouraging. Some preparatory work to clear a runway had been completed by local labour, but deep snow covered the ice between the edge of the lake and the runway and everything had to be moved to the runway edge by horse drawn sledge. Work continued throughout the night and by the morning of the 24th the improvised airstrip was as ready for operations as it ever would be. Two guns from a battery of Royal Navy Oerlikons under Sub-Lieutenant Goodale provided a modest anti-aircraft capability. Fuel and ammunition had been laid out alongside the runway, and although recognisably vulnerable to air attack, there was little alternative if the aircraft were to be refuelled and re-armed reasonably quickly. Only two refuelling troughs had been sent and so every available jug or container which could hold fuel had been pressed into use. The starter trolleys were useless as their batteries were discharged and there was no acid. Finally, there was only one armourer for eighteen aircraft, or seventy-two guns.

263 Squadron's aircraft were meanwhile on their way to Norway on the aircraft carrier *Glorious*. One aircraft had already been lost when it crashed into the sea on its approach to the carrier, but a replacement was soon found. On the afternoon of the 24th the Squadron flew off whilst still one hundred and fifty miles from the Norwegian coast in two waves of nine aircraft, each wave led by a Fleet Air Arm Skua to assist with the navigation. All aircraft arrived safely at Lesjaskog by 1800. Even as he flew in, the Commanding Officer, Squadron Leader J. W. Donaldson, recognised the enormity of the problems he faced. He saw the extent of the bombing at Aandalsnes and the difficulty of obtaining supplies, and although 263 was tasked with co-operating with the Army, he recognised that protecting themselves and their landing strip would

itself be a difficult enough task. A meeting with the Norwegian Liaison Officer, Captain Ewin, did nothing to allay his fears. The Germans had been seen overflying the lake and were almost certainly aware of what was going on. He also warned that the lake was totally defenceless against an assault by parachute troops and that the Germans were already using them in large numbers – something of an exaggeration. The runway was already rough because snow from the banks on the edge of the strip which had melted during the day had refrozen in ruts overnight. There was no flarepath and landing at night would have been extremely hazardous. Nevertheless, Donaldson agreed that from dawn the following morning he would undertake standing patrols at Kvam where the most recent defensive position in the Gudbrandsdal had been established.

The night was bitterly cold and dawn on the 25th found all the flying controls frozen solid and engines difficult to start. Even so two aircraft were airborne at 0445 to patrol the lake and within fifteen minutes had shot down a He 115 reconnaissance aircraft. However, whilst the patrol was occupied with the 115, a He 111 bombed the lake although without hitting either aircraft or runway. Bombing continued throughout the day, the enemy usually approaching in vics of three aircraft bombing and machine gunning the lake from various heights. After a while the ground staff took shelter in the woods leaving the officers and the NCOs to refuel and re-arm the aircraft. Whilst undoubtedly reprehensible, none of the ground crew had ever been subjected to air attack before, and nor had they in any way been pyschologically prepared for the ordeal. They had been trained in a Service which regarded the aircrew as the fighting men leaving the ground tradesmen in the security and safety of the home base. They did not even have the benefit of the camaraderie of squadron spirit, for they were brought together at the last minute, neither knowing each other nor their officers and SNCOs. Fortunately, this lesson was quickly learned and only months later on the airfields of southern England the ground crews soon became very familiar with the trauma of air bombardment.

Whenever there was a Gladiator patrol airborne the German attacks were wild and inaccurate, but one early bombing run caught all aircraft on the ground, destroying four and injuring three pilots, fortunately none seriously. In those taxing conditions it took ninety minutes to turn round aircraft for another patrol. At 0900 six aircraft were able to get airborne and actually provide some air support over the ground positions at Kvam. Their role was to deter aircraft spotting for artillery fire, but they were able to remain on task for only thirty minutes. Meanwhile, Flight Lieutenant Mills shot down one of six He 111s attacking the lake. One Gladiator was lost with engine failure, but there was something of a morale boost to the hard pressed pilots and ground crew when an attack by Pilot Officer McNamara on a He 111 over the lake itself so disconcerted the pilot that he stalled and spun into the ground in full view of everybody on the lake.

Nevetheless, by midday the incessant bombing attacks had destroyed ten aircraft on the ground and by mid afternoon the runway was virtually unusable and the belted ammunition exhausted. Squadron Leader Donaldson with the remaining four aircraft flew off to a small strip at Setnesmoen near Aandalsnes, and after destroying any useful stores remaining at Lesjaskog, the whole Squadron had joined them by midnight. The following day Pilot Officer Craig-Adams had to abandon his aircraft by parachute after an engine failure and by evening the remaining three aircraft were unserviceable with engine problems. In any case aviation fuel had now run out and the three aircraft left were destroyed to prevent their falling into enemy hands. By the evening of the 27th the pilots had embarked in the cargo ship *Delius* to return to Scapa Flow. Even then they could not escape the harassment of the Luftwaffe and were subjected to regular bombing until they eventually escaped out of range.

They had been in Norway just three eventful days. They claimed six aircraft destroyed and eight possibles, and although all eighteen Gladiators had been lost, none had been destroyed in combat. Some valuable lessons had been learnt, the Gladiator was too slow if an attack developed into a stern chase and therefore it was essential to get into position for a diving beam attack with a deflection shot, which whilst more difficult to achieve, gave a much higher chance of success. This was the same lesson learned by the Bf 110s just four months previously against the RAF bomber formations. But, of course, the Squadron's primary task had not been self defence but support of the Army, and in this role they had mounted just one short patrol on the morning of the 25th. Their contribution to the ground battle which was so badly needed had been virtually negligible. However, as will be recounted later, 263 Squadron was not yet finished with Norway, returning to Bardufoss less than a month later. Once again, in rather different circumstances, 263 lost all her aircraft.

Fleet Air Arm Intervention

It required very little time to discover that Bomber Command could do little to prevent the steady but remorseless advance of German troops into Central Norway and that the establishment of fighter aircraft ashore was severely constrained by the lack of suitable airfields and the inadequate lines of communication. The only remaining option therefore for providing air support for the hard pressed soldiers on the ground in Central Norway was from the sea. The Fleet Air Arm as an independent formation had been in existence for only three years in 1940, and the dogma of a strategic role for the RAF in the inter-war years had paralysed the development of maritime-air operations just as it had resulted in the neglect of land-air operations.

It is no part of this book to examine the arguments for and against the creation of an independent Naval Air Arm which had raged back and forth between the Royal Navy and the RAF in the inter-war years. Suffice to say that today many of the arguments paraded by distinguished proponents on both sides seem narrow and unconvincing. Even after the war, that doyen of air strategists, Marshal of the Royal Air Force Sir John Slessor was able to write.

> I cannot call to mind any warlike action against an enemy maritime objective carried out by a Naval aircraft from a carrier, that was not done more often and just as effectively by an RAF aircraft from a base on the shore.[12]

Despite the fact that he was on the Joint Planning Staff in 1940, he appears to have forgotten the campaign in Norway. For whilst defence of the bridgeheads, although of enormous importance to the Navy, is not strictly a maritime objective, the proponents of land based air power would have even less readily admitted the efficacy of carrier borne aircraft against land objectives. Nevertheless, the only practicable way of bringing fighter support to Central Norway was by means of the aircraft carrier, as it was in the war against Japan in the Far East and again in the South Atlantic in 1982. The area of operations in Central Norway was far beyond the radius of action of fighters based in Scotland and the aircraft carrier had a unique opportunity to prove its worth. But despite many worthwhile individual successes, it did not really influence the campaign as its advocates might have wished.

One of the main reasons stems from the indecision and lack of purpose between the wars. There were only seven aircraft carriers available at the outbreak of war of which six were of First World War vintage or earlier, with only the *Hermes* actually designed as a carrier. The only exception was the *Ark Royal* which had made her appearance in 1938. The aircraft were also equally obsolescent, Sea Gladiators, Skuas, Rocs and Swordfish.

The Sea Gladiator was identical to the RAF version except for the provision of an arrester hook and catapult launch points, and whilst it could be expected to perform creditably against the He 111, Ju 87 and Do 17, it would be hard pressed by the Ju 88 and outclassed by the German fighters. The Blackburn Skua was the first operational monoplane in the Fleet Air Arm and the first aircraft designed for dive bombing, but it was a hybrid aircraft expected to double as both fighter and dive bomber and in 1940 was not really effective in either role. Its top speed was only 225 mph and its nominal range 760 miles. It too was outclassed by its more modern opponents. The Roc was an unsuccessful fighter derivative of the Skua, but the remaining aircraft in the Fleet Air Arm inventory, the Swordfish, has a mythology all of its own. Designed as a torpedo, spotter and reconnaissance aircraft, it could also double as a bomber and minelayer. Its maximum speed in level flight was only 139 mph and barely 200 in the steepest dive, and its nominal range with weapons only 546 miles. The Swordfish, despite its antiquated design and appearance, had a number of heroic feats to its credit, including as we have already seen at Narvik and later at Taranto and elsewhere. Because of its very slow speed and tight turning circle, it was not such an easy aircraft for fighters to destroy as its mediocre performance might have suggested. Nevertheless, the situations, even in Norway in 1940, in which the Swordfish could be effectively used were constrained by the overall unfavourable air situation.

Ark Royal and *Glorious* had both been carrying out training in the Mediterranean until they were summoned home in early April 1940. It had been intended originally that they would participate in 'Hammer', but when this operation was cancelled the Admiralty undertook instead to use them to provide air support for operations already in hand in Central Norway. The first of the modern aircraft carriers, *Ark Royal* displaced 27,700 tons and could embark up to seventy-two aircraft. *Glorious*, a much older ship, could only carry about forty aircraft comfortably and she was also ferrying the eighteen Gladiators of 263 Squadron on their way to Lesjaskog which further reduced her own complement of aircraft. The total complement of aircraft embarked, excluding 263 Squadron, were eighteen Sea Gladiators and eleven Skuas in *Glorious* and another eighteen Skuas, twenty-one Swordfish and five Rocs in *Ark Royal*.

The Carrier Task Force under Vice Admiral 'Nutty' Wells who flew his flag in *Ark Royal*, consisted of the *Glorious*, the cruisers *Berwick* and *Curlew* and six destroyers.[13] The Carrier Task Force was another innovation of the new war and this was the first occasion on which the Royal Navy had mounted such an operation. The *Curlew* was a particularly valuable addition as she was one of the few ships fitted with radar with a range of seventy miles or so against high flying targets. The objectives assigned to the Task Force were to protect naval ships and convoys, to give cover to the troops at the landing places and to attack the German occupied air bases in Norway. They left Scapa Flow early on the morning of 23 April and embarked the Skuas of 800 and 801 Squadrons from Royal Naval Air Station Hatson, many of whose crews had already seen action over Norway during the sinking of the *Königsberg* at Bergen on 10 April.

Their first problem was that perpetual concern of all naval task forces, the need for self protection. It is axiomatic that a major weakness of a carrier task force is that the scale of effort needed for self protection can often outweigh the residual balance available for offensive action. In the worst case, the task force has to devote its whole effort to self protection, or alternatively is forced to operate from an area where its own strike capability is severely inhibited. Admiral Wells was certainly not confident of the ability of the Sea Gladiators and Rocs to protect his ships and decided not to come closer than one hundred and twenty miles to the Norwegian coast where he might hope to remain undetected. The fighter patrols which could be maintained over Namsos and Aandalsnes were thus very small, never normally more than three Skuas, and only on station for short periods.

The weather on the 24th was bad for most of the day, but eighteen Gladiators of 263 Squadron were eventually launched in the late afternoon. At the same time six Skuas were dispatched to attack opportunity targets in the Gudbrandsdal Valley. One He 111 was claimed destroyed and one damaged, but an early encounter with Ju 88s clearly showed they had the legs on the Skua and escaped without difficulty. Two aircraft were lost as a result of running out of fuel. The following day a raid was planned against shipping and airfield targets at Trondheim by Swordfish of 810 and 820 and Skuas of 800, 801 and 803 Squadrons. The Skuas were also to provide fighter escort for the Swordfish whilst the Gladiators maintained a patrol over the carriers. The main target was supposed to be a cruiser in the harbour, but in fact there were no warships although two oilers and a large transport were damaged. A hangar and a petrol dump were set on fire at Vaernes. The formations encountered heavy ground fire but saw few enemy aircraft, only one Heinkel was definitely claimed although other aircraft were destroyed on the ground. But four Swordfish and four Skuas were lost, five to enemy action and the rest for other reasons. This was a poor rate of return and did nothing to stem the German attacks on Namsos and Aandalsnes which were now almost constant throughout the day.

On 26 April the Task Force was tentatively brought into eighty miles offshore and an attempt made to maintain a regular patrol over Kvam and Otta. One He 111 was destroyed for the loss of a single Skua, which was proving no match for the Ju 88. In the afternoon the Germans made a major attack on Aandalsnes, but the lack of communications and the distance of the Task Force offshore precluded the Skuas arriving in time to intercept the enemy bombers. They patrolled the smoking town until dusk, but no further raids developed.

By the morning of the 27th, only four Skuas remained serviceable, but they continued to operate as far as resources allowed and accounted for another He 111 over Aandalsnes. Throughout this brief campaign, the ability to assist ground forces was severely hampered by the lack of air-to-ground communications: there was no way of directing the air effort towards the most hard pressed troops or the most profitable targets. Encounters with enemy aircraft were mere chance and the scale of effort required to mount a standing patrol over the front line was simply not available.

Captain Partridge RM, CO of 801 Squadron, had an amusing encounter. He shot down a He 111, but in return a stray bullet hit and stopped the engine of his Skua and he had to force land on a road. Not being quite sure on which side of the front line they had landed, Partridge and his observer took shelter in an empty farmhouse. A few minutes afterwards, hearing footsteps in the snow, they were somewhat startled to be joined by the crew of the Heinkel which they had shot down shortly before. After making the appropriate introductions in broken English, they settled down to await developments. Fortunately, it turned out to be a Norwegian ski patrol which eventually discovered them.[14]

At 0430 on 28 April, Vaernes was heavily raided by Swordfish with a Skua escort. Several aircraft were destroyed on the ground and five Heinkels claimed in the air as well as damage to hangars and other ground installations. However, the Task Force was itself attacked on the 28th, although none of the ships were hit, Admiral Wells decided to withdraw further out to sea for a period of recuperation after five days of heavy fighting and serious aircraft losses. On 30 April *Ark Royal*, rejoined the following day by the *Glorious* which had meanwhile been back towards Scotland to refuel and to fly on additional aircraft, returned to cover the evacuation from Aandalsnes and Namsos.

The evacuation itself was however proceeding reasonably quietly as much of the enemy air effort on 1 May was devoted against the Task Force. On this occasion there were several very near misses, but once again all the ships escaped unscathed. The Gladiators, which flew constant patrols throughout the day, had very little success either and one Skua was shot down by the home side; fratricide that was to occur with alarming frequency throughout the war.

Manoeuvring ships at sea had once again proved immune to attack from the level bomber. Nevertheless, the scale of the Luftwaffe assault was sufficient for the Admiralty to decide that the risk of losing their scarce aircraft carriers was no longer commensurate with the advantages of maintaining air support in the area as the evacuation now had only two more days to run. By 3 May, *Ark Royal* and *Glorious* were back at Scapa Flow, the ships undamaged, but with their aircraft complement severely depleted. The final score sheet did not look too unfavourable, twenty-one enemy aircraft were claimed destroyed in the air or on the ground for the loss of four Swordfish and nine Skuas. But this was a mere pinprick given the numbers of enemy aircraft now deployed at airfields in Denmark and Norway. The ships had survived prolonged heavy air attack, but it had done little to assuage the fears in the Admiralty for the operation of capital ships in a hostile air environment.

Several other lessons were driven home, the most potent of which was that the Skuas and Rocs were no match for the aircraft ranged against them. Several of the claims for aircraft destroyed were for the very slow He 115 seaplane which would have been easy prey for almost any fighter. The Skuas could only hope to catch a He 111 or the Ju 88 if they could creep up unobserved and catch the enemy unawares: if they were seen the pilot could simply accelerate out of range. The Rocs, with no forward firing gun, were totally useless. It is arguable that the Sea Gladiators should perhaps have achieved better results than they did against aircraft attacking the Task Force in the latter stages, after all 263 Squadron was to perform very creditably in the Narvik area and had achieved some success in Central Norway in the short period before their frozen lake was destroyed beneath them. One of the limitations of the fighter patrols was the poor quality of the radar and the inexperience of the radar operators. It was virtually impossible to differentiate between friend and foe and the method of broadcast control employed quickly became chaotic: the fighters spent much of the time chasing their own tails. There was much food for thought, but as the war in the Pacific was to show, the carrier task group was eventually to become a very formidable force.

So ended the air war in Central Norway. The losses in terms of modern aircraft were modest, fortunately so with the Battle of Britain only weeks away. But the achievements were negligible apart from the single highlight of the successful Fleet Air Arm attack on the harbour at Bergen. A handful of German bombers and reconnaissance aircraft were destroyed, but virtually no support was rendered to the troops on the ground and the two bridgeheads were left almost totally unprotected.

Nevertheless, as we have already seen, without adequate air support the ground operations in Central Norway were simply not sustainable. How did we get into this unenviable situation? The RAF had neither the means nor, for good reasons, the will to provide wholehearted support in Norway and warned both the War Cabinet and the other Chiefs of Staff accordingly. But their warnings went unheeded, the politicians, driven by Mr Churchill's overriding obsession to prosecute the war whenever the opportunity appeared, either did not recognise the deficiency or allowed themselves to be persuaded that this critical missing link could be disregarded. The equation was simple, if the Allies felt impelled to intervene in Central Norway they should have endeavoured to ensure that the necessary air support was provided. This could have been achieved only by securing the use of at least one suitably located all-weather airfield, supplemented from the outset by the all out support of the Fleet Air Arm stationed sufficiently close inshore to provide the maximum level of support over the bridgeheads and the lines of communication. It is doubtful if these requirements could have been met successfully, but what is certain is that no real effort was made to meet them. The conclusion is therefore self evident, the Allies should not have tried to intervene in Central Norway – it was an operation doomed from the outset.

The Master Card – Luftwaffe Operations in Central Norway

'The moral effect of bombing stands to the material in a proportion
of 20 to 1.'

Lord Trenchard[1]

The Rise of the Luftwaffe

The inability of the RAF and the Fleet Air Arm, heavily constrained as they were by a shortage of modern aircraft and the lack of suitable airfields, to provide adequate air support for the operations in Norway is indisputable. But how did the Germans fare in providing for this essential element of combined forces in the new style of modern warfare? That the Luftwaffe made a major contribution to the ability of the Wehrmacht to achieve their objectives is equally irrefutable, not only during the initial invasion phase, but also in establishing their stranglehold on the whole of Southern and Central Norway and thwarting the attempts of the Allies to regain ground lost. German air superiority by day was virtually complete, and the Luftwaffe was able to apply all the advantages of air power without fear of serious interference. The Luftwaffe did not by any means have it all its own way in the Narvik area, but even here the influence of air power proved to be significant: we shall look at air operations in the northern theatre later.[2]

The much publicised growth of the Luftwaffe in the pre-war years had caused profound apprehension in the minds of the politicians, the military and even the general public, and more than any other factor had stimulated the climate for British rearmament in the late 1930s. Although most of the hysteria in Britain was concentrated on the supposedly devastating affect on civilian morale of strategic bombing, it was not in fact in this area that the Germans had concentrated their efforts. Throughout the war they never managed to introduce a truly strategic bomber, but the aircraft they did introduce into service in the pre-war years were more versatile, capable of supporting ground operations as well as carrying out precision bombing in good weather. The Luftwaffe, unlike the RAF, had not forgotten how to support the army during the inter-war years. Even so, the much vaunted proficiency of the Luftwaffe was in some respects a chimera; in its conception and development it contained fundamental flaws which ultimately led to its subjection and defeat – but that is not part of this story.

In Norway in 1940, as in Poland eight months earlier, the Luftwaffe's contribution was well planned and in most, but not all aspects, effectively applied. It was nevertheless in the circumstances prevailing in Norway at the time utterly decisive. The first year of the war proved to be the apogee of German air power and although its subsequent decline was neither rapid nor dramatic, it was rarely able in subsequent years, with notable exceptions such as Crete in 1941, to impose again such a decisive influence on the outcome of land warfare. This is not to denigrate the impact of air power itself, but it reflected the gradual swing in the balance of capability and effectiveness as the war progressed. In Central Norway in 1940 German air superiority was unchallenged and its role of crucial importance; but later in the war, as at El Alamein in 1942, it was the RAF's ability to control the skies over the battlefield which made such a substantial contribution to General Montgomery's historic victory – one of the major turning points of the war. Later in France in 1944, it was the United States Army Air Force and the RAF which prevented the concentration of the German Panzer units against the bridgehead so precariously established in Operation 'Overlord'. By 1944, the RAF had learned again how to support the Army.

The Aircraft

In support of 'Weserüebung', the Germans used fighter, bomber, reconnaissance and transport aircraft over both Norway and Denmark from bases in Northern Germany. The fighters were represented by Messerschmitt Bf 109s and Bf 110s. The single engine 109, an all metal monoplane powered by a Daimler Benz engine and armed with 20mm canon as well as machine guns, was similar in performance to the early marks of the Spitfire. Blooded in Spain in the Condor Legion where it achieved a remarkable ascendancy over Republican fighters, it remained in 1940 far superior in performance to all aircraft encountered in Norway or over the sea approaches. In conjunction with the 110, it forced the RAF to abandon daylight attacks by its heavy bombers and constrained the Blenheim to operating only when weather conditions were such that it could make a dash for concealment in cloud. There was little call on the Bf 109 in Norway itself and it was not as much used as its larger twin engined sister.

The Bf 110 was a long range fighter (Zerstorer) with a crew of two. The design was the result of an uneasy compromise between endurance and performance, but the 110 also made an effective contribution against the RAF bombers although taking some losses in return. As often as not these were due to faulty tactics rather than inferior performance. Displaying its hallmark of versatility, the Bf 110 was also used for low level strafing attacks, tactics which it was able to indulge almost with impunity against troops who could oppose it with nothing larger than a Bren gun. Even so, the Luftwaffe lost a number of 110s during the Norwegian campaign both to the Gladiators and to ground fire.

The Luftwaffe had enthusiastically embraced the concept of dive bombing from the moment that General Udet had brought two American Curtiss Hawks to Germany in 1933. This event led directly to the development of the Ju 87, the Stuka, a light, rugged, single engined aircraft which could dive at a very steep angle and recover quickly to level flight. No German aircraft attracted greater notoriety or aroused so much controversy as the Stuka: its proponents believed it was invincible, its detractors were just as virulent. The arguments excited airmen in the late 1930s in much the same way as the controversy over vertical take off and landing when the even more revolutionary Harrier arrived on the scene in the 1960s. Level precision bombing in 1940 was an under-developed science on both sides, and as we have seen, the probablility of hitting a moving target was not high. On the other hand the diving attack significantly improved the accuracy of bomb release given the very primitive bomb sights then available. Although the Ju 87 soon proved to be far too vulnerable both to fighters and anti-aircraft fire, in Norway in 1940 in conditions of absolute air superiority, its greater accuracy achieved some success against both ships and land targets.

The Ju 88 was also evaluated as a dive bomber, but it was generally unsuccessful in this role despite its greatly superior all round performance compared with the Stuka. However, the concentration by the Luftwaffe on the concept of dive attacks had led to a neglect of the development of the conventional bomber, represented in 1940 by the Dornier Do 17, the Heinkel He 111 and the Ju 88. Although they were soon to meet their match in the skies over the Channel, the bombers available in April 1940 were quite adequate for most of the tasks demanded of them in 'Weserüebung', particularly in Central Norway. Only the He 111 and the Ju 88 were used in Norway, the Do 17 was confined to the Western Front.

The use of transport aircraft to move troops quickly over relatively long distances had been demonstrated in the Spanish Civil War. Hitler had sent twenty Ju 52s to Spain in August and September 1936 to transport General Franco's Moroccan troops from Tetuan to Seville. In all, some 12,000 men were transported in 677 flights.[3] Incorporated into the infamous Condor Legion, the Ju 52 eventually flew some 5,400 missions in Spain. Nevertheless, despite the lessons of the Spanish Civil War, Hitler did not fully comprehend the role of air transport and was forever trying to adapt the Ju 52 as a bomber rather than allow it to perform in its natural role in which it so obviously excelled.

The workhorse of the Luftwaffe transport force, the Ju 52 was rivalled only by the DC 3 Dakota as the most versatile transport aircraft of all time. Conceived in 1930 and remembered mainly for its tri-motor design and corrugated skin finish, it remained in service for forty years in airlines and airforces throughout the world. Known affectionately in the Luftwaffe as 'Tante Ju' (Auntie Junkers) it could carry between twenty and thirty men with all their equipment. It looked obsolete almost from the day of its introduction, but appearances were deceiving, for it was arguably the most influential German aircraft of the Second World War. It was the ideal vehicle for the rapid deployment of troops to reinforce key areas which would come under threat if more conventional but slower methods of transport were not appropriate. Furthermore, transport aircraft could be used in the initial assault against lightly defended areas either by dropping paratroops or air landing soldiers under the cover of a fighter escort. The Ju 52 was destined to play a vital role in Norway.

The Organisation

In 1939 the Luftwaffe was divided into four Luflotten or air fleets within which were Flieger-Divisionen (air divisions) and Fliegerkorps (air corps). X Air Corps under Lieutenant General Hans Geisler was assigned to 'Weserüebung' with units taken from Luflotten 1 and 2. Three days after the invasion a new air fleet was formed for Norway (Luflotten 5) with its headquarters in Oslo. It was initially commanded by the second ranking officer in the Luftwaffe. Generaloberst Erhard Milch who had a hankering for an operational command, but he returned to Germany on 7 May, handing over to General Hans-Juergen Stumpff.

Although a unified land/air command had been proposed initially, X Corps remained under the tactical control of the Air Commander after protests from the Luftwaffe. It was a concept ahead of its time, Goering was too conscious of his own status and influence to subordinate the Air Force to Army control: inter-Service jealousy was just as potent in the German as in the British military structure.

X Air Corps set up a headquarters in Hamburg's Hotel Esplanade in the first weeks of 1940 when detailed planning was commenced. The forces assigned for the invasion were substantial with the main striking force consisting of the 4th, 26th and 30th Bombardment Wings (Geschwader), each composed of about one hundred aircraft divided into three Groups (Gruppe). Each Gruppe was in turn divided into three Squadrons (Staffeln). It was reinforced by one dive bomber gruppe (Ju 87), two twin engine fighter gruppe (Bf 110), one single engine fighter gruppe (Bf 109), one coastal reconnaissance gruppe and two long range reconnaissance staffeln. Its transport forces were composed of eleven gruppes, mostly Ju 52s but also including Ju 90s and FW 200s. The 1st Special Purpose Transport Wing, which had been specially trained in paratroop and air landing operations, was also assigned to X Air Corps. In all it totalled more than 1,000 aircraft, 330 bombers, 100 fighters, 70 reconnaissance aircraft and over 550 transports. It was this last figure which highlighted the most obvious difference between the German and Allied concepts and capabilities in 1940. No less than 573 Ju 52s were gathered together for the invasion of Norway under Oberst von Gablenz.

If the RAF had had 500 available transports of similar capacity to the Ju 52, it would have been technically possible to have placed as many as 15,000 soldiers ashore in one wave. This would have been sufficient, with Naval support, to secure the few available airfields and the major ports in Central Norway and to have changed the entire complexion of the campaign. However, it is not profitable to pursue this line of thought, the concept of air mobility for land forces did not exist in Britain in 1940.

The Plan

All the Corps' senior commanders were gathered together in the Hotel Esplanade on 6 April for a detailed briefing on the planned operations. The main role of the bomber geschwader on 'W' day was to attack Royal Navy ships which might seek to intervene against the invasion forces, one staffeln being transferred as quickly as possible to Stavanger to maintain the same task from a forward location. Other bomber gruppes were to 'demonstrate' over Oslo, one over Kristiansand-Bergen, and one staffeln over

Stavanger. The physchological threat of terror bombing had been carefully fostered by the Luftwaffe to cower the civilian population. Only a few days before the invasion, the German Minister in Oslo had shown to a selected audience a graphic film of the impact of air bombardment in Poland. Physchological warfare was always to the forefront in German strategic thinking. These 'demonstration' aircraft were to support the invasion force as necessary, drop leaflets and to provide reconnaissance. One staffeln of Ju 87s was to deploy to Stavanger, the other two going to Aalborg in Northern Denmark. The Bf 110s were earmarked to support the initial operation and subsequently to escort the Ju 52s. Some of these were to land at Oslo (Fornebu) and Stavanger on the completion of their first mission. Further dive bombers and fighters used against Denmark on 'W' day were to transfer to Norway on the following day. The whole operation had been carefully thought through to provide the maximum effect.

The transport operations had also been planned in the minutest detail by Von Gablenz. It was after all the first time ever that airborne forces were to be employed to capture key points ahead of the main thrust. Only four airfields were to be used, Aalborg (East) and Aalborg (West) in Denmark and Oslo (Fornebu) and Stavanger (Sola) in Norway. The former were needed to maintain subsequent operations against Norway and the latter for use as a forward operating base against the British fleet. Timing was to be absolutely precise, for example the parachute troops were to drop at exactly 1005 at Fornebu to be followed at 1025 by an air landed infantry battalion. This would be followed throughout the day by a steady stream of Ju 52s bringing technical and administrative staffs and General Falkenhorst's command staff.

The Action

On the day, air support proved important in a number of ways, and in one area in particular proved decisive in the accomplishment of the objective by the invasion force. As we have seen in Chapter 5, the ships of Group 4 intended for Kristiansand ran into difficulties in penetrating the fiord and were twice repelled by fire from the coastal batteries. The captain of the *Karlsruhe* was forced to call upon air support to subdue the coastal batteries and it was only after two bombing raids against the forts at Odderöy and Gleodden that the guns were silenced and the ships were able to enter the harbour, some six hours later than intended. At Bergen also, four bombers assisted by gunfire from the *Köln* and the *Königsberg* were needed to subdue the coastal forts, although the delay in entering the harbour and capturing the forts was not as long as at Kristiansand. In Oslo Fiord, successive waves of bombers including Stukas were called forward to attack Horten and the forts at Kaholm and Dröbak, which had achieved such a notable success in sinking the *Blucher*. Whilst they did not succeed in destroying the guns, they forced the defenders to shelter underground, facilitating their capture subsequently by ground troops. Other bombers attacked the airfield at Oslo (Kjeller). It was not until the morning of the following day that the last of these strongholds surrendered to the invader, thus allowing unrestricted access from the sea to Oslo. The low level 'demonstration' missions over Oslo were entrusted to thirty six He 111s, and as already recounted, they did not escape unscathed from the attentions of the Gladiators of the Norwegian Air Force.

One of the more vulnerable aspects of the invasion plan was the use of specially selected companies of paratroops to capture key points in both Denmark and Norway. Twelve Ju 52s were assigned to carry two platoons of paratroops of General Student's elite 7th Airborne Division to capture the important bridge between the Danish islands of Falster and Seeland, the key to Copenhagen. They landed on the little island of Masnedö exactly on 'W' hour and rushed to the fort that was supposed to be watching the bridge. All was peaceful, the whole area wrapped in the blissful quiet of a spring dawn: the guards were rounded-up before they could even shake the sleep out of their eyes. Seizing bicycles, the paratroops pedalled furiously to the other side of the bridge where once again the unsuspecting guards offered no resistance. At that precise moment the advance troop of the Wehrmacht appeared along the road: it was all too simple, a perfect *coup de main* without a shot being fired. Despite the ease with which it was accomplished, it was noteworthy as the first paratroop assault of the war; few were to be achieved as easily as this. A single paratroop platoon was equally successful in a similar bloodless coup on the airfield at Aalborg some forty five minutes later.

Airborne troops were used to good effect in Norway as well as Denmark. The sinking of the *Blucher* and other consequential difficulties encountered in reaching Oslo from the sea meant that the air landing at Fornebu airfield had suddenly become crucial to the success of the whole operation. Only two companies of paratroops were assigned to Fornebu and they were allowed only twenty minutes to capture the airfield and to prepare it for the first of the Junkers bringing in the air landed troops. Captain Erich Walther was delegated to lead the assault and the twenty nine transports were to be escorted over the dropping zone by eight Bf 110s under First Lieutenant Hansen, which were themselves to land as soon as the airfield had been captured.

The plan was immediately beset by difficulties. A meteorological forecast for fog and low cloud extending up to 2,000 feet ruled out a passage below cloud, and in the absence of precise navigation aids, a descent through the weather would be an extremely hazardous exercise in the mountainous areas surrounding Oslo. Nevertheless, the transports led by First Lieutenant Drewes optimistically set course across the Skagerrack in ever worsening weather. Two aircraft disappeared, probably as a result of a collision, but the rest still pressed on. However, with some forty five minutes still remaining before reaching the dropping zone, Drewes could no longer hold his formation together in the deteriorating weather conditions and reluctantly turned back towards Denmark.

Gablenz was now faced with a difficult dilemma. Goering had given specific orders that if the paratroops failed to capture the airfield, the air landed battalion following up immediately behind was to turn back. But news of the disaster afflicting the naval invasion force was filtering through and the success of the airborne landing was now rapidly becoming of paramount importance to the capture of Oslo. Gablenz, supremely confident, intuitively believed that the airfield could still be secured and pleaded with General Geisler commanding X Air Corps to let the formation press on and take its chance. But Geisler was not one to disobey orders, particularly those emanating from Goering himself, and ordered the formation to turn back. In the event, this potentially disastrous divergence of view was to prove irrelevant, for there now followed one of those happy accidents which so influence the course of success or failure in war. Captain Wagner leading the follow-up wave believed that the order to turn back was an enemy ruse and decided to press on; he was after all nearly overhead Oslo and he could see that the weather was steadily improving. Looking down on the small airfield through a break in the cloud, he could see little sign of life except the burning wrecks of two aircraft: there seemed no reason for calling off the operation at this late stage and he decided to land.

Lieutenant Hansen leading the Bf 110s had meanwhile pressed on to Fornebu completely unaware that the first Ju 52s had turned back towards Denmark. As they approached the airfield they were met as already described by the gallant but outnumbered and outgunned Norwegian Gladiators, Hansen's fighters soon brushed-off this impertinent challenge, but even so, two of his Bf 110s had now disappeared and the remainder were beginning to run low on fuel. As they circled, waiting anxiously for the paratroops to arrive to capture the airfield they soon had to land on come what may, they took the opportunity to destroy two more Gladiators on the ground, those seen by Captain Wagner when he arrived some twenty minutes later.

Eventually the Ju 52s arrived, but instead of dropping paratroops as Hansen had expected, the first one seemed to be preparing to land. It was Captain Wagner making the first approach, but his Ju 52 was hit and Wagner himself wounded, and so the co-pilot overshot the runway and climbed away. The six Bf 110s were now desperately short of fuel and Hansen could wait no longer, he decided to land whatever the consequences. The runway was short and the first one overran the landing run and disappeared down a slope. Hansen, discouraged, but with little in the way of an alternative, decided to have a go himself and managed to stop on the runway with ten yards to spare. The sporadic fire from the airfield had now died down and he quickly ordered the rest of the 110s to make their approach. Safely on the ground they quickly formed up on the edge of the airfield with their machine guns pointing towards the woods where it was believed the opposition was concealed. But all was silent, the Norwegians had fled. Many of the Ju 52 pilots, with less resolution than their leader, turned back on seeing that Wagner's aircraft had been hit, but a handful landed and the airfield was secured. For a full three hours the vital landing strip was held by this tiny group whilst the rest of the Ju 52s were gathered in, and by the afternoon the whole of Infantry Regiment 324 had arrived.

It was a remarkable *coup*, and it must be said one which owed a considerable debt to boldness, *force majeure*, and good luck. The Norwegians should have been able to hold the airfield against a handful of 110s and even if they could not have prevented the aircraft landing, they should at least have quickly rounded-up the crews. In the event, it was this air landed regiment which occupied Oslo as the main invasion force coming by sea was still tangling with the coastal forts and making little progress. Even a military band was flown in on the first day in a Junkers G38, a large four engine civilian transport from Lufthansa still sporting its peacetime name of *Generalfeldmarschall von Hindenburg*.

Two days later General Geisler himself arrived at Fornebu. He was quick to congratulate Lieutenant Hansen – 'but for your squadron' he said 'things might have turned out very differently':[4] in the circumstances, this was something of an understatement.

The other objective to be captured from the air was the airfield at Stavanger, also known as Sola. It was in many respects the most important from the German viewpoint, being one of the few serviceable airfields in Norway, the occupation of which would enable the Luftwaffe to extend their air operations into Central Norway and to range far out over the North Sea. Its capture in a useable condition would ensure that the XXI Army could move north of Oslo to link up with the Trondheim Group under the complete protection of an air umbrella. It was, however, imperative to seize it by a *coup de main* to preclude the Norwegians demolishing the installations and even the runways, although the latter are notoriously difficult to put out of commission for any length of time.

Fortunately from the German viewpoint, the Norwegians were as unprepared for an attack on Stavanger as they were elsewhere in the country on the morning of 9 April. The sole means of ground defence was a section of machine guns and a rifle platoon, seventy men in all. There were vague and, as it transpired, unexercised plans to place demolitions on the airfield, but the only action on the day was the last minute erection of barricades on the runways. The half dozen Fokker aircraft at Stavanger were capable of dropping 50 kilogram bombs, but their commander was given clear orders not to use them. The plaintive, if understandable, response was 'in that case I do not understand what I am supposed to do at Sola'.[5] Unable to dispute this incontrovertible logic, the Norwegian High Command then ordered him to disperse the aircraft away from the front line. In practice, they could have achieved little of value other than perhaps to try to destroy their own facilities if no other demolition explosives were available. The main problem was perceptual, the Norwegians, if they expected a threat to the airfield at all, thought it would arise from troops landed on the coast where two German cargo boats had been spotted early on the morning of 9 April.

But the assault was not to come from the sea, but from the air. At about 0930, the airfield was attacked by two Bf 110s which strafed aircraft on the ground and some of the airfield installations. At almost the same moment, eleven Ju 52 transports led by Captian Gunther Capito appeared over the airfield. They too had encountered difficulty with the weather and one aircraft turned back. But the rest broke out into brilliant sunshine some way short of Stavanger and Capito quickly gathered his formation together and descended to low level. Creeping up a side valley they approached the airfield completely unseen and, pulling up to 400 feet, twelve paratroops were accurately dispatched from each aircraft, their weapons containers being thrown out immediately afterwards.

The paratroops were armed with revolvers, hand grenades and automatic rifles. A few who were unfortunate enough to drop within range of the hastily mounted machine gun defences were killed, but the majority were able to assemble elsewhere on the airfield from where they quickly launched an attack on the sole point of defence. A few hand grenades through the embrasures of the machine gun post quickly discouraged the defenders and induced their surrender, and within an hour or so of the initial assault the airfield was under German control.

The third phase of the operation at Stavanger was the landing of troops and equipment from Ju 52 transports of which nearly one hundred arrived during the course of the day bringing some 2,000 fully armed troops. By 11 April, no less than two hundred German aircraft were on the ground at Stavanger and anti-aircraft batteries had been located at five positions on the airfield.

The capture of Stavanger airfield is particularly interesting in that it was the first significant independent operation mounted solely from the air ahead of the front line of ground operations.[6] It was boldly conceived and carefully planned, and was totally successful even though the rather imprecise air drop might have led to difficulties against less feeble opposition. It was the precursor of many more elaborate missions, not always successful, during the course of the war. The concept was used most successfully in Crete, although it proved exceptionally costly in casualties and it has been recognised in retrospect that it could so easily have been thwarted. Nevertheless, the airborne operations in Denmark and Norway were a splendid example of air mobility, illustrating both the spectacular success which may be achieved, and how, far more than in most other forms of warfare, success or failure can hang on the thread of each individual element of the operation.

To complete the summary of air operations on the morning of 9 April, we should perhaps note again the remaining tasks of the bombardment wings – to prevent the Royal Navy interferring with the eleven naval groups delivering the invasion force to Norway and Denmark. This was accomplished by forty one He 111s of Kg 46 and forty seven Ju 88s of Kg 30. Despite the difficulties of hitting ships at sea, this raid was unusually successful. The destroyer *Gurkha* was sunk, the *Devonshire*, *Southampton* and *Glasgow* damaged, and the *Rodney* had a lucky escape.[7]

Closing the Ring

The British Intelligence Summary in the week following the invasion suggested that the Germans had allocated to the Danish and Norwegian theatres ten long-range bomber, three reconnaissance, three fighter and three army co-operation squadrons, about two hundred aircraft in all.[8] In fact, as we have seen, this estimation was significantly lower than the actual allocation of five hundred offensive aircraft to Weserüebung in addition to the substantial number of transports. With all the serviceable airfields in Central and Southern Norway now in their hands, the build-up of offensive aircraft in theatre was very rapid. Six squadrons of Ju 88s at Vaernes and Kjeller (Oslo), no less than thirteen squadrons of medium range bombers at Vaernes, Kjeller and Fornebu, three squadrons of Bf 110s at Vaernes and three of Bf 109s at Kristiansand were known to be in position by 17 April. Reconnaissance and army co-operation aircraft were also available in some numbers at different locations within Norway. In addition, there were up to three hundred transport flights every day.

The airfields were rapidly enhanced to provide the necessary levels of support, spares and administrative infrastructure, and were soon ready to clamp an iron ring round the airspace above the troops who were by now pushing forward from the invasion ports. The Luftwaffe was given the following main roles: air defence against daylight bombing raids, attacks against ships at sea, reconnaissance, and the bombing of troop concentrations, communications, and most importantly, the bridgeheads at Aandalsnes and Namsos.

In forcing the RAF to suspend daylight bombing except by Blenheims, the fighters were totally successful although they suffered some unnecessary losses whilst they sorted out the best method of attacking bombers in tight formations. At this stage of the war, air fighting at night was a very hit or miss affair. Without the assistance of either ground or airborne radar, the only chance of achieving a kill was by a lucky encounter on a moonlit night: in fact only one aircraft was definitely shot down by a fighter at night during the Norwegian campaign. Fortunately, the chances of a bomber hitting its specific target at night were also equally slim. In daylight, on the other hand, the fighters were able to maintain almost total air superiority over the coast and land areas, thus allowing other friendly offensive aircraft to operate without hindrance.

In their attacks against shipping, the Luftwaffe achieved only modest success. Only one transport was sunk on its way to Central Norway and although naval ships were repeatedly attacked until the final evacuation in early May, surprisingly few successes were achieved after their initial coup on 9 April when the *Gurkha* was sunk. It was neither the accuracy or lethality of the ships' anti-aircraft guns which saved them, their successes were comparatively few although the amount of ammunition blasted into the sky almost certainly deterred the more cautious pilots from approaching too close or too low. The main reason was the already well recognised difficulty of hitting ships at sea with the existing aircraft and bombsights. Even when a ship's defences were silenced, as happened to the *Suffolk* on her return from bombarding Stavanger, the Luftwaffe was still unable to send her to the bottom despite almost seven hours of constant attack. The poor returns did not justify the effort expended in terms of the ships sunk or damaged, but the indirect effects were more substantial, for the potential risk persuaded Admiral Forbes to abandon surface operations south of Bergen and in other ways constrained the effort which the Royal Navy could bring to bear on the campaign, most noticeably in the positioning of the *Ark Royal* and the *Glorious* when supporting land operations around Trondheim in the last week of April.

The bombing and strafing of troops and vehicles on the ground was almost constant during the campaign in Norway, although again the results in terms of vehicles destroyed and troops killed was surprisingly low. In many parts of Norway, the mountainous terrain with the roads winding through the valleys made precision attacks difficult, and the proximity of trees close to the road provided ready cover. Both the Luftwaffe and the RAF were to discover in the early years of the war that attacking moving targets on the ground even under conditions of absolute air superiority was not as straight forward as they had envisaged. As late as 1942, when the circumstances were reversed, the Desert Air Force in North Africa encountered surprising difficulty in destroying moving columns even in the open expanse of the desert. In Norway the conditions were far more exacting, for the pilot had to be constantly aware of the terrain when planning his approach and his escape path from the target. The unpredictable weather provided an additional hazard to the aircrews and sometimes, if not often enough, brought welcome relief to the troops moving along the narrow roads. Frequent air attack of course made moving along the roads difficult and this undoubtedly had a major effect on the ease and speed with which reinforcements and supplies could be moved. Furthermore, the hours of darkness were very short, only about four hours in Central Norway at this time of the year, and thus the harrassment could be maintained over a long period. But the results achieved were not impressive, and the Luftwaffe would undoubtedly have done better to concentrate on focal points, for example bridges and tunnels, rather than attack targets of opportunity which could, with some degree of warning, disperse into the surrounding forest.

It was not however in attacks against the troops on the ground that the Luftwaffe's bomber forces made their greatest contribution to the success of Weserüebung, but in their systematic destruction of the two Allied bridgeheads at Aandalsnes and Namsos. It took them a little time to recognise that these two small and insignificant ports were the sole lifeline of the armies committed ashore, but when it was realised some five days after the initial landings that severing the umbilical cord was simpler and more effective than trying to destroy the body, the Luftwaffe set-to with a grim determination to remove the ports from the face of the earth. The timber jetties and the settlements themselves, being also largely constructed of wood, were quickly reduced to flattened, smoking ruins, but the bombers never managed to completely destroy the stone quays. Thus although they effectively prevented supplies coming ashore except in small dribbles, the quays were still sufficiently intact to use for the embarkation of troops when the time came for evacuation. Perhaps too greater proportion of their effort was directed against the shipping in the fiords rather than the port facilities themselves, for success in the former was limited. But wherever directed, neither Namsos or Aandalsnes was to function with anything approaching the efficiency needed to give a glimmer of encouragement to General Paget or the troops ashore. This achievement, more than any other of the many roles undertaken by the Luftwaffe in Norway, was the 'mastercard' which ensured the success of Hitler's gamble in Scandinavia.

As the campaign developed, reasonably secure lines of sea and land communication were gradually established between the north German ports and the forces operating in the Gudbransdal and the Österdal. But for the isolated bridgeheads at Trondheim and Narvik, air supply was the only lifeline with the bulk of the German troops in the south. Almost continuous streams of Ju 52s flowed to Trondheim (Vaernes) carrying reinforcements, equipment, medical supplies and ammunition. Unopposed by the RAF or any anti-aircraft guns on the ground, the pilots flew just far enough away to be safe from the itching fingers of the British troops in the Gudbransdal armed only with Bren guns and other light weapons. In all, Ju 52s flew 3,018 sorties in Norway including 1,830 carrying troops and 1,188 with supplies. Nearly 30,000 men and 2,500 tons of supplies as well as a quarter of a million gallons of aviation fuel travelled in the cabin of this remarkable transport. About one hundred and fifty aircraft were lost, mostly in accidents, due either to the weather or the limitations of the airfields.[9]

The Ju 52 was not the only aircraft pressed into use by the Luftwaffe as a military transport. Several unusual aircraft saw service in the campaign, many in support of the more isolated garrison at Narvik. Civilian aircraft tasked in an unaccustomed role by the Luftwaffe included the Blohm and Voss Ha 139, a gull winged four engined float plane, and the Ju 90 a large and sophisticated four engined transport which could carry up to forty passengers. It is an indication of the overstretch imposed on the Luftwaffe transport force that these often unsuitable aircraft had to be brought into service with variable success.

Flying boats were also used to transport troops, again particularly in the support of Narvik. In addition to the Do 18, two of which were used to move a company to Hemnesberget in support of Operation 'Wildente',[10] the larger Do 24, of which two prototypes were available in Germany, and the Do 26, a long range, four engined flying boat which could be modified to carry twelve fully equipped troops also gave valuable service. A general purpose reconnaissance and transport gruppe (Küstenfliegergruppe 406) was formed to carry-out difficult and dangerous missions into remote fiords in support of troops who might otherwise have been bereft of food, ammunition and other essential supplies. The Do 26 in particular suffered severely in supporting Narvik when two were shot down by Hurricanes on 28 May, one crash landing with the capture of its ten passengers.

Maritime patrol was mainly in the hands of the Do 18 flying boats, powered by a tractor and pusher engine mounted on a high wing. It was slow and vulnerable and some were lost to ground fire whilst operating in Norwegian coastal waters. The Blohm and Voss Bv 138, of which only two production aircraft were available, was also used in the reconnaissance role in Norway. The He 115 was used for mine laying and reconnaissance. The Norwegian Naval Air Service also used He 115s, and in the Narvik area the Germans had the misfortune to be attacked by one of their own aircraft types two of which were captured machines. These aircraft were used subsequently by the RAF for clandestine operations.

One remarkable success by a German maritime aircraft was the capture of a British submarine. Küstenfliegergruppe 706 commanded by Major Lessuig was based at Aalborg in Denmark equipped with obsolescent Heinkel He 115 and Arado Ar 196 seaplanes to reconnoitre the sea lanes in the Skagerrak and Kattegat for British submarines. It was generally unrewarding work, for their aircraft were not equipped with any detection devices and could only achieve a sighting if they surprised the submarine on the surface, an unusual occurrence as they only normally surfaced during the hours of darkness. But on 5 May, Lieutenants Mehrens and Schmidt took off in their Arados in the dark to arrive at their allotted patrol area at dawn. It was still dark when Mehrens suddenly spotted a dark shape on the surface – it was the submarine *Seal* which had been laying mines in the Kattegat when it had itself struck a stray mine. After several hours on the bottom Lieut Commander Lonsdale had surfaced to survey the damage. The inspection was not encouraging; the hull was holed and the boat could only make a few knots, and realising that the chances of getting home were negligible, Lonsdale was therefore making slowly for safety in neutral Sweden.

Mehrens attacked with 100 lb bombs which missed, but Schmidt now joined in and managed to plant a bomb very close to the submarine. Her engines stopped as the water level rose and this was sufficient to induce the appearance of a white sheet of surrender at the *Seal's* conning tower. Schmidt landed his Arado alongside the submarine and signalled for the captain to swim over. Lonsdale had few options left, it was getting daylight and his boat was now sinking, it could not be long before more formidable reinforcements arrived to take over from the Arados. He complied with the request and was flown back to Aalborg. Mehrens meanwhile had located a fishing boat which was able to take the *Seal* in tow to Frederikshaven. This unlikely combination had not only taken prisoner a submarine commander, but had captured his submarine as well.

But it proved to be an isolated occurrence, further successes against submarines were achieved only by the German surface ships. Nevertheless, the German maritime air forces continued to maintain a valuable observation role in locating and shadowing British surface ships. On the only other occasion when a He 115 ventured too close to a warship, it was promptly shot down by the anti-submarine trawler *Arab*.

In all of these many facets of air operations, the Germans were able to assess in operational conditions many types of military aircraft as well as those impressed from civilian service. For most of the time they were able to do this with only minimum interference from fighter or anti-aircraft defences. Rather like Spain and Poland, Norway provided valuable opportunities for training and evaluation for the Luftwaffe in readiness for the sterner tasks which lay ahead. The whole operation was conducted with precision and flair even though their effort was sometimes misdirected. But unlike their British counterparts, the German planning staff fully appreciated the key role of air power. In some areas, notably in the capture of the airfields and in the elimination of the Allied bridgeheads, the role of the Luftwaffe was decisive.

Operation Rupert –
Misplaced Optimism

'Our staff work at this time had not been tempered by war experience, nor was the action of the Service Departments concerted except by the meetings of the Military Co-ordination Committee over which I had just begun to preside.'

Winston Churchill[1]

An Inauspicious Beginning

Admiral Whitworth had toyed with the idea of landing a naval force at Narvik after the successful action on 13 April when the *Warspite* and her supporting destroyers had annihilated those ships of Group 1 which had survived Warburton-Lee's raid four days before. But caution prevailed, and in the early morning of 14 April he extricated his battered ships from the confined waters of the Ofotfiord leaving General Dietl to consolidate his position ashore with his meagre and isolated force of Austrian mountain troops and stranded sailors. It was to take almost two months before the town was eventually occupied by Norwegian, French and Polish troops, the British component of the Allied force having by then been dispatched to the south to fight a desperate delaying action against a German relieving force marching relentlessly north from Trondheim.

The Allies had been thrown into some confusion as the news of the successful German invasion arrived in London during the morning of 9 April. At first it was thought that Narvik could still be occupied without opposition, but that illusion had disappeared by the time the Supreme War Council met in London that same afternoon when it became known that, contrary to all expectations, the Germans had succeeded in capturing Narvik as well as the more accessible ports further south. By the evening, the Military Co-ordination Committee had decided, in line with the French preference, that all the available resources should be devoted to the recapture of Narvik, and the War Cabinet readily endorsed this priority on the following morning.

Admiral of the Fleet the Earl of Cork and Orrery was appointed Flag Officer Narvik to command the naval forces assigned to recapture the town. Although retired from active service, he had been recalled by Mr Churchill at the age of 65 in October 1939 to plan in detail 'Operation Catherine', the proposal to insert a strong naval presence into the Baltic. He was even more delighted to receive a summons from the First Lord on the afternoon of 10 April to serve his country again in a more active role.

But he had precious little time to assimilate the details of what was expected of him and received no written orders. He attended a meeting of the Military Co-ordination Committee, had a conversation with the First Sea Lord, and a chat in the car with Mr Churchill. His Army counterpart, General P. J. (Pat) Mackesy, was more fortunate, he had been involved in the planning for operations in Scandinavia for some time. With Admiral Sir Edward Evans, Mackesy had been working on the plan to occupy the Gallivare orefields under the pretext of going to the aid of the Finns. After this unlikely scheme had collapsed with the demise of the Finnish resistance, he had been appointed to command the land forces assembled under the codename 'Avonmouth' which were to occupy Narvik if the laying of mines in the Leads precipitated a German invasion of Norway. But once this eventuality had slipped away, he was the obvious choice to command the North West Expeditionary Force now being reorganised to recapture Narvik. This was to prove a far more exacting proposition.

Mackesy's 49th Division consisted of the 24th Guards Brigade of three battalions under the command of Brigadier the Hon W 'Willie' Fraser DSO, MC, supported by a second echelon of Chasseurs Alpins and Polish troops. The 24th Brigade had existed on paper since December 1939, but the Headquarters staff were only hastily brought together during the first week of April. The 1st Battalion Irish Guards (Lieutenant Colonel W. D. Faulkner) and the 1st Battalion Scots Guards (Lieutenant Colonel T. B. Trappes-Lomax) had been undergoing intensive training in the first few months after the outbreak of war, but since December had been kicking their heels in London anxiously waiting to discover where their freshly honed skills would be needed. Rumour succeeded rumour, plans were hatched, feverishly developed, and then summarily cancelled. Their training had suggested that they were destined to join the British Expeditionary Force in France, but events in the north made Scandinavia an outside chance which attracted increasing support as time passed. King George VI watched the Scots Guards in training on 3 April and visited the Irish Guards on the following day, suggesting to the men, quite correctly as it turned out, that a move was imminent. Finally on 6 April, the first elements departed London by train for an unknown destination, although the personal kit with which they had been issued confirmed a destination far to the north. The full complement of the Brigade was made up by the 2nd Battalion South Wales Borderers (Lieutenant Colonel P. Gottwalz) which had only recently returned from a long tour of duty in India, hardly the most effective acclimatisation for a unit destined to fight north of the Arctic Circle. The 'Micks' and the 'Jocks' were old campaigners together, but neither knew the Borderers and regarded their new found Welsh comrades with understandable suspicion. The whole Brigade had never trained together, an omission which would be viewed today with disbelief and alarm, but which was by no means unique in 1940.

The Scots Guards were the first to embark on the Clyde in the Polish transport MV Batory on 8 April. They already knew that their equipment had not been tactically loaded, with all they needed for an opposed landing at the bottom of the hold hidden by the non-essential items on top. Even though as a part of 'Avonmouth' they were not expected to have to make an opposed landing, it shows little forethought or contingency planning, which characterised the operation from the start. The Guards at least had the time to do some re-arranging and reloading, others following along behind were not so fortunate. They sailed at nightfall on 9 April in company with the Hallamshires who were destined originally for Trondheim, safely negotiating the treacherous waters of the Minch, and arrived at Scapa Flow at 0600 on the 11th. The same day they were joined by General Mackesy who was still awaiting his written orders.

The Irish Guards had a little more time to prepare themselves. Extra bren guns were drawn from stores to provide one for each section and an anti-tank rifle was allocated to each platoon. By the morning of 10 April the newspapers had headlined the breach of Norwegian neutrality, and it needed little imagination now to guess their destination. The Green Line buses which were drawn up in Birdcage Walk to take the battalion to Euston station were crudely inscribed in chalk with slogans such as 'See the Midnight Sun' and 'North Pole Express', or less imaginatively, simply 'To Norway'. Wives and girlfriends came to say their fond farewells and, more formally, the Major General Irish Guards and the Regimental Lieutenant Colonel wished the Battalion well, thrusting a bottle of champagne into the Commanding Officer's compartment as a farewell gesture. By the morning of the 11th they were in Glasgow and embarking on the liner *Monarch of Bermuda*. Meanwhile the South Wales Borderers, with rather less ostentation, had embarked on the *Reino del Pacifico* and the K.O.Y.L.I., who as we have seen ended up at Namsos, in the *Empress of Australia*. Merchant shipping played a vital role in the mounting of the Norwegian campaign, as it was to do in the evacuation of a few weeks later, and as it had on the launching of so many expeditionary forces – from Galliopoli to the Falklands. It is another reminder of why the rundown of the British merchant fleet is causing such concern in military circles today.

The Seeds of Confusion

Although the expedition was now launched on its way, there was still a large degree of confusion as to the actual situation. *The Times* headline of 11 April ran 'Recapture of Bergen and Trondheim' following a Swedish report that the British had reoccupied Bergen and the Norwegians Trondheim. The War Office well knew that this was not true, nevertheless official intelligence was by no means complete or unambiguous and this was reflected in the orders hastily taken by hand of Brigadier Lund to General Mackesy. These arrived around midday on the 11th directing Mackesy to establish control of Narvik after making a preliminary landing at the port of Harstad on the island of Hinnöy, about 35 miles as the crow flies from their final objective. The instructions were far from precise, and a handwritten message from General Ironside accompanying the formal orders brought little additional enlightenment, but its opening sentence ran:

> Owing to naval difficulties in escorting, we have decided to send 4 Bns together, the whole arriving 30 hours after the arrival of 2 Bns with a week's interval before the arrival of the other 2 Bns.[2]

If Mackesy sought to unravel this ambiguous declaration from the accompanying formal instructions, he would have been equally disappointed. However, he would doubtless have been heartened by the clear accounting instructions contained further on in General Ironside's short note:

> There should be considerable numbers of ponies in the village and neighbouring ones. Let no question of paying trouble you. Issue payment vouchers and we will see that you get a paymaster as soon as possible. Don't allow any haggling over prices.

His final exhortation ran:

> You may have a chance of taking advantage of naval action and you should do so if you can. Boldness is required.

This was in stark contrast to the injunction in the formal instructions that:

> It is not intended that you should land in the face of opposition.

The advance element consisting of General Mackesy, the Brigade Commander, two companies of Scots Guards and some staff officers sailed from Scapa Flow in the cruiser *Southampton* at 1300 on 12 April. They arrived at Harstad at 0600 on 14 April after enduring a mild gale and widespread seasickness, but otherwise unscathed. They were struck immediately by the wild and beautiful scenery, but equally noted with a mounting degree of apprehension the snow which lay in considerable depth right down to the waters edge: they had been told by the War Office before departure that there would be little or no snow at this time of the year. Whilst the General and his staff established themselves ashore, the Scots Guards immediately carried on in the *Southampton* to Sjövegan in the Salangenfiord, some thirty three miles north of Narvik as the crow flies, but rather more by road. Late in the afternoon they landed to a hospitable welcome from the local population, who were impressed in turn by the discipline and bearing of the Guards.

The remaining two and a half battalions of the 24th Guards Brigade and the three battalions of 146th Brigade also left home waters on the same day as their General on transports escorted by the battleship *Valiant*, three cruisers, *Manchester*, *Birmingham* and *Cairo*, and eleven destroyers. Their orders were to occupy Narvik and the peninsula, but this was soon changed as Colonel Faulkner succinctly explained to his officers:

> Gentlemen, I have just heard that neither of these is possible. The maps are in another ship and the Germans are in Narvik. HQs are now trying to choose another base.[3]

However, the orders were to be changed yet again, and as we have seen, 146th Brigade was diverted to Namsos on 14 April when the transports were just one hundred and thirty miles from Harstad. This caused numerous residual problems. Quite apart from their brigadier who was carried on to Harstad, some of the 146th Brigade equipemnt was in ships carrying the Guards Brigade, and none of the equipment had been tactically loaded and had to be sorted and re-allocated after the ships had arrived.

The Naval Commander, Lord Cork, had also set sail from Rosyth in the cruiser *Aurora* on the same day as General Mackesy. He had never met Mackesy, but he too had been encouraged by the injunction that 'the utmost boldness is required'. As his official report confirmed, he was in no doubt as to what was expected of him:

> My impression on leaving London was quite clear that it was desired by HM Government to turn the enemy out of Narvik at the earliest possible moment and that I was to act with promptitude in order to attain this result.[4]

It was certainly by now the Cabinet's intention to make a dash for Narvik even though this was contrary to the orders given to General Mackesey. The operation was given, unofficially it appears by Mr Churchill, the codename 'Rupert', although it did not officially replace 'Avonmouth' as the codename for General Mackesy's force until 19 April. The seeds of confusion had been well and truly sown.

A Missed Opportunity?

Lord Cork's naval task force consisted of seven cruisers and five destroyers. The Naval Commander was a very senior officer, outranking even the Commander-in-Chief Home Fleet, a post that Cork himself had held between 1933 and 1935. This was an uncomfortable arrangement, particularly for Admiral Forbes, and inevitably led to misunderstandings as the campaign progressed. Lord Cork was well recognised as a man of action, an officer not frightened to take a risk or miss an opportunity to steal the initiative, and this certainly characterised his approach to his new command. Approaching the Norwegian coast, he received a signal from Admiral Whitworth suggesting that Narvik could be taken by a small force with the aid of substantial naval gunfire support. This accorded with both Cork's orders and his instincts, and quick to react, he immediately signalled the *Southampton* that they should meet in the Skjelfiord and that the two companies of Scots Guards supported by two hundred marines and seamen from his own ships should attempt a landing at Narvik on the following morning, 15 April. Unfortunately, the *Southampton* did not receive this message as a result of unfavourable atmospheric conditions until the Scots Guards were actually disembarking at Sjövegan. Mackesy immediately responded that he did not think the Admiral's plan was feasible, and the Admiralty weighed in with a signal saying that the two forces should act together in concert. This was the first of a series of disagreements between the two senior commanders which soured their relationship from the outset.

Whether Narvik could have been captured by an immediate *coup de main* has remained a matter of controversy ever since. Mr Churchill and Lord Cork certainly continued to claim after the war that an assault on 15 April would have succeeded, and they have been supported by a number of military historians. But analysis of the circumstances suggests that the chances of success were at best problematical.

The first point to clarify is the actual state of the defences at Narvik over this period, and this is where the difficulty really lies. Without doubt the Germans were still in some disarray at this time. After his successful landing on 9 April, General Dietl had pushed forward many of his mountain troops from the town in the expectation that the approach from the Ofotfiord would be guarded by Bonte's destroyers. The second battle of Narvik on the 13th was therefore a severe setback to his defensive plan. But what actually was the strength of the Narvik defences between the 13th and the 16th during which an assault might have been made? According to Mr Piers Mackesy[5] who quotes a German source, one battalion of mountain troops supported by mortars, machine guns and two mountain guns was dug in and around the town from the 10th onwards, and that it would have required a force of at least 1500 men to have mounted a successful landing even at this early stage. On the other hand, there have been reports, mainly traceable back to Theodor Broch who was the Mayor of Narvik at the time, that the town was almost deserted after the naval battle on the 13th and the Germans were in complete disarray. But his book in fact does not really substantiate this assertion and although there was a degree of dis-organisation, it was not necessarily such as to allow the British the luxury of disembarking at the quayside.[6]

I think we may reasonably conjecture that the defences at Narvik were neither quite as secure as indicated by Mr Mackesy nor in quite the state of disorganisation indicated by Theodor Broch. After the naval debacle on 13 April, Dietl would have been foolhardy not to have taken urgent steps to improve the defences of a town no longer protected from the sea, and Dietl was one of the more astute and experienced of the German generals. We may conclude therefore that whilst a *coup de main* might have been successful in the immediate aftermath of the second battle of Narvik on 13 April, it was becoming a progressively more difficult proposition thereafter.

In fact, the assault could not have taken place until the morning of the 16th. Most of the two Scots Guards Companies were already ashore at Sjövegan in the early evening of the 14th when Lord Cork's message to the *Southampton* was belatedly received. They would have had to re-embark, sail round to the Vestifiord, join up with Lord Cork and General Mackesy (who was at Harstad), prepare a plan for the combined assault and position in the Ofotfiord to carry it out: it is inconceivable that they would have been ready to mount the attempt until dawn on the 16th at the earliest. It also has to be remembered that only the scantiest of information was available as to the true state of the defences of Narvik at this time, and this would have undoubtedly added to the complexity and uncertainty of the plan.

Another question is how effective would the naval bombardment have been in quelling any defences that existed. Experience was to show that it was extremely difficult against the blanket covering of snow on the hillsides to locate the German machine gun nests guarding the narrow beaches. There was also the technical problem of bringing the low trajectory naval guns to bear effectively in the narrow fiords on targets close inshore. Whilst the town itself could have been ravaged, this was hardly likely either to cause serious distress to the defenders mainly dug in round the periphery or to endear the British to the Norwegians whose active assistance would be needed if the Allied objective of recapturing Norway was to be achieved.

Finally, there was the problem of the landing itself. This aspect will be considered in more detail later, for it increasingly monopolised the two commander's attention; suffice to say at this stage that the only reasonable place to land in Narvik was at the town quay as the Germans had demonstrated a week previously. Without landing craft, artillery and mortar support, and perhaps above all better weather conditions, a landing on the so-called beaches in the vicinity of Narvik even against minimal opposition would have been an extremely hazardous enterprise.

The inescapable conclusion is that whilst there might have been a chance that a *coup de main* would have succeeded immediately after the Warspite's action on the 13th whilst the defenders were in greater disarray, the window of opportunity had disappeared by the 16th. Lord Cork's naval force, for no very good reason, had delayed its departure from Scotland for a full twenty four hours after the orders were issued and had prepared no co-ordinated plans for an immediate assault. Thus the only chance of a quick victory rested with Admiral Whitworth himself immediately after the action on the 13th, and he had decided, I believe prudently, that the risk even at that time was too great.

The blame for this so called missed opportunity, for it was certainly seen as such in London, was nevertheless laid firmly at the door of General Mackesy, leading eventually to his dismissal from the command and subsequent retirement from the Army. A more reflective analysis of the situation at Narvik in this dramatic week suggests that the opportunity was by no means as clear-cut as was thought in London at the time. Even under the injunction that 'boldness is required', a direct assault against Narvik on either 15 or 16 April would most probably have ended in disaster.

Settling-in

His first plan for the capture of Narvik thus thwarted, Lord Cork now took his naval force round to the west of Hinnöy and joined the *Southampton* in the waters off Harstad.

Harstad, on the eastern shore of the large island of Hinnöy, was a small town of some 4,000 inhabitants in 1940 with three small quays and anchorage for about six vessels. In peacetime its main *raison d'etre* was as a centre of the fish processing and canning industry. The sea approach to Narvik from Harstad is via the narrow Tjeldsund Fiord to the south and thence into the Ofotfiord, a distance of some seventy miles. Although hemmed-in by mountains to the south, the inner reaches of the Ofotfiord are flanked on the opposite shore by more gentle wooded slopes with the peaks now forming a backdrop rather than the foreground. The mountains close-in again around Narvik itself which lies at the head of the Ofotfiord, dominated to the south-east by the mass of Fagernesfjell and Taraldsvikfjell, over 3,000 feet high, their steep slopes riddled with gullies and ravines and carpeted at the lower levels by birch trees wherever they can gain a precarious foothold. The town nestles round a natural harbour at the neck of the Beisfiord, with the iron ore processing plant and a few wooden quays on the south side of the Narvik peninsula, a low, rocky outcrop jutting out into the Ofotfiord. Across the Beisfiord, less than a mile away, lie the more gentle foothills of the Ankenes peninsula, clothed with birches and other deciduous trees, with the small fishing village of Ankenes itself facing Narvik across the water. To the north Narvik looks across the wide and more open Herjangsfiord with the village of Bjerkvik at its head. Finally to the north-east is the long narrow finger of the Rombaksfiord, stretching some twelve miles into the mountains towards the

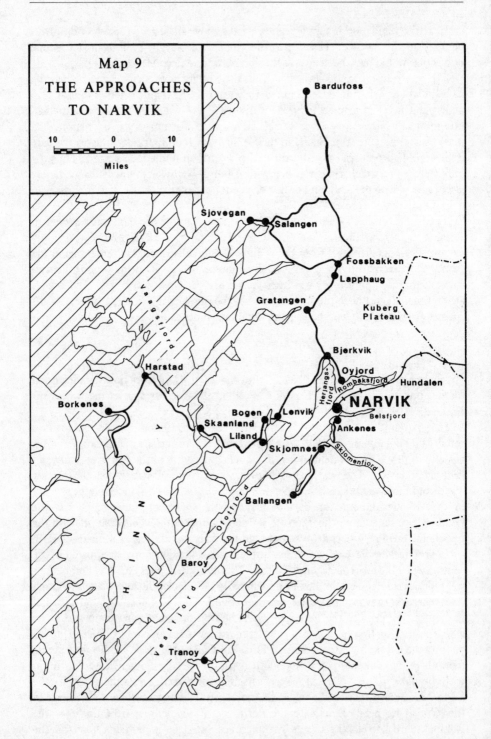

Map 9

THE APPROACHES
TO NARVIK

10   0   10

Miles

Bardufoss

Sjovegan
Salangen

Fossbakken
Lapphaug

Gratangen

Kuberg
Plateau

Bjerkvik

Oyjord
Rombaksfjord   Hundalen

Harstad

Herjangs-
fjord

NARVIK

Borkenes

Bogen   Lenvik
Skaanland   Belsfjord
Liland   Ankenes

Skjomnes

Skjomenfjord

Ofotfjord

Ballangen

Baroy

HINN OY

Vaagsfjord

Vestfjord

Tranoy

Bjornfjell and the Swedish border, only five miles further up the valley. Across the mouth of the Rombaksfiord from Narvik is the small village of Öyjord, the two connected by ferry. All of these quiet villages and rugged mountain slopes were to feature prominently in the struggle for Narvik. Despite being some one hundred and fifty miles north of the Arctic Circle, it is an attractive and benign landscape on a quiet sunny day, the waters blue and clear, and the soft green of the ubiquitous birch clothing all the slopes up to about 1,500 feet. But when the cloud and mist rolls in it becomes ominous and forbidding, the waters turning grey and surprisingly rough for such a sheltered location. More than most places, Narvik assumes an entirely different and more menacing character as the season and the weather changes.

There was no direct land approach to Narvik from Harstad. On the mainland, a road of sorts ran from Skaanland, about fifteen miles south of Harstad, to Öyjord, on the opposite bank of the Rombaksfiord from Narvik. Öyjord could also be approached by road from the north from Gratangen or Salangen. However, unlike today, there was no road from Öyjord round the Rombaksfiord to Narvik, only a ferry. On its own bank of the Ofotfiord, Narvik could be reached from Skjomen or Ankenes round the head of the Beisfiord or down the railway from Sweden. Beyond that, further to the south, lay rugged, inhospitable tundra, indented with fiords and studded with lakes creating a formidable barrier to travel. Aside from direct assault from the sea, there was no doubt that Narvik was a very difficult place to get at.

General Mackesy had already made contact with the civil authorities at Harstad on the morning of the 14th and ascertained that the Germans had not yet reached the area. He established his Headquarters in the most comfortable building in town, the Grand Hotel, but for the time being decided to leave the two companies of Scots Guards ashore at Sjövegan in accordance with his original plan. The main force started to arrive off Harstad on the 15th. It was a perfect day, the sun shone out of a clear blue sky, dazzlingly reflected off the glistening snow. Lining the decks of their transports the new arrivals, like the Scots Guards on the previous morning, marvelled at the grandeur of the mountains mirrored in the still waters of the Vaagsfiord; clouds of eider ducks rose gracefully from the water disturbed by the approach of the convoy. But suddenly the serenity of the scene was disturbed by the muffled roar of depth charges, and a destroyer rushed past, her crew signalling triumphantly that they had sunk a U-boat. The cruiser *Aurora*, soon to become a familiar sight in the Narvik fiords, steamed slowly and majestically past, the flag of the Naval Commander flying proudly aloft. The local population bewildered by the sudden turn of events which had shattered their peaceful lives came out from their little wooden houses in the fishing villages lining the shore to wave to their new found allies. The 'puffers', the small Norwegian fishing ketches, added their welcome and busily escorted the convoy into Harstad. The town itself was disappointing, just a cluster of wooden buildings round a bay with more isolated farmsteds on the lower slopes of the mountains scattered among the bare birch trees – no sign of spring yet in this quiet, barren landscape. Soon after midday, the troops started to disembark in destroyers and 'puffers', stepping tentatively ashore to regain their land legs, muffled in their newly issued sheepskin coats against the sharp chill of the Arctic air. The North West Expeditionary Force had arrived.

They were accompanied by the 3rd Light Anti-Aircraft Battery, RA, but still without their guns, and a large number of divisional and base troops. They had no transport other than bicycles, which were not well suited to carrying heavy mortars in deep snow. The 2 inch mortars, which could be carried by hand, were not accompanied by HE bombs, only smoke. As the official Scots Guards' historian remarked 'The keynote of the expedition had been resonantly struck'.[7] Each soldier had two or three kit bags of personal equipment as well as the usual battalion stores. One bonus was the lavish scale of protective clothing for the Arctic winter; the British troops rarely suffered from the cold throughout the campaign. As well as their sheepskin coats, they had white fur caps and mittens, long woollen socks and underclothes, and kapok bedding. The son of Ernest Shackleton, the Arctic explorer, had been called in to advise the Ministry of Supply on what was required. Some of the more enterprising included their salmon rods in their baggage in expectation of sampling the renowned Norwegian game fishing. Most of this equipment was eventually abandoned unused. Despite the foresight which had attended its acquisition, the weight of ·personal kit and copious bedding quickly became an impedence after landing because of the lack of transport. Indeed, getting around was the major problem, the troops had no skis or snowshoes; even if they had, few would have known how to use them.

The disembarked troops slowly settled themselves into more or less comfortable billets in and around Harstad. Already the difficulty of moving in the snow which still lay on the few roads was having its effect – Lieutenant Powell-Edwards of the Irish Guards was overheard remarking, 'Oh, for a hot bath, a week's leave, and a mention in despatches'.[8] On 16 April, the German bombers appeared. The first bomb landed only fifty yards from the Irish Guards Orderly Room, quickly followed by a second which threw to the floor the battalion officers who were gathered together for a conference – 'Have we too many eggs in one basket?' remarked Colonel Faulkner drily.[9] Bombers continued to arrive in pairs throughout the afternoon, but only one military policeman was killed although several buildings were damaged or destroyed.

The initial unloading was completed by the 18th, but the arrival of further base troops added to the congestion and the confusion. Some were even sent straight back to Scotland because of the lack of facilities ashore. The Expeditionary Force had hardly got away to a smooth start, and all the time the Germans were slowly consolidating their position in Narvik. The continued attention of the Luftwaffe added to their troubles. Still lacking any anti-aircraft protection the Guards set up anti-aircraft posts which were little more than small snow forts containing a bren gun; the occupants of such establishments were without doubt at greater risk than the aircrew! Fortunately for the troops ashore the bombers tended to concentrate on the ships which zig-zagged back and forth across the fiord to escape their attention. In all, Harstad was to suffer one hundred and forty separate air raids, all of which disrupted the laborious process of unloading supplies from the tiny wharves which could only handle about two ships every five days.

With all this shipping threading its way around the fiords, the presence of U-boats in the area would have posed a very real threat. In fact there were four U-boats in the area, but the Navy had had a remarkable stroke of luck. As the convoy made its way up the Andfiord on 15 April, a message had been received from the Norwegians of a submarine lying in wait on the surface. Two destroyers, the *Fearless* and *Brazen*, were sent in pursuit. They gained an asdic contact on the U-boat which had submerged almost immediately and dropped depth charges. To their delight, perhaps even surprise, the U49 immediately surfaced and the crew started to jump overboard. The U49 then sank and the *Brazen* stopped to pick up survivors, forty of whom were rescued. But the greater prize was a bundle of documents which were also picked up containing the U-boat dispositions in the Norwegian Sea. Following this coup the submarine threat in the area completely subsided although there were several sightings, probably most, if not all, spurious. This removed what would have been a very formidable threat to the warships which were constantly moving around the fiords. Air attack was to prove a sufficient, but containable threat, the presence of submarines as well might have prejudiced the whole expedition.

The operations at Narvik over the next two months may be conveniently divided into four separate phases, the second and third of which ran concurrently. Firstly, until early in May, consideration was still being given to a direct assault on Narvik from the sea. Secondly, the 24th Brigade was dispatched to the south of Narvik to hold or delay a German advance by land from Trondheim which had been opened up by the withdrawal of British troops from Central Norway. The third phase culminated in the capture of Narvik by French, Polish and Norwegian troops, and the final phase was the evacuation of all Allied troops from northern Norway.

A Favourable Balance?

Lord Cork and General Mackesy met face to face for the first time on 15 April on board the cruiser *Southampton* to survey the situation and decide on their next move. Despite the failure to seize Narvik on their first arrival, the situation was not unpromising. General Dietl had at his disposal some 4,600 men, but 2,600 of these were seamen from the sunk destroyers and could not be expected to double as infantry with the same effectiveness as the specialist mountain troops even though they were well provided with weapons and ammunition captured from the Norwegian depot at Elvegaardsmoen.

The mountain troops belonged to the 139th Gebirgsjäger Regiment of the 3rd Gebirgs Division. Descendants of the first Alpine units of 1915 and recruited largely from Bavaria and, following its annexation in 1938, from Austria, they were hardy, resourceful and trained in winter warfare. Although they looked very professional in their Alpine boots, stout leggings and coats enlivened by brightly coloured scarves, in fact they had no quilted suits and were to suffer severely from the extreme cold. Their commander, Major General Eduard Dietl, had joined a Bavarian Regiment as early as 1909 and specialised in winter warfare. Ironically, between the wars he had undergone winter warfare training at the Norwegian Army and Shooting School, a course also completed by his forthcoming adversary General Bèthouart. He was small, wiry, tough and resilient.

Two battalions of the Gebirgsjäger had been deployed about twenty miles north of Narvik as far as the Gratangen Fiord and Lapphaug on the road to Bardufoss. The remaining battalion had returned to Narvik and taken up positions in the town itself and at Ankenes on the opposite side of the Beisfiord to the south west. There were thus about 750 combat troops in the vicinity of the town supported by six heavy and eighteen light mortars, four mountain guns and machine guns. The hastily formed Naval Battalion was deployed on either side of the Herjangsfiord and along the railway to the Swedish border at Björnfjell which they reached on 16 April. General Dietl's main worry was how to support his force with food, clothing, medical supplies and ammunition. The prospect of supply from the sea was slim in view of the absolute superiority of the Royal Navy although the occasional seaplane managed to land in the fiords when the Navy was looking the other way. On 14 April ten Ju 52s landed on Lake Hartvig with a mountain battery of 7.5 cm guns, but four aircraft were lost as the ice began to melt before the aircraft could take off again. Although some supplies were air dropped, these were quite inadequate for a force of this size. Indeed, to relieve the pressure on his supplies, General Dietl elected to return some of the seamen to Germany along the rail link through Sweden. The only means of sustaining the garrison was by this railway from Sweden and although negotiations had been started promptly, supplies did not begin to flow along this route until 26 April, and the Government would not permit the movement of ammunition through Sweden. Not all of this information was of course known to the British commanders at the time who tended throughout to over-estimate the strength of German forces in the area.

General Dietl's predicament in Narvik looked even bleaker in Berlin during this period, and Hitler in particular suffered major bouts of depression. As early as 14 April, Jodl reported in his diary that Hitler was becoming terribly agitated. By the 16th, he was talking to Keitel of evacuating Narvik and ordering Dietl to fight his way south to Trondheim. But Jodl's steadfastness and more pragmatic recognition of what was militarily possible sustained Hitler through this crisis and by the 18th he was ordering Dietl to hold on as long as possible. Colonel Walter Warlimont, Deputy Chief of the OKW Operations Staff, recorded meeting Hitler at this time:

> It so happened that I had to see Jodl in the Reich Chancellery and there was Hitler hunched on a chair in a corner, unnoticed and staring in front of him, a picture of brooding gloom . . . I could not however help making a mental comparison with the great commanders of German history: they must have felt themselves destined to be leaders on the basis of their character, self-discipline and experience.[10]

The great commander faces crises of command, or even defeat, with the same imperturbable composure as he contemplates success: Hitler still had this lesson to learn and in the elation of the eventual victory in Norway he soon forgot this timely reminder. Instead he sought to lay the blame on others and increasingly meddle in the minutae of tactical decision making – another lesson that he might have heeded.

The regular battalion of Norwegian troops in Narvik had surrendered on 9 April except for about two hundred who managed to slip away in the mountains. But General Fleischer commanding the 6th Norwegian Division still had five battalions which he was mobilising in the area of Bardufoss and Tromso, and forward patrols were at Fossbakken, rather more than halfway between Bardufoss and Narvik. The two companies of Scots Guards which had landed at Sjövegan were by now in contact with these advance forces and their arrival did much to stiffen the resolve of a confused and demoralised army. The Guards were made most welcome by the local population and the next few days were spent in reconnaissance and learning to use the four hundred pairs of skis presented to them on their arrival. Some of the officers had skied before, but all-round, their efforts were not very successful, the Guardsman did not take readily to this unfamiliar mode of movement. This inability to adapt to the terrain was a continuing and frustrating impediment for the British troops in North Norway. But overall the balance of force seemed to favour the Allies, and they had superior lines of communication through Harstad compared with General Dietl who was short of almost everything he needed. Even so, Narvik was to prove a hard nut to crack.

Inter-Service Wrangling

Such was the situation which Lord Cork and General Mackesy reviewed on 15 April. The two men were very different in character and temperament; both had distinguished records, but whereas Cork was energetic, determined and impulsive, Mackesy was cautious, thorough and methodical. Although Lord Cork was by far the senior in age and rank, he had been given no authority over the land force commander, that there quickly developed a divergence of view was not in the circumstances altogether surprising. Given their different briefs and lack of central direction, they immediately found difficulty formulating an agreed course of action. Lord Cork was still in favour of a direct assault on Narvik from the sea, to be launched as soon as possible. The destroyers *Faulkner* and *Zulu* had reconnoitred the harbour approaches and the Rombaksfiord on the 15th and Captain de Salis had suggested that a landing to the north-east of the town would not be opposed by fixed defences and could be supported by naval gunfire. But General Mackesy, quite correctly, pointed out that he had no troops available for an early assault. The main force was about to disembark, and as the transports had not been tactically loaded, they required a few days to organise their equipment. Furthermore, he had hardly any mortar ammunition, no artillery, and no landing craft with which to mount an assault. He reminded the Admiral that the beaches generally around Narvik were rocky and totally unsuitable for a landing. The few areas where it might be feasible to get ashore were covered in three or four feet of snow and could easily be swept by concealed machine gun nests. Once on the beach, the foreshores were so narrow that no formation larger than a platoon could be concentrated at any one time. Finally, no operation could be mounted under the cloak of darkness, already in mid April there were only a brief few hours of twilight. Mackesy was quite adamant, and it is difficult in retrospect to question this judgement, that an opposed landing in these circumstances was likely to end in disaster. Reluctantly, Lord Cork was forced to call off his plan to mount a direct assault on 16 April.

By the following day, the War Office and the Admiralty had conspired to press for immediate action. They pointed out that the *Warspite* could only remain in the area for two or three more days and that the Chasseurs Alpins, diverted to Central Norway, would not be coming to supplement those forces already available. However, as those in London had even less reliable information to hand than the commanders on the spot, it must be concluded that this injunction was mostly wishful thinking provoked by the First Lord's impatience to achieve an early success. There was undoubtedly a feeling in London that Narvik was there for the taking and the military heirarchy were already losing confidence in General Mackesy. Churchill described the decision not to mount an immediate assault on Narvik as 'unexpected and disagreeable'[11] and sent Lord Cork a personal signal with a thinly veiled invitation to tell the Admiralty if he thought Mackesy was mishandling the situation.

Lord Cork was not yet ready to give in. On 18 April he tried again to persuade Mackesy to gamble on a naval bombardment breaking the enemy's resolve, thereby opening the way to an unopposed landing. The General was not convinced, but with obvious reluctance agreed to have troops ready for a landing if the bombardment appeared to have achieved the desired result. A personal reconnaissance of Narvik in the *Aurora* did nothing to relieve his misgivings and on his return stated with renewed vigour that a landing was not feasible unless the bombardment had induced the total surrender of the defending troops. To achieve this would require the shelling of the town itself which was totally against his own directive and contrary to standing instructions forbidding the intentional bombardment of civilian populations. Mackesy signalled a report of his reconnaissance to the C.I.G.S.:

> Owing to the nature of the ground, flat trajectory of naval guns, and the impossibility of locating the concealed machine guns, I am convinced that the naval bombardment cannot be militarily effective, and that a landing from open boats in the above conditions must be ruled out absolutely. Any attempt of this sort would involve not the neutralisation but the destruction of the 24th (Guards) Brigade.

In private he put it more graphically: a landing could result in the 'snow of Narvik being turned into another version of the mud of Passchendaele'.[12]

Fortunately, blizzards which commenced with increasing frequency and vigour on 20 April came to the General's rescue and brought the wrangling to a temporary halt. It became abundantly clear even to the Admiral that a landing in these conditions was not viable. Lord Cork finally gave in to General Mackesy's misgivings on 21 April when he agreed that troops would be landed only if the naval bombardment forced the defending troops to raise the white flag of surrender. It is rather ironic that it was on that same day that Lord Cork was given supreme command of all naval and land forces in the area. If this had been conceded a week earlier, there can be little doubt that the Admiral's plan for a direct assault would have prevailed. The results would have been interesting.

Wrangling in Whitehall

In London 'Operation Hammer' had by now been cancelled and the Cabinet and the Military Co-ordination Committee had reluctantly recognised that it was not going to be possible after all simply to walk into Narvik. Released from 'Hammer', the *Warspite* was sent north again to Narvik and Churchill in particular believed that this powerful boost in maritime capability might hold the key. He held few of Mackesy's reservations regarding the bombardment of Narvik town as was revealed in a signal to Lord Cork:

> We are sending you an ammunition ship as fast as possible. Of course the less the town is knocked about the better for our own accommodation, but we must get into Narvik or its ruins as soon as possible.[13]

Mr Churchill, his attention now focussed firmly again on Narvik, was becoming increasingly concerned that once the Baltic was free of ice the Germans would advance through Sweden both to secure the ore fields and to reinforce the garrison at Narvik. From now on he stressed again and again the need for a quick result, the political wish completely subsuming the military realities. He had been encouraged to a certain extent by Lord Cork in a letter dated 20 April to think that Army lethargy was the main stumbling block to an early conclusion of this disagreeable delay. But although Cork himself now recognised that climatic conditions and shortage of equipment were the main obstacles, the First Lord now had the bit firmly clenched between his teeth and was convinced that Mackesy was to blame for the lack of progress. On 22 April he signalled Cork:

> If this officer appears to be spreading a bad spirit through the higher ranks of the land force, do not hesitate to relieve him or place him under arrest.[14]

Mr Churchill was not at his best over this tense period. He had come so close to confrontation with his colleagues within the Military Co-ordination Committee over 'Operation Hammer' that he had been forced to invite the Prime Minister to take the chair himself on 16 April, whilst at the same time some members of the War Cabinet were becoming increasingly concerned that too many strategic decisions were being taken within that Committee without Cabinet consideration or approval. Admiral Keyes' dramatic intervention in the Commons had stirred up the back benches, and although Churchill's popularity with the public at large was as bouyant as ever, he was increasingly coming under criticism in Whitehall. After all, he had been the most conspicuous in pressing for action in Norway and could hardly expect to escape the opprobrium when things were going so badly.

A bid by Churchill to be appointed Chairman of the Chiefs of Staff Committee was not helping to lower the temperature either. Churchill recognised clearly enough that planning and decision making by committee was causing alarming shifts in priorities and tactics – the espousal and subsequent rejection of 'Hammer' was a case in point. No responsibility without authority became Churchill's theme of the moment and he was increasingly seen to be angling to become Deputy Prime Minister, responsible for all aspects of defence. Even so, he was outwardly totally loyal to Mr Chamberlain who was also not unexpectedly facing severe criticism of his conduct of the war at this time. Soon enough Mr Churchill was to assume full power, but that did not seem the likely outcome in the last week of April.

The Mailed Fist Approach

By the end of the third week in April the 24th Brigade was established ashore. The weather during the first few days was clear and sunny although the temperature dropped to at least ten degrees of frost every night and the sun was not warm enough to melt the snow in the day. The troops were mostly billeted in the small wooden houses and continued to receive a generally cordial welcome from their still bemused hosts. There was, nevertheless, widespread apprehension, certainly exaggerated, of fifth columnists among the local population and at one point even the Mayor of Harstad was briefly detained. Their main problem continued to be the lack of transport: transport officers and drivers had arrived, but their vehicles were still awaiting ship space in Scotland. On the 29th the weather gradually deteriorated, the snow slowly intensified to a blizzard, depositing another two feet or so over the roads and the surrounding countryside and making movement even more difficult. Some of the soldiers were learning to ski, although most did not progress beyond toboganning, their commanders lamenting the absence of the 5th Battalion Scots Guards who had been specially trained in winter warfare when earmarked for service in Finland. It is yet another example of the ironies of this campaign that they had been irretrievably dispersed shortly before the 1st Battalion sailed for Narvik.

The South Wales Borderers had been landed on the mainland at Skaanland directly on their arrival from Scotland and it was now decided to move the Irish Guards across to join them, leaving Harstad as the main administrative headquarters and logistics base. They were embarked on 18 April on the converted repair ship *Vindictive*, destined to play a vital part in this role in the forthcoming months, and taken the long way round the west coast of the Lofoten Islands to enter the Vestfiord from the south west. Although shadowed by the Luftwaffe on both leaving Harstad and again the following morning, the small convoy was not attacked. That afternoon they landed at Liland in Bogen Bay, only ten miles by sea from Narvik, but still twenty five miles by road and ferry. Local reports indicated that German ski patrols were operating as close as ten miles to the east having bypassed a small Norwegian Army outpost at Lenvikmark, midway between Lenvik and Bjerkvik. Lieut Colonel Faulkner had been ordered originally to occupy Lenvik, but he decided first to concentrate his force at Bogen itself at the head of the bay which he achieved on the afternoon of the 20th, leaving only No. 4 company at Liland. He also received that afternoon the only communication he received from Norwegian Divisional HQ stating that 'Norwegian volunteers at Bogen are not to be used by British troops as their task is only to defend their homes'[15] – not a happy omen for Allied co-operation. The following morning he heard that the Norwegian outpost at Lenvikmark had been abandoned. The lack of transport proved an even larger handicap on the mainland than it had on Hinnoy. In fact, the Battalion was never able to get its hands on its allotted transport:

> When the transport eventually arrived, it remained at Harstad, being cleaned, oiled and polished until it was driven for the first time in Norway – into the sea.[16]

Furthermore, the one hundred and forty 'puffers' which were commandeered to maintain the lines of communication with Harstad proved totally inadequate.

Brigadier Frazer, the Brigade Commander, also established his headquarters ashore at Skaanland leaving only the two companies of Scots Guards behind at Harstad to guard the burgeoning depot. The Brigade was now established in a favourable location to launch an attack on the Narvik area if the weather should improve and the caution of the army commanders could be overcome, although Lord Cork had by now reluctantly accepted that the landing could only be made in the most favourable conditions induced by naval bombardment. But one problem remained, that of discerning just how effective a bombardment had been. The German machine gun emplacements overlooking the rocky shore were difficult to locate in the blanket of snow and were unlikely to reveal their presence to the warships. The extent and residual fighting efficiency of the opposition might only become apparent therefore as the troops stepped ashore on this rocky and inhospitable coast. There was still only one landing craft available and landing a sizeable force would be a protracted operation; the first elements ashore were thus facing a grave risk of being cut down before they could establish a secure lodgement on the beach. On the other hand, the almost total absence of land transport, the poor roads which needed constant clearing, and the inability of the troops to make their way across country suggested that the approach from the sea was the only viable option. Narvik was indeed proving a difficult objective to get at.

Now in supreme command, Lord Cork was in a stronger position to return to his favoured concept of the direct approach. General Mackesy's resolve was slowly weakening, his strategy of the indirect approach out of tune with both the wishes of the commander on the spot and the exhortations from London. Even so, Lord Cork had agreed that the landing would be undertaken only if it appeared that it would not be opposed. The Irish Guards, drawing the short straw, were detailed to make the assault and prepared as best they could. They were hardly overborne with confidence and those chosen to remain behind as base troops had severe misgivings, or as the Irish Guards' official historian remarks 'Their hearty "Wish I was coming with you" had the genuine ring of insincerity'.[17] Colonel Faulkner himself presciently remarked 'It is a curious fact that the 24th is the anniversary of Gallipoli'.[18] The Irish Guards carried out another reconnaissance of the Narvik area on 23 April in the destroyer *Bedouin*, each of the soldiers being given a naval officer's hat to wear to avoid alarming the watching defenders. All appeared quiet as they surveyed the area to the north-east of the town, the intended point of landing, but there was an ominous grey curtain of snow racing across the fiord as they returned to their quarters at Bogen.

The bombardment was timed to begin in the early morning of 24 April. Lord Cork transferred his flag from the *Aurora* to the cruiser *Effingham* and was accompanied by the *Warspite*, the cruisers *Aurora* and *Enterprise* and the destroyer *Zulu*. It was a bitterly cold morning with a howling wind lashing the narrow waters of the fiord into tempestuous waves; but every cloud has a silver lining, for the bad weather prevented the Luftwaffe from putting in an appearance to disrupt the operation. The bombardment lasted three hours and was restricted to military targets, the harbour area receiving the greatest attention where a ship was sunk and piers and rolling stock destroyed. But if an assault was to be mounted in the wake of the bombardment, the concealed machine gun posts had to be put out of action, and of these there was no sign under the dark cloud and the thick blanket of snow. There was no indication whatsoever that the Germans were ready to surrender, or even of the degree of damage they had sustained; the conditions under which the Irish Guards' assault was to be mounted had quite clearly not been met. The Guards, who had embarked unenthusiastically on the *Vindictive* earlier in the morning, were ashore again before midday, not without difficulty in what had developed into a very wild day. It was a wise decision, and the Battalion was thankful that their first encounter with the enemy might be joined in a more predictable and controlled situation. The mailed fist was blunted, and a more subtle approach was now surely indicated.

Relieved, at least temporarily, of pressure from Lord Cork to mount a frontal assault, General Mackesy was now able to develop what was for him a far more workable and congenial plan. He intended to advance against Narvik simultaneously from three sides. From the north, in conjunction with the Norwegians, he would advance down the road from Bardufoss towards Öyjord. From the west, he would seek to occupy Ankenes, just across the Beisfiord from Narvik. Finally he would take control of the railway from Sweden at Hundalen, thus both cutting off the main source of German resupply and blocking their most obvious line of retreat. Once in control of the Ankenes and Öyjord peninsulas, it should be possible over a period of time to locate the hidden enemy machine gun nests and neutralise them with his artillery. Meanwhile, naval bombardment would steadily weaken the resolve of the beseiged garrison. The plan was conventional, economical and safe provided that it could be completed before Dietl received help from the south, and at this stage, that was not an immediate prospect. The Norwegians, more aware of the difficulties of climate and terrain in this inhospitable land, would have preferred a joint push down the road from Bardufoss: as they pointed out, whilst movement was difficult on the snow, in the thaw it would become impossible.

The Norwegians opened their offensive on 24 April, the day of the sea bombardment of Narvik. They had already made limited contact with the Germans to the south of Fossbakken and determined to advance towards Gratangen with four battalions. General Dietl had two battalions of mountain troops in this area with well dug in machine gun posts commanding the road, but their mobility was already circumscribed by the Royal Navy's control of the fiords, maintained by a squadron of two cruisers and five destroyers under the *Aurora*. This forced Dietl to avoid the obvious supply route from Öyjord to Bjerkvik and to establish a difficult line of communication across the mountains from Bjornfjell at the head of the Rombaksfiord. Whilst three Norwegian battalions moved directly on the German forward position at Lapphaug, one battalion advanced from the north across the mountains direct to Gratangen to cut off their line of retreat. The Scots Guards held a position in the rear, the cautious Mackesy had no wish to involve them directly in the fighting until the Chasseurs Alpins, who were now on their way from Scapa Flow, could deploy their more specialist skills in the snowbound terrain. The Guards were by now slowly adapting to their unfamiliar environment, their tents buried deep in the snow surrounded by snow walls five feet high. Despite the worsening weather, they were mildly surprised how a simple stove or brazier could bring a glow of warmth and security to the stark interior of a canvas shelter. The Norwegians even stabled their horses in snow trenches where they seemed quite comfortable and content.

The blizzards which had so hindered the naval action against Narvik proved to be too much even for the better acclimatised Norwegians. The deep snow prevented the movement of artillery and the advance towards Lapphaug was easily repulsed by the well entrenched German machine guns. The battalion moving directly across country from the north fared better and by the evening was astride the road at Gratangen. However, because the main advance had been halted, it was now in grave danger of being cut off and a second battalion was sent forward in support on the right flank. It was too late. The German machine gunners, encouraged by their success at Lapphaug, now turned round to meet the threat in their rear. Surrounding the village of Gratangen and pouring lethal machine gun fire into the Norwegian positions, they forced them to make a desperate break for safety. Some succeeded, but about one hundred were killed and one hundred and fifty taken prisoner – the battalion was for all practical purposes destroyed as a fighting force. Nevertheless, despite its lack of success, the action persuaded the Germans of the vulnerability of their forward positions and within a few days they had withdrawn from both Lapphaug and Gratangen.

28 April saw the welcome arrival of the first demi-brigade of Chasseurs Alpins under General Bèthouart. Even the Chasseurs, used to winter conditions, found the climate difficult, only a part of each battalion was trained in the use of skis and there were insufficient snow shoes available for the rest. They found moving around almost as difficult as the British and suffered from snow blindness and frostbite. Two battalions were assigned to help the Norwegians advance on Narvik from the north and were dispatched immediately to Sjövegan, a third battalion was sent to Bogen Bay to join the Irish Guards.

Despite their increasing familiarity with the conditions, it was nevertheless with some relief that the Scots Guards now rejoined the rest of the battalion in Hinnöy. They had received a warm welcome from the Norwegians, but this could never entirely overcome a strong feeling of isolation and vulnerability in an unfamiliar environment in which the weather rather than the Germans seemed to be their biggest obstacle. Movement in the six feet of snow was always difficult, and when the weather deteriorated, sustaining themselves with food and shelter became an all-consuming challenge; any aggressive intent seemed out of the question in such disagreeable conditions.

The planned advance on Narvik from the west could take two forms, either on the north side of the Ofotfiord along the road from Bogen to Bjerkvik and Öyjord, or on the south side from Ballangen. The former had the disadvantage that the road cut inland from Lenvik into the mountains, thus not only introducing the difficulty of moving in deeper snow, but more importantly depriving the troops of naval covering fire from the fiord. A battalion of Chasseurs Alpins had now taken over the forward position at Lenvik from the Irish Guards who had retired to Liland and the Brigade HQ moved forward from Skaanland to Bogen. The southern route, whilst following the coast, was cut by the deep inlet of the Skjomenfiord which had to be crossed by ferry at its narrowest point.

The southern route was thought to be the better alternative and the South Wales Borderers the chosen instrument. Between 26 and 28 April the Battalion was transferred from Skaanland to Ballangen and was joined by the Brigade Headquarters on the 29th. On the same day, the Battalion supported by one ski troop of Chasseurs Alpins was carried forward by the Navy to land unopposed at a small jetty near Haakvik. They had leapfrogged the Skjomenfiord in a bold and imaginative stroke and now posed a direct threat to Ankenes. They immediately advanced round the peninsula towards the village, and although coming under German artillery fire, managed to establish their forward position at Baatherget on the north-east corner of the promontory beneath the gently rolling and wooded slopes above the Beisfiord. Narvik was at last in view. The weather had also relented and patrols were sent inland towards Lake Storvatn to protect the flank of the British advance. Brigadier Fraser had landed ahead of the Borderers and began walking with his escort towards Ankenes. Although they could not prevent the landing, the Germans were certainly not prepared to let the Brigade Commander just walk unsupported into the village. A burst of machine gun fire forced the party to take refuge in a church where the intrepid Brigadier soon reappeared on the tower to review the situation. But a stick of three mortar bombs drove him back into the church which was then systematically bombarded until the Brigadier and his party decided to make a dash for the beach. Although they just made it, a fragment from a mortar shell hit the Brigadier who, somewhat chastened, was evacuated by a watching destroyer to Harstad. The advance recommenced rather more sedately and carefully with Lieut Colonel Trappes-Lomax now in command of the Brigade.

Whilst the operation had proceeded quite smoothly so far, it was now difficult to see what to do next. The main approach to Ankenes along the coast road was commanded by artillery in Narvik, and until the weather improved, it would not be practicable to advance in strength across the mountains to the west of Beisfiord to approach Narvik by land from the south east. General Dietl had one battalion of infantry and one less effective naval battalion in the area, but the German mountain troops were once again more adept at moving across country than the British. They attacked the British patrols strung out towards Lake Storvatn and on 2 May a small company of about one hundred men made a determined advance on the road from Storvatn towards Haakvik. It was eventually driven off with heavy casualties with the help of the guns of the *Aurora*, but a further British advance across the neck of the promontory towards Beisfiord was considered too hazardous. The Chasseurs, rather more suited to the conditions than the Borderers, succeeded in dislodging isolated German patrols from the mountain tops to the north of Storvatn on 9 May, but the prospect of occupying Ankenes by this route was still likely to take some time. Stalemate had settled on operations in the Ankenes peninsula which in any case was hardly likely on its own to provide a real threat to the security of Narvik. The Chasseurs now gradually took over operations in the Ankenes area: the British were soon to be required to meet a new and more immediate threat from the south.

Frontal Assault – Again

In following the South Wales Borderers and the Chasseurs in the Ankenes peninsula, we have moved slightly ahead of the main stream of events, for towards the end of April Lord Cork's thoughts once again turned towards a frontal assault on Narvik from the fiord. The long awaited thaw arrived on 29 April and two days later he made another reconnaissance of Narvik from the sea. On 3 May he was further encouraged by a signal from the Admiralty pressing for action 'even at severe cost':[19] the First Lord was still restless. The plan this time was more ambitious and involved landing two battalions three miles to the north-east of Narvik. In preparation, the Scots Guards (less two companies) moved forward to Skaanland on 1 May where their left flank joined up with the Irish Guards who were to be their partners in the assault. On the 3rd Lord Cork issued orders for the attack to be mounted on the 8th, an alternative plan to land on the north shore of the Rombaksfiord was soon abandoned. General Mackesy, now firmly under the hand of the Admiral, had acquiesced to the plan but the two battalion commanders, Trappes-Lomax and Faulkner, made another reconnaissance of the proposed landing sites in the *Aurora* on 4 May. Whilst cruising round the fiord, they came under heavy air attack and watched the Polish cruiser *Grom* receive a direct hit and sink almost immediately with the loss of fifty nine lives: there is a striking memorial to the Polish sailors now hidden away in a housing estate in a quiet corner of Narvik overlooking the Rombaksfiord. The battalion commanders were not impressed with what they saw and Major H. L. Graham, second in command of the Scots Guards, who accompanied them on the *Aurora* recorded their reservations:

a. There was no darkness.

b. Landings from the warships could only be made by tows or in small local steamers, both vulnerable to all forms of fire. There were no landing craft as we knew them later in the war.

c. The enemy had complete mastery of the air . . .

d. The only artillery support was from the guns of the warships, but unfortunately these guns have a very flat trajectory and therefore had to cease fire on the beach defences and lift to targets further inland at the most critical moment when we were actually landing.

e. No wireless sets had been provided, so communication was extremely difficult: moreover the 2 inch mortars had only smoke bombs and no HE.[20]

In fact, four landing craft had by now arrived, but these were totally inadequate for the numbers that would have to be put ashore to achieve any chance of success. The need to supplement the landing craft with 'puffers', which had a deeper draught, restricted the available landing sites, and there was also now an increasing awareness of how devastating attack from the air would be for men in open boats. Even if they achieved against the odds a successful landing, there were no suitable assembly points which were not within range of enemy artillery and mortars in which they could prepare for the assault on the town. It is not surprising that the two battalion commanders earmarked for this attack were no more sanguine of the outcome than when the similar, if less ambitious, plan had been shelved on 24 April. Yet another reconnaissance in the *Aurora* by the Company Commanders reinforced the view that this operation was simply not feasible.

The *Aurora* was also attacked by He 111s on the 4th, suffering casualties when an accurately aimed bomb scored a direct hit on a gun turret. The German bombing was getting more accurate particularly when, as in the case of the *Aurora*, the bombers caught the ships in a narrow part of the fiord where they had difficulty in manoeuvring. In fact the Germans had quickly learnt to lie in wait above the narrow parts of the Ofotfiord for the ships to enter the restricted waters before pressing home their attacks.

Lord Cork was now in a very difficult position. He was being strongly pressed by the Admiralty, particularly by the First Lord himself, to achieve quicker results by adopting a more aggressive approach. Although this was undoubtedly in line with his own instincts, his military commanders on the other hand were unanimously opposed to a direct assault. Whilst by now formally nominated as the Supreme Commander, it would have been a very brave officer indeed to have overridden such a strong front of opposition from his army 'experts'. He signalled to London for advice, setting out quite fairly the Army's reasons for holding back. Whilst the First Lord in his reply expressed every confidence in Lord Cork's judgement, the guidance fell short of directly ordering the assault against the advice of the army commanders on the spot: it would have been rash for him to have done so, and Lord Cork had been somewhat naive to ask in the first place. Rather weakly, the reply from London also informed Lord Cork that a new army commander would shortly be arriving. As we shall see, even that was not strictly true.

Lord Cork at last succumbed to the inevitable and the views of the Army prevailed. From now on, if Narvik was to be captured at all, it would be taken by the indirect approach which General Mackesy had advocated from the beginning. It is nevertheless somewhat ironic that when Narvik was eventually captured some three weeks later, the final plan for the attack on the town itself from across the Rombaksfiord supported by naval gunfire was not very far removed from that which Lord Cork had been advocating throughout the first three weeks of the campaign. However, the conditions were by then very different, the snow had gone and the weather was much improved. Landing craft of sorts were available, and troops wading ashore were not likely to contract frostbite or worse as a result. The assault could be supported by artillery from the Öyjord peninsula as well as aircraft from Bardufoss, the former being much more effective than naval bombardment because of the higher projectory. Lord Cork's assertion that he could see little difference between the two occasions smacks of obstinacy.

Time for Reflection

The overhanging threat of having to fight their way ashore in most unfavourable circumstances at last finally removed, the troops in Bogen Bay now settled-down into a more comfortable routine of waiting and training. The weather improved and one or two intrepid souls even ventured into the fiord for a swim although fishing was a more popular pastime for most. The soldiers were comfortably billeted in local houses, purchasing meat, vegetables and fish to supplement the bully beef and biscuits which occasionally arrived from Harstad.

> A few miles down the fiord a 5,000 ton German store ship had been driven ashore by the Navy. It was loaded with guns, tracked vehicles, motor cycles, hundreds of sets of horeshoes, crates of cigars and tinned food. Official and unofficial salvage parties went through the holds like a swarm of locusts.[21]

Messes were established, vying with each other to bring life back to normal even though hospitality was curtailed by the shortage of suitable beverages. But there were no baths, and one company of the Irish Guards built an improvised bath house in a dairy using the big boiler installed for sterilising milk churns as an eight man communal bath tub. Letters and newspapers at last arrived on the 9th, the troops smiling wryly at the front page headline of a *Daily Mirror* asserting 'Narvik in Allied Hands'. The Irish Guards moved forward to Lenvik again as the Chasseurs pushed into the mountains towards Bjerkvik, but the latter soon became bogged down in the snow without adequate provisions and under threat from machine gun emplacements and mines in an area which was thought to be free of Germans. No. 1 Company of the Irish Guards crossed the Ofotfiord to support the South Wales Borderers at Skjomnes, but were not needed for the action on the Ankenes peninsula which had now reached stalemate.

In London, however, the situation looked less encouraging. The optimism of the Military Co-ordination Committee on 13 April when they believed that the early fall of Narvik was virtually assured had proved to be misplaced. The presence of the 146th Brigade which had been diverted to Namsos would not have changed this situation, for it was not the shortage of troops, but topography, climate and the lack of the necessary transport and equipment which made an early conclusion improbable. By the end of the first week of May, almost a month since the first and perhaps the only opportunity of an early victory was missed, the Allies were little further forward in the battle for Narvik. On the other hand, the German supply position, although still serious, was slowly improving with the opening up of the railway line from Sweden. Furthermore, following the evacuation of Central Norway, the Luftwaffe was able to concentrate its attention on the Narvik area and the German forces in Trondheim could now move northwards unimpeded to relieve the beleagured Dietl. The prospect of capturing Narvik by frontal assault having been abandoned, the North West Expeditionary Force now had to turn on to the defensive to prevent the loss of Norway altogether. We shall therefore leave the investing of Narvik for the time being and turn towards the new threat from the south.

13

'Scissorsforce' – Retreating Again

North from Trondheim

The first two weeks of May were a particularly low period in the progression of a war which in its first nine months had provided depressingly few highlights for the Allies. Their first venture in arms in Central Norway had ended in disastrous and humiliating defeat in little more than two weeks, relieved only by the near miraculous evacuation of those who had escaped the relentless drive of the German divisions through the Gudbransdal and the Österdal. In the far north, the North West Expeditionary Force inexplicably appeared to be making little or no progress against a far smaller and ill-provided German outpost after the ground had been so well prepared by the Royal Navy in the two battles of Narvik. But these same two weeks were also to provide a momentous turning point in the future direction of the war. The beleaguered and indecisive Chamberlain Cabinet reached the nadir of its political fortunes and some days before the long expected invasion on the Western Front, the whispers in the corridors of power grew to an irresistible surge which culminated in the King sending for Mr Churchill on 10 May to form a new government.

But in the first few days of May, the First Lord of the Admiralty was more concerned with urging the seemingly lethargic commanders at Narvik to mount a decisive thrust against their stubborn adversary. Time was not entirely on their side, for with the final evacuation of the Allied forces from Namsos on the night of 2/3 May, it was only to be expected that the Germans would intensify their efforts to bring succour to their isolated comrades in Narvik. Assistance could take three possible forms. In the air, the release of aircraft no longer required for operations in Central Norway would enable a greater effort to be applied in the resupply and reinforcement of Dietl's garrison as well as the bombardment of enemy ships, troops and installations ashore. Secondly, ground forces could move northwards overland from Trondheim to Narvik; and finally, troops could be transported by sea to a suitable jumping-off point south of Narvik from which a counter stroke could be eventually mounted against the forces besieging the town. In fact, the Germans adopted all three options, thus complicating the task of the Allies still desperately trying to find a way of unlocking the door to Narvik.

From Trondheim to Narvik is about three hundred and fifty miles in a straight line, although this was an academic calculation for troops following the incomplete and tortuous road north to the Arctic Circle. The narrow strip of land between the coast and the Swedish border, only fifteen miles wide at its narrowest point, is mountainous throughout, deeply indented by fiords, and in early May still clinging to the fading rigours of winter. The only town of any size is Bodo, some one hundred miles south of

Narvik, although there are other smaller settlements further south of which Mo-i-Rana and Mosjöen are the most notable. In 1940, the railway had not yet been completed in its entirety beyond Grong and the road south of Bodo was interrupted by ferries. Beyond Bodo there was no direct road or rail connection with Narvik, just a wild, inhospitable plateau of tundra.

General Carton de Wiart had already surveyed the road north of Grong at the end of April and pronounced it impassable for any sizeable force of infantry, and the thaw to be expected in May would, albeit temporarily, worsen the road conditions. He appears to have ignored the fact that a Norwegian battalion had successfully moved south from Mosjöen to Grong on 21 April. In London, however, General Massy remained convinced that it was essential to install a considerable force in the Mosjöen-Mo area, supported by anti-aircraft guns and the establishment of an airfield, if the Germans were to be prevented from making an irresistible march to the relief of Narvik. He was supported by the French, and General Audet commanding the Chasseurs Alpins at Namsos actually received a direction from General Gamelin to leave a detachment of ski troops at Grong to delay the German advance. Even as the evacuation commenced, Massy still wanted to transfer a substantial element of 'Mauriceforce' by sea to Mosjöen. But the view of the generals on the spot prevailed on the grounds of the lack of any defence against air attack and the impossibility of establishing a secure base at Mosjöen. Furthermore, if it was physically impracticable for 'Mauriceforce' to withdraw along the road to the north, it would prove to be equally difficult for the Germans, or so it was thought.

In truth, Carton de Wiart was frustrated and fed-up with his Norwegian campaign and wanted only to complete the evacuation and return to a more familiar and potentially rewarding form of warfare. He was of course correct in his assumption that operating without a secure port and air support which had so constrained him at Namsos would be equally evident further north. But that the difficulties of passage north of Grong were exaggerated was clearly demonstrated when the Norwegian battalion which had travelled south in April returned just as easily to Mosjöen in the first week of May; and Colonel Getz, the Norwegian commander, had reported to his legation in London on 1 May that there were good road connections between Grong and Mosjöen. In the end, only one hundred Chasseurs Alpins and two British light anti-aircraft guns were sent by destroyer to Mosjöen on 30 April.

'Mauriceforce' had not been involved in heavy fighting and there is no doubt that at least a significant element should have been transferred further north to supplement or even replace those elements of 24th Brigade which had to be detached to the south from Narvik to delay the German advance. The argument that a large force centred on Mosjöen could not survive for long unless provided with adequate air and logistic support was of course perfectly valid, but if it was deemed essential to delay the German advance to the north at whatever cost until the objective in Narvik could be attained, it was clearly counter productive to remove much needed forces from Narvik when those evacuating from Namsos could so easily have been transferred northwards.

The establishment of a main defensive base at Fauske at the head of Bodo Fiord with air protection from an offshore carrier does not appear to have been given serious consideration. Tactical thinking centred only on delaying measures, rearguard actions with small forces and the inevitable gradual relinquishing of ground; tactics which had proved so fallible in the Gudbransdal. All of these possibilities were of course fraught with difficulties and dangers, but the threat from the south was considered real enough, perhaps excessively so in view of the exceptionally difficult terrain to the north of Bodo. It illustrates once again the failure of the Military Co-ordination Committee to formulate a cohesive strategy for the Norwegian campaign as a whole, but rather to react to events in turn as though they occurred in a vacuum of their own.

Although General Massy's wishes were overruled, the War Office was very much alive to the threat from the south. Of particular concern was the small airfield at Bodo, which although under snow and still unuseable at the end of April, could have been taken by a pre-emptive paratroop landing to prepare it for operations when the snow melted. Lord Cork was therefore directed to send a small force to Bodo to counter such an eventuality and 'C' Company of the Scots Guards was dispatched by the destroyer *Ardent* from Harstad on 29 April. The War Office had already decided to use Independent Companies, of which more later, to harass and delay any German advance to the north of Trondheim. The main problem, as always, was the shortage of airfields from which some progress towards air parity could be developed. On 30 April the Air Ministry directed that a reconnaissance party should look for possible landing sites near Bodo, Mosjöen or Mo; and on 4 May they arrived at Bodo in two flying boats chartered from Imperial Airways which were promptly wrecked by German bombing. Although work to clear and improve the airfield at Bodo was put in hand, it was only too apparent that there was no immediate prospect of providing air support, galling though it was to observe the Luftwaffe roaming freely over the area from their main base at Trondheim (Vaernes).

The Germans wasted little time in pressing forward from Trondheim. On 4 May, Group XXI directed the 2nd Mountain Division to push northward from Grong to Mosjöen and Bodo, and thence try to establish overland contact with General Dietl at Narvik. General Fuerstein, commanding the 2nd Division, had available immediately two battalions plus one company of mountain infantry, one battery of mountain artillery and a platoon of engineers. The rest of the division was still in transit from Germany, and motorised units and a mountain regiment which had executed the original landing at Trondheim were promised as soon as they could be made available. The move forward started on 5 May and ninety miles were covered in four days along roads which had been judged impassable by General Carton de Wiart. In front of them was the single Norwegian battalion which had already marched to Grong and back. Although ill-trained and too demoralised to offer serious resistance to a larger force, they can hardly be excused for failing to demolish road and railway bridges as they retreated untidily northwards.

The Nascent Commandos

Some of the more percipient minds in the War Office were already recognising one of the apparent lessons of the campaign so far. The longstanding principle of employing infantry in at least brigade strength and preferably in even larger formations was well tried in more conventional situations where support services were to hand at the appropriate level. In addition to artillery, engineer, signals and supply, air co-operation was also now recognised by the Army, if not yet the RAF, as an essential component of a balanced infantry force. But none of these were available in Norway in sufficient quantity, if at all, and so forces operating at even battalion strength became immobile and inflexible – forced to apply at least as much effort to sustaining themselves as inflicting damage on the enemy. Despite the generally static character of warfare in the past, small, mobile, hardhitting, independent units, capable of living off the land had surfaced from time to time in military history. The principle of 'special forces' was acknowledged as far back as the Peninsular War, but perhaps the best remembered First World War exponents of this unfamiliar role were T. E. Lawrence's raiding parties in Arabia in 1916 which had fallen out of the desert with such devastating effect on the Turkish controlled railway line south from Damascus.[1] The Germans had also recognised the value of specialised troops operating in smaller numbers during that same conflict with the formation of their mountain battalions (Gebirgsjäger), the descendants of which were playing such a decisive role in this campaign. But the concept had never found real favour with the military authorities in Britain still imbued with finding more conventional ways of replacing trench warfare.

Nevertheless, as early as 18 April the War Office had recognised that small, self-sufficient units, with an approach more akin to that of the guerilla fighter than the traditional infantryman, might be better suited to the terrain and circumstances in Norway which did not appear to favour static all arms set piece confrontations. A small group under the Director of Military Intelligence known as MI(R) had kept alive the notion of irregular warfare and proposed that Independent Companies should be formed from the Territorial Army to operate between Namsos and Narvik. They were to be transported by ship, but were not to have any indigenous transport of their own. Their role was demolition, ambush, to strike and retire; and above all, not to get involved in set piece battles. The method by which the Independent Companies was formed is interesting. Within the divisions of the Territorial Army, each brigade recruited a platoon composed of a section from each battalion. Three platoons were welded into an Independent Company consisting in total of twenty one officers and two hundred and sixty eight other ranks: all were volunteers.[2] The Company Headquarters contained small support sections of Royal Engineers, Royal Army Service Corps, Royal Army Medical Corps and Intelligence. In the first instance, ten companies were assembled at various locations throughout the country and equipped with Arctic clothing and snow shoes, each soldier carrying his own hard pemmican rations. In fact, each man's kit weighed one hundred pounds and was far too heavy to be carried by a supposedly mobile soldier operating in rough country. Inevitably, as the Independent Companies retreated through Northern Norway, articles of equipment and clothing were indiscriminately discarded, often to be regretted later. The Royal Marines yomping across the Falklands, far fitter and better trained than the Independent Companies of 1940, carried only sixty pounds.

The plan to use Independent Companies in Norway was approved by the Military Co-ordination Committee in preference to General Massy's wish to use some elements of 'Mauriceforce', and the first five companies were ordered to Norway. Their intended destinations were frequently changed, but No. 1 Company was landed at Mo, 2 and 3 at Bodo and 4 and 5 at Mosjöen, replacing the one hundred Chasseurs Alpins who had been transferred north from 'Mauriceforce'. Their commander, Colonel Colin Gubbins,[3] established his Headquarters at Bodo and on 5 May was placed under the overall command of Lord Cork, still flying his flag in the cruiser *Aurora*, thus making communications tenuous at best. The codename of the operation was 'Scissorsforce' which rather aptly described their intended mode of operation. They were directed to prevent the Germans occupying Bodo, Mo and Mosjöen by employing harrying tactics from the flanks and were specifically ordered not to attempt to offer prolonged resistance.[4] Their main objective therefore was to disrupt the German lines of communication and they were enjoined to 'get to know the country intimately, make use of locals . . . use wit and low cunning, be always on guard'.[5] In practice, their opportunities to act in the desired way were few and they were increasingly forced to act in concert with the regular infantry transferred from Narvik. But it was nevertheless an imaginative, far seeing concept, and is of particular interest because the Independent Companies were the direct forerunners of the Commandos who were to play an ever increasing role later in the war.

Colonel Gubbins wasted no time in getting into contact with the Norwegian battalion which had retreated from Grong and found them at Fellingfors, some twenty five miles south of Mosjöen. As he travelled south he was able to see at first hand the terrain over which the battle would be fought during the next month. The roads were appalling, water ran off the hills during the day, froze overnight, and gradually broke up the roads in the process. The Norwegian battalion was only four hundred strong, disorganised and in low spirits, and it was immediately apparent to Gubbins that they were not going to make any significant contribution to delaying the German advance. In fact on 9 May, only four days after leaving Grong, the Germans easily ran through the Norwegian positions.

No. 5 Independent Company established itself about ten miles to the south of Mosjöen where the Björnaa River forms a narrow lake, with the road taking the eastern shore and the railway following the west bank. It was a good location for an ambush, carefully selected with the help of the Indian Army mountain warfare 'expert' attached to the Company. Two platoons with two Norwegian companies guarded the road which was exposed to fire from the steep hillsides running down to the water's edge whilst the other platoon protected the alternative line of approach along the railway. The railway bridge over the Vefsna River, a tributary of the Björnaa running in from the south west, was demolished by the Independent Company. On the morning of 10 May, the vanguard of the German force came into sight cycling down the road, looking for all the world like some youth organisation sampling the delights of the fresh air and the countryside. The Independent Company and their new found Norwegian comrades held their fire, and the Germans cycled blindly into a perfectly laid trap. About fifty fell almost at once in a jumbled mass of bicycles, helmets and rifles: the Wehrmacht had certainly not learnt from their experience in the Gudbransdal where they frequently made the same mistake and were to do so again. Although the Germans did not follow up in force, it was decided about midday to fall back on Mosjöen. This was, of course, in accordance with their original orders;

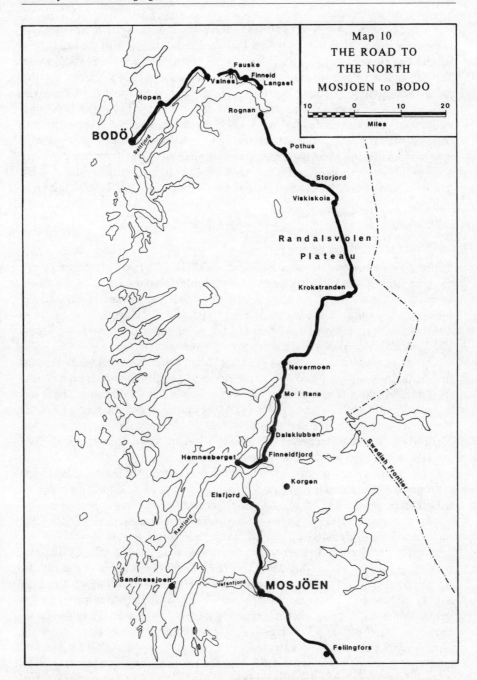

Map 10
THE ROAD TO
THE NORTH
MOSJOEN to BODO

Miles

Independent Companies were not intended to be used as defensive infantry, a role for which they were neither designed nor equipped. Fortunately for No. 5 Company, there was low cloud throughout the day and no Luftwaffe activity.

Colonel Gubbins quickly recognised that there was no obvious defensive position at Mosjöen, so he ordered No. 1 Company forward from Mo to guard the head of the Ranfiord at Hemnesberget. There was a break in the road about halfway between Mosjöen and Mo requiring a ferry crossing from Elsfiord to Hemnesberget, and this could be expected to impose at least a temporary halt on the German advance. In the meantime No. 5 Company, with whatever help they could gain from the Norwegians, would stage delaying actions north of Mosjöen. Already there is a clear indication that Gubbins was beginning to think of the Independent Companies in terms of a conventional infantry company rather than as the irregular force for which they were equipped. However, the Germans now took a bold initiative which rapidly changed the situation between Mosjöen and Mo and nullified the measures Gubbins had set in train.

Leapfrog

Whilst the initial German invasion had exploited all the advantages of boldness, speed and surprise, the subsequent enlargement of the bridgeheads was carried out in a more methodical, cautious way, pushing steadily along the obvious lines of advance and consolidating their lines of communication behind them. Their next move therefore was unexpectedly daring and might well have failed had it not thrown the British Headquarters in Bodo into a temporary state of panic.

Operation 'Wildente' was a joint land, sea, air operation to leapfrog up the coast from Trondheim. Their objective was the Hemnesöy peninsular which projects into the Ranfiord about fifteen miles south-west of Mo. They would thus divide the Independent Companies, leaving Nos. 4 and 5 Companies and the remnants of the Norwegian battalion to the south with just No. 1 Independent Company and a few Norwegians between themselves and Bodo. But there was a further bonus, their immediate objective was Hemnesberget, the northern terminus of the ferry from Elsfiord. Nos. 4 and 5 Companies would therefore apparently be trapped unless some other way could be found to move quickly from Elsfiord to Finneidfiord, the village on the isthumus between the Hemnesöy peninsular and the mainland.

On the morning of 10 May, a large infantry company of about three hundred men was transported to Hemnesberget in the Norwegian coastal steamer *Nord Norge* with an escort of two aircraft. Another half company followed in two Dornier Do 18 flying boats. The passage of the *Nord Norge* was reported on the morning of the 10th by Norwegian coastguards to Naval Headquarters at Harstad and within two hours the anti-aircraft cruiser *Calcutta* and the destroyer *Zulu* were dispatched to intercept. But despite this quick response, valuable time was lost whilst the two ships joined up off the Myken Light at 1700, and as a result they actually entered the Ranfiord behind the *Nord Norge*. Lord Cork, who had had full command of 'Scissorsforce' since 5 May had clearly not expected this move, and with his mind still hankering for a naval assault on Narvik, he had neglected the seaward flank of his Independent Companies south of Bodo. In mitigation it must be added that the *modus operandi* of Independent Companies did not really require such support, but in fact, the Companies were already beginning to act more like regular infantry units than irregular forces.

The Germans landed at Hemnesberget by 1900. No. 1 Independent Company had already deployed a platoon to this attractive little port with its wooden houses running down to the quay, and a somewhat startled platoon commander immediately contested the landing. But they were quickly forced to withdraw after a brief period of concentrated street fighting. The *Calcutta* and the *Zulu* now arrived on the scene and promptly sank the *Nord Norge*, but not before the whole company and two mountain guns had been landed. No. 1 Company had meanwhile concentrated with about one hundred and twenty Norwegian troops with four heavy machine guns at Finneidfiord at the neck of the Hemnesöy peninsular and about eight miles from Hemnesberget.

The Germans entered Mosjöen early on 11 May and advanced rapidly forward with the aim of joining up with the amphibious operation at Hemnesöy. Nos. 4 and 5 Companies, with their backs to the Elsfiord ferry which no longer had a further terminus, fell neatly into the trap. If they had retreated quickly either across country or by ferry to Finneidfiord where No. 1 Company was now established, they could have remained in the action. That such a route was feasible was subsequently demonstrated by both the Norwegians and the Germans, but Gubbins was taking no chances and decided to evacuate the Companies by sea. They embarked on a coastal steamer for Sandnessjöen at the mouth of the Vefsenfiord where the majority transferred to two destroyers and were taken to Bodo. The anti-aircraft battery which had originally accompanied the Chasseurs Alpins went with them but had to abandon their guns.

This hasty move was undoubtedly a mistake. Whilst Gubbins could not be blamed for the unenviable situation he now faced, it hardly improved his circumstances to remove at a stroke two of the three companies he had at his disposal. Even if he was not sure of the feasibility of withdrawing 4 and 5 Companies direct to Finneidfiord, he could have moved them round to Mo where they could have joined up with the Scots Guards who had by now arrived and were already warned to move south. In effect, he could have leapfrogged in turn over the Germans rather than remove his pieces from the board altogether. Two more companies would have proved invaluable to the Scots Guards a few days later at Dalsklubben.

11 May had not been a happy day for 'Scissorsforce', four out of the five companies were now marooned in or close to Bodo leaving No. 1 Company and a few battered Norwegians terribly exposed. The Norwegians north of Mosjöen withdrew down the road towards Elsfiord, but their further retreat by the normal route was blocked by the German occupation of Hemnesberget. Instead they were taken round by ferry to a landing point on the road north of Korgen and completed the journey to Mo by road. Although the remnants of the battalion were saved, they had to abandon their heavy equipment and their capability, never very high, was even further diminished.

The Germans reached Elsfiord by the 15th, a rather slow advance by their standards, and three and a half companies were sent across the mountains to Korgen whilst the remainder were eventually ferried to Finneidfiord. That such a move was possible indicated how misguided it had been to withdraw 4 and 5 Companies to Bodo. It is also incredible that the Norwegians had not destroyed all the available boats at Elsfiord before withdrawing. Far too often in this campaign, insufficient attention was shown to placing physical obstacles in the path of the German advance.

The Hemnesberget landing had struck another blow against the Allied cause in Norway and there was no longer confidence in either London or Harstad that any substantial delay could be imposed upon the inexorable German advance along the length of Norway. Already almost all of Norway south of the Arctic Circle was under their firm control leaving only a narrow strip of mostly mountainous, barren land north to the North Cape. The Norwegian Legation in London conferred with the French Government and lamented the inadequate response and military performance of the British, but in truth their own performance hardly justified this sanctimonious stance. In any case Britain and France now had weightier issues on their minds as the Germans had launched their long awaited offensive on the Western Front on 10 May. Norway was now even more of a sideshow and the seeds of the eventual withdrawal were already being sown. On 14 May the Chiefs of Staff confirmed that operations south of Bodo should be confined to the Independent Companies with the aim of making Mosjöen and Bodo into a 'no mans land'.[6] Even so, the desire to capture Narvik was still strong, and on the same day the new Prime Minister, Mr Churchill, telegraphed to Lord Cork 'I hope you will get Narvik cleaned up as soon as possible and then work southwards with increasing force'.[7] A large measure of wishful thinking now pervaded messages from London.

The Scots Guards Move South

We now need to move back a few days to set the scene for the next stage of what was soon to become a desperate rearguard action reminiscent in many respects of the retreat in the Gudbransdal. Although caught by surprise by the Hemnesberget operation, Lord Cork was still acutely aware of the need to hold firmly on to the southern approaches to Narvik and on 9 May both the Scots and Irish Guards were warned of a short notice move to Mo. Brigadier Fraser, still recovering from his injury sustained at Ankenes, was placed in charge of all troops operating south of Bodo. The Scots Guards departed for Mo carrying supplies for fourteen days early on the morning of 11 May in the cruiser *Enterprise* accompanied by the destroyer *Hesperus*, the sloop *Fleetwood* and a small merchantman, the *Margot*. They suffered another rough passage and many of the troops again succumbed to sea sickness. A request that they should be joined at Mo by 'C' Company which was still at Bodo was turned down. They were accompanied by four 25 pounders and three Bofors anti-aircraft guns, and some Royal Engineers. The weather apart the passage was uneventful, but the length and narrowness of the Ranfiord immediately aroused naval concern because of the difficulty of manoeuvring in the event of air attack. This is understandable, most of the fiord is very narrow, in places no more than a mile across. Even at this early stage the Navy confirmed that they could not support the force through the Ranfiord and that supplies would have to come overland from Rognan, eighty miles to the north. The fear of being cut off was ever present, either as a result of another leapfrogging move by sea or paratroops, or by a flanking movement to landward by mountain troops.

On 11 May a counter-attack against the Germans at Hemnesberget was made by Norwegians under Captain Ellinger, a spirited Dane who later attached himself to the

Scots Guards and fought with distinction. But it was driven back some way short of its objective although the *Enterprise* shelled Hemnesberget for good measure in the early hours of the 12th on its way to Mo which was reached at 0500. As they surveyed in the half light the uninviting snow-shrouded terrain on their way up the Ranfiord, the Guards were not exactly confident of their ability to make a stand in this difficult position. It is, in passing, interesting to note that when they passed Hemnesberget on their way up the Ranfiord, the Scots Guards passed within at most a few hundred yards of the Germans they were subsequently to face at Dalsklubben. The Luftwaffe arrived at Mo soon after the *Enterprise*, but most of the troops were ashore and only one 'puffer' was sunk. The *Margot* however rammed the quay in the excitement and confusion and the captain could only be persuaded with difficulty not to retire immediately with the artillery still on board which it was estimated would take three hours to unload.

> The Gunner Battery Sergeant-Major bet her captain a bottle of whiskey that he could do it in an hour, and he agreed to wait. They did it in thirty-five minutes – and got two bottles.[8]

Lieut Colonel Trappes-Lomax commanding the Scots Guards considered making another assault on Hemnesberget immediately after his arrival, but instead took up a defensive position at Dalsklubben, midway between Mo and Finneidfiord.[9] No. 1 Independent Company was still at Finneidfiord, quite a strong defensive position, but could not be expected to remain there for very long. To break out from Hemnesöy the Germans had to pass through Finneidfiord where the large triangular peninsular is connected to the mainland by a narrow strip of land. On the landward side, steep tree-covered slopes would have made an encircling move difficult and well dug in troops in sufficient strength should have been able to hold the neck of land bordering the fiord for some time. However, Dalsklubben was potentially an even stronger position than Finneidfiord and Trappes-Lomax should not be criticised for deciding that this would be the best location to make his stand. Furthermore, it allowed the troops time to dig in before the enemy approached, an advantage frequently denied in the campaign in Central Norway.

The road north from Finneidfiord hugs the side of the fiord and is flanked by very steep mountain slopes. At Dalsklubben, the River Dalselva rushes down a narrow valley into the Ranfiord, bordered on both sides by high precipitous spurs running right down to the edge of the fiord. Between the spurs at the mouth of the river is a bay about half a mile across and half a mile in depth, the road running round the bay and across a bridge at its apex.[10] The bay at Dalsklubben is rather like a wineglass on its side – the Germans could either come round the rim or down the narrow stem which is the Dalselva river valley. Looking at this position today, it is difficult to imagine how the Germans could clamber over the southerly ridge which is mostly precipitous rock in its upper parts and clothed in dense woods nearer the river. There was another bridge about a mile up the river, but apart from these two crossings which could be easily demolished, the river was in spate in the spring thaw and very difficult to cross. Even if attacking troops went all the way round the head of the valley, they should still have had some difficulty descending to its mouth against determined opposition. The ridge on the north side of the Dalselva River is even more formidable than that on the south. A well disposed and dug-in force watching the road round the spur to the south and the lower slopes of the valley to the east should have been able to hold their position for some time even though the birch trees in the valley bottom and on the lower slopes restricted the field of fire. Furthermore, the valley floor and lower slopes were covered in heavy snow making movement down the valley even more difficult. Dalsklubben was certainly not encirclable quite as easily as many of the positions in the Gudbransdal or on other stretches of the road north from Mosjöen. All in all, Trappes-Lomax should have been reasonably content with the Dalsklubben position even though the presence of another battalion would have been extremely valuable to really seal up the Dalselva valley. It is here that the two Independent Companies which had been shipped back so hastily from Sandnessjöen to Bodo would have proved useful. Trappes-Lomax would have been even more confident if the Irish Guards had arrived in time to support their Scottish comrades.

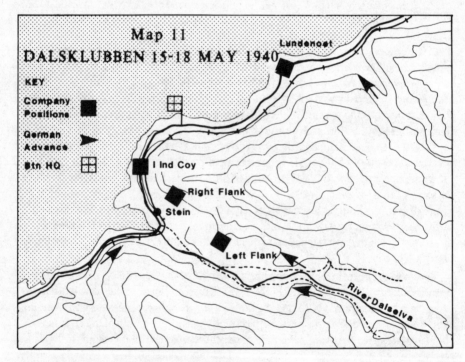

The Guards started to dig in to their new positions on the 13th, constructing log barricades where the rock made entrenching impossible. But their capability was further weakened when 'B' Company was withdrawn north towards Mo to forestall a possible German approach along the opposite side of the Ranfiord. Trappes-Lomax placed 'Right Flank' on the lower slopes of the headland to the north of the bay where they could wait for the enemy coming round the spur and 'Left Flank' up the valley on the northern slopes near the upper bridge. No. 1 Independent Company, when withdrawn from Finneidfiord, was to be placed in reserve on the road by the northern spur, but it would have been able to make a greater contribution to the forthcoming battle if it had been placed higher up the valley to reinforce 'Left Flank'. This would have helped to resist the inevitable encircling movement, for it would have been suicidal for the Germans to make their main approach along the road and round the headland of the southern spur. Three small detachments of Norwegian ski troops were posted on the hill tops but achieved little. Another weakness in the plan was that the four 25 pounders were placed too far to the rear along the road in a position where they could command the southern spur, but not the valley. Their siting, along with that of the Independent Company, suggests that Trappes-Lomax underestimated the likelihood of the Germans preferring the indirect approach down the valley. In any event, the guns were to play little part in the action because their communications which ran along the road were soon disrupted.

The night was miserably cold for men exhausted by the sea crossing, their forced march from Mo, and a day spent digging in. They had no sleeping bags or hot food and dare not light fires for fear of exposing their position. On the following morning, the 14th, Major Graham, second in command, went forward to Finneidfiord to review the situation, but had to withdraw rapidly when the German attack started at about 1700. The Independent Company was quickly withdrawn from Finneidfiord under the cover of the 25 pounders and a timely intervention by a destroyer which arrived in the Ranfiord at an opportune moment. They took up their designated position in the rear vacated by 'B' Company.

During the long clear night German bombers put in an appearance to supplement sporadic mortar fire, but there was a welcome success in the early morning when one of the Bofors shot down a bomber and the troops jubilantly apprehended the pilot and gunner.

The Guards held their position firmly throughout the 15th inflicting some casualties although the Unit Diary recorded that the situation was 'anything but satisfactory'. At midday on the 16th the main bridge was blown and a Dornier flying boat shot down by Bofors in the fiords with the capture of four of its crew. Towards nightfall the other bridge was demolished, the Diary commenting 'a good time was had by all, as there is nothing more fun than a nice bit of destruction'.[11]

The 2nd Mountain Division under General Fuerstein had by now been diverted to Norway from the Western Front by direct order of Hitler in a bid to make a high-speed dash to Narvik, and by the 17th the German strength had built up to about 1,750 although the difficulty of access prevented all of these being deployed against Dalsklubben. Nevertheless, large numbers were observed advancing down the road from Finneidfiord supported by artillery and mortars. A few who penetrated round the spur and attempted to repair the bridge were quickly dispatched by 'Right Flank', but smallish numbers of mountain troops were already beginning to outflank the Guards' position. To add to their worries, about one hundred and fifty paratroops were dropped on a frozen lake seven miles to the south-east from where they could advance down the Dalselva valley or follow the mountain ridge to the north.

A major attack developed down the valley at 2130 on the 17th and was at first stoutly resisted. Guardsman Bryson in the leading platoon particularly distinguished himself, inflicting several casualties and twice rescuing wounded men under fire for which he was awarded the DCM. However, by midnight 'Left Flank' appeared in danger of being surrounded and it was becoming extremely doubtful if the position could be maintained for another day. Adding to their problems, news arrived that more paratroops had landed in the rear and were engaging 'B' Company south of Mo. At 0200 on the 18th the Battalion was ordered to withdraw. Despite being under almost continuous fire for three days, casualties were light, only three killed and about seventy injured: testimony to the good defensive position and the fact that they had nearly two days to dig-in, a luxury which was rarely possible in the similar actions in the Gudbransdal. The German mortar bombs were also proving ineffective, their force being dissipated in the deep snow. But the continual harassment from the air was very wearing on the troops' nerves, and although they were regularly promised air support of their own, they saw none. In fact, there was no prospect of air patrols this far south until the airfield at Bodo was ready and that was not to be accomplished for another week.

A defensive position was briefly taken up about four miles to the north of Dalsklubben at Lundenget, but at 0900 further orders were received to retreat to the north of Mo leaving 'B' Company to guard the rear. Dumps of petrol and ammunition in the town were destroyed, but the Germans arrived only minutes after the last party had vacated the town. 'B' Company failed to get through Mo in time but later joined up again with the battalion after bypassing the town through the mountains. The Battalion had now lost almost all its equipment and personal kit, the troops retaining only their weapons: the lack of transport was again proving to be a serious liability. How they envied the Norwegian battalion which had passed through Dalsklubben comfortably ensconced in lorries.

A walk along the road north of Finneidfiord can leave no doubt that Dalsklubben was the best defensive position in this area, but did Trappes-Lomax make the most of it? It must be acknowledged right away that he was well short of the ideal number of troops to cover the likely lines of advance despite the physical advantages of the site. Only two of his four companies were available, 'C' Company was still at Bodo as a precaution against a paratroop assault on the airfield and 'B' Company had been withdrawn northwards to Mo to counteract a possible German advance on the west bank of the Ranfiord which never materialised. He had one Independent Company under command, but they were scratch troops playing a role for which they had not been intended, and by his dispositions at Dalsklubben he did not appear to have great confidence in their capacity as a regular infantry company. The straightforward line of advance round the southerly spur was stoutly held, as indeed it should have been given the hazardous nature of this line of approach. The situation in the Dalselva valley was more fluid. It was very difficult to ascertain in the thickly wooded country just how many Germans had infiltrated round the head of the valley. In retrospect, it appears that the numbers were small enough to have been held by a well dug in company, but when reports were received that further parachute troops had dropped in his rear, Trappes-Lomax's concern at the possibility of being totally surrounded can be well understood.

My conclusion, with the benefit of hindsight, is that Dalsklubben might have been held for longer although retreat would have become inevitable eventually. But given the lack of support in the rear, and the uncertainty of just how many Germans were working their way round the left flank, the decision to withdraw was reasonable – as Trappes-Lomax saw the situation at the time. However, Brigadier Gubbins, now in command of the Brigade after Willie Fraser had returned to Harstad not yet recovered from his injury, clearly felt that Dalsklubben had not been held as long as it might have been and his confidence in Trappes-Lomax began to waver. Their disagreement was to come to a head after the later retreat from Krokstranden.

It is true of course that the Guards suffered very few casualties in the action at Dalsklubben, and it could be inferred, and perhaps was by Gubbins and later by Auchinleck, that this indicated a lack of commitment. But the scale of casualties does not necessarily reflect lack of effort. The Guards were securely entrenched to contest the two lines of approach they could reasonably command – round the spur and down the valley. But their equipment and training simply did not allow them to match on equal terms the specialist mountain units in a mobile action on mountain slopes feet deep in snow. Although Gubbins had seen for himself when he arrived in Norway the conditions along the road north of Mosjöen, only one other member of his staff, a GSO 3, had been to the front line, and this lack of awareness of what conditions were really like became a source of irritation and contention between Brigade HQ and the troops on the ground. If the Irish Guards had arrived at Bodo as intended and moved rapidly south, or if Nos. 4 and 5 Independent Companies had not been evacuated to Bodo, it is quite conceivable that the German advance could have been stemmed for longer. But the overriding factor was always, as it had been in the Gudbransdal, the inability of the British battalions to overcome the constraints of terrain and climate. As soon as the Germans took to the mountain slopes, their inexorable advance was unstoppable.

The Scots Guards had held Dalsklubben for five days against increasingly superior numbers, but had succumbed again to the familiar encircling movement through the mountains. The Norwegian battalions, although diminished in size and short of equipment, might have been expected to operate more readily in such conditions, but were proving of little value. Indeed their main contribution was to commandeer what little transport was available.

The fundamental problem was however even more deep seated. The Allies had no coherent strategy for preventing the Germans marching to the relief of Narvik. The War Office placed its faith in the Independent Companies, but totally failed to recognise that the Territorial Army, despite its enthusiasm, was simply not the right vehicle at this stage of the war for providing the special qualities needed of irregular forces. On the other hand, the regular formations were not deployed in sufficient strength in the right place to offer a realistic chance of placing more than a temporary halt to the relentless German advance. If the real aim of sending troops to the south of Bodo was to prevent the Germans reaching Narvik rather than to retain ground for its own sake, there was little to be gained by stringing penny packets of troops all the way along the road from Mosjöen to Bodo. It was the Gudbransdal all over again – the lessons were not being learned quickly enough.

Disaster at Sea

Lieutenant General Claude Auckinleck had by now arrived at Harstad to take command of all the land and air forces in northern Norway.[12] He needed little convincing of the vital importance of maintaining a strong Allied force to the south of Narvik and decided to commit the whole of the 24th Guards Brigade to that area and leave the capture of Narvik to the Norwegian, French and Polish troops who were now beginning to make worthwhile progress. General Mackesy had already ordered the Irish Guards to the south on 11 May and on the morning of the 14th the South Wales Borderers were given similar instructions.

The Irish Guards embarked in the transport *Chrobry* from Skaanland, but spent most of the 14th cooped-up in the ship in the bay under regular air attack waiting for clearance to depart. At last, at 1830 the *Chrobry* weighed anchor and set off slowly down the fiord escorted by the destroyer *Wolverine* and the sloop *Stork*, and ominously shadowed by a German observation plane. The inevitable air attack arrived at midnight, still in broad daylight at this time of the year, and unimpeded by any anti-aircraft defence, three He 111s were successful in hitting the aft quarters of the *Chrobry* occupied by the Battalion officers. Lieut Colonel Faulkner and five other senior officers were killed instantly and others were lucky to escape. Fire spread rapidly, the sprinkler system had been wrecked, and no water was forthcoming from the hydrants when the hoses were ran out. The Guards mustered on the deck and began to throw overboard mortar bombs and ammunition which were threatened by the flames; most of the surviving officers were in the rear of the ship, isolated by the fire from the men.

The bombers were meanwhile circling overhead, their crews enjoying the unaccustomed spectacle of actually hitting a moving ship, and inviting speculation down below that they were only waiting for the men to get into the boats before attacking again with machine guns. But with the ship's power cut off the forward lifeboats could not be lowered, and there was no alternative but to wait for the escorting destroyer to come alongside. A few lifeboats were launched aft with mixed loads of soldiers, sailors and wounded and were rowed to the sloop *Stork*. Many were dressed only in pyjamas, others had their rifles and kitbags from which they were reluctant to be parted, reinforced by a reminder from a sergeant that they should 'take care of those rifles, they are government property'.[13] Most of those who could not get into the boats stayed on the burning ship rather than face almost certain death from exposure in the icy water although a whaler from the *Stork* rescued about twenty from the sea. Despite the danger of explosion, the *Wolverine* came alongside to starboard and a gangway was quickly put in position. Commander Craske, captain of the *Wolverine* later wrote:

> We closed in on the burning and sinking ship. I never before realised what the discipline of the Guards was. We got a gangway shipped forward and the men were ordered to file off on to us. There was no confusion, no hurry, and no sign of haste or flurry. I knew that there might be only a matter of minutes in which to get them off. I had four ropes fixed so as to hurry up the transfer. They continued to file steadily off in one line. I cursed and swore at them, but they had orders to file, and they filed. I saw someone who seemed to me to be a young officer and in no measured terms I told him to get them off by all four ropes. In a

second they conformed to this order by one of their own officers still steadily and without fuss or confusion. Their conduct in the most trying circumstances, in the absence of senior officers, on a burning and sinking ship, open at any moment to a new attack, was as fine, or finer than, the conduct in the old days of the soldiers on the *Birkenhead*. It may interest you to know that 694 were got on board in sixteen minutes.[14]

The praise did not go unreciprocated. On 16 May, the new Battalion Commander wrote to Commander Craske:

> I wish to convey to you the deepest gratitude and admiration of all ranks for the bravery and skill displayed by the officers and crews of HMS *Wolverine* and *Stork*. It was entirely due to your gallant action that so many lives were saved.[15]

Commander Craske, who was killed at sea the following year, was awarded the DSC. It was indeed a gallant and well ordered rescue. But the loss of the *Chrobry* had left the Scots Guards dreadfully isolated as they dug in at Dalsklubben.

The Irish Guards were landed on the quays at Harstad early on the following morning, there were amazingly few casualties apart from the senior officers who had died in the initial attack. The Battalion reorganised under the command of Captain H. C. McGildowny, the most senior officer remaining, and began to refit as best it could from what was available at Harstad. One of the more important losses was three light tanks of the 3rd Hussars which were the only British tanks landed in Norway. Although Norway was by no means good tank country, in certain circumstances, as had already been demonstrated at Tretten, they could tie down a disproportionate number of infantry not equipped to deal with them. Four days later on 19 May the Irish Guards were ordered back to Bodo.

The transfer of the South Wales Borderers to Bodo was hardly less dramatic, although the injury in this case was self-inflicted. With the Brigade Headquarters, the Battalion was embarked on the cruiser *Effingham* on the evening of 17 May for the move to Bodo. Sailing outside of the Leads to lessen the risk of air attack, the *Effingham* escaped the bombers, but ran aground at twenty three knots with an escorting destroyer on the Faksen shoal only twelve miles short of their destination. The sea approaches to Bodo are infested with rocks and shoals and was not an easy place to enter in more favourable conditions. The whole Battalion was rescued without loss by an accompanying anti-aircraft cruiser and returned to Harstad early in the morning of the 18th, but again most of their equipment was lost. The *Effingham* herself was eventually abandoned and sunk after efforts to refloat her failed. To add to their problems, most of the Borderers' reserve equipment had now been issued to the Irish Guards who had returned in similar circumstances two days before. Even so, two Companies were refitted and sent again by destroyer to Bodo that same night, this time successfully, to be followed by the remainder of the Battalion a few days later.

Crossing the Snow Belt

As a result of these setbacks, it now became important for the German advance to be delayed, or Bodo would be overrun before it could be reinforced. We must therefore return to the Scots Guards and the Independent Company which we left retreating from Dalsklubben on 18 May. They were still one hundred and thirty five miles from Bodo along a narrow inferior road which ran mainly along the western bank of the River Rana until reaching a snow-covered plateau north of Randalsvollen. Beyond this watershed the road picked up the River Saltdal following it down into the Saltfiord at Rognan to the south-east of Bodo. The battalion continued the weary march north, resting for about eight hours at Strandjorden before pressing on to Sandheim. Enemy air activity was not heavy and one aircraft was actually shot down by Bofors. 'B' Company had meanwhile rejoined the battalion after their arduous cross-country march reminiscent of similar adventures in the Gudbransdal and at Steinkjer. They had also at last been joined by 'C' Company who had been hurried down by road from Bodo.

On the 20th, orders were received from General Auckinleck to make a stand at Krokstranden, some thirty miles north of Mo.

> You have now reached a good position for defence. Essential to stand and fight denying enemy opportunities for outflanking in less difficult country further north. I rely on Scots Guards to stop enemy.[16]

As the Guards surveyed Krokstranden, they could see little to substantiate the confidence implied in the message. A better position to attempt another delaying action might have been a gorge about ten miles to the north of Mo near the village of Nevermoen. Here the river valley narrows to about half a mile with precipitous slopes on both sides of the river and the road. There was of course no real confidence that the position would not be encircled after their experience at Dalsklubben, but it was certainly a more promising location than Krokstranden. It would have been a particularly good location for the Independent Company to have been used in the way intended as a harassing force. But it was passed-by and eventually Trappes-Lomax surveyed, with a good deal of apprehension, the ground at Krokstranden.

A reconnaissance of the site quickly confirmed that however good a defensive position it might have appeared on the map at Harstad, the reality was totally different. The valley at Krokstranden is wide with the road, gently rising towards the snow plateau, running close to the east bank of the river. The ridge to the north-west is not steep and was clothed in birch and douglas fir, restricting fields of fire. It was by no means difficult country for mountain troops equipped with snow shoes. The hill to the south-east was even more friendly and would prove no problem at all; whilst the mountains at Dalsklubben dominate the scene, at Krokstranden they merely form the backcloth. The road was surrounded by snow six feet deep and all supplies would have to come down the road from Rognan, still some sixty miles to the north and subject all the time to air attack. It was Trappes-Lomax's view that it would have taken a brigade to hold this position.

Trappes-Lomax recognised immediately that there was no chance of preventing the usual outflanking manoeuvre by mountain troops able to cross the snow-covered hills with a facility quite beyond the capacity of his own Battalion, and represented his views to Brigadier Gubbins. Nevertheless, Gubbins, who was himself being pressed by General Auchinleck, gave Trappes-Lomax written instructions to 'only withdraw from any position you hold if in your opinion there is serious danger to the safety of your force': it was a widely held view within the Battalion that this situation had already been reached.

In fact, as Trappes-Lomax recognised only too clearly, the Battalion was in grave danger of being trapped. The single track road across the plateau to the north of Randalsvollen could only be kept open by continuous ploughing and was lined by sheer walls of snow several feet deep. The snow plateau was totally different country to any that the Guards had seen before in Norway; bleak, flat moorland with isolated outcrops of rock and not a tree in sight, the Arctic Circle actually traverses the plateau about halfway across. There was no shelter whatsoever, the road just cutting straight across an Arctic wasteland. Even in summer this looks an uninviting and forlorn place, in winter it resembles the surface of the moon, featureless as far as the eye can see. And with the Luftwaffe's all seeing eye, it was no place to linger in daylight which existed for most of the day at this time of the year. There was no escape from attacking enemy aircraft and a well placed bomb could close the road for several hours.

Major Graham had crossed the snow belt twice to reconnoitre the ground on the other side and had already experienced the feeling of utter helplessness when trapped between the snow walls by a low level machine gunning aircraft, but he had survived to complete the crossing. The situation was exacerbated by the untidy withdrawal of the Norwegians, and to crown the confusion, handfuls of civilian refugees were now mingling with the soldiers.

The Scots Guards set up three positions either side of Krokstranden. Position A, three miles on the road to the south[17] was manned by 'C' Company and 'Right Flank' and came under attack on the afternoon of the 21st. They quickly retired to Position C which was at Randalsvollen on the edge of the snow belt. Position B, with 'B' Company and 'Left Flank', was attacked at dawn on the 22nd. The usual outflanking manoeuvre was commenced immediately and penetrated well past the left flank, and another hasty withdrawal was made to Position C despite the heroic efforts of Captain Ellinger and his three machine guns who had attached themselves to the Scots Guards after the capture of Hemnesberget. With only a tortuous line of retreat behind them, Randalsvollen was clearly no position to mount a major defensive action. Another outflanking manoeuvre, which was inevitable as night follows day, would have spelt disaster for the whole Battalion. But the snow belt could only be crossed by lorry and that only during the few brief hours of twilight. Trappes-Lomax had fortunately foreseen the problem and arranged for a Guardsman to accompany every lorry which had moved the Norwegian battalion across the area on the night of 19/20 May to ensure that the vehicle returned.

The Germans had temporarily halted their advance after moving into Position B, but it was essential that they did not recognise that Position C was only an assembly point for the crossing of the snow belt rather than another defensive position. A reconnaissance aircraft appeared, but despite orders not to fire to avoid revealing their position, it was engaged by a bren gun and with unexpected if undeserved good luck was shot down; fortune for once favouring the indisciplined. An advance party of twelve German cyclists was also summarily accounted for by a rear party with a machine gun carrier which had been salvaged from the wreck of the *Effingham*. Even so, if the Germans had pressed on with their attack, there is every likelihood that the Scots Guards would have been annihilated, their escape cut off and starved or bombed into surrender. It is incredible that the Luftwaffe neglected to bomb the road just before the twilight period – this would almost certainly have closed it for long enough to prevent their escape.

However, the Battalion was successfully evacuated over the brief hours of semi-darkness, and by early morning on the 23rd was established at Viskiskoia on the far side of the snow belt. Brigadier Gubbins clearly felt that the Krokstranden position had been abandoned too readily, but it was undoubtedly indefensible for any length of time and posed a very real risk of losing the whole Battalion. As in the Gudbransdal, the British tactic of defending every inch of the way rather than establishing a good defensive position in strength and depth was risking the decimation of the force in penny packets. As Major Graham has observed, the military axiom which says 'disperse for movement and concentrate to fight' was never observed throughout the campaign.[18]

Nevertheless, the Brigade Commander decided that Colonel Trappes-Lomax should be relieved of his command and on the 23rd he was sent back to Harstad. Whilst he may have been cautious, it was not without good reason. The Battalion, despite being under-strength, had held the Dalsklubben position for five days and it is impossible to argue that any protracted defence of Krokstranden was feasible. Brigadier Gubbins had not examined the terrain for himself and there can be little doubt that if he had he would have agreed with Trappes-Lomax.[19] The decision at this time to remove their colonel, a respected leader, was hardly calculated to improve the morale and fighting efficiency of a force already exhausted and beginning to suffer the demoralisation of being subjected to fighting one rear-guard action after another. It was a harsh decision and not one justified by the events of the past ten days. One officer recorded in his diary:

> CO comes back and says he has been sacked! For saving his Battalion presumably? Anyway someone is nearly lynched. This is quite monstrous. Battle develops . . .[20]

Feelings were running high and Brigadier Gubbins was now losing the confidence of both the regular battalion and the Independent Companies. It was rumoured that Gubbins himself was relieved shortly afterwards for having the effrontery to sack a Guards Battalion commander. In fact, he had received a clear instruction from General Auchinleck to remove the Battalion commander if he was dissatisfied with his performance. Auchinleck himself was not familiar with the terrain and the conditions under which the Guards were fighting, and he may well have recognised later that the sacking was unjustified. Fortunately, unlike General Mackesy, it was to have no detrimental impact on Trappes-Lomax's career and he was promoted to brigadier two years later.

No Respite – Viskiskoia

Viskiskoia was hardly a better position than Krokstranden. The road now ran downhill alongside the River Saltdal through some lovely scenery. The mountains closed in again with their dense cloak of birch trees on the lower slopes, but the valley bottom is more open with fields and scattered farmhouses. It is almost a carbon copy of the country to the south of the snow belt. The problem as always was the ability of the Germans to outflank the more static British troops confined largely to the valley floor. The road crossed the river to the east bank at Viskiskoia close to the position where the Junkerdal Valley runs off to the east. The latter is an idyllic spot, but its scenic attractions were not so well appreciated by the Scots Guards at this moment, they were more concerned that it provided another indirect approach to their already vulnerable defensive position.

The Scots Guards were now joined by Nos. 2 and 3 Independent Companies which had marched forward from Rognan, their original role almost totally forgotten. The Guards were deployed to cover the demolished bridge, 3 Company to the left rear to cover the approach from the Junkerdal and 2 Company on the right flank guarding the lower mountain slopes where the false crests provided excellent protection for advancing troops. Indeed one of the main limitations of Viskiskoia was that the enemy was always advancing from the higher ground. By now the Scots Guards were reduced to one 3-inch mortar and there was no ammunition at all for the 2-inch mortars. The field guns could be used only for direct sight line of fire because the field signalling equipment had been lost: in this terrain a hopelessly inadequate mode of operation as the enemy when they appeared were always too close to engage.

The Battalion was by now exhausted and suffering the demoralising effect of perpetual rearguard actions, long marches under arduous conditions, almost unremitting assault from the air, and the loss of most of their personal kit. Their orders were to hold the position until the 27th. The men settled down wearily to snatch some sleep before the all too early dawn heralded the relentless attack from the air and the unseen enemy on their flanks.

The Germans approached the Viskiskoia position at about 1500 on the same day, 23 May. Once again, the leading section of German cyclists was decimated by fire from an ambush laid by No. 3 Independent Company – would they never learn! But within an hour they were in command of the high ground on the right flank, supported by machine gun attacks from the air which seriously impeded the limited manoeuvrability left to the Guards. The solitary 3-inch mortar had some success, but it quickly became apparent that the position was untenable. Indeed it had always been so, and at 1800 Brigadier Gubbins, who had dismissed the Battalion commander for withdrawing too quickly from Krokstranden, immediately ordered the withdrawal from Viskiskoia as soon as he came forward to see the position for himself.

By midnight the Battalion had withdrawn to Storjord, five miles to the rear, where it was originally planned to defend another bridge in a similar situation to that at Viskiskoia. The enemy air reconnaissance began again at dawn, and to add to the troops' discomfort, machine-gunned any targets of opportunity in the open. The new Commanding Officer and his Intelligence Officer were attacked from the air while they were snatching a brief sleep in their cars. Major Graham laconically recorded in his diary:

> A bullet each through the cars and a canon between. We were so sleepy we scarcely moved, but just watched rather interestedly. However we heard him coming back and scuttled off to the woods to finish sleep.[21]

Their orders were to hold the position until 1800 whilst the Irish Guards, who had at last arrived at Bodo, settled into position at Pothus some thirteen miles further north. The Germans on this occasion were rather slow to follow up their advantage and did not commence an attack until the Guards had already started their withdrawal which was skilfully and expeditiously executed, and apart from some interference from the air was achieved without the need to engage the enemy. Shortly after midnight the weary Scots Guards passed through the positions occupied by the Irish Guards in the Pothus woods: at last they had another battalion between themselves and the German vanguard after twelve days of either continuous marching or fighting. This was the day that the War Cabinet finally decided to abandon northern Norway, but we shall examine that decision later. On the 26th, after frustrating delays in Rognan while some order was brought to the chaotic transport arrangements, they at last stopped in the vicinity of Hopen, about ten miles to the east of Bodo, for their first day's rest in a fortnight. Their respite was shortlived.

The Battle of Pothus Wood

After their near disastrous first attempt to get to Bodo, the Irish Guards sailed again on 20 May. Under the command of Captain McGildowny and accompanied by 166 Field Battery, RA, the Battalion embarked on destroyers and 'puffers' to the almost inevitable accompaniment of a bombing attack on Harstad. Even as they clambered aboard their transports, the sight of a tanker burning furiously in the harbour with an eerie glow was an ominous reminder of their last eventful trip on the *Chrobry*. Soldiers do not take to the sea readily any more than any military man is comfortable operating outside of his own familiar environment, but in the light of their experience just a week before, anybody who felt in the least sanguine about the forthoming voyage must have been singularly bereft of imagination.

The destroyers *Walker* and *Firedrake* carrying Nos. 1, 2 and 3 Companies made a wide diversion round the minefields in the Vestfiord. The 'puffers' on the other hand with the HQ and No. 4 Company preferred to hug the coast, taking their chance with the mines. One 'puffer' hugged the coast so closely that it ran aground and had to be dragged clear by its passengers. Nevertheless, they all arrived safely at Bodo at midnight and settled down to sleep on the quayside amid equipment rescued from the *Effingham*. Some of the SNCOs, never slow to miss a chance, rooted around the piles of stores, with some success, to see whether there was anything useful to supplement their own meagre equipment.

Their orders from General Auchinleck were to establish a defensive line to halt the enemy advance which had now begun to bear the semblance of a rout. The following morning they moved forward to the hamlet of Hopen, about ten miles to the east, whilst Captain McGildowny sought out Brigadier Gubbins to obtain more detailed instructions. It had been decided to combine all the remaining forces with the codename of 'Stockforce' under the command of Lieut Colonel H. C. Stockwell who had previously commanded No. 2 Independent Company. But it was not until the senior officers had made a reconnaissance of the Saltdal Valley on the 23rd that it was decided to make the stand at Pothus, ten miles up the valley from Rognan.

The Battalion marched into its new position on 24 May to sporadic air attack. As they moved south, they immediately observed how much more hospitable the country seemed compared with the bleak barrenness of Narvik. There were far more trees scattered round the wooden farmhouses, good for cover against marauding aircraft, but they also noted that it would provide equally good protection for an infiltrating enemy. For the moment they were content to enjoy the shelter of the trees; the omnipresent Luftwaffe was becoming tiresome. Despite one or two alarms and dashes for cover, the Battalion reached Pothus without casualties and surveyed the scene. For most of them, their first ground action of the war was imminent: after their adventures at sea and the relentless pounding from the air, they at least had the consolation that it was to be a contest with which they would be more familiar and one over which they had a greater degree of control.

The river was now swollen by the melting snow and had become unfordable in most parts. The tiny hamlet of Pothus clings to the east bank of the river where a minor tributary joins the main stream. The main road from the south crossed the river to the west bank by an iron girder bridge just to the south of the hamlet and then ran through a dense fir wood – the Pothus Wood – towards Rognan. To the west is a wooded ridge running parallel to the road, not high, but with sheer slopes at the top above the Pothus Wood. A much steeper razor backed ridge lies on the east side, much closer to the river and the road and nosing into the confluence between the river and its tributary. A rough track climbed over the summit of this ridge, crossed the tributary by a light suspension bridge and continued for three miles along the eastern bank before rejoining the main road across another footbridge. The valley bottleneck was a good defensive position, but it could be outflanked, particularly to the west where concealment was afforded by the trees. Not for the first time, the consensus was that a brigade supported by an artillery regiment could have held the position for a long time. But with only one battalion, two Independent Companies, a troop of 25 pounders and some Norwegian mortars and machine guns, the cover inevitably had to be spread too thinly to safeguard against all the options.

The two Independent Companies, Nos. 2 and 3, were detailed to cover the surrounding hills and the Guards were concentrated in the valley. No. 1 Company was placed on the ridge to the south-east of the river junction where it commanded a good view of the road, but its field of fire in other directions was limited. As the leading company it was particularly exposed – in front of the bridge which was to be demolished and with the tributary at its back. Furthermore, it was on the reverse slope of the ridge and could be dominated from above. No. 4 Company dug in to the west of the river overlooking the girder bridge with No. 3 Company immediately behind the crossing. No. 2 Company was held in reserve in Pothus Wood and Norwegian machine gun detachments located ahead of the bridge on the west side.

It was a perfect day, the scenery was sublime and the sun was beginning to make its presence felt after the hard winter; even the soil was suitable for digging. The midges were also enjoying a first run out as the troops set-to to prepare their defensive positions. The silence was broken only by the occasional passing aircraft. Wireless sets were again in short supply, the only communication between Force HQ in Pothus Wood and No. 1 company east of the river was by runner.

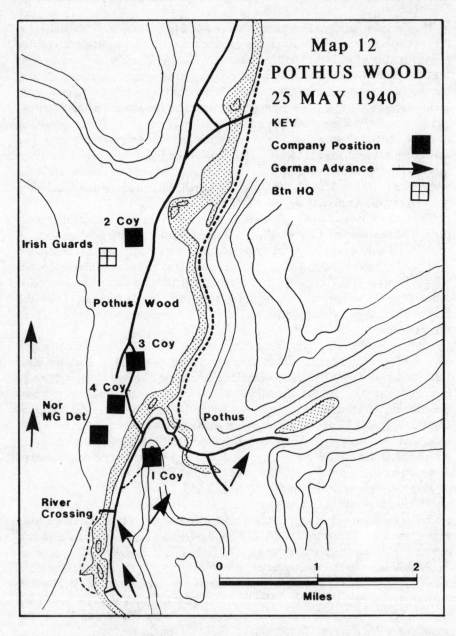

Map 12
POTHUS WOOD
25 MAY 1940

KEY

Company Position

German Advance

Btn HQ

2 Coy

Irish Guards

Pothus Wood

3 Coy

4 Coy

Nor
MG Det

Pothus

I Coy

River
Crossing

0   1   2

Miles

They broke to rest, the night now as cold as the day had been hot. At midnight the
Scots Guards appeared from the south, exhausted, demoralised, dishevelled;
'Tottering columns, crumbling ruins, defeat of an empire' muttered Lieutenant
Powell-Edwards.[22] There was little inclination to engage in the lighthearted banter
one would have expected when the 'Jocks' ran across the 'Micks' in such a remote
location. The next day, the 25th, was to be the turn of the Irish Guards and this

encounter with their fellow Guards Regiment did little to raise their spirits. Sleep was difficult and the men sat idly in small groups, smoking, reading, making small jokes as men do in such situations, each man apprehensive at the prospect of his first direct contact with the enemy, and each showing it in his own individual way. Their defensive preparations were as complete as possible with the tools available, but there was a widespread feeling that it might not be enough. Such nights can seem endless.

Unknown to the men in Pothus Wood, there was one encouraging announcement that day. The airfield at Bodo had been declared ready and the following day three Gladiators were sent down from Bardufoss. Unfortunately, the pilots were less happy with the state of the runway, and after one crashed on take off from a wire-covered grass surface, the building of a wooden runway nine hundred feet long was put in hand. Remarkably, it was finished by midnight and the two remaining Gladiators were ready to make their brief appearance to the south of Bodo.

After the Scots Guards had passed through, the main Pothus bridge was blown leaving No. 1 Company even more exposed. The demolition was premature, for it left the frail suspension bridge across the tributary stream as their only lifeline with the rest of the Battalion. At 0800 the German advance echelon appeared as usual on bicycles along the road. Equally predictably, they were accounted for by the Norwegian machine guns on the other side of the river: the Germans in Norway never lost the knack of sticking their heads into the noose on the first encounter.

The next German advance was more cautious as they worked their way steadily across the eastern ridge towards the leading Irish Company. It was extremely tough going, even for German mountain troops, but the rock-strewn, scrub-covered ground provided good cover and enabled the Germans to work their way close enough to throw grenades. Small arms fire, whilst it forced the men to keep their heads down, was ineffective and the Guards replied with grenades of their own and 2-inch mortar bombs, thrown rather than fired. This was an unorthodox and hardly to be recommended practice:

> The grenadier must unscrew the cap, bang the nose hard on a rock to arm the bomb and then throw it high in the air so that it lands on its nose and explodes.[23]

The 25 pounders and the Norwegian mortars laid a barrage across the bottom of the hill and the Germans, discouraged, temporarily withdrew.

But their own mortar and machine gun batteries were now brought into play and at about 1400, during an air attack by five Heinkels which methodically machine-gunned Pothus Wood, the German infantry again appeared over the ridge hurling grenades. Once more No. 1 Company was able to drive them back by bren and rifle fire, but the Germans were also now working around their left flank and it became obvious to Captain Eugster, who himself had been wounded in the shoulder, that this would be their last opportunity to escape. Two platoons were withdrawn across the suspension bridge, but the final platoon when it arrived found the bridge already blown. The river, although only a short tributary, was in spate from the melting snow and looked unfordable. The Germans, quickly recognising that the Company position had been abandoned, re-appeared over the ridge and opened fire on the men below.

There was no alternative but to surrender or take to the river. Led by Guardsman Murphy and using knotted rifle slings as a chain, they pulled themselves laboriously across the roaring torrent. The wounded Captain Eugster, who had placed himself as an anchor in the middle of the stream, was so exhausted that he lay on the far bank for two hours to recover despite the attention of rifle fire from the other side.

The German mountain units were by now making their customary wide encircling movement to the east, although this can have been no more than a probe as the terrain on that side of the river was far more rugged compared with the west bank. The importance of countering this manoeuvre had however still not been fully absorbed by the British command and it was only at this late stage that Lieut Colonel Stockwell ordered No. 2 Company to climb to the highest point on this flank, a 2,500 ft peak, supported by an Independent Company on the slopes below.

It was now the responsibility of No. 4 Company on the west side of the demolished girder bridge to confront the enemy advance along the road and they inflicted some casualties. But it was inevitable that the Germans would cross the river further south in their own time, and sure enough a forward observation detachment observed them constructing a pontoon bridge during the night half a mile upstream from the demolished girder bridge. As the hidden watchers saw the infantry disappear into the woods on the west bank in the early morning of the 26th, it was only too apparent that another outflanking movement was underway. Contact was re-established on the ridge above Pothus Wood, and already the Pothus position was in danger of being encircled.

Brigadier Gubbins gave the order to withdraw at 1130, but it was 1600 before Stockwell could get most of his Company Commanders together to brief them on the withdrawal plan: the absence of wireless communications was again proving a serious handicap in concerting action. Meanwhile the Luftwaffe kept up their relentless assault on Pothus Wood. The original Battalion HQ had already been destroyed, but Stockwell had taken up a new position in the corner of the wood. A Norwegian Army arms dump well hidden on the edge of the wood exploded in spectacular fashion, it seemed at the time that the Luftwaffe must have been aware of its exact location. No. 4 Company withdrew at 1900 with the unexpected help of a Gladiator which appeared on the scene, shot down one Heinkel, and distracted the others. For good measure, it machine-gunned the astonished Germans for long enough for an orderly withdrawal along the road to be hastily arranged. No. 4 Company had not lost a single man or any of their equipment. They actually finished with one more bren gun than they started with as Guardsman Wylie was awarded the DCM for retrieving a weapon that had been abandoned by another company. They collected support troops as they passed through Battalion HQ and set out to march back to Rognan. Except for No. 2 Company which was isolated on its hill to the east, the final withdrawal from Pothus was accomplished by 2000. Some of the forward observation sections who were unaware of the order to withdraw eventually made their way back independently. The Germans made good progress along the flanks and several groups of men finding their way back to Rognan came under isolated machine gun fire. One section of No. 3 Company came under such pressure that they had to make a hazardous crossing of the main river using rifle slings as a chain in emulation of No. 1 Company earlier in the day.

Meanwhile, No. 2 Company, who had made the summit despite a rigorous climb over 1,500 feet of often near perpendicular rock, were blissfully unaware of what was going on. It was not until nearly midnight that a Norwegian liaison officer eventually gave them the information that the rest of the Battalion had been ordered to withdraw several hours earlier. It was ironic that in the last major battle of the campaign, the British troops had at last outclimbed the Germans, albeit to no avail. Nevertheless, most of the stragglers found their way into Rognan during the following day, and by evening only twenty men from Battalion HQ were still unaccounted for.

The hamlet of Pothus still slumbers in its tributary valley. The main bridge across the river has been replaced, but the suspension bridge has gone for ever. The scene today on the west bank is totally different. Much of Pothus Wood remains, although doubtless replanted, but the coming of the railway along the west bank has led to the development of a new settlement, Rokland, to the south of the wood. Few people now remember the dramatic events of 1940, in fact the majority I spoke to were even unaware that this was the scene of one of the main confrontations of the war in north Norway.

The dramatic and timely intervention by the single Gladiator at Pothus on the evening of the 26th was not to be repeated. On the following day the German bombers inevitably turned their attention to Bodo and the airfield, starting at 0745 with twelve Ju 87s and four Bf 110s and repeated at intervals during the day. The two remaining Gladiators made a valiant attempt to stem the tide, but after shooting down two aircraft and damaging two others, one more was destroyed on the ground and the last was forced to flee back to Bardufoss. The runway was wrecked beyond immediate repair and in the town petrol dumps, food stores and 25 pounder ammunition were destroyed. As elsewhere in Norway, most of the houses were of wood and were burned to the ground. The hospital was also heavily attacked. The unhappy events of Lake Lesjaskog had been repeated, albeit on a lesser scale. A substantial intervention by the RAF in Bodo would undoubtedly have had a major impact on the retreat from Mosjöen, but the tiny force that was actually provided could make no more than a token impression on the overwhelming German air superiority.

The Final Act – Concentrate to Withdraw

The Irish Guards, the stragglers apart, did not remain long at Rognan, and by midnight were embarking on 'puffers' for Finneid on the north shore of the Saltfiord. On the morning of the 28th the whole of 'Stockforce' was concentrated on a peninsular at Valnes where it could block the main road to Bodo. Two Norwegian battalions guarded the passes and hills to the north and the 2nd Battalion of the South Wales Borderers, whose last company had finally arrived on 25 May, were held in reserve on the north-west side of the peninsular. The Scots Guards had already retired to Hopen only ten miles to the east of Bodo. 24th Brigade had at last managed to concentrate its forces. For the first time since the Scots Guards arrived at Mosjöen over two weeks before, there was more than one battalion in the same location to provide a reasonable opportunity of manning a defensive position in some strength and depth. On the 27th, the day on which Bodo was bombed, the Scots Guards were ordered back to the town, but the only company to arrive found it in ruins, and the following day the Guards prepared to take up defensive positions between Hopen and Bodo. The 28th was relatively quiet, only the occasional German aircraft was seen and on the following day only one seaplane came over. The weather was at last on the side of the defenders.

But it was too late. The decision had already been made to withdraw from northern Norway. On the Western Front, disaster had followed disaster and the evacuation from Dunkirk had started on 26 May. France was all but defeated and it was clear to all in London that the battle for Britain could not now be long delayed. In such a climate the defence of Norway had become irrelevant to all, that is, but the Norwegians. The final act at Narvik was still to be played out, but it was no longer intended to maintain a presence there afterwards, and thus there was no longer a need to try to prevent the Germans linking Trondheim with Narvik. The lack of a road north of Bodo would provide sufficient delay to enable the final act to be accomplished. Ironically, the destroyer which brought the Borderers' last Company also brought the staff officers to co-ordinate the withdrawal.

The evacuation was now in full swing with four of the Independent Companies going first on the 29th followed by the Irish Guards who had seen no action at Valnes. The Scots Guards who had borne the main brunt of the action south of Bodo had the somewhat dubious honour with No. 3 Independent Company and the South Wales Borderers of providing the rearguard and the last engagement fought by British soldiers in Norway. The German advance troops were in strong pursuit of the Irish Guards as they retreated from Pothus and made contact with the forward echelon of the Scots Guards at Hopen where the bridge had already been blown. During the evening, heavy machine gun and mortar fire was laid on the British positions, but the Germans also suffered as artillery pounded their positions to the east of the bridge. By 0200 it became apparent that the British left flank was being turned and the forward companies were withdrawn under covering fire from the Borderers' carriers. But the Germans did not follow up on the 31st, and as at Dunkirk inexplicably allowed the British force to slip through their fingers. By midnight the last man had withdrawn through the ruins of Bodo and embarked for Harstad. The evacuation will be covered in more detail later, for some their adventures were by no means over.

The actions south of Bodo were in many respects a replay of the events in the Gudbrandsdal a month before. Inadequate numbers, poorly supplied through long and unreliable lines of communication from a bridgehead which was itself insecure. It is surprising that the Luftwaffe had not paid more attention to Bodo sooner than it did, and certainly the availability of equipment and stores never became quite as critical as it had in Central Norway. Casualties south of Bodo were surprisingly light. The Scots Guards who had seen the most prolonged action had suffered eighty nine casualties of whom only thirteen had been killed and thirty six taken prisoner. The Irish Guards had also not suffered badly; apart from their disaster on the *Chrobry* when they had lost six of their senior officers (one more had died later in hospital) and two Guardsmen, only another eleven men had been killed and some thirty or so wounded. The surprisingly small number of casualties can largely be attributed to the amount of cover which existed in these Norwegian valleys. Air attack in particular, although persistent, never quite achieved the expected impact, its effects were disruptive rather than lethal. But whatever protection it afforded against air attack, it was ideal terrain for infiltrating ground forces, particularly on the flanks, and it was the greater mobility of the German mountain troops rather than the weight of fire power their infantry could muster which frequently forced the more static British battalions to withdraw. At the end of this short campaign, the total numbers available to both sides were not significantly different, the British eventually had some 3,500 troops south of Bodo whilst at the end of the campaign the German force was about 4,000. What was different was the German ability to concentrate its force where needed.

Although the actions south of Bodo appeared to be another British defeat, they had delayed the German advance for almost a month. They had, in fact, achieved the objective of preventing the Germans moving up from Trondheim joining forces with their beleaguered comrades in Narvik. Although it seemed small consolation to those long suffering troops who were being pushed steadily backwards along the Saltdal Valley, Narvik had finally fallen to the Norwegian, French and Polish troops on 28 May, and it is to this final phase of the Allied action in Norway that we must now turn.

14

The Capture of Narvik –
Success at Last

'You all know our men are fighting on the sea and in the air and in France and Belgium against much heavier odds than we are faced with. It is up to us all here to FIGHT TO WIN so that we too may claim that we have done our part in saving the country from the Hun. Every German killed here is one the less to fight in France. Man for man you are more than a match for the Germans. So give them what they deserve.'

Lord Cork's Order of the Day, 24 May 1940

A New Commander

As the stalemate at Narvik became increasingly irritating to Mr Churchill and correspondingly frustrating to Lord Cork, the threat from the south had assumed a rather larger dimension than it really deserved given the almost impenetrable tundra north of Bodo. But despite constantly having to look over his shoulder to the south, Lord Cork had at last reluctantly forsaken the frontal assault and was now persuaded that the indirect approach, always favoured by General Mackesy, was the only feasible way to winkle General Dietl out of his beleaguered and uncomfortable garrison. It was ironic therefore that steps were already well in hand in London to replace Mackesy who was held responsible for what was seen as an over-cautious and unimaginative approach to the task. By the end of April there was widespread misunderstanding and frustration at the turn of events in Norway, and as usual at such times, thoughts turned towards alternative methods and new leaders. The mantle fell upon General Claude Auchinleck.

General Auchinleck had spent most of his formative years in India, but he was well regarded, particularly by the C.I.G.S. who commented in his diary 'the best officer India had, who was not contaminated by too much Indian theory'.[1] He had been summoned back to England in the winter of 1940 to train and command No. IV Corps which was intended to join the British Expeditionary Force in France in June 1940. He had only just returned from a reconnaissance to France when on the evening of 28 April he was ordered to report to the War Office. He was taken immediately on his arrival to the C.I.G.S.'s room where General Ironside told him that he and part of his staff would be required to proceed in the immediate future to Narvik.

By 1 May Auchinleck with about a dozen officers from his Corps staff had assembled at the War Office to contemplate their new task. Intelligence Officers began collecting information on northern Norway, and immediately encountered the same

252

problems which had beset planning staffs less than a month before. Maps and weather data were scarce and unreliable, northern Norway might as well have been on another planet for all the information available in London in May 1940. Tourist and motorist's guide books were borrowed and after some difficulty a copy of *The Norway Pilot* obtained from the Admiralty. Nevertheless, Auchinleck had prepared an initial appreciation which was handed to General Sir John Dill, recently appointed as Vice Chief of General Staff, on 3 May. But already doubts of the wisdom of pursuing the operation in the way prescribed were fermenting in his mind and he concluded his summary with one statement and three simple but realistic questions.

He recognised first of all that Narvik was not essential to the Germans for at least the next six months and questioned whether it was necessary to go there at all. Would it not be better to look for an anchorage further south and should that not be combined with an army and an airbase?

These questions fell on stony ground: Narvik had become a festering sore and not only with Mr Churchill. Following the withdrawal from Central Norway at the end of April, the capture of Narvik had become as much a political as a strategic commitment, a matter of prestige rather than a military or economic necessity. The following day Auchinleck submitted his shopping list: four brigades of infantry, one or two machine gun battalions, one regiment of light tanks and one or two squadrons of armoured cars. Support troops and one hundred and forty four 4.7-inch guns and one hundred and thirteen Bofors light anti-aircraft guns completed the list. He also specified a requirement for airfields at Bardufoss, Harstad and possibly also at Bodo, capable of operating both bomber and fighter aircraft. It was a formidable and, at the time, an unrealistic assessment.

On 6 May he received his orders from the Secretary of State for War, Oliver Stanley. The objectives of the expeditionary force were to secure and maintain a base in northern Norway to deny iron ore supplies to Germany through Narvik, to interfere as far as possible with ore supplies to Germany via Lulea, and to preserve a part of Norway as a seat of government for the King and his people. The directive went on to describe in broad and not very accurate terms the scale of enemy opposition he might expect to meet. Significantly, no mention was made of the most likely German development, an overland advance from Trondheim which was already underway. Auchinleck was nominated as C-in-C designate of the Anglo-French military forces and the RAF, but was not to be subordinate to Lord Cork despite the fact that a unified command had been set up under the Admiral only two weeks before. In fact the orders went further, stating that he was not to interfere until the unified command structure was terminated by the Government – a clear indication of their intention. The principles of a truly joint command – so important when an integrated tri-Service approach is the key to success – were simply not recognised by the military hierarchy in 1940. Nevertheless, in the best traditions of the contradictory orders which permeated the campaign, a most secret and personal letter from General Dill accompanying the formal orders authorised him to take over from General Mackesy if he thought it necessary and subject himself to the command of Lord Cork.

There is no evidence that General Mackesy was given any indication of this covert authority to replace him before the unified command was disbanded. Indeed, the notification of the intended arrival of Auchinleck in Norway merely stated that he was not to interfere with the existing plans, merely to report in conjunction with Lord Cork on the 'requirement to secure and maintain a base in northern Norway'.

There is little doubt that a very strong feeling existed in London that Auchinleck should take over immediately from Mackesy; and it was dishonest to have fudged the issue so blatantly.

On Tuesday 7 May, Auchinleck sailed from Leith with an escort of destroyers in the *Chrobry*, the merchantman that a few days later was to be so tragically sunk whilst transporting the Irish Guards to Bodo. There had been many changes since Admiral Cork and General Mackesy had first reviewed the forces at their disposal aboard the *Southampton* in mid-April. By the time of Auchinleck's arrival in Norway on 11 May, the composition of forces in northern Norway looked very different.

Skaanland, the small village on the mainland fifteen miles south of Harstad had become the main naval base. The Royal Marines were preparing sites for coastal defence batteries although the guns were never actually installed. Two Bofors anti-aircraft guns were transferred from Harstad at the end of April and additional heavy anti-aircraft guns arrived on 8 May. But the main burden of defence against air attack fell upon two anti-aircraft cruisers and two sloops which, between other duties, ceaselessly patrolled the Vaagsfiord and the Tjeldsund. Nevertheless, ships could rarely anchor and were attacked regularly whenever the skies were clear throughout the long hours of daylight. Fortunately, the naval base was not subjected to submarine attack thanks to the tenacious activity of the escort vessels described earlier, and only one attempt was made to lay mines from the air. Although constantly harassed, the Navy had not suffered serious damage from air attack apart from the loss of the Polish destroyer *Grom* and about half its complement of trawlers. The battleship *Resolution* had replaced the *Warspite* which had provided such valiant service in these northern waters, and the cruiser *Southampton* had temporarily returned home after assisting with the evacuation from Aandalsnes. But the *Effingham* (soon to be lost carrying the South Wales Borderers to Bodo), *Aurora* and *Enterprise* remained. The aircraft carrier *Furious* which had patrolled the area until only eight of her complement of Swordfish remained serviceable had been replaced by the *Ark Royal* on 6 May. Unlike the *Furious*, the latter carried fighter aircraft, and although this comprised only the slow and cumbersome Skua, it at least brought some moral uplift to those on the ground subjected to relentless unopposed air attack for nearly a month. Up to fifteen destroyers were usually available and very active patrolling the fiords, heartening the local population and constantly reminding General Dietl and his troops of the threat from the sea. At this stage of the battle for Narvik, the Navy's control of the sea approaches was as complete as the Luftwaffe's supremacy in the air.

The administration of the main base at Harstad and the support of the scattered outposts was always a problem. There were very few jetties which were suitable even for the destroyers, and the few Motor Landing Craft available were needed for the military operations. The only means of transport between the various locations was the 'puffers', the largest of which were about 50 tons and therefore unsuitable for carrying major items of military equipment. Furthermore, their crews were becoming less than enthusiastic in the face of the continuing assault from the air and Army personnel were eventually placed on board the 'puffers', in the words of General Auchinleck 'to ensure a measure of availability of the crafts themselves, together with their personnel'.[2] It was eventually decided that another main base would be required at Tromso which could offer better and more secure facilities.

Although the somewhat chaotic build-up of ground forces had continued after the arrival of the 24th Brigade on 15 April, it had been mainly in the form of administrative support until the 27th Demi-Brigade of Chasseurs Alpins sailed from Scapa Flow on 24 April. They were followed on 6 May by two battalions of the French Foreign Legion forming the 13th Demi-Brigade and on the 9th, a Polish brigade of four battalions under General Bohusz-Szyzko known as the Chasseurs de Montagne, or alternatively the Carpathian Chasseurs. The former had the resilience and resourcefulness for which the Foreign Legion was traditionally noted, and some of the latter had already experienced combat in Poland although, despite their name, most of them had never seen a mountain before. They were a heterogeneous group who after the rapacious assault on their homeland had made their escape, often suffering great privation, to carry on the fight elsewhere. They eventually found their way to Coëtquidan in Brittany to be moulded together into an army.

> But no luxuries awaited the volunteers at the end of their journey. Sleeping on a hard floor under a single blanket in a cold barracks, eating from the same pot, paddling through the mud of the parade ground from dawn to dusk for ten hours a day . . . Shoulder to shoulder there stood an old professor, past his prime, with shaking, rheumatic knees and a seventeen year old schoolboy whose shoulder was numb under the weight of his rifle, a barrister and a baker, a peasant who had scarcely ever seen anything more exciting than a cow and a journalist who had interviewed kings. The refined pale faces of the intellectuals and the weathered sunburnt faces of the manual workers, all were equally attentive, equally eager to master the soldier's trade, to go and fight.[3]

But what they lacked in martial skills they made up for in determination and a burning hatred of the enemy. Although cordially received by the local people, there was nevertheless a high degree of suspicion between the Norwegians, who at this stage were understandably wary of offending the Russians camped on their most northerly boundary, and the Poles who if anything loathed the Russians even more than they did the Germans.

The stage was now set at last to claim the main prize – Narvik. There were, discounting the Norwegians, some 27,000 Allied soldiers ranged around Narvik although many of these were base and lines of communication troops. The artillery support now consisted of twenty four guns, twelve French 75s and twelve British 25 pounders, and the anti-aircraft artillery had been built up to one heavy and four light batteries. There was also one troop of tanks of the 3rd Kings Own Hussars although these were destined never to see action, being lost on route to Bodo. The craft available for an opposed landing were still woefully inadequate: four Assault Landing Craft (ALC) and six Motor Landing Craft (MLC) for vehicles. After the loss of a battalion at Gratangen on 24 April, General Fleischer had slowly re-organised his Norwegian troops into two brigades, one with three battalions and a mountain battery, the other with two battalions and a mountain and motorised battery. There was as yet no air support for the Allied forces apart from that from the *Ark Royal*.

The strength of the Germans in Narvik was hardly any better than a month before. A few paratroops and mountain infantry, in total no more than three hundred, had been dropped on Bjornfjell, but the JU 52s which could only carry one ton of payload to Narvik were mainly used for dropping vital stores and ammunition. The seaplanes had been driven out of the Rombaksfiord but could still land in the harbour. On 5 May, Dietl's force which since 15 April had been under the direct command of the OKW was returned to Group XXI. This was the lowest point for Dietl, it seemed an indication that Hitler had given up the position as hopeless and on the following day, for the first time, he considered abandoning Narvik.

On 8 May Dietl received a personal message from Hitler saying that if forced to abandon Narvik he should first destroy the iron ore workings and the railway before withdrawing towards Bodo, or in an emergency across the frontier into Sweden. Ironically, the act which terminated the flow of iron ore which the Allies had so long sought to achieve was in the end to be accomplished by the Germans themselves. Food was now very short, between mid-April and the end of May, most of the men had only three hot meals. The standard daily ration was sometimes only five slices of bread washed down with melted snow water; the only roof over their heads was a tent and there was little combustible material on the mountain tops to kindle a fire. Not surprisingly sickness was rife and spirits at rock bottom.

Some of the 2,000 stranded sailors had returned to Germany through Sweden; their capacity for scarce food, clothing and medical supplies exceeding their utility as infantry. Three companies of naval personnel were assisting one mountain battalion in guarding Narvik itself and the Navy was also still responsible for protecting Dietl's lifeline, the vital rail route to Sweden. Two more mountain battalions faced the Norwegians to the north who were regarded as the main threat at this time. The Germans' strongest card was their overwhelming air superiority; a new command under Colonel General Stumpff had been formed on Hitler's direct orders and two hundred bombers were based at Trondheim. Even so, by the time Auchinleck arrived at Harstad on 11 April, the Allies were in a position of overwhelming numerical strength and the forces of Group XXI advancing from the south were unlikely to arrive in time to raise the seige before the Germans were forced to abandon Narvik and retreat towards Sweden. Dietl's situation was becoming desperate.

Auchinleck's arrival in Harstad had been completely overshadowed on the day before, 10 May, by the momentous news of the German invasion of the Low Countries. The Battle for Flanders and France and the withdrawal of the British Expeditionary Force from Dunkirk inevitably occupied the Cabinet and the Chiefs of Staff to the almost complete exclusion of events in Norway, they paused merely to order the evacuation some two weeks later. Auchinleck was thus left in comparative peace to tidy up events in Narvik. He met General Mackesy, who he had known in India and for whom he had a high regard, and the latter readily explained the situation and his battle plan – unaware, at least at this time, that Auchinleck had come other than in a purely exploratory capacity. Auchinleck himself reinforced this misapprehension, explaining that his mission was to report to the Chiefs of Staff on the situation in Norway, existing and potential. Nevertheless, he was immediately struck by the fact that Admiral Cork retained his HQ on board the *Effingham* whilst Mackesy was ashore at Harstad. Many of the problems of co-ordinating action arose from the Admiral's natural resistance to leave the environment in which he was most comfortable and establish a unified command HQ ashore where it could operate more logically and effectively. It was an error which Auchinleck determined to redress.

Action at Bjerkvik

Following the abandoning on 6 May of the last proposal by Lord Cork to mount a direct assault on Narvik, General Mackesy issued detailed orders on the 8th for a careful and deliberate advance on Narvik. A battalion of Chasseurs and the South Wales Borderers, shortly to be replaced by the 2nd Polish battalion, would press along the Ankenes peninsula towards Beisfiord as soon as weather conditions permitted, thus threatening Narvik from the south-east. The two battalions of the French Foreign Legion would land at the head of the Herjangsfiord at Bjerkvik and advance the eight miles to Öyjord on the opposite side of the Rombaksfiord from Narvik. Finally, the Norwegians, supported by the Chasseurs, would resume their advance from the north in the Gratangen area. Narvik would thus be gradually encircled and forced into submission with far less risk than that entailed in one speculative lunge at the hostile beaches. A sea reconnaissance had been made on the night of 7 May disclosing no sign of enemy activity near Bjerkvik where the beach appeared reasonably suitable for a landing.

Bjerkvik was a pleasant little settlement, nestling in a wide open bay at the head of the Herjangsfiord. Mountains loom over the village to the west and the east, but between them lies a gentle valley leading north to Gratangen. The road between Öyord and Bogen ran round the bay against the shore line, which was generally sandy although liberally sprinkled with boulders. The final goal, Narvik, lay well within sight overlooking the Herjangsfiord just eight miles to the south. Looking from Bjerkvik, the troops must still have wondered how they were going to get into Narvik; screened by the high range of mountains behind, it looks almost impregnable from this position.

General Auchinleck approved of the plan which seemed perfectly sound in this difficult environment; but already sensing that the unified command was not working smoothly, determined to meet with Lord Cork as soon as possible. After a journey of several hours by car and launch which emphasised the absurdity of the command organisation, Auchinleck at last met with Cork later that same night on board the *Effingham*. The two men, both of strong personality, immediately struck a chord, although it soon became clear to Auchinleck that relations between Cork and Mackesy were far from harmonious.

Lord Cork gave Auchinleck his view of the prevailing situation. He had by now accepted that Narvik would be captured only by an encircling movement, the first steps of which were already in progress, and soon to be reinforced by the landings at Bjerkvik. Nevertheless, he repeated his strongly held view, never to be relinquished, that a direct assault in the early stages of the campaign would have involved less risk

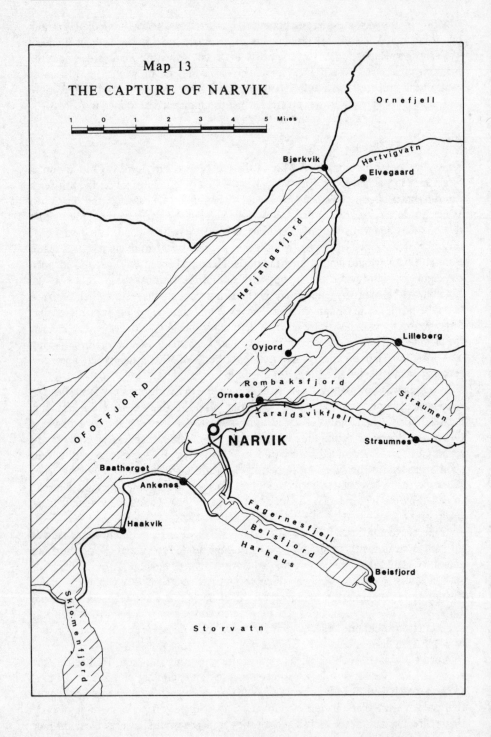

and effort. He was concerned about German reinforcements arriving from Sweden, but thought that Bodo could be held. The most alarming aspect for Auchinleck, however, was that he believed the British troops had developed a defeatist attitude towards the attack on Narvik.

It was becoming quite clear now to Auchinleck that he would have to invoke his secret authorisation from General Dill to take over responsibility himself under Lord Cork for the direction of the ground forces. Not only was there the obvious divergence of view between the naval and ground commanders, but Mackesy, who had been unwell earlier, was now sick again. However, he did not wish to take command until the impending assault on Bjerkvik was complete and sought the Admiral's agreement to remain on board the *Effingham* to watch the landing which had been postponed until the night of 12/13 May.

On the 12th the *Effingham* proceeded up the Ofotfiord, ostensibly to bombard Narvik, but in reality to embark the Foreign Legion from Ballangen. In addition to the *Effingham*, the naval force consisted of the battleship *Resolution*, the cruiser *Aurora*, five destroyers, the training ship *Vindictive* and the net-layer *Protector*. In command of the assaulting forces was General de Brigade Béthouart, an officer of redoubtable courage and resource. The initial landing force consisting of 120 men travelled in the four ALCs whilst the cruisers, carrying most of the rest of the 1,500 infantry, each towed three small craft. Four French Hotchkiss tanks travelled in the battleship, with two MLCs to put them ashore, with one more going independently in a more modern MLC. By 2100 the whole party was silently negotiating the twenty miles up the fiord to Bjerkvik: it was still light, but low cloud and poor visibility grounded both the Luftwaffe and the supporting aircraft from the *Ark Royal.*

It had not been intended to bombard the town before the landing although surprise was hardly possible in the prevailing daylight. In the event, the five destroyers in the van opened fire at midnight as soon as they approached within range, provoking enemy machine gun posts along the shore, in the town, and in the woods behind to return the fire. By 0100, the planned time of the assault, it was quite clear that they had not all been silenced.

An old resident of Bjerkvik who showed me the invasion beaches remembers the night well. He was asleep when the bombardment began exactly on midnight, and as the townspeople cowered in their homes or fled to the hills behind the town, the shells reigned all around, looking for, but not always finding the German strongpoints. The whole town was soon ablaze, and when the people were able to return on the following morning, hardly a building remained standing.

The men in the ALCs were to go ashore first along with the tanks from the *Resolution*, but it took so long to load the MLCs that the more modern MLC under its own power proceeded independently to the beach with a single tank. The fire from the beach forced the first wave to put ashore about half a mile to the west of the intended position, but they gained control of some high ground overlooking Bjerkvik and the single tank, now joined by two more and the rest of the battalion, quickly silenced the machine gun posts in the vicinity. The second battalion and the two remaining tanks were landed less than half a mile to the south-east of the village and quickly joined up with the first battalion. Bjerkvik was quickly under control and one battalion advanced along the road towards Gratangen and Hartvigvatn: sixty prisoners were taken and an ammunition dump destroyed. To protect his left flank, General Béthouart put another company ashore on the road towards Bogen where, to their immense surprise, they met a Polish battalion which had marched the fifteen miles from Bogen on a road which hitherto was regarded as impassable.

The whole of the north shore of the Ofotfiord was now in Allied hands, but to complete the encirclement of Narvik to the north, it was necessary to capture Öyord on the opposite bank of the Rombaksfiord from Narvik. The Germans still held Elvegaard, the former Norwegian regimental depot which had proved such a profitable source of ammunition and stores when they had first arrived at Narvik. General Béthouart had hoped to use two companies of the Polish battalion from Bogen for this task, but they had thwarted this intention by setting out to walk to Bjerkvik instead of waiting for their sea lift. Nevertheless, with the forces at his disposal and with the assistance of the light tanks which were proving so useful in countering the enemy machine gun posts, the Foreign Legion stormed the depot building by building. Their attack was swift and successful, the Germans were quickly driven into the hills and one hundred machine guns and other equipment captured.

Thirty motorcycle troops were despatched along the road to Öyord, eight miles to the south, screened from the fiord by the destroyer *Havelock* to which General Béthouart had transferred his headquarters. The few Germans quickly evacuated the village towards Lilleberg, their only line of retreat, and the motorcyclists entered Öyord without opposition, to be greeted on the quayside by their own general staff who had landed meanwhile from the *Havelock*.

The landing at Bjerkvik had been impressively undertaken. The assault had been completed under difficulties because of the limited number of landing craft and the opposition from concealed machine gun posts, which had been mauled but not destroyed by the preliminary naval bombardment. The officers leading the assault had shown their flexibility and control by changing the chosen point of landing to evade machine gun fire from the shore. They had not dallied to regroup once ashore and the tanks, small in number, had been used aggressively to quell the pockets of resistance. The naval support was also well judged and effective, and the whole operation had been completed at a cost of only forty casualties. The essential springboard had been established which made the fall of Narvik inevitable – the only line of retreat now open to the Germans was the railway line to Sweden. General Auchinleck, from his grandstand seat in the *Effingham* was impressed by what he had seen, lamenting only that no British units had been involved. The bad weather which had prevented interference from the air was of course a considerable bonus, emphasising once again how the impact of air power, or in this case the lack of it, could make such a difference to operations in Norway. In particular, the Navy could not have provided the necessary support in the narrow waters of the Herjangsfiord if they had been harassed by bombing from the air. It was the most satisfactory land engagement of the Norwegian campaign so far, and it was with a less disturbed mind that Auchinleck was able that night to put together his first report to General Dill on the situation in north Norway. Even so, he expressed concern about the threat from the south, the vital need for land-based air support and anti-aircraft guns, and requested another British brigade to support the land operation:

> . . . it would be criminal to pretend that one can make bricks without straw. If HMG think that the commitment involved in the preservation of northern Norway is worth adding to their other commitments, I trust that they will set aside definitely the forces required for the purpose. I feel very strongly that if they are not prepared to do this, it would be better to come away now than to risk throwing good money after bad by failing to provide the necessary forces.

Auchinleck was by no means convinced of the desirability of extending our stay in north Norway, he went on:

> If there is any chance of it being decided to evcacuate Norway the sooner the decision is taken the better, as every day's delay must increase the difficulty of the operation of withdrawal. In any event, land-based aircraft and anti-aircraft artillery will be needed to cover the evacuation, so the development of landing grounds and the installation of artillery must continue.[9]

A Miscarriage of Justice?

Lord Cork and General Auchinleck were back at Harstad before lunch on the 13th and the latter now took the opportunity of informing Lord Cork that he had decided to invoke his remit to take over from Mackesy. The Admiral immediately agreed and a signal was sent to Dill asking that Mackesy be recalled for consultation. The conspiracy to remove the unfortunate Mackesy had now been fulfilled. He was strongly criticised both at the time and later for his failure to make progress with the capture of Narvik. His inability to establish a sound working relationship with the Admiral undoubtedly contributed to the lack of progress, but the Chiefs of Staff and the War Cabinet must take a large share of the responsibility for failing to establish an unambiguous line of command, a coherent strategy and common objectives. Equally, Lord Cork, who refused to move his headquarters ashore and only reluctantly admitted the limitations upon the ground forces, contributed to the lack of empathy between the two men. As by far the more senior officer, a greater responsibility rested on Lord Cork's shoulders to establish the right working environment, for the soldiers did have many problems of equipment and organisation which were totally out of Mackesy's control.

The chaotic way in which the troops had been equipped and embarked inevitably meant that Mackesy had to establish a large administrative base in Norway to try to bring some order to his Brigade before they could be expected to mount an effective operation. The failure to supply amphibious craft for an opposed landing, the shortage of vehicles and support arms, the lack of adequate air support; none of these can be laid at Mackesy's door. Even the Navy's amphibious expert, Captain Maude, agreed with Mackesy against the view of his Admiral that a direct assault posed an unacceptable risk. The comparative ease with which it was achieved on 13 May at Bjerkvik by no means proves that it would have been feasible in the far more difficult terrain of the Narvik peninsula itself at the end of April. Mackesy was not alone in resisting the Admiral, his battalion commanders who each made an independent reconnaissance of the possible landing areas were equally opposed to the frontal assault. It will of course remain a matter of conjecture whether such an assault would have succeeded. We now know that General Dietl's troops were less numerous and less well supported than was believed at the time, and in retrospect it seems incredible that no greater effort was made to establish the real situation by seeking wider contact with the inhabitants of Narvik, if necessary through General Fleischer's Headquarters. But the art of cultivating informants from within the enemy's camp, which no mediaeval commander worth his salt would have neglected, appears to have been lost in these early months of 1940.

That General Mackesy was a cautious commander is indisputable, but the more one reflects on the conditions existing in Narvik in 1940, the more one is convinced that his refusal to countenance a direct assault on Narvik was correct. It is even more certain that he was right to reject Lord Cork's proposal to rush ashore at Narvik with little more than five hundred troops immediately after their arrival in Norwegian waters on 14 April. Nevertheless, no matter how unjust to Mackesy personally, it was a sensible move for General Auchinleck to supercede him on 14 May. The need was for a new man to establish a better relationship with Lord Cork and to ensure that Mackesy's plans were pushed forward in a spirit of co-operation and harmony. However, it is appropriate to note that history should not condemn the original commander with the certainty which seemed so self-evident in London at the time.

Despite the circumstances of his dismissal, General Mackesy showed no rancour against the Navy; indeed, in his report after his return home written on 15 May he paid a fulsome tribute to the Senior Service.

> I wish to place on record my deep appreciation of the co-operation and assistance afforded by the Royal Navy at all times to the troops under my command. Without that help it would have been impossible to make any progress . . . The naval staff, particularly Captain Maude RN and Commander Hubback RN worked in intimate and unflagging co-operation with my own staff: I owe these officers a deep debt of gratitude for their ever close and cordial assistance.[4]

Mackesy was retired from the Army shortly afterwards, but his stand against a direct assault on Narvik was largely vindicated later by Auchinleck himself who noted in his report:

> Reconnaissance after the capture of the town revealed the full difficulties of landing on the beaches close to the town and the wisdom of the plan finally adopted.[5]

Seeking the Tools for the Job

The Norwegians were now making better progress in their renewed offensive on Narvik. The reconstituted Norwegian 6th Brigade had been fighting General Dietl's Group Windisch on the mountains to the south of Lapphaug since 6 May. The conditions were still very difficult, the thaw had not reached the high mountain tops, many of which were still clothed in deep inpenetrable snow in places nearly ten feet deep. Neither the Norwegians or the German mountain troops, accustomed though they were to these conditions, could make much progress. The Germans had generally established themselves on the accessible mountain summits, up to 3,000 feet high, commanding the paths along which the Norwegians had to advance and maintain their lines of supply. The Norwegians had timed a renewed advance to coincide with the attack on Bjerkvik, but in the event had moved forward on the night of 11/12 May, unable to comply with Lord Cork's last minute postponement of the French landing. They had the support of a miscellaneous collection of Norwegian aircraft acting as bombers, for all practical purposes largely ineffective, but a timely morale boost for troops who had only been on the receiving end of air attack. In the course of two days' fighting the Norwegians gained several mountain summits and advanced to the edge of the Kuberg plateau. This mountain plateau, lying about ten miles to the east of the Bjerkvik-Öyord road, was the key to the control of the area to the north and east of Narvik. One of the two German battalions was virtually eliminated as a fighting force during this action.

The Chasseurs Alpins on the Norwegian right flank also advanced on the 13th along the line of the Gratangen-Bjerkvik road. The Norwegian 14th Battalion joined up with the Foreign Legion above Bjerkvik just after midday on the 14th, but the 6th Battalion advancing across country to the east of the road found the going more difficult, and many of the Germans in the Öyord peninsula managed to escape before their back gate could be closed. The situation at nightfall on the 14th therefore was that the Germans faced the Norwegians to the north on the edge of the Kuberg plateau and the Hartvigvatn valley; and the French to the west, inland from the Bjerkvik-Öyord road. Even so, with the forces available, the final investing of Narvik and the subsequent stabilisation of the situation was likely to be an arduous task.

Now in command of the land forces, Auchinleck had several tasks to undertake. Firstly, he needed to persuade Lord Cork to move his Headquarters ashore so that combined naval/ground force planning could be undertaken effectively without having to chase the *Effingham* around the Norwegian fiords. Using Captain Maude as a tactful intermediary, he successfully accomplished this on 16 May. Secondly he had to establish a command structure. Brigadier Fraser had been sent south to Bodo and so General Béthouart, who Auchinleck admired as a spirited, intelligent and resourceful commander was placed in command of all French and Polish forces in the Narvik to Bardufoss sector. Next he had to establish a better working relationship with the Norwegians. The latter, bruised by events in Central Norway and far from satisfied with the support they were getting from their allies, were at times tiresome colleagues. Quick to take offence, defensive in attitude, it was proving difficult to formulate a co-ordinated plan for the capture of Narvik. The King and Government were established at Tromso and the Supreme Commander, General Ruge, had his headquarters at Maalselvdal to the north-east of Bardufoss. Relations between the two were neither close nor co-ordinated. General Ruge was not content to maintain contact with the British only through Lord Cork's Headquarters or his own Government, he also wanted a direct link with the British military authorities in London. He pressed therefore for the appointment of an attaché to replace Colonel King-Salter in addition to Colonel R. C. G. Pollock who had recently been appointed as head of the British Military Mission to the Norwegian Government. He also wanted a Norwegian commander to take overall command of forces in the Narvik area as well as the Bodo area – a solution that was clearly not acceptable to Lord Cork or the Government in London: the British naval force was still the key to the capture of Narvik. The control of the civilian population and property in the battle area was also a source of friction. General Ruge held that this was entirely a matter for the Norwegians whereas Auchinleck believed the civilian community was riddled with spies and fellow travellers. He met Generals Ruge and Fleischer at Harstad on 17 May and although the temperature was lowered, misunderstanding and suspicion remained. Lord Cork made another more formal effort on 23 May to improve both the spirit and the practice of co-operation by visiting the King and his Government in Tromso and also General Ruge's headquarters. He was cordially received and the atmosphere gradually improved. Auchinleck's final task was to prepare the report which was his original reason for coming to Narvik.

He began by stating that the first objective of the British presence in the Narvik area had been achieved – the supply of iron ore to Germany had ceased. He saw no way, for political reasons, of attaining the second objective which was to interfere with the supply of ore to Germany from Lulea. He saw his task therefore as establishing and maintaining a foothold in northern Norway as a home for the Norwegian Government and a base for future operations. He regarded the retention of Bodo as essential to this aim and described the action – the complete transfer of the 24th Brigade to the south – that he had put in train to meet this requirement. He indicated the need for the establishment of a military base, including a 1,200 bed hospital, at Tromso, but noted that the Norwegian Government required the establishment of anti-aircraft defences as a condition of their acceptance of this proposal. He then went on to detail the forces required. On the naval side he indicated the need for four additional cruisers and six destroyers as well as escort vessels, submarines and anti-sumbarine trawlers. His requirement for ground troops was seventeen infantry battalions, two hundred anti-aircraft guns, seven batteries of artillery and some armoured troops. He also required four squadrons of aircraft, two fighter (Hurricanes), one bomber and one Army Co-operation. It was a formidable shopping list.

The Chiefs of Staff had also meanwhile been considering the force structure in Norway. Their appraisal of what was possible was vastly different to Auchinleck's list, and in a signal dispatched that same evening, they stated that the forces available would be the 1st French Light Division, the 24th Guards Brigade and ten Independent Companies with support troops to scale. Although their signal did not specifically include them, it was also presumably intended to retain the Polish brigade. The air complement was to be one Hurricane and one Gladiator squadron, and possibly one Army Co-operation Flight. The anti-aircraft guns had been scaled down from two hundred to one hundred and eight. The signal concluded, rather lamely, that re-organisation and galvanisation of the Norwegians must be pushed firmly.[6] Auchinleck was with Lord Cork when this signal was received and, not surprisingly, both were dismayed by its contents.

But it was really inevitable, given the tide of events elsewhere in Europe, that the Cabinet and Chiefs of Staff now regarded Norway as a sideshow. The fighting in the Low Countries was only seven days old, but already the writing was on the wall. Lord Gort had earnestly stressed the need for additional fighter aircraft on 13 May; and even more vehemently on the following day, M. Reynaud in a personal telephone call to Mr Churchill had implored him to send ten more fighter squadrons to France. With Sir Hugh Dowding fighting tooth and nail to retain every single aircraft for Fighter Command in Britain, the Chiefs of Staff may even be thought over generous in releasing even two squadrons for Norway.

The response from Norway was twofold. Lord Cork, in a signal drafted by Auchinleck and released on the evening of 20 May, set out the strategic situation. It pointed out that Narvik was not yet in Allied hands, that the security of the area was indivisible from the individual security of Bodo, Harstad and Narvik, and upon these three was dependent the security of Tromso. It referred scathingly to galvanising the Norwegians who 'were few in number and not proving of great value'. It stressed in particular the essential requirement for 'a sufficient air force' and the provision of ample anti-aircraft artillery.[7]

Auchinleck's signal put the meat on the bones. He nominally reduced his main force requirement to fifteen battalions, twelve French and three British, plus the ten Independent Companies. But including the latter this marginally increased the original requirement of seventeen battalions. He also required five artillery batteries and reiterated his need for the full complement of anti-aircraft guns. On the air side he required a minimum of two Hurricane squadrons and one bomber squadron. Of the offer of one flight of Army co-operation aircraft, he merely stated that it was entirely inadequate.

Before this signal reached London, Mr Churchill had once again blasted into print. On 20 May he exhorted Lord Cork to get on with it:

> I am increasingly disappointed by the stagnation which appears to rule in the military operations around Narvik, and at the delay in occupying the town itself . . . I should be very much obliged if you would enable me to understand what is holding you back.[8]

As with Lloyd George in the earlier conflict, the seeds of Churchill's disillusion with his generals were already germinating and for Auchinleck in particular, would flower in the Western Desert two years later when he was abruptly dismissed for being over-cautious.

The reaction to Auchinleck's signal in London, which led more or less directly to a recommendation by the Chiefs of Staff on 22 May to abandon Norway will be considered later when we look at the evacuation. We shall also look later at the impact of British air power on the campaign at Narvik which at last obtained a land-based component when the airfield at Bardufoss was declared operational on 21 May. For the time being we shall continue to examine the continuing quest for the key to Narvik.

Closing the Ring

As detailed planning progressed, the situation in the Narvik area, if not Bodo, began to look more promising and the increasing air of optimism in the combined headquarters was now more soundly based. Although between 23 and 25 May Dietl had received his first major reinforcements – two companies of a parachute battalion, the balance of which arrived in early June – he still believed he was some 2,000 short of the number of men he needed to mount an effective defence of Narvik. On the Allied side, relations and co-ordination with the Norwegians were gradually improving as the latter slowly battled their way south on the Kuberg plateau. On their right, the Foreign Legion and the Chausseurs were consolidating their position on the Öyord peninsula and along the road to Gratangen, and some degree of order was replacing the administrative chaos at Harstad. The weather was also improving and the snow disappeared around the shores of the fiords; but inland, conditions in the valley bottoms were still vile, a morass of melted snow water making the movement of wheeled vehicles almost impossible.

The final plans for the capture of Narvik were discussed at a meeting under General Auchinleck on the afternoon of 23 May. The operation had originally been planned for the night of 24/25, but it was decided that unless the weather conditions were exceptionally favourable, it would be prudent to await the arrival of the Hurricane squadron to provide additional air support. In the meantime, the newly established Gladiator squadron would mount extensive air patrols to test the strength of the air opposition, and the Navy would monitor activity from the fiords. However, whilst this group was meeting at Harstad, the Cabinet in London were authorising the preparation of a plan for the withdrawal of all Allied troops from Norway, and the signal signifying this intent was received by Lord Cork the following morning. But it did leave open the possibility of capturing Narvik first, indeed it actually encouraged it. At this stage Lord Cork and General Auchinleck needed no further incentive, they had now come far enough to regard the capture of Narvik as a matter of honour. Henceforth, however, planning for the latter was conducted in parallel with that for the evacuation of both Narvik and Bodo; a task made immeasurably more difficult by the need to keep the plans for withdrawal from the Norwegians whose capitulation at this stage would have placed the Allies in extreme jeopardy. General Béthouart was brought into the secret and bravely and generously supported the proposal to capture Narvik first: relations between the commanders were now entirely harmonious, but all were acutely distressed at having to deceive the Norwegians, essential though this remained.

The attack was now ordered for the night of 27/28 May. The final plan envisaged a direct assault across the mouth of the Rombaksfiord from Öyord by two battalions of the Foreign Legion, a Norwegian battalion and a section of tanks. The Poles at the same time would make a two-pronged attack on Ankenes at the neck of the Beisfiord. This would leave the Germans only one line of retreat along the railway to Hundalen. To cut them off and apply the *coup de grace*, a Polish Company and the ski troops of the Chasseurs Alpins would cross the mountains to seize the railway in the enemy rear. The Norwegians meanwhile would mount increased pressure on the Haugfjell which they had reached on 22 May. Conditions in the mountains were hardly better than at the beginning of the month; rivers were in spate and difficult to cross and on the highest slopes the snow still lay several feet deep. Resupply was by packhorse, but even this entailed man-packing ammunition and food up the slopes to the mountain summits; for weeks on end neither the Norwegians nor the Germans had enjoyed a warm meal or a bed other than in a snow trench. The troops were exhausted, but for the first time in the campaign, the Norwegians were tending to gain more from any sporadic action that was possible in the conditions. This phase of the battle for Norway was by far the best effort made by the Norwegians – they were at last recognising that they had to fight with more spirit and tenacity if they wanted to preserve a future for their country. It had taken more than a month of war and an almost unmitigated string of disasters to raise the Norwegian ethos from the numbness of years of faceless neutrality. It is all the more ironic therefore that the Allies were already planning to desert their cause as soon as the conquest of Narvik was complete.

There were now only three ALCs and two MLCs available for the short crossing from Öyord which between them could carry less than three hundred men. The Navy, although now without a battleship, would open the proceedings with a twenty minute bombardment. Four destroyers were posted in the Rombaksfiord, and the anti-aircraft cruisers *Cairo* and *Coventry* with one destroyer would operate from the Ofotfiord. The *Southampton*, the only ship available with the longer range 6-inch guns would target both Narvik and Ankenes. Both the Hurricane and the Gladiator squadrons would provide air cover during the landing with the support of the sloop *Stork*. This was to be the first truly combined air, sea, land assault that had ever been mounted by the Allies, and the need for fighter protection for ships had been demonstrated only too clearly just the day before the assault when the anti-aircraft sloop *Curlew* had been caught and sunk by a salvo of bombs near Skaanland.

The bombardment began accurately at twenty minutes to midnight. The main targets were the machine gun posts on the north facing slope of the Taraldsvikfjell, nearly 5,000 feet high, towering over Narvik to the south-east. Unfortunately, these had still not been accurately located, and although the fire was intense, many escaped unscathed. Other targets were the entrances to the railway tunnels which ran along the south shore of the Rombaksfiord. Bombardment of the actual landing zone to the east of the town was entrusted to two French and one Norwegian battery posted behind Öyord.

The landing was made promptly at midnight on a beach to the east of Orneset and encountered little opposition. The Germans were taken by surprise as the ALCs had been loaded in a little bay hidden round the corner from Narvik in the Rombaksfiord. The first group ashore worked their way rapidly towards the town across the rugged slopes of the hill meeting only desultory opposition. Surprise lost, the second flight was to have embarked from Öyord itself, but the quay came under mortar fire and it was necessary to return to the original loading point out of sight of the guns. Unfortunately, the 'puffers' could not use this spot and the transfer of troops was inevitably slowed as the MLCs were used to ship across the tanks. Belatedly, the Germans at last recognised the threat and brought machine guns into action from the east against the landing beach and sniped at the invaders from the higher slopes of the Taraldsvikfjell. The disembarking troops suffered several casualties including Commandant Paris, General Béthouart's Chief of Staff. But the German counter attack had been delayed too long; within the first hour it might have succeeded in isolating the small force working its way towards the town, as it was there were now enough troops ashore to repulse the threat. The last gun to the east was finally silenced by the French manhandling one of their own guns up the steep, tree-covered slope until at last it reached a position from which it could dominate the railway line below. By 0400, one French and the Norwegian battalion were safely lodged on the south shore of the Rombaksfiord, together with two French tanks which unfortunately immediately became bogged down and took no further part in the advance.

So far the operation had been proceeding remarkably according to plan, but this good fortune was not to last. Little German air activity had been seen during the initial landing, but at 0415 a sea fog suddenly swept across the airfield at Bardufoss temporarily grounding the fighters. The Luftwaffe, however, operating from airfields to the south basking in the early morning sun had no such problems and the fiords were clear as well. The Ju 87s soon arrived on the scene and had the area to themselves for almost two hours. The ships in the narrow fiord were the main target and were forced to evade furiously, thus at a stroke almost completely removing their ability to provide gunfire support to the troops ashore. The *Cairo* was straddled by two bombs, one landing very close to the operations room from which Lord Cork, General Auchinleck and General Béthouart were directing the operation. There were nearly thirty casualties but the *Cairo*, battered but still able to manoeuvre remained in action.

Despite the unwelcome attention of the divebombers, by 0600 the Allies were clearly gaining the upper hand. Three RAF fighters had at last reappeared over the battlefield and were able to make constant patrols throughout the rest of the day. The Foreign Legion was established on the shoulder of the Taraldsvikfjell, the way to the town now open. Naval bombardment as far up the Rombaksfiord as Straumnes had closed the railway line, the only route by which reinforcements could approach the town. At 0630, the Naval forces withdrew apart from the *Coventry* and two destroyers; the attack had been fought-off with unexpected success, with only one 'puffer' actually sunk, although the second French battalion was prevented from getting ashore until 1100 on the 28th.

Narvik was not yet, however, ready to capitulate, fighting continuing as the two battalions moved westwards both on the approach to and within the town itself. The lower slopes of the hillside are quite steep, clothed with birch trees and threaded with gullies bearing flood water down to the Rombaksfiord from the peaks of the Taraldsvikfjell. The rocky, broken ground beside the railway line which runs some way up the mountain side was good defensive terrain, and it was hard and painful going for the 1st French Battalion who had to clear every little gully in turn. The 2nd Battalion, ashore at last, proceeded along the lower slopes which was easier going and soon established themselves on a little knoll to the north of the railway station where they were joined by General Fleischer and the Norwegian Battalion.

By midday, it was clear to the dwindling number of defenders that the town was lost. One officer and one hundred men escaped to the south-east along the road to

Beisfiord, but a boat containing sixty men escaping across the Beisfiord was sunk by the Poles now well established on the Ankenes peninsula.

The Poles also launched an attack on Ankenes to coincide with the main assault. Although it was essential to clear the Germans out of Ankenes to prevent them bringing their artillery to bear on Narvik when it was captured, it was not in itself an easy line of approach to the town. The southern shore of the fiord is virtually impassable as the Harhaus falls steeply into the waters of the fiord, and although there was a narrow road hugging the north bank from Beisfiord at the head of the inlet, this is flanked by the even steeper slopes of the Fagernesfjell, heavily wooded and threaded by gullies and clefts in the rock. It would be very difficult to make progress into Narvik from this direction against any determined opposition. Two French Hotchkiss tanks leading the assault of two Polish battalions were quickly put out of action by mines, but with the support of naval bombardment and the British 25 pounder guns, one company gained a foothold in Ankenes almost immediately. A German counter-attack on their right flank restored the situation and some positions which had been held since the first day had to be temporarily given up. Even the Brigade Headquarters was threatened. The Poles were also subjected to air attack during the day, but by now the RAF were back in the air in strength and these were largely ineffective. The Poles gradually encircled Ankenes on the gentle wooded slopes which lie above the town and the Germans for the first time were on the receiving end of their own favoured tactic in Norway. By midday they began to retreat along the south shore of the fiord and although stubborn resistance continued in the hills, by early evening the Polish right wing had pressed on some way towards the small town at the head of the fiord. That night the Poles joined up with a French motorcycle section which had advanced from Narvik along the north shore of the Beisfiord.

The Norwegians were afforded the courtesy of entering the town first which they did at 1700 to a warm welcome from the town's 6,000 inhabitants. The quays, ore handling plant and warehouses were in ruins, as was much of the town, and there were more than twenty wrecks littering the harbour. At 2200, General Béthouart formally declared that the whole of the Narvik peninsula was in Allied hands together with some three hundred prisoners. The cost was about one hundred and fifty casualties, thirty killed, more or less equally shared between the French and the Norwegians. The Norwegians established themselves in the town which could expect to be subjected to renewed air attack, and the French pursued the retreating Germans along the railway towards Sweden.

It had taken six weeks since the arrival of Lord Cork and General Mackesy on 14 April to capture the town. Most of the first month had been taken-up with the argument between the two as to how to tackle the problem – by direct assault or encirclement. But since the landings at Bjerkvik on 13 May, the operation had been conducted with exemplary precision and careful planning, and with the minimum of casualties. All the troops, Norwegian, French and Polish had performed well, and the naval support was carefully planned and effectively delivered.

Lord Cork still believed that the town could have been carried by direct assault much earlier. The final thrust across the Rombaksfiord had many similarities to the plans which he had so strenuously tried to foist upon General Mackesy in the first weeks of the campaign. But there were essential differences. There was now air support, and even though this was grounded by fog during a part of the assault, its pyschological boost during the initial landings should not be underestimated. There were now MLCs and ALCs, albeit few in number, whereas Mackesy would have had to approach the shore in open boats. The troops involved had been blooded by the rather more straightforward landing at Bjerkvik, unlike 24th Brigade which would have been facing its first ever engagement in most trying conditions. Perhaps above all, there was a significant improvement in the weather and movement, once ashore, became easier. We shall never know, but as viewed by the Army commanders in April, it is still difficult to convincingly argue against their decision. It did not prevent Lord Cork rather sourly remarking in his report:

> . . . the carrying out of this operation proved more simple than expected. He (General Béthouart) was good enough to give much credit to the naval assistance he had received. That, however, would always have been forthcoming to any force that had attempted the task.[9]

Eventual success was really inevitable, General Dietl with a much smaller force at the end of a precarious line of supply could not be expected to withstand for long a concentrated attack from all sides except the south-east. His only chance of success lay with the opening of a reinforcement and supply route from the south. Although, the story of the 24th Guards Brigade and the Independent Companies had been a series of desperate actions and unseemly retreat, they had in fact succeeded in their aim of preventing the join up of the 2nd Mountain Division and Dietl's besieged garrison. However, even if Bodo had been lost, the last one hundred miles or so across the desolate, trackless wilderness would have caused immense difficulties for the Germans in linking up with Narvik. General Dietl himself had indicated at an earlier stage that it was quite impracticable for his garrison to retreat to the south towards Bodo because of the exhaustion of his troops and the nature of the terrain.

The Allies had gained their first success in Norway, indeed their first success on land of the war. The invincible progress of German troops across Europe to the West and North had at last been halted and repulsed. What an ironic paradox therefore that even before the ink was dry on the signal announcing the capture of Narvik, all of the Commander's attention was now directed towards giving up what had been so dearly won.

15

The Gladiator's Revenge – Air War in the North

'All our available Metropolitan air strength must be devoted to operations against Germany with the primary aim of the defence of the United Kingdom.'[1]

Chiefs of Staff Appreciation
The Situation in the Event
of War Against Germany

Preparing the Ground

It was a novel and unwelcome experience for the Royal Air Force to see how easily a whole squadron of fighters had been decimated within forty eight hours in its first venture into Norway in April 1940. But Dowding was not too worried, he did not pin great faith in the Gladiator for salvation in the skies of Britain, and the Air Ministry consoled themselves with the knowledge that the circumstances were unique, and in any case army co-operation was not really their business! Nevertheless, when a month later the equally pressing requirement arose to provide air support in the north of the country, the task was inevitably approached with caution and some foreboding. As in Central Norway, therefore, the ships in the fiords and the troops on land had to endure over a month of almost continuous battering by an unopposed Luftwaffe before they obtained anything but token relief. In fact, the decision to evacuate north Norway was taken almost coincidentally with the arrival of the first RAF squadron and so the impact on the ground operations was again short-lived.

Nevertheless, air operations in the Narvik area were eventually rather more successful for the Allies than had been the case in Central Norway, and before picking up the story of the last flourishes of the campaign and the evacuation, we need to look in a little more detail at the air war in north Norway. We have seen how important the Luftwaffe's superiority had proved over Central Norway, and released from this commitment, it was only to be expected that they would seek to achieve the same advantage in the north. Narvik was within range of the Heinkels and Ju 88s from Vaernes (Trondheim), but until a forward landing strip was prepared near Mosjöen towards the end of May, Narvik was outside of the normal operating range of the dreaded Stuka.

The Air Ministry had never been very enthusiastic regarding the employment of squadrons in Central Norway, and the end result had unfortunately vindicated their scepticism. But the problem of containing the Luftwaffe remained, and was reinforced by those returning from Aandalsnes and Namsos who had suffered the demoralising effect of unfettered air bombardment. Resources were limited; in addition to the eighteen Gladiators lost at Lesjaskog, the four batteries of anti-aircraft guns sent to Central Norway also had to be abandoned. Replacements were hard to find. The British Expeditionary Force in France had only half of its complement of anti-aircraft guns, and the number of heavy and light guns available for the air defence of Great Britain represented only forty and nine per cent of scale respectively: in number 900 and 166.

The 3rd Light Anti-Aircraft Battery R.A. arrived in Harstad on 15 April with 24th Brigade although they had to wait another week for their twelve Bofors guns. The first consignment of heavy guns, eight 3.7s, did not arrive until 8 May, by which time three more batteries of light guns were on their way. Five more heavy and one light battery were also loading and were authorised to sail on 10 May. This brought eventually the total complement of anti-aircraft artillery in north Norway to 48 heavy and 60 light guns. Auchinleck, meanwhile, in his original shopping list sent on 17 May had asked for two hundred guns: thirteen heavy batteries totalling 104 guns and eight light of 96. The Vice Chiefs of Staff had earlier reached an even higher estimate of the requirement, 144 each of heavy and light guns, but the claims of Lieutenant General Sir Frederick Pile, GOC in UK Anti-Aircraft Command were paramount and no more guns were sent. Given the staggering shortfall in the requirement for the air defence of Great Britain, the Chief's allocation for Norway may even be thought generous, but predictably Auchinleck was far from satisfied.

It was another of those dreadful dilemmas posed to a Government so woefully unready for war. There is a dreadful risk of dissipating inadequate resources to meet so many disparate requirements that in the event none of them are satisfied. It was to arise again and again during the early years of the war, most notably in the Mediterranean and North Africa in 1941.

In practice, anti-aircraft guns were not particularly effective in the prevailing environment in Norway. The mountainous terrain made it relatively straightforward for low flying aircraft to use the contours of the land to shield themselves from guns whose arc of fire was necessarily limited. Only in the more open areas did the guns force the bombers to fly high where their bombing accuracy was diminished and the fighters could get at them. In these areas, the guns deterrent effect was quite valuable. Even so, the anti-aircraft artillery claimed twenty three victims and contributed to the limited ascendancy in the base areas achieved by the RAF towards the end of the campaign. The importance of protecting the airfield at Bardufoss was fully recognised and given priority in the provision of the limited number of guns available.

Despite the early evidence of the impact of enemy air power in Central Norway, the Air Ministry was still slowly off the mark in assessing the feasibility of deploying squadrons to the Narvik area. Although the land forces were assembling at Harstad in the middle of the month, it was not until 30 April that a survey was begun of the available airfields in north Norway. Wing Commander R. L. R. Atcherley, one of two brothers who subsequently made such a mark in the RAF of later years, was sent to advise on possible sites for the location of the air component, at that stage intended to consist of two fighter and one bomber squadron (40 Squadron Blenheims) and grandly called the Royal Air Force Component of the North Western Expeditionary Force.

Atcherley and his deputy, Squadron Leader Bell, quickly borrowed a Fleet Air Arm Walrus to reconnoitre the area. The only possible site for a bomber squadron was considered to be Banak,[2] two hundred miles north of Narvik at the head of the Porsangerfiord, and only a few miles from the North Cape. It was generally snow free, but could only be supplied by sea round the North Cape in an area which would be vulnerable to the German submarines which had been forced out of the waters around Harstad. Its use would have placed a heavy strain on the naval forces available and in the event it was never used, despite the formidable efforts in preparation of some one thousand Lapps led by an exceptionally resourceful Able Seaman. Banak was far too distant from the main scene of the ground action to be of any use for the basing of the shorter range fighter aircraft.

Three possible sites were considered suitable for the fighter squadrons: Bardufoss, which already had a small airfield with two short grass runways, Skaanland, the naval headquarters which had no airfield but provided a level drained area, and a site just outside Bodo where there was another small airfield still deep under snow. Wing Commander Atcherley assumed direct responsibility for Bardufoss and Banak and sent Squadron Leader Bell to Skaanland and Flight Lieutenant Masterman to Bodo. Although Skaanland was the best geographical site being closer to Harstad and Narvik, the existing airfield at Bardufoss had the greater potential as a fighter base. But it was seventeen miles by narrow track to the nearest access to the sea for re-supply, a small wooden jetty at Sörreisa. The airfield was still under nearly five feet of snow, but work was put in hand immediately to clear the airfield and reconstruct the road to Sörreisa. General Fleischer, the Norwegian army commander, at first resisted the introduction of British or French troops to help prepare the airfield, a symptom of the uneasy relationship which existed between the Allies. He also wanted, in the light of the recent withdrawal from Central Norway, a written promise, for what it was worth, that there would be no precipitate withdrawal.

The Norwegian Air Force was more constructive, arranging two teams each of three hundred local men to work around the clock removing snow, clearing away the ice and rolling the ground by means of a roller improvised from two forty gallon drums filled with concrete. One of the problems encountered at all the airfields was that beneath the frost layer the soil was soft and peaty and quickly became spongy and dangerous when the thaw set in. The lessons of Lesjaskog where so many aircraft were destroyed on the ground between sorties were well heeded and twenty log and gravel blast-proof shelters were constructed in the surrounding forests, connected to the runway by a network of narrow taxiways. Eventually a runway 715 yards long by 95 yards wide was completed, but the second runway proved too rough for use and an extension of the single runway was put in hand. Air-raid shelters and a rudimentary operations room were built, and in most respects the airfield became a satisfactory base for the two squadrons which eventually arrived. Even so, more feverish digging was required when the thaw arrived to prevent the cleared area being submerged by water. The road to Sörreisa was repaired and two hundred mules co-opted to transport stores.

The preparation of Skaanland proved more difficult even though the snow was not as deep as at Bardufoss, and in the end it never became fit for use. A great effort was made to improve the airfield at Bodo where part of the original field had been ploughed and the site was criss-crossed by power and telephone lines. Unfortunately a misguided attempt to help by the Chief of Police appealing on the radio for five hundred volunteers to assist the rehabilitation of the airfield was answered by the Luftwaffe and restricted the efforts of a willing workforce. Even so a rolled strip was ready by 26 May and three Gladiators flew down from Bardufoss. But as we have already seen, their effort was largely in vain.[3] The runway was quickly made unusable by bombing attacks and two aircraft were destroyed on the ground.

The search continued for additional airfields. The main problem was in deciding what might constitute a usable landing strip when everything was covered by several feet of snow. A level area of sufficient size might prove to be totally unsatisfactory when the snow was cleared as happened at Skaanland. A possible site was found at Elvenes near Salangen and another at Elvegaard near Bjerkvik. In the end, only Bardufoss, and very briefly Bodo, proved capable of supporting the few fighters that were made available.

The anti-aircraft defences at Bardufoss were provided by one heavy battery of eight guns and a light battery of twelve. Radar early warning in its infancy even in Great Britain, could not be provided in the time available, and in any case the topography was not really suitable for radars unless they could be located on the high ground which was clearly impracticable. Instead, two observer chains were developed made up of about two hundred and seventy five airmen and soldiers. One ran from Bodo eastwards to Fauske at the head of the Saltfiord which should have provided about twenty minutes warning of aircraft approaching Narvik, but whose effectiveness was limited because it left a clear channel for enemy aircraft about thirty miles wide between Fauske and the Swedish border. The other lying across the Lofoten Islands was designed to cover approaches from the west. But the pack wireless sets supplied to alert the airfield operations room of an incoming raid were almost useless in the mountainous terrain and in practice the observers had to report in by telephone.

Although the warning time to Harstad was eventually reduced to between two and ten minutes, in practice the RAF could not rely on the late and intermittent warning available and had to mount standing patrols most of the time to provide a reasonable chance of intercepting the German aircraft before they could release their bombs. This was a most wasteful deployment of resources, the small number of fighters that could be spared for each patrol was invariably outnumbered by an enemy who could choose the time and place to concentrate his force. It is a sad reflection on the co-operation between the Allies that the existence of a well established Norwegian observer chain from Tromso in the north to as far south as Mosjöen was unknown to the RAF when they were making their own arrangements. It would have proved far more beneficial to have reinforced the Norwegian chain with better communications than to set up a competing organisation.

Relations with General Fleischer were however slowly improving, and a company of Chasseurs Alpins was eventually provided to supplement a reserve Norwegian battalion to guard against a surprise paratroop attack on the airfield at Bardufoss. It was absolutely imperative that the raid which had been so successful at Stavanger on 9 April should not be repeated.

Redressing the Air Balance

Group Captain M. Moore and his headquarters staff arrived with General Auchinleck in the *Chrobry* on 11 May. Work on preparing the airfields proceeded apace throughout the first three weeks of May, and it says much for the initiative, resource and organising ability of Atcherley and his team that his original estimate for the availability of the first airfield was missed by only one day: Bardufoss was declared ready for operational use on the morning of 21 May.

The first aircraft to arrive were the Gladiators of No. 263 Squadron, rejuvenated in spirit and re-equipped with eighteen Gladiator 11s to replace those lost at Lesjaskog. Squadron Leader J. W. Donaldson still commanded the Squadron, Flight Lieutenant R. S. Mills returned as flight commander, and twelve more of the pilots had been with the Squadron on its last ill-fated visit to Norway. Four of them, including the squadron commander, were still carrying injuries sustained in that expedition, but Donaldson had the consolation of a DSO in recognition of his earlier endeavours. As on the previous occasion, they were ferried out to Norwegian waters in the aircraft carrier *Glorious*. The ground crew had travelled earlier in the *Chrobry*, and seven spare pilots went in the *Sobriesti*, arriving at Bardufoss on 20 May.

After several days waiting at sea for the completion of the airfield, their arrival in Norway on 21 May was marred by misfortune. Eager to reach their destination and to avenge the disastrous interlude of Lesjaskog, they took off in appalling weather conditions in two flights each led by a Swordfish to help with the navigation. One prudently returned with its accompanying Gladiators to the carrier, but the other Swordfish pressed on. The pilot, however, soon became completely lost in deteriorating visibility and flew into a mountain taking two of the Gladiators with him. Having escaped without losing any pilots at all on their first visit to Norway, 263 had suffered casualties on this occasion before even getting into action. The following day they made another attempt to get ashore and eight aircraft managed to reach Bardufoss.

Safely ashore, they did not waste any time settling in, flying no less than fifty four sorties in what remained of the day. Only three enemy aircraft were seen, but one more Gladiator was lost, probably in a collision with a He 111. The pilot, Pilot Officer Craig Adamas was still strapped in the cockpit of his aircraft when it was found just a few yards from its victim. Six more Gladiators arrived on the 23rd, bringing the total ashore to fourteen, but another aircraft was lost that day when Sergeant Whall had to abandon his aircraft after running out of fuel.

The task of 263 Squadron was to maintain patrols over Bardufoss and Harstad and over the fleet anchorage in the Vaagsfiord, a task which was maintained throughout until the evacuation was completed. Predictably, maintaining standing patrols soon proved difficult and the problem was exacerbated when it was decided to operate only in formations of at least two aircraft so that more fire power could be concentrated against intruders who rarely appeared in less than flights of three or more.

The Luftwaffe did not for long neglect the new base, indeed it is surprising that they had not made a greater effort to disrupt its preparation. On the 24th, Bf 110s and a He 111 appeared over Bardufoss, and although a dogfight with the twin engine fighters was inconclusive, the Heinkel was shot down and its crew captured. The following day, the Squadron encountered a new type, the four engine Junkers Ju 90. The Ju 90 was a transport derivative of Germany's only attempt to produce a strategic bomber, the Ju 89; it was a modern looking four engined aircraft which had entered service with Lufthansa before the outbreak of war, but which was quickly pressed into Luftwaffe service to supplement the Ju 52s in Norway. They nevertheless proved easy meat for the Gladiators and three were shot down during the course of the day.

Three more Gladiators were lost on the brief detachment to Bodo although the pilots had a most profitable time while it lasted. Flight Lieutenant Hull downed two Ju 52s and damaged two He 111s on his first sortie. But the following day, two pilots were injured and their aircraft destroyed in an encounter with Ju 87s escorted by a superior number of Bf 110s. The third Gladiator, flown by Lieutenant Tony Lydekker RN, who had only joined the squadron from the *Glorious* on the way out to Norway, was forced to flee back to Bardufoss chased by Bf 110s. His aircraft was damaged beyond repair.

The numbers were now dwindling, but fortunately a respite ensued for a few days as the weather deteriorated again. It was during this period of generally overcast weather that the final attack on Narvik was launched and successfully concluded, although on that particular day the weather conditions favoured the Luftwaffe during a critical period of the assault. The Squadron, taking advantage of the weather which grounded the enemy bombers, indulged themselves in a little ground attack whenever the local conditions were suitable. This was a welcome change from air combat, with lorries, staff cars, railway stations and an enemy strongpoint, which turned out to be the German headquarters at Hundalen, all providing targets of opportunity.

263 Squadron had now been joined by 46 Squadron equipped with Hurricanes which eventually arrived on 26 May. Commanded by Squadron Leader Ken (Bing) Cross, 46 was a rather more experienced unit than many of the Hurricane squadrons which were to contest the skies over Britain during the following months. Many of the pilots had four hundred hours or more and had already been blooded in patrols over the North Sea from their home base at Digby in Lincolnshire. Their eighteen aircraft had been embarked on the *Glorious* on 12 May and their ground crew followed on the *Batory* a day later. However, the *Glorious* was destined to shuttle back and forth across the North Sea for a fortnight before an airfield was ready for them in Norway.

The intention was that they should operate from Skaanland, but two of the first four aircraft to land tipped onto their noses on the soft ground, and the rest of the Squadron was diverted to Bardufoss from which they operated for the remainder of the campaign. The Squadron quickly got into its stride, and on the day after their arrival, a Ju 88 was claimed near Narvik and two large flying boats destroyed on the water in the Rombaksfiord.

From now on the two squadrons worked in unison and a new operating concept was quickly produced. Four distinct patrol areas were devised; in the north at the head of the Solberg Fiord, to the east over Gratangen and the Rombaksfiord, to the south over Ballangen and to the west in the area of Harstad. Although the early warning system was improving, it was still not sufficiently fast or reliable to allow aircraft to be scrambled and arrive over the patrol area before the enemy aircraft appeared. On the other hand, standing patrols in sufficient strength to take on large enemy raids were still usually impracticable even with two squadrons. The problem was exacerbated by the impossibility of redirecting fighters from one patrol area to another because of the poor quality of the ground to air communications in the mountains. Standing patrols had to be mounted at about 12,000 feet as attacking aircraft came in at variable heights between 8,000 and 16,000 feet.

The busiest day of air operations throughout the campaign was 28 May, the day of the assault on Narvik, when despite bad weather ninety four sorties were flown, forty two by 263 Squadron and fifty two by the Hurricanes. However, the fighters made little contact with the enemy, achieving only three throughout the day. Unfortunately, the weather cleared in the south to the advantage of the Luftwaffe at the same time as fog rolled into Bardufoss, grounding the squadrons at a critical point of the attack on Narvik early on the following morning. Despite the eventual success in capturing Narvik, this was not in other respects a good day for the Allies. The cruiser *Cairo*, Lord Cork's flagship from which the assault was being controlled, was damaged in the Rombaksfiord whilst the fighters were fogbound, and at about 1130 *Coventry* was attacked near Skaanland. The French positions on the approaches to Narvik were attacked at lunchtime and again at 1700. No enemy aircraft were destroyed and no fighters lost. The problems of mounting continuous standing patrols were exemplified on this day. The following day was almost as busy with eighty four sorties, eight combats and one aircraft lost. Enemy bombers attacked Harstad, Skaanland and shipping in the Narvik area.

After another lull, 2 June also proved to be a very busy day with over two hundred German bomber sorties escorted by Bf 110s in a sustained attack between 1200 and 1300 on naval vessels in the Narvik area. Despite their reduced number of aircraft, fourteen had now been lost altogether, the two squadrons still managed seventy five sorties, achieving twenty four combats. 263 Squadron's Pilot Officer Jacobsen had a particularly fruitful day. Engaged in several successive combats with Ju 88s and He 111s, he shot down at least three Heinkels and possibly more. But another Gladiator was lost and only ten now remained serviceable.

The evacuation was now in full swing, fortunately protected by mist and low cloud. The squadrons saw little activity: only forty two sorties were flown between 3 and 6 June, but no enemy aircraft were seen. They continued flying patrols right up until the last man had been evacuated, and indeed on their last sortie on 7 June they claimed three more bombers. But their ground crew had by now been evacuated and the squadrons were to follow immediately afterwards. Their final act was to deny the use of Bardufoss to the enemy by blowing one hundred and twenty craters diagonally across the airfield: five hundred yards of runway was left for the Norwegian Fokkers.

It had always been a part of the plan to recover the Gladiators onto the *Glorious* at the end of the evacuation, after all, the RAF pilots had already demonstrated their ability to land on the carrier when their first attempt on 21 May to reach Bardufoss had been thwarted by the weather. After completing their final sorties on the evening of 7 June, ten aircraft led by a Swordfish landed on the carrier and were duly tucked away below without incident.

It had, however, been intended to destroy the Hurricanes because it was thought impossible for these aircraft, not equipped with arrester hooks, to stop on the carrier's deck which was only 465 feet long. Landing on trials had been held in England before the squadron embarked and was then deemed not to be feasible for the average operational pilot. When the squadron left for Norway the aircraft had been hoisted on board by crane. Nevertheless, aware of the desperate need in England for every available Hurricane, Squadron Leader Cross begged to be allowed to try – after all what was to be lost, the aircraft were going to be destroyed anyway. Group Captain Moore agreed and volunteers were requested to attempt the task. Predictably, all eighteen squadron pilots offered their services and ten were selected for the remaining serviceable aircraft. The first three led by Flight Lieutenant Jameson departed in the early evening to attempt the impossible. Fortunately, it was a clear Arctic evening and the *Glorious* was making a good thirty knots with a stiff wind along the deck to help. All three aircraft made a safe, if not always immaculate landing, and each aircraft was stopped well within the short landing run available. The remaining seven aircraft followed soon after midnight. None of the pilots had ever landed on a carrier before, but all got down safely with only three suffering minor damage. It was a remarkable achievement – what an ironic twist of fate therefore that decreed less than twenty four hours later that all the aircraft and nearly all the pilots would be lost in the major naval disaster of the campaign.

The Fleet Air Arm's Contribution

It would be remiss to leave this account of the air war over north Norway without a brief mention of the contribution of the three aircraft carriers which were successively in the area, *Furious*, *Ark Royal* and *Glorious*.

Ark Royal had returned to the Norwegian Sea on 6 May. The weather was frequently unsuitable for flying, but in the breaks in the cloud and rain, the fighter aircraft mounted combat patrols over Skaanland and Harstad and the Skuas attacked targets ashore. Fighter aircraft covered the landing of the French Foreign Legion at Bjerkvik on 14 May, but there was no interference by the Luftwaffe.

For most of the time, however, the Luftwaffe remained active enough, concentrating on the ships in the fiords, and now achieving greater accuracy than was evident in the early stages of the campaign. Quite apart from the limitations imposed by the weather, it was too demanding on the limited resources available to mount standing patrols over the fiords, but occasional chance encounters resulted in air combats with mixed success.

After belatedly launching the Hurricanes on 12 May, the *Glorious* held off shore and was requested by Lord Cork to support the ground forces south of Bodo and to attack the airfield at Mösjoen. It was very desirable that this airfield be denied to the Luftwaffe, for its use brought within range of Narvik the Ju 87 Stuka, the most dangerous of the German bombers for the ships in the fiords. But the *Glorious* carried only Sea Gladiators and Swordfish and was not really equipped for this type of operation. In the event, the raid was cancelled and the *Glorious* returned to Scapa Flow on the evening of the 28th. It had been a frustrating cruise: having unloaded its indigenous Skuas in order to make room for the Hurricanes, it lacked a real offensive capability of its own, and was merely acting as a transport carrier for the RAF. Furthermore, tensions created between the captain and his senior flying executives during this operation may have contributed to the disaster which was to befall the *Glorious* later. It had however sent a Walrus flight to Harstad on 18 May, and within its very modest capability, it carried out useful transport, reconnaissance, and even bombing duties until re-embarked on 6 June.

Ark Royal, with *Glorious* and an escort of five destroyers, departed again for Norwegian waters on 31 May. *Ark Royal* was intended to help with the provision of fighter cover for the evacuation whilst the *Glorious* was once again required to act in the role of an aircraft tender to recover the RAF's Gladiators from Bardufoss. She carried only six Gladiators for self defence and six Swordfish. *Glorious* was therefore detached to the north-west to stay out of harms way and to conserve fuel. This may have proved rather a waste of resources: *Glorious* could have carried a larger complement of aircraft and still had room to embark the Gladiators of 263 Squadron. As it turned out, the weather came to the aid of the evacuation and *Ark Royal*, together with the shore-based squadrons, proved quite capable of maintaining local air superiority over the fiords and the rendezvous areas. Bombing sorties were also launched by *Ark Royal*'s Skuas and Swordfish against troops working their way north from Bodo, but apart from the satisfaction of administering to the Germans some of their own medicine, these sorties now had no impact on the campaign itself as they could never arrive in time to impede the evacuation.

A More Successful Balance Sheet

During this brief campaign, with considerable help from the weather, the two squadrons had established a reasonable degree of air parity in northern Norway, and at the end even air superiority over the immediate evacuation areas. In all, the squadrons operated on twelve days, 263 Squadron mounting 389 sorties achieving sixty nine combats, whilst 46 Squadron made 249 flights and engaged enemy aircraft on twenty six occasions. This was overall a very high rate of utilisation given the periods of poor weather, the declining number of aircraft and the makeshift conditions under which they were forced to operate. Most of their engagements had been in the Harstad or Narvik areas and the pilots claimed thirty seven kills, 263 Squadron claiming twenty six and 46 Squadron eleven. But the losses must be seen in the perspective of the scale of the Luftwaffe operations. If they had been equally distributed, each Staffel would have lost only its three reserve aircraft and the number of operational sorties would have been undiminished. Indeed statistics show that the scale of enemy operations was not reduced by the arrival of the RAF on 22 May and further fighter reinforcements would have been needed to sustain operations for much longer. Nevertheless, the main base at Harstad and the anchorage in the Vaagsfiord remained tenable throughout, and not one soldier was lost during the evacuation. Furthermore, much of the equipment and stores which both the Government in London and the commanders on the spot had expected to leave behind were successfully embarked. That the evacuation was so efficiently carried out in accordance with the plan was due both to the skill and foresight of those who organised it, and particularly to the efforts of the two squadrons which kept the hostile aircraft off their backs whenever the weather allowed the enemy to fly, which fortunately during the evacuation period was not very frequently.

16

Evacuation

'I hope before any fresh appointment is given to General Auchinleck, the whole story of the slack and feeble manner in which the operations at Narvik were conducted, and the failure to make an earlier assault on Narvik town, will be considered. Let me know the dates when General Auchinleck was in effective command . . .'[1]

Winston Churchill

Unremitting Gloom

General Auchinleck's report of 21 May was the decisive nail in the coffin of the ill fated Scandinavian campaign which had begun with such mismanagement and muddle barely more than six weeks before. The Cabinet and the Chiefs of Staff were now absorbed in the struggle for France in the increasing realisation that the battle for Britain could not now long be delayed. The news from the Western Front was almost universal unremitting gloom: the long expected strike on Holland and Belgium had erupted at dawn on 10 May. General Auchinleck heard the news on the Chrobry during his protracted journey to Harstad, he was already dubious of the strategic benefit of this adventure beyond the Arctic Circle when the fate of Europe, even of the world, was being enacted in the heartland of Western Europe. By 14 May, the German Panzer Divisions were across the Meuse and the Netherlands was already negotiating terms of surrender, the centre of the historic city of Rotterdam lying in smoking ruins after a savage attack by the Luftwaffe Stukas. The French, still half clinging to the chimera of their invincible army, were finding to their horror that it was a paper myth as it crumbled almost without a fight. Guderian and Rommel's thrust through the Ardennes, country considered quite unsuitable for armoured warfare, was as unstoppable as it was unbelieveable: on a large canvas, it was reminiscent of General Carton de Wiart's appreciation of the passability of the road north of Grong a month before.

On 18 May the Panzers were rumbling across the 1916 battlefields of the Somme in that relentless push that was to reach Bordeaux and Lyon five weeks later. General Weygrand replaced Gamelin as Chief of the General Staff, one old, tired traditional warrior replaced by one even older and more out of touch with the nature of modern armoured warfare. The British Expeditionary Force, which had not been heavily involved in the early fighting, was now forced to retreat rapidly towards the coast as General Blanchard's 1st French Army disintegrated on their right flank. By the 20th, the 2nd Panzer Division reached the Channel at Abbeville. Air Marshal Barratt's

Advanced Air Striking Force of Blenheims and Battles had been decimated and the French Air Force had hardly put in an appearance. This was the situation when the Chiefs of Staff considered Lord Cork's signal of 21 May, preparing the scene for Auchinleck's more detailed statement which was on its way to London that same night. It was hardly surprising in this situation that it was difficult in London to concentrate on the campaign in Norway.

On 20 May the Cabinet, frustrated by the delays in capturing Narvik, had considered ordering a direct assault and Mr Churchill signalled that delay was costing more men and ships than vigorous action. But, in the event, as had become endemic in the Government's handling of Norway, a decision was postponed. In fact, there was too little knowledge or understanding in London of what was actually happening in Norway, of the constraints imposed by climate and the impact of the overwhelming air superiority of the Luftwaffe. There was a strong feeling that we should be doing better, but no clear idea of how to achieve it. Indeed, the lack of any coherent strategy in London in the few days before the Cabinet elected to evacuate Narvik was very reminiscent of the days before the decision was made to abandon Central Norway. Half-hearted support for the venture had sporadically continued without any clear sense of direction or purpose. On 10 May, an additional regiment of anti-aircraft artillery was allowed to sail for Norway and the 2nd French Light Division, despite events on the continent, was held waiting in readiness on the Clyde to embark for Norway until 15 May. The three battalions of the Chasseurs Alpins, re-equipped after their return from Namsos, were actually ordered to sail for Harstad with the five remaining Independent Companies on 22 May, but delayed by General Auchinleck for administrative reasons. One squadron of Hurricanes, which had originally been authorised to go to France were finally diverted to Norway on the 21st when the airfield at Skaanland was alleged to be ready for use. Once started rolling, the campaign had built up its own inertia, only the co-ordination was lacking. There was even a feeling, expressed by Mr Churchill on 15 May, that the Allied presence in Norway was tying down a disproportionate number of German forces away from the main theatre of war. This forlorn hope was matched by M. Reynaud's observation, born of desperation rather than reality, that a success in Narvik would do something to offset the bad news from other quarters.

It was in this climate that the Allied Governments considered what Auchinleck scathingly described as the 'so called Mowinckel Plan'. Mowinckel, a former Norwegian Prime Minister who had rejoined the Government in Tromso, suggested the neutralisation of Norway to the north of a line through Mösjoen. The idea had apparently been conceived in discussions with the Swedish Foreign Minister in Stockhom, 'as a passing thought' as early as April, but nothing of substance had materialised. The Swedes by now were feeling acutely uncomfortable, hemmed in on one side by the Russian invasion of Finland and on the other by the German occupation of Norway, and proposed that their forces should occupy Narvik, replacing both the Germans and the Allies. Lord Halifax and the Foreign Office gave some support for the scheme, and even the Germans were thought to be favourably disposed to the idea although the Norwegian Government was lukewarm. Discussion rambled on, but the plan received no support from Mr Churchill at this stage who was still more concerned to dismember by force any future economic and military advantage that might accrue from the continued German occupation of the port.

By 20 May, ahead of his Chiefs of Staff, Mr Churchill was already thinking in terms of capturing, destroying and then abandoning Narvik. Only one day after extolling the virtues of tying down German troops in Norway, he now considered that Narvik was in fact a greater drain on our own resources. But again no decisions were reached by the new Defence Committee. The Chiefs of Staff also began to doubt the wisdom of maintaining a force in Narvik, citing the weakness of the Norwegians in both material and will as being insufficient upon which to build a base for continued resistance. They pointed out that no less than half the total available number of destroyers was required to escort convoys to Narvik and that one and a half Allied divisions were opposed to eleven German divisions.[2] Their appreciation continued:

> The Germans employed their forces to overcome southern Norway, and there is no reason for them to lock-up large forces in Norway merely because we are at Narvik. Moreover, the air forces that the Germans had stationed in Norway could operate against the United Kingdom, and were not in any sense diverted from the main theatre. And furthermore the expedition to Norway was absorbing forces that would be better employed elsewhere. The naval forces in the Narvik zone now numbered:
>
> > 3 Aircraft carriers
> > 2 Anti-aircraft cruisers
> > 4 Cruisers (one of them a modern 8″ cruiser)
> > 15 Destroyers
> > 2 Sloops
>
> In addition to this, 43 heavy and 60 light AA guns were needed for the defence of the aerodrome and of the base, and thus was a heavy burden; for these guns were much needed for the defence of the United Kingdom. The two squadrons at Bardufoss would not suffice to defend the base or the town of Narvik, if it were severely attacked, and it was not going to be easy to maintain even these two squadrons in Norway: their losses would be high; Hurricanes could not be spared; Gladiators were no longer being manufactured and very few of these aircraft were to be found in the aircraft storage units.
>
> As against this it was not to be disguised that there were substantial reasons for remaining in Norway: discredit would attach to us if we abandoned the Norwegians altogether; moreover, if we captured Narvik, and held it, certain quantities of timber, iron ore and high grade steel would be assured to us. The reasons for holding on could not, however, have the same weight as the reasons for withdrawing: the campaign in France was going ill; and the advance of the German armies was endangering Great Britain and France. The security of France is essential; the retention of northern Norway is not.[3]

On 23 May the Chiefs of Staff formally recommended the abandonment of Narvik. The increasing recognition that an invasion of Britain was becoming a very real prospect gave added force to their proposal. As they indicated, evacuation would take twenty-eight days, and if an invasion occurred during this time, the whole naval force would have to be brought back to defend home waters.

The War Cabinet was generally in agreement that Norway had to be evacuated, but some were less happy with the plan to capture Narvik first. In the midst of the melodramatic tidings from France, the capture of Narvik would not provide the political coup that might have followed success in April. Churchill in particular was concerned at the morality of asking troops to risk casualties for an objective that was to be given up immediately afterwards. Although the Cabinet directed that plans for the evacuation should be set in hand, no decision was actually taken at the meeting on the 23rd.

The following day it was decided to act as the Chiefs of Staff had proposed and a signal was prepared for Lord Cork indicating that troops, ships and guns were now needed for the defence of Britain. This was indeed true, as invasion scares were now a daily occurrence and the evacuation from France was already underway with the withdrawal of 1,000 troops from Boulogne. It was concluded that, for the time being, the decision to leave would not be divulged to the Norwegians. The evacuation was finally endorsed by the Supreme Council on 31 May but as a sop to the French, it was agreed that after re-grouping the troops would be dispatched to France – a decision not likely to be fulfilled as the retreat from Dunkirk was now in full swing.

Even now, the agreement was challenged in the Cabinet on three subsequent occasions, finally on 2 June by Churchill himself who, heartened by the successful evacuation from Dunkirk, suggested that we should maintain a garrison in Narvik, at least for some weeks. Meanwhile, the Mowinckel plan had resurfaced and on 1 June, at the same time as the Norwegians were advised of the Allies intention to withdraw, formal support for the plan was notified to the Swedish and Norwegian Governments. The Norwegians asked for and were granted a twenty-four hour stay of execution, but the proposal came to nothing anyway as the Germans, predictably, had by now lost any interest they might have had in the idea. There was also a scheme for leaving independent forces behind to succour the resistance movement, but this was stillborn as well. In a completely opposite vein Lord Cork was ordered to bring home all the small guns and ammunition even though the Norwegians complained on 1 June that they had received only one thousand of the twenty thousand rifles they had requested. A counter order to leave behind for the Norwegians four thousand five hundred rifles and two million rounds of ammunition was received some hours after the last ship had left Narvik. True to form, confusion reigned right up until the very end.

The Evacuation from Bodo

The signal ordering the withdrawal from Norway was received by Lord Cork during the night of 24/25 May. It stressed the desirability of first capturing Narvik both to facilitate the evacuation and to ensure that everything would be destroyed that might help the Germans to resurrect the flow of iron ore from Narvik. As we have seen, Narvik was duly captured, but as it was now intended that we should withdraw shortly thereafter and the delaying role of the 24th Brigade would thus no longer be needed, there was no point in risking further losses south of Bodo. The Scots Guards were heavily depleted and in need of rest, and the last companies of the South Wales Borderers were still on their way to Bodo. The Irish Guards had not yet seen action, but were concentrated at Pothus, the last defensible location in the Saltdal Valley.

Colonel 'Pop' Dowler, G.S.O. 1 in Auchinleck's headquarters was sent down with the last company of the Borderers in the *Beagle* on 25 May to advise Brigadier Gubbins of the intention to withdraw. He found Gubbins in the early hours of the 26th still remarkably resilient in the face of his many difficulties, but he was in the middle of the battle for Pothus and little time could be devoted to thinking of the evacuation. Nevertheless after the withdrawal from Pothus, 24th Brigade ignored a previous plan to make another stand at Finneid and withdrew to the less satisfactory defensive position on the Fauske isthmus on the opposite side of the bay from Finneid. The Norwegians were justifiably mystified by this decision as they had previously brought another battalion down from Bardufoss to reinforce Finneid and it was under protest that they joined the British at Fauske. The facade was already looking transparent and the secret of the withdrawal could not in these circumstances be kept from the Norwegians any longer. They were told accordingly of the intention to withdraw from Bodo, although no mention was yet made of the plan to abandon Narvik. The Norwegians quite naturally considered the proposal absurd, for it negated all that had been done to protect Narvik from the south – it is perhaps not surprising that they remained suspicious of the British motives and real intentions throughout the campaign. Nevertheless, there was no question of the Norwegians staying in the area on their own, and so they requested a three day delay while they organised their own withdrawal from Rösvik, some fifteen miles to the north of Fauske and the terminus in 1940 of the road to the north.

The Norwegians eventually extricated themselves from their difficult position at Fauske, but not before losing a few prisoners in the process. The Germans pursued them along the road to Rösvik, although not in any great strength, and a Norwegian rearguard managed to hold off a motorcycle detachment while the majority were evacuated to the Lofoten Islands in 'puffers'. One company was trapped however in Finneid and made its way, too late, across the Blaamannsis glacier and into captivity.

The original intention was to evacuate the British force from Bodo on 2 June in four fast passenger ships protected by an aircraft carrier. However, the Luftwaffe, who had been provoked by the arrival of the three Gladiators, turned their attention to Bodo, not only upon the airfield, but also the town and the port. It was deemed prudent in the circumstances to get out as quickly as possible and a new plan was conceived to embark 1,000 men in two destroyers on 29 May, and 1,500 men on each of the two succeeding nights on three destroyers. Gubbins was not made aware of these arrangements until 29 May and he had already signalled Auchinleck requesting the evacuation be brought forward two nights as he doubted his ability to hold on until 2 June.

In the event, the evacuation from Bodo went very well; after all, following Aandalsnes and Namsos it was an operation in which the Navy was becoming well versed. The first group of 1,000 men was duly taken off the quaysides which had remarkably escaped serious damage in the German bombing and ferried out to the repair ship *Vindictive* lying well out to sea which took them directly back to Scapa Flow. On the second night, another 1,300 were transferred on two destroyers to Borkenes to the west of Harstad, and the remainder, mainly comprising the Scots Guards battalion, were cleared on the third night in two more destroyers, the *Echo* and *Delight*, whilst two Gladiators and two Hurricanes patrolled overhead. By midnight on 31 May, the last man had passed through the ruins of Bodo and was on the first stage of his journey home. Virtually all of their equipment had to be abandoned, but air attacks during the embarkation period were unexpectedly light. Once again, the Luftwaffe missed the opportunity, as they had in Central Norway and also at Dunkirk, of pressing home their advantage when their opponents were most vulnerable. Although they possessed an overwhelming numerical advantage, they were strangely unable to capitalise on their superiority to turn a retreat into a rout. General Auchinleck was disappointed that it had not proved possible to send the whole of the 24th Brigade and the Independent Companies straight home – in coming to Harstad they merely compounded the problems of extricating the rest of the Allied forces. Nevertheless, when he inspected some of those who had arrived back from Bodo, he was pleased to see that they were still in good heart despite their ordeals at sea and in the valley of the Saltdal.

A Painful Disengagement

By 30 May Norwegian suspicion of the Allied intentions boiled over. They could hardly be expected to believe that our known intention to vacate Bodo did not presage a complete withdrawal from Norway. Colonel Pollock, the Military Liaison Officer, telephoned Auchinleck from Tromso to advise him of the disquiet regarding the evacuation of Bodo which was now public knowledge. He travelled down to Harstad later the same day to discuss the situation and said that it was only with difficulty that he and the British Minister had persuaded the Norwegian Government not to open armistice negotiations with the Germans. Auchinleck confirmed to Pollock that it was the Government's intention to withdraw, but that the Norwegians were not yet to be told.

The evacuation planning had meanwhile been proceeding in great secrecy and a list of those privy to the plan was drawn up under the codename 'Alphabet'. They were told that a deception plan was to be mounted suggesting that troops were to be deployed from Narvik to more advantageous locations, and that Tromso was to be established as the main base because it was less vulnerable than Harstad to air attack. The plan not only deceived the Norwegians. The Royal Marines base organisation actually set off for Tromso, but were redirected to Scapa Flow en route where they were held incommunicado to prevent this change of plan becoming general knowledge. The Scots Guards believed as late as 4 June that their destination was Tromso, but when their Transport Officer begged to be allowed to drive his brand new unused trucks to Tromso rather than destroy them as he had been ordered, he was curtly refused. The myth was becoming difficult to sustain!

On the following day, 31 May, the British Minister at Tromso, Sir Cecil Dormer, and Colonel Pollock conferred with Lord Cork and it was agreed that the Norwegians would have to be told of the Allied intentions. Dormer agreed to go back and speak to selected Norwegian Ministers individually, and then if satisfied with their response, to advise the Government formally of the situation. It was both a disagreeable mission and one unlikely to be very productive – the lid could hardly be left on after even an informal approach to the Norwegians. It was suggested by the Foreign Office that a revival of the Mowinckel plan might help to sweeten the pill, but they could hardly expect this to succeed in the light of a British withdrawal which the Germans would soon know of, if indeed they were not aware of it already. Sir Clive Dormer consulted Ministers as instructed on 1 June and told the King and his Cabinet formally on the following morning. The news was received with better grace than might reasonably have been expected and an attempt was made to revive Sweden's interest in the neutrality plan for north Norway. Vice Admiral Cunningham was entrusted with making arrangements for the evacuation of the King, his family and the Government ministers, and indeed anyone else who wished to accompany him. Lord Cork wrote to Admiral Diesen expressing a hope that any remaining Norwegian ships would be sent across to the Shetlands to continue the fight and this request was also graciously agreed. On the whole, the Norwegians accepted the abandonment of their country by Allies who had promised much more than they had delivered with remarkable dignity and generosity.

The fighting had not ended with the capture of Narvik. General Dietl had received instructions to hold out to the bitter end and managed to escape from Narvik with most of his troops and withdraw in the only possible direction along the railway line towards the Swedish border. Here they were forced into the mountains and were running short of ammunition, but even at this stage they still held to a slender hope of being relieved: they did not of course know at this time of the Allies intention to withdraw which would have given a boost to their will to continue the battle. They established themselves on the Haugfjell which overlooks the north shore of the Rombaksfiord, and on the two mountains behind it, the Bjornfjell and the Rundfjell. To the north lay the Norwegians who, encouraged by their recent successes, were organising themselves on the Kuberg plateau for a further push. But their lines of communication and supply were long and tortuous, and between them and the Germans lay the Jernvatnene, a tundra landscape of lakes and barren ground which had become very difficult to negotiate in the thaw which was now in full flood.

General Béthouart's original plan to send a detachment of Polish and French troops to cut off the German's escape route had been abandoned, but the Foreign Legion pursued the Germans along the Rombaksfiord to just beyond Straumen. The Poles had also moved across country from Beisfiord towards the railway and joined up with the French on 2 June.

The Norwegians had three battalions available for the final thrust to round up the remaining German fugitives, and even after having been officially informed of the Allied intentions, they still hoped to complete the action before the final withdrawal. Their intention was to attack the Rundfjell, and after its capture, turn towards the Haugfjell where the Germans faced the French and Polish troops. This in turn would force the Germans towards Bjornfjell where the *coup de grace* could be delivered. The final attack was to be launched on 8 June.

General Ruge, despite his periods of depression in the Gudbrandsdal, was now grimly determined to press on to achieve a victory in at least one part of Norway, token though it might be in the overall picture. Their success in Narvik had revived the Norwegian spirit, and a desire to recoup some of their tarnished pride had begun to replace the earlier defeatism. How different this whole story might have been if only this same spirit had resurfaced in the Gudbrandsdal and the Österdal a few weeks before. But it now posed a particular problem for the Allies who had to withdraw without leaving their erstwhile comrades in an impossible and dangerous situation. General Béthouart, who had worked most closely with the Norwegians on the final phase of the attack on Narvik, was particularly concerned that the Norwegians should not be left in a position which would compromise their safety – 'I am operating with Norwegian troops whom for reasons of national honour I will not abandon in difficulties on the battlefield'.[4] The French are perhaps particularly sensitive to the need to sustain the esprit and pride of their fighting troops – only days later a last counter-attack on the Panzer divisions in France was to be mounted to salvage the pride of the French Army rather than to achieve any military or strategic gain, sacrificing the British 51st (Highland) Division in the process.

But it was not to be. Whilst it is often necessary to fight a defensive or delaying action whilst implementing a withdrawal – as had been so vividly illustrated at Dunkirk just days before – it is not so easy to launch an offensive simultaneously with the withdrawal of your rear echelons. The Norwegians disentangled themselves from their forward position and the French and Poles withdrew towards Narvik.

A Model Evacuation

But whilst the final chapters were being enacted, plans for the withdrawal were proceeding apace. By now the Allied forces were spread around several locations ranging from Balangen on the south side of the Ofotfiord to Tromso in the north: in all, there were some 24,500 troops to withdraw. In their original signal authorising the evacuation, the Government had laid down a priority for the recovery of equipment and stores. Not unexpectedly, in the context of events at home, the light anti-aircraft guns and their ammunition headed the list, followed by the 25 pounders and the heavy anti-aircraft guns and ammunition. Unfortunately, it was these very anti-aircraft guns that Auchinleck most needed at this stage of the operation even though he had little faith in the effectiveness of their shooting.

Ships to effect the evacuation slowly gathered together at a rendezvous point one hundred and eighty miles to the west of the Lofoten Islands, well out of reach of the German bombers. Ships such as the *Monarch of Bermuda* which were more familiar with cruises in tropical waters, transatlantic liners like the *Franconia* and *Lancastria*, and humble ferries more used to plying between Liverpool and Belfast such as the *Ulster Monarch* – all now assembled in unfamiliar waters with a common objective. In all there were fifteen troopships under the command of Rear Admiral Vivian in the *Coventry*. Although the smaller ferries were to come right into the habour at Harstad, the larger ships would be moored in the Vaagsfiord where their passengers would transfer from destroyers.

Apart from the risk of attack from the air General Auchinleck considered other possible ways by which the Germans might impede the withdrawal. The most likely eventuality seemed to be that German troops now free in the Bodo area might try to make their way across to Narvik. In fact, the terrain was too difficult and no serious attempt was made to move north in this way. The earlier fears of a sizeable paratroop landing had receded as the specialist troops needed had been redirected to the Western

Front, although a few paratroops were dropped near Balangen during the final stage of the evacuation, for what reason is not clear. But there was still a possibility of a seaborne landing on the south or west coast of Hinnöy, although this could have been little more than an irritant against the large number of troops now ashore in the Narvik area. It was not attempted. Mining from the air or sea was an obvious possibility, although after an abortive attempt on 29 May to lay mines from the air in the Tjelsund, no further attempt was made. In fact, any injection of ground or naval forces was unlikely: the Navy controlled the seas and the RAF was slowly establishing a degree of parity in the air for the first time in the campaign. The weather also joined in on the Allied side as the evacuation was conducted under lowering grey skies which impeded the German bombers and forced them to operate inefficiently at high altitude. Nevertheless, the two squadrons of fighters maintained a constant vigilance and from 2 June they were re-joined by the *Ark Royal*.

The destruction of the port and ore handling facilities to preclude their early re-use by the Germans was not difficult. Much had been destroyed by the naval bombardment, and the Germans themselves demolished the ore crushing plant before evacuating the town. They also burnt the railway workshops and locomotive sheds and blew up the engines. Over thirty wrecked ships littered the harbour, many with only their masts poking forlornly above the waves: it resembled a huge ships graveyard. German bombers carrying firebombs added to the destruction on 2 June, causing widespread damage to the wooden houses which the Allies had been so careful to avoid. The centre of the town was totally destroyed, the stone tower of the church standing gauntly amid the smouldering remains. It was not surprising that the Allies felt that the Germans had made such a thorough job of the destruction that there was nothing further they could do themselves. Brigadier Pyne – the senior Royal Engineer Officer – reported on 5 June:

> In view of the work entailed in clearing the harbour and rebuilding the ore quays and railway in this climate, it is clear that not less than one years work will be necessary before ore could be exported in appreciable quantities. This presupposes that work could not be interfered with from the air or the sea. The ore companies' Norwegian Engineers estimate the time at two years, but it is considered that more energetic people could produce the result in a year under the conditions mentioned above.[5]

The evacuation began on the night of 3/4 June, although night was really a misnomer at this time of the year as some light remained throughout the 24 hours. Five thousand men were lifted off the quays at Harstad, Bokenes and Skaanland each night with remarkable efficiency and smoothness. Admiral Cunningham went north to Tromso in the *Devonshire* to embark the King to exile in London in company with his son, the Crown Prince Olaf, and members of the Government. General Fleischer who had commanded the Norwegian division in North Norway went with them, but General Ruge remained at his post with his troops. The final break was sad, but there was now remarkably little acrimony. One of the bravest and most unselfish decisions the Norwegian Government made during these troubled weeks was not to seek an armistice as soon as the Allies decision to leave became known. They withdrew from their forward positions in the mountains above Narvik with dignity and courage – some of them to continue the fight from Britain and elsewhere.

By the evening of 7 June the evacuation was almost complete, rear parties from the Chasseurs Alpins, the Royal Engineers and the Military Police were all that remained ashore. Far more of the stores and equipment were recoved than had originally been thought possible, but even so much was lost and lorries which would have been invaluable on the road down to Mo were pushed, unused, into the water. General Auchinleck remained ashore until the last man had climbed aboard the *Ulster Monarch* before being ferried out to join Lord Cork in his flagship, now the *Southampton*. General Béthouart joined them in a destroyer from Narvik and about the same time, the French rearguard of two battalions was lifted out of Narvik by 'puffer' and transferred to destroyers lying offshore. The *Southampton* and the destroyers followed the last troopship to sea – not a single man had been left behind. The RAF flew throughout the day until nearly midnight to cover the final stages of the evacuation, but there were remarkably few interruptions. Even on the afternoon of the 7th when, in a break in the weather, dive bombers attacked the *Stork* and *Veteran*, the pilots did not appear to notice that anything untoward was afoot as there were no follow-up raids to harass the end of the evacuation.

The German Fleet Intervenes

There was good reason to expect that the evacuation could be completed without any serious intervention by the German fleet. Not a single vessel had been lost in all the many crossings of the North Sea to Narvik by both naval ships or transports: Admiral Forbes could justifiably claim that he had wrested and maintained control of the open sea. Furthermore, the *Ark Royal* and the *Glorious* were available to cover the voyage home and in addition, the escort comprised the cruiser *Southampton*, the fleet repair ship *Vindictive* and ten destroyers. The whole operation was under the control of Admiral Vivian who flew his flag in the anti-aircraft cruiser *Coventry*. Unfortunately, the ordeal was by no means over for at least some of those who had departed Norway, many with a profound feeling of relief, in this impeccably ordered evacuation.

Lord Cork would have preferred to form all the transports into a single group so that the escort forces provided for their protection could be more effectively deployed. But the troopships were urgently required for other duties and thus the first group departed for Scotland at 0300 on 7 June. Escorted only by the repair ship *Vindictive*, six large liners with 15,000 men provided an attractive target, and their concern would have been magnified had they known that the German battle fleet was roaming the North Sea no more than one hundred miles away. Lord Cork had signalled Admiral Forbes requesting additional protection from the Home Fleet and the latter, well aware of the risks the unprotected convoy would face, immediately ordered the *Renown* and the *Repulse*, escorted by nine destroyers, to sail from Scapa Flow to meet the convoy.

But once again fate, followed by miscalculation, intervened. The Q ship *Prunella*, two hundred miles north-east of the Faroes, reported the presence of two warships heading south. Admiral Forbes immediately ordered the diversion of the two battleships, supported by the cruisers *Newcastle* and *Sussex* and five destroyers, in search of this phantom enemy which has never been traced. In thinking that the German fleet was breaking out into the Atlantic, he had succumbed to exactly the same obsession that had influenced the Admiralty when they launched the Home Fleet on 7 April. The urge to confront the German capital ships in a duel to the death was hard to dispel, but in so doing he left the Narvik convoy, and in particular the first Group, dreadfully and unnecessarily exposed. Although Forbes dispatched the aged battleship *Valiant* to replace the original escorts, the best she could achieve was to meet up with Group 1 at 0100 on the 8th, nearly twenty-four hours after they had left the rendezvous. It was a mistake that could have proved disastrous and one for which Admiral Forbes would not have been readily forgiven.

With undeserved good fortune, however, he was not called upon to pay the price. Apart from a mild air attack on the 8th from which they were rescued by enveloping fog, the convoy made its way uneventfully to safety. Also on the 7th, a convoy of eight slow merchantships carrying most of the equipment which had been retrieved also left for home escorted only by two sloops and the trawlers which were still usable. This too had an uneventful voyage.

The second main group which was made up of four large liners and three Irish Sea packets with 10,000 men left on the 8 May. The liner *Orama* which was not required was sent back alone, another mistake which as we shall see did not end so happily. Group 2 was escorted by the *Coventry*, the *Southampton* and the five remaining destroyers. They were joined by the *Ark Royal* with three more destroyers and also had an unimpeded journey home.

The good fortune however was not to be sustained, for the German fleet had decided to intervene. Their original intention, under the codename Juno, had been to attack ships and shore installations in the vicinity of Harstad in an attempt to bring some relief to General Dietl and his hard pressed troops still fighting in the mountains near the Swedish border. The operation was originally timed for 25 May, and if it had been launched on time would have proved a serious distraction for the final assault on Narvik.

But for various reasons the Battle Group did not get away from Keil until the morning of 4 June; repairs to the *Scharnhorst*'s engines took longer than expected and the *Gneisenau* on a trial run struck a mine in the mouth of the Elbe. When it eventually departed, the Group consisted of the *Scharnhorst, Gneisenau, Hipper* and four destroyers[6] under the command of Admiral Marschall and intended to attack Harstad on the night of 8/9 June, proving conclusively that the secrecy surrounding the evacuation had clearly deceived the Germans. As the Norwegian Government had been told of the Allies' plan on 1 June, it is surprising that it had not filtered through to Germany by the 4th, suggesting that the presence of collaborators in Norway was nothing like as serious as the British continually believed. What is even more surprising is that the German's ability to intercept and decypher Naval signals did not reveal the true purpose of the congregation of additional ships in the Lofotens area, but they interpreted this instead as an intensification of the effort in support of Narvik rather than its evacuation.

Marschall was well aware of the hazards involved in taking the greater part of Germany's remaining striking fleet into the constricted waters of the Vaagsfiord; indeed even as the Group left Kiel it is clear that his resolve was wavering. On the 7th he briefed the taskforce captains gathered aboard the *Gneisenau* who were to say the least less than enthusiastic at the prospect of entering the fiords, and Marschall himself was reported as saying 'You can rest assured that I shall not send the ships on any senseless foray'.[7]

Aerial reconnaissance had been mounted to the west of the Lofotens from the 5th onwards, but the early reports were inconsistent and at this stage there was no indication that an evacuation was in prospect. On the 7th, however, the Group received reports from U-boats as well as aircraft of the presence of three convoys heading away from the Lofotens. It was by now dawning upon Marschall that something unusual was afoot and by the evening he decided to investigate these reports before continuing north towards Harstad. The Group spread out and at about 0600 the *Admiral Hipper* was the first to stumble across a target. It was the tanker *Oil Pioneer* escorted by the trawler *Juniper* which were quickly dispatched by gunfire and torpedo. Significantly, neither ship was able to raise the alarm, and the Royal Navy still remained oblivious of the fact that the German striking fleet was now at sea. Some two hours afterwards, alerted by one of her own Arado floatplanes, the *Hipper* spotted the transport *Orama* in company with the hospital ship *Atlantis*. The latter was spared, but the *Orama* was also quickly sent to the bottom, Captain Heye and his destroyers rescuing 268 survivors from the sea including some German prisoners of war who were the only passengers on an otherwise empty transport.

Marschall was by now convinced that an evacuation was in progress and ignored another order from Navy Group West received in the early morning of the 8th to leave the convoys to the *Hipper* and the destroyers and proceed as planned to Harstad. Instead, he dispatched the *Hipper* and the destroyers to Trondheim for refuelling, unwilling to run the risks of refuelling at sea, and the *Scharnhorst* and *Gneisenau* continued alone to scour the open wastes of the North Sea for better quarry than the *Oil Pioneer* and the *Orama*. In fact, Marschall had been chasing small fry even though he had been warned of the positions of the major warships, and turning his two battle cruisers to the north he determined to make up for lost time.

He soon succeeded. It was a gloriously clear sunny day with almost unlimited visibility, and in the late afternoon the *Scharnhorst*'s lookout spotted a smudge of smoke on the horizon. It was the aircraft carrier *Glorious* escorted by only two destroyers – the *Acasta* and the *Ardent* – and the most serious naval disaster of the campaign for the Royal Navy was now but a matter of minutes away.

The Sinking of the Glorious

The loss of the aircraft carrier *Glorious* excited speculation and controversy immediately after the event which has not yet entirely subsided. The story has been admirably told by John Winton in his book *Carrier Glorious*.[8] It is only necessary here to recount briefly a few salient points.

The *Glorious* was not a happy ship. Her captain, Captain D'Oyly-Hughes, could be variously described as single-minded, courageous and determined; or alternatively idiosyncratic, megalomanic, or simply mad. Whilst his attitude towards the ratings was fair and caring, he appeared to regard aviators with distrust and contempt – hardly an engaging attitude for the captain of an aircraft carrier. He quarrelled ceaselessly with the Commander (Flying), J. B. Heath, a very experienced pilot, and the other senior flying executives, to the extent that Heath had been left at Scapa Flow awaiting court martial when the ship returned on 30 May from her first foray in Norwegian waters.

For a man of D'Oyly-Hughes' temperament, the secondary role allocated to *Glorious* of acting as a transport tender for the RAF must have been frustrating in the extreme. He was not perhaps therefore in the best of humours when he requested permission after landing-on the Hurricanes to proceed independently to Scapa Flow. The official reason subsequently given for his move was that the *Glorious* was short of fuel and could not wait for the rest of the convoy. This may be so, it has never been conclusively proved one way or the other. But the story has been muddied by another report which alleged that D'Oyly-Hughes had signalled 'for permission to part company and proceed ahead to Scapa Flow for the purpose of making preparations for impending courts martial'.[9] If correct, this suggests that D'Oyly-Hughes was over-concerned with administrative matters which may have affected his tactical judgement. Whatever, the real reason for proceeding independently, it was approved by Admiral Vivian and by implication agreed by Lord Cork. These officers must therefore be held ultimately responsible for allowing the *Glorious* to sail separately.

In fact, in the circumstances prevailing at the time, the decision was not quite as stupid as it now seems in retrospect. Naval ships and transports had been proceeding across the North Sea almost with impunity for the whole period of the campaign in Narvik, and Lord Cork had no reason to suspect that a German task force was at sea. Once clear of the Luftwaffe, a carrier proceeding at speed even with only a small escort of two destroyers should have been reasonably secure against U-Boats and surface ships. Given his known concern regarding the vulnerability of the slower ships, Lord Cork perhaps believed that the *Glorious* would be safer on its own than in a slow convoy.

Whatever the truth may be, the *Glorious* was certainly caught unawares by the two marauding German raiders. She had no reconnaissance aircraft airborne and was totally unprepared to defend herself. It was subsequently suggested that the presence of the Hurricanes on board had prevented the ship's own aircraft launching, but there is good evidence that this was not true. In any case her sixteen 4.7 inch anti-aircraft guns were quite useless compared to the 11 inch guns of the German battle cruisers and thus her only hope of salvation was to avoid the German battle cruisers.

At 1630 the *Scharnhorst* opened fire at a range of 28,000 yards. The German gunnery had already demonstrated its accuracy earlier in the campaign and this proved to be no exception. Heavy shells were soon hitting the *Glorious*, impeding belated efforts to get the torpedo bombers airborne. Her wireless equipment was almost immediately destroyed, permitting nothing more than a brief corrupted message which was heard only by the *Devonshire* some eighty miles away. It was not understood. The *Acasta* and the *Ardent* immediately tried to lay a smoke screen between the battle cruisers and the *Glorious*, but it was too late – and for thirty minutes shells rained on the defenceless carrier, one scoring a direct hit on the bridge, probably killing the captain and the senior executives. During the early part of the bombardment the *Glorious* was still making nearly 30 knots and there was just a chance that she might escape despite the damage received. But a hit in the area of the boiler room put paid to this hope and the engine revolutions began to run down. By now *Scharnhorst* and *Gneisenau* were aligned in line abreast either side of the carrier and mercilessly pumping shell after shell into the stricken ship whilst carefully remaining out of range of the carrier's own smaller calibre armament. Stopped and burning, the order was given at about 1740 to abandon ship and only twenty minutes later she rolled over and sank. In the meantime, the *Ardent*, all her torpedoes gone, was overwhelmed by the devastatingly accurate gunfire and also sank.

But Commander C. E. Glasfurd in the *Acasta* was not yet ready to give up the unequal struggle. In an action very reminiscent of the *Glowworm* at the beginning of the campaign, the *Acasta* briefly retired behind her own smoke screen before turning about and re-appearing steering straight for the *Scharnhorst* with all guns and torpedoes firing. She was so close that it seemed she could not miss but the evidence suggests that on this attack none of the torpedoes found their mark although she may have scored with her guns. Briefly retiring again into the smoke, she made one more run towards the *Scharnhorst* to deliver the remainder of the torpedoes and at much longer range one torpedo struck home below the aft turret. But Captain Hoffman was not prepared to let her escape into the smoke screen again, and as soon as she re-appeared he ordered every gun to fasten onto her immediately. After a massive explosion aft, Glasfurd gave the order to abandon ship, but shells continued to strike home and she soon sank. There was only one survivor.

Only forty one of the three ship's complements were saved, although perhaps as many as 1,000 actually escaped the sinking vessels. It was some time before the extent of the disaster was recognised and rescue ships dispatched to the area led by the *Ark Royal*, but although wreckage and bodies were found, the survivors in their carley floats had now drifted far away from the scene. The North Sea is still terribly cold even in June and many did not survive the first night and were heaved overboard by the ever shrinking number that remained, cold, thirsty, hungry and suffering from shock. Occasionally aircraft were seen and once or twice a ship on the horizon, but they had nothing with which to attract attention and the survivors looked on helplessly as every hope of rescue faded away. Eventually, only thirty eight men (of whom three later died) were picked up by the Norwegian merchantman *Borgund* two and a half days after the sinking. Five more (one of whom died) were rescued by another Norwegian ship the *Svalbard II*, and two from the *Ardent* by a German seaplane. In all, 1,452 sailors and marines and 59 airmen were lost. All the Gladiators and the Hurricanes which had been so bravely and skilfully recovered from Bardufoss went down with the ship and only two of their pilots escaped, Squadron Leader Ken Cross and Flight Lieutenant Pat Jameson, who were eventually picked up from a carley float on which twenty two men had died.

The *Acasta* and the *Ardent* had maintained the fighting tradition of the Royal Navy against overwhelming odds even though the performance of the *Glorious* hardly lived up to her name.

The *Scharnhorst*, shipping water heavily, limped off to Trondheim with the *Gneisenau*. Meanwhile, Lord Cork's convoy which was to the east and unknowingly sailing directly towards the area of the engagement returned home unscathed. Without reflection on the other three VCs awarded to Royal Naval officers in the campaign, Glasfurd's exploits seem worthy of similar recognition. The circumstances in which he determined to attack the *Scharnhorst* despite the almost inevitable loss of his own ship were almost identical to those facing Lieutenant Commander Roope in the *Glowworm* at the beginning of the campaign. But in this case the stakes were much higher. If the *Scharnhorst* had been allowed to continue to roam in the North Sea, she might well have found the main evacuation convoy and caused even greater havoc than actually occurred. In removing the *Scharnhorst* from the action, Glasfurd probably prevented a major catastrophe.

Grand Admiral Raeder was not satisfied with his Battle Fleet's performance despite the sinking of the *Glorious*. Admiral Marschall had failed to obey orders – a cardinal sin in the eyes of a sailor brought up in the rigid traditions of the Imperial German Navy. Furthermore, to allow the *Scharnhorst* to be so badly mauled by the tiny *Acasta* was considered grossly inept seamanship, as indeed it was despite the ferociously determined assault that Glasfurd had inflicted upon her. Admiral Marschall was removed from his command and replaced by Admiral Lütjens who was later to go down with the *Bismarck* in one of the great naval encounters of the war.

The loss of the *Glorious* was not immediately recognised by Admiral Forbes. Indeed until the *Atlantis* met the *Valiant* on the morning of the following day, it was not even realised that the German battlecruisers were at large in the North Sea. Once again, the signs had been misinterpreted. The Government Code and Cypher School at Bletchley had become quite adept at interpreting from the volume of intercepted messages the presence and positions of German ships at sea even if they could not yet decipher individual messages. For some days they had been reporting increased activity suggesting major movements into the Norwegian Sea. But all of these were ignored by the Admiralty's Operational Intelligence Centre which had turned a Nelsonian blind eye to the possible presence of the German capital ships at sea.

Admiral Cunningham carrying the King and his entourage in the cruiser *Devonshire* heard the broken and corrupt message from the *Glorious*, but decided not to risk giving away his own position by passing it on. It was not until nearly twenty four hours later that an account of the action was revealed by German radio and an increasingly concerned Admiral Forbes made aware of the grim facts. He had, however, on hearing from the *Atlantis* of the presence of German raiders at large in the North Sea, already left Scapa Flow with the *Rodney* and six destroyers to escort the remainder of the returning convoys.

Admiral Forbes' confidence in his control of the sea had clearly been misplaced. Whilst Lord Cork and Admiral Vivian must accept the responsibility for allowing the *Glorious* to travel independently, Admiral Forbes had the main responsibility for ensuring that the convoy, once clear of Norwegian waters, returned with the same degree of safety as had attended their departure. In ordering the *Repulse* and the *Renown* to proceed on a wild goose chase into the Iceland/Faroes gap, he had put the whole operation inexcusably at risk. But the presence of a more senior officer, Lord Cork, in the task force may well have blurred the lines of responsibility. As this campaign was to demonstrate time and time again, forces on the ground or at sea cannot expect to operate coherently unless the chain of command and control is absolutely and unambiguously defined.

But Admiral Forbes and Lord Cork were not the only senior commanders at fault. The Commander-in-Chief of Coastal Command had been advised in greatest secrecy of the evacuation, but his Command staff were not advised and thus no aircraft were launched to monitor the path of the returning convoy. It should have been recognised by the Air Ministry as well as the Admiralty that the safety of slow moving convoys at sea would be at serious risk if the location of the German fleet was not known. Despite the fact that the war was now nine months old, the need for effective and routine reconnaissance of the German ports was simply not recognised, nor was a system for locating and shadowing German raiders at sea ever effectively organised. Once again, whilst the maintenance of secrecy had merely confused the enemy, it had proved catastrophic for the home side. It was not without justification that Admiral Forbes reported to the Admiralty on 15 June:

> The quite unexpected appearance of enemy forces . . . in the far north on 8th June which led to the sinking of the *Glorious*, two destroyers and a liner . . . shows that it is absolutely essential that our scheme of air reconnaissance should be overhauled . . . The enemy reconnoitre Scapa daily if they consider it necessary. Our reconnaissance of the enemy's main bases are few and far between . . . It is most galling that the enemy should know just where our ships . . . always are, whereas we generally learn where his major forces are when they sink one or more of our ships![10]

The Final Act

The concluding flourish of the war in Norway fell to the Skuas of 800 and 801 Squadrons in a final attempt to destroy the two battle cruisers which had turned an unhappy campaign into a disaster. The first real indication that a German raiding party was at sea was received by Admiral Forbes on the morning of 9 June after the hospital ship *Atlantis* crossed the path of the battleship *Valiant*. He immediately ordered the *Repulse* and two cruisers to proceed to the German ships last reported position, and shortly after noon left Scapa Flow himself with the *Rodney*. At about the same time, the *Ark Royal* with the second group of transports was also well placed to join in the hunt. The Home Fleet thus had an overwhelming numerical superiority – if only the quarry could be found.

The *Scharnhorst* was soon located in the Trondheimfiord by RAF reconnaissance on 10 June. Although their report indicated the presence of a battle cruiser and two cruisers, in fact their ship recognition was again awry and only the damaged *Scharnhorst* and two destroyers lay in the fiord: the *Gneisenau* with the *Hipper* having already returned to sea in search of further prey. Having found the target, the RAF assumed the responsibility for making the first attack, but Hudsons bombing from high level could not achieve a single hit. Once again, therefore, the Fleet Air Arm was left to pick up the challenge.

The *Ark Royal* had by now joined up with the rest of the Home Fleet on a course towards Trondheim, and on the 12th her captain was ordered to prepare all aircraft for a strike against the harbour on the following morning. It was a daunting prospect. The fiord was known to be protected by heavy anti-aircraft defences and the airfield at Vaernes only twenty miles to the east was estimated to house about one hundred and twenty bombers and eighty fighters, including some Bf 109s. Furthermore, as Trondheim lay eighty miles inland from the coast, the aircraft could hardly expect to creep in unseen. To add to the risk, the Fleet had been shadowed throughout the day and could therefore expect an attack from the air at any time. Admiral Forbes was certainly being more adventurous than he had been earlier when the Luftwaffe had driven the Home Fleet out of range of its bombers surprisingly quickly. Perhaps the successful attack against Bergen which led to the sinking of the *Konigsberg* had stiffened his resolve, although this raid was to be flown in very different circumstances.

The attacking force, which was originally intended to consist of both Swordfish and Skuas, needed both the protection of the weather and the advantage of surprise to stand a reasonable expectation of success. In the event, neither condition was met. The night was clear and cold, although a belt of cloud on the horizon promised more favourable weather conditions towards the coast. Even so, it was decided to abandon the plan to use the vulnerable Swordfish and just after midnight fifteen Skuas launched, formed up around the carrier, and headed east for Trondheim. The promise of cloudier weather over the target did not materialise, for it was crystal clear over Trondheim and conditions could not have been less favourable. The plan optimistically called for a synchronised attack by four Beauforts on Vaernes to hold the fighters on the ground and a flight of six Blenheims to provide a fighter escort for the Skuas, tasks for which both aircraft were inherently unsuitable. Predictably neither proved successful. Both Bf 109s and 110s were scrambled and soon mixing with the Skuas, each of which was laden with a 500 lb armour-piercing bomb and thus even less agile than usual. However, as the Skuas approached sedately at 11,500 feet, the anti-aircraft fire appeared even more lethal than the fighters although the targets at least were easily identifiable in the good visibility. Leading the attack, Lieut Commander Casson of 801 Squadron entered a shallow dive to bomb from bow to stern at 3,000 feet whilst Captain Partridge of 803 Squadron made a steeper attack from 7,000 feet. But even as they dived the pilots were forced to take violent evasive action to avoid the pursuing fighters, manoeuvres hardly conducive to a steady aim. After hurriedly releasing their bombs the formation scattered, each pilot making off independently as fast as possible at sea level. By 0400, the first seven aircraft had staggered back to the carrier. Lieutenant Spurway, the first to land-on, thought he had achieved two hits on the battle-cruiser, but later reports soon dimmed the early euphoria, and in fact only one bomb hit the *Scharnhorst* which failed to explode.

All eyes continued to peer with mounting apprehension into the brightening horizon, but no more stragglers appeared. The weather turned hazy and cloud soon shrouded the waiting ships, conditions which had been so badly needed when the target was approached only hours before. By 0545 all hope of recovering more aircraft had disappeared, not only would they by now be running out of fuel, but a white mist was blanketing the fleet, reducing visibility to a few yards. Both squadron commanders, Casson and Partridge were missing, although both survived along with about half the aircrew who had not returned. The loss of Captain Partridge was felt particularly keenly, for he had led the successful attack on the *Konigsberg* on 10 April and thus had the distinction of participating in both the first and the last air raid on ships in the Norwegian ports.

The *Scharnhorst* and the *Gneisenau* eventually struggled back to Germany, but not before the former had again been subjected to heavy air attack by Swordfish and Hudsons and forced to run for cover in Stavanger Fiord, and the latter had been torpoedoed but not sunk by the sumbarine *Clyde*. The German battle-cruisers had survived a hazardous few weeks in support of the invasion of Norway; both had been damaged on several different occasions, but their original mission of escorting Group 1 to Narvik had been successfully concluded and they had accounted for the *Glorious*. Their captains may have reasonably claimed that they finished ahead on points at the end of this brief but furious campaign.

Nevertheless, the *Scharnhorst* was not to re-appear in action again until December 1940 after repair at Keil where she was joined by the *Gneisenau* after being damaged by the *Clyde*. Despite their frequent contact with the two ships, the Admiralty remained oblivious of the damage inflicted by the *Acasta* on the *Scharnhorst*, believing that it was the latter rather than the *Gneisenau* which had been the *Clyde's* victim. It was not recognised until the end of July that both battle-cruisers had been damaged. It is a sorry reflection upon the aerial reconnaissance and other intelligence sources that it took so long to establish the status of these two ships – the two most important vessels in the relatively small German Navy.

The Allied intervention in Norway had drawn to its inevitable and disappointing close and, sporadic commando raids apart, was not to be revived in the duration of the war. In Narvik General Dietl re-occupied the town with the remnants of his once proud Gebirgsjäger; he was to remain in Norway in command of all mountain troops and was eventually killed in an air crash in Austria in 1944. His 139th Regiment was awarded the distinction of the Narvik arm shield containing a propeller, an anchor and an edelweiss surmounted by the word 'Narvik'. It was a hard earned and well deserved recognition for troops who had endured greater hardships than most of their comrades in the capture of Norway.

On the Allied side, the latter part of the campaign had proceeded reasonably smoothly compared with the acrimony and distrust which had marked the earlier phase. Auchinleck and Cork immediately struck up a close and harmonious relationship which had never existed between the Admiral and Mackesy. General Béthouart proved the ideal complement to these two senior officers – always willing, co-operative and ever anxious to get at the enemy. In his reports Lord Cork paid a fulsome compliment to both officers: of Auchinleck he wrote:

> Finally I must express my gratitude to Lieutenant General C. J. E. Auchinleck in whom I could not wish for a better colleague. His sound and soldierly views on all subjects were of great assistance and support and the period of our service together will for always be a pleasant memory.[11]

Of General Mackesy he made no comment.

Mistaken Strategy –
Faulty Execution

'What we will not do is to rush into adventures that offer little prospect of
success and are calculated to impair our resources and to postpone ultimate
victory. One lesson that military history teaches is that that road leads to
disaster. Strategy is the art of concentrating decisive force, at the decisive
point, at the decisive moment.'[1]

Neville Chamberlain
20 September 1939

Post Mortem

With the sinking of the *Glorious* bringing the Allied campaign in Norway to an
inglorious finale, it might seem kinder to draw a decent veil over the proceedings at
this stage and not seek to carry out a post mortem of what went wrong. But post
mortems are a very necessary feature of military operations, for so rarely does a
campaign follow precisely the plan which preceded it that the planners can bask in the
reflected glory and march confidently along the path towards inevitable victory. In
fact, the cynic might even suggest that in respect of the Scandinavian campaign there
was no worthwhile plan, and thus little need to dissect the reasons why it failed. Nor,
incidentally, is there much evidence that a post mortem was conducted, although
perhaps it is understandable in the dark days of June 1940 when far greater potential
disasters clouded the horizon.

The Germans had unequivocally won the battle for Norway, but did Hitler achieve
his strategic aims which Admiral Raeder had warned him could be at the cost of the
German Navy? Some of the advantages foreseen by the possession of Norway were
overtaken by the unexpectedly rapid collapse of France. The acquisition of ports and
airfields in France which were much closer to Britain and provided a better outlet to
the Atlantic to a certain extent negated the potential value of those in Norway,
although the airfields did force the RAF to maintain a larger fighter presence in
Scotland than would otherwise have been necessary. The Norwegian ports also proved
valuable to the Germans, particularly against the convoys to Murmansk which after
the advent of 'Barbarossa' were Russia's most important link with her new allies in
the west. Furthermore, the Royal Navy could henceforth only enter the two hundred
mile wide Shetland-Bergen gap in strength, and as a result had to intensify their
surveillance of the much wider Iceland-Faroes gap to locate German raiders breaking
out into the Atlantic. The ownership of both littorals of the entrance to the Baltic Sea

also provided a greater degree of security of Germany's northern flank. In sum, the foreseen maritime advantages to Germany of owning the Norwegian ports were generally fulfilled, with the added bonus of a convenient launch point for attacks against the Russian convoys.

The economic advantages of the control of Norway also favoured Germany. The Swedish iron ore was secured as was the flow of other raw materials for Germany's armaments industry; and conversely the export of ore and timber products to Britain was stopped. But these factors should not be overrated, they never attained the influence that was credited to them in the heady arguments which preceded the campaign.

On the debit side, Germany had to maintain a garrison in Norway for the rest of the war which eventually built up to 300,000 men, and which became an increasingly onerous burden when the balance of manpower resources swung dramatically towards the Allies as both the Americans and the Russians mobilised their sleeping masses.

The overall conclusion must be that by the capture of Norway, Germany improved her strategic position at the expense of Britain although some of the foreseen advantages were overtaken by the far more important occupation of France during much the same period.

There is, however, one more indirect outcome of the battle for Norway which should be mentioned. In simple numerical terms, the losses of the Royal Navy and the Kreigsmarine were roughly similar. The former lost one aircraft carrier, three cruisers, eight destroyers and a number of submarines and miscellaneous craft, whilst the Germans lost three cruisers, ten destroyers, four U boats, and suffered serious damage to their two battle cruisers, the *Scharnhorst* and the *Gneisenau*. But in comparative terms measured against the overall size of the two navies, the German losses were far more serious. As prophesied by Admiral Raeder, a major part of the German Navy was sunk or disabled as a consequence of the Scandinavian operation, and this had an important bearing on the outcome of Operation 'Sea Lion', the projected invasion of Britain in the Autumn of 1940. At best, the Navy could support only a single crossing point between Calais and Dover as opposed to the much wider front preferred by General Halder and the Army Staff. This lack of adequate naval resources was but one of the many complex and interactive factors which eventually led Hitler to abandon 'Sea Lion', but it was one of the few benefits which came out of the Allies otherwise disastrous intervention in Norway.

The difficulties which faced the Allied ground forces in Norway require little more explanation than that already described in these pages. The rigours of the climate and the terrain, and the inability of the troops to overcome them by comparison with their opponents was probably always the deciding factor. The number of occasions were legion when the better equipped and trained German units were able to outflank a static Allied position and force a hasty and often unco-ordinated withdrawal. It is true that the Allies did not help themselves by trying to stem the tide with troops in penny packets rather than by concentrating force in good defensive locations. Lieut General Massy's official report on Central Norway highlights this point; but it arrived too late to prevent the same mistake being even more blatantly exposed in the actions south of Bodo.

> A more effective solution of the problem therefore would have been the establishment of the Brigade on a selected naturally strong position some distance in the rear of the Norwegians where they would have had time to dig-in and organise a proper defence. Such a position might well have enabled the Brigade, ill equipped as it was, with the aid of proper demolitions, to obtain protection against the attacks of Armoured Fighting Vehicles and to get sufficient cover to withstand bombardment and to hold off infantry attacks for a prolonged period. Behind such a position the Norwegians would have had a better opportunity to re-organise than was in fact ever given.[2]

This was undoubtedly the major tactical blunder in the conduct of the campaign, but it cannot be claimed that it led ultimately to the defeat and withdrawal. The reasons for this were far more deep-seated. The inability to provide reliable lines of communication for reinforcements and supplies through secure bridgeheads would inevitably have sapped eventually the ability and will of the troops to withstand the continued pressure of German forces who suffered, except at Narvik, no such insurmountable handicap. The lack of fighter aircraft to defend the bridgeheads in Central Norway against air attack, far more important in real terms than the higher profile action of supporting troops actually fighting on the front line, meant that delaying the German advance for more than a limited period was quite unsustainable no matter how tactically adroit the dispositions on the ground. This was quite clearly shown at Narvik where the boot was on the other foot; the Allies in this case were able to develop a supportable bridgehead and thus eventually overcome their opponents whose supply life line was even more tenuous than that of the British in Central Norway. In the earlier campaign in the south, even that equipment which did penetrate to the front was either grossly inadequate in quantity, for example, vehicles and signals equipment, or, like field artillery and armour, missing altogether.

This very brief summary therefore clearly shows that the execution of the campaign was by no means without fault, and the planning in logistic terms was quite inadequate. But many of the latter deficiences, given the overall state of Britain's resources in 1940, were totally inescapable. The main question therefore is why were the Allies involved in Norway at all if defeat and ignominious withdrawal was the almost inevitable conclusion. Was the security of Norway such an essential plank in the strategy of the Allies in 1939/40 that almost any risk was worthwhile to ensure its protection? What was the grand strategy for the progression of the war, and bringing it to a speedy and successful conclusion?

In so far as the Allies had a grand strategy at the outbreak of war, it was to continue that which had dominated the First World War – to blockade Germany into submission. Certainly the Allies were inadequately prepared to fight an offensive war on land in 1939 and quickly discovered they were ill equipped to pursue a strategic policy in the air, but the one area in which they had a clear superiority was in the strength of their naval forces. Although the development of the Kriegsmarine, set in motion by Defence Minister von Schleicher in 1932, had been dramatic whilst the

Royal Navy in the same period had been in comparative decline, the balance of power still apparently resided under the aegis of the White Ensign.

The strategic blockade of Germany was therefore a sensible policy to pursue in the first year of the war even if, as in 1918, it could not ultimately prove a decisive weapon. It is in pursuance of the economic blockade therefore that we should judge the Allied Government's policies towards Scandinavia, even though more esoteric factors such as bringing an end to the phoney war and the idealistic support of Finland often apparently clouded the issues involved.

To what extent therefore was the action in Norway justified in pursuance of this strategy? The answer hinged on the perceived value to Germany of the iron ore which was imported from Sweden through Narvik. Although the Leads were used by other vessels making for German Baltic and North Sea ports, this activity was insufficient to justify the violation of Norwegian territorial rights that was an inevitable concomitant of a positive Scandinavian policy. The impact of the cessation of the flow of iron ore from Narvik on Germany's industrial capacity, was frequently exaggerated; but even so, the complete bottling-up of the Swedish ore throughout the winter of 1939/40 would have made a significant dent in Germany's capacity to wage war. The minor strategy of stopping the flow of iron ore in pursuit of the grand strategy of blockade was thus probably justified, particularly if it could be achieved without resort to occupation of Scandinavian territory. The mining of the Leads towards the onset of winter in 1939 was thus a credible strategy to pursue at that time although this was no longer true when it was actually initiated in April 1940.

In terms of grand strategy, therefore, the boat was missed when the Allies procrastinated throughout the winter on the question of mining the Leads. The next issue, the support of Finland against Russia was a potentially disastrous strategy for the Allies that was only narrowly avoided by the much more sensible Finns knowing when it was expedient to forsake the struggle. The hidden advantage of capturing and controlling the iron ore mines at source was certainly not worth the risk of consolidating the Russo-German alliance and aligning the dormant but potentially enormous power of the Russians on the opposite side of the fence.

It is strange that one other consideration which should have influenced Allied strategy, the value of Norway to Germany, seems to have occupied very few minds during these months. It should have been apparent that there were a number of quite substantial reasons for Germany wishing to control the Norwegian coastline with its multitude of safe anchorages, both to counter the Allied strategy of the blockade and to prosecute an offensive naval strategy of her own. That these considerations did not worry the Allies seems to stem from the clearly unjustified premise that the occupation of Norway was not physically within Germany's capability if the Allies wished to prevent it. The tragedy of Norway was thus twofold – not only did the Allies omit to follow through the implications of their own grand strategy, but they also failed to recognise and counter the strategy of their opponent. Although Hitler himself did not immediately recognise the benefits of occupying Norway, he did at least see the importance of Norway remaining benevolently neutral, and following the *Altmark* incident was quick to adopt a more positive approach to the Scandinavian problem.

Nor were the Allies to immediately recognise and learn from the failures in strategy highlighted by the debable in Norway. The definition of a direct, achieveable strategy to defeat Germany was not to be realised until 1943 and implemented in 1944 with the re-invasion of continental Europe. In the intervening years there were to be several fruitless adventures in the Mediterranean and elsewhere which illustrated only too clearly the poverty of Britain's grand strategical aim.

The real tragedy therefore of Norway was that there was no sound strategical reason for the intervention at all in April 1940, at least not in the way and at the time it was carried out. There was a case for preventing Germany gaining control of Norway, but the resources available for that were totally inadequate. It would thus have been sounder strategically for the Allies, having conceeded the initiative – arguably largely inescapable in political terms for democratic countries resisting aggression – to have stayed out of Norway altogether. The drift into Norway was largely a result of Mr Churchill's unbridled impatience to prosecute the war, to grasp an initiative almost irrespective of the strategic realities and the availability of resources to carry out the task. There were of course other lesser figures who aided and abetted his prodding, and he was misled to a certain extent by the Service Chiefs who never unequivocally warned of the military difficulties which would be faced in resisting a German invasion of Norway. Indeed, it might be more correct to say that they themselves never recognised the problems involved.

It is therefore ironic that the man at whose door much of the responsibility for the Scandinavian debacle should be laid was thrust into the foremost position of power in the state in the midst of the crisis. It probably never occurred to Mr Churchill that he had made a major strategical mistake in leading the country down this path, and he always preferred to blame the military for the incompetent way they progressed this 'ramshackle campaign'. The sequence of events which propelled Churchill into power bears an almost uncanny resemblance to the way that Lord Palmerston acceded to the prime ministership shortly after the start of the Crimean War. He too had goaded a reluctant government into mounting a campaign that would have better been avoided, and was then thrust into national leadership by popular acclaim – an elevation which would have seemed inconceivable in other circumstances.[3]

But the fundamental lesson of the misadventure in Scandinavia was that a nation should not undertake military commitments it does not have the means to fulfil. Mr Churchill was to make a very similar misjudgement in Greece and the Balkans little more than a year later. He had still not grasped the lessons of Gallipoli and Antwerp in the First World War, and more lately the reminder in Scandinavia.

Not only, however, was there a deficiency in the strategic rationalisation of the intervention in Norway, there were also glaring weaknesses in the strategic direction and the command and control of the forces assigned to the operation after its instigation. Although there was a Joint Planning Staff, albeit working under extreme pressure, each Service department issued its own orders and there was no established means of ensuring that these were properly co-ordinated. Inevitably there were often quite blatant contradictions, for example in the directions given to Lord Cork and General Mackesy before their hurried departure for Narvik. The Military Co-ordination Committee was dominated by Mr Churchill who, although nominally only responsible as First Lord for naval operations, frequently blatantly interfered in other aspects of the operation: he had few scruples regarding harnessing authority without assuming responsibility. Neither Lord Chatfield or Mr Chamberlain were able to restrain his bold initiatives which they only reluctantly supported against their better judgement. The result was frequent changes of direction which left the Service Chiefs bewildered, with little chance of re-organising their resources to attain the new objectives.

But even if strategic direction was chaotic, the individual Services had little reason to be satisfied with their own means of command and control. It was always unclear who was directing naval operations, witness the first battle of Narvik in which the Admiralty, Admiral Forbes and Admiral Whitworth all issued conflicting instructions to subordinate formations because it was not clear which of them was actually running the operation – in the end Captain Warburton-Lee as the man on the spot made his own arrangements with spectacular results.

The Army fared little better. General Massy was given overall command of all land forces in Norway without the means to implement the responsibility and indeed never left London. Once again, therefore, the commanders on the spot were thrown back on their own resources with little appreciation of the overall picture. Co-operation with the Norwegian forces was equally *ad hoc*, although there were undoubtedly more difficult problems to reconcile in this sphere. In Narvik, the situation was more complicated. Success here depended on a joint naval/land operation, but the two commanders were independent of each other and responsible to separate Service departments. The outcome was thus totally dependent on their striking up a harmonious, co-operative relationship, and this as we have seen was never achieved until Auchinleck replaced Mackesy. The solution – a supreme commander – was only belatedly tried in a final effort to break the stalemate. The higher authority in London gave the principle lukewarm support, and with the decision to send General Auchinleck to Narvik soon indicated their intention to rescind it. These are just a few examples of the more glaring deficiencies in the command and control arrangements, the preceding narrative provides evidence enough of other cases where control at all levels was painfully inadequate.

Of all the many lessons which might have been learned from the events in Scandinavia – how best to command, control and conduct a combined land, sea, air operation was undoubtedly the most important question which the campaign raised. It was to take a number of years before this problem was really recognised as the key to a war which was to be fought from the outset in all three elements, interfacing and interacting in a way which, by comparison, had only been hinted at in the First World War. General Eisenhower in Europe and Earl Mountbatten in the Far East were the eventual inheritors of a combined tri-Service organisation which was so obviously needed in Narvik in 1940.[4]

Aftermath

The departure of the last Allied soldier from Narvik on 8 June marked the end of direct British involvment in Norway for the duration of the war apart from occasional special forces raids and intelligence activity. In terms of actual casualties, the cost of the war to Norway in 1940 was relatively light, about two thousand military personnel and civilians. But the pyschological blow was immense, the speed and efficiency of the German invasion, the dramatic collapse of the Norwegian defences, and the fumbling and ill-prepared Allied response conditioned most Norwegians to expect a long period under Nazi hegemony if not direct rule. The initial reaction, as always when a country is beset by disaster, was to blame the government, but the success of the blitzkrieg on the Western Front completed the disillusionment of the majority of the Norwegian people and fostered at worst collusion and at best sullen acceptance of German rule.

The King and his government meanwhile established themselves in London. Some of the latter were resentful of what they regarded as a British betrayal in the defence of their country, but in truth they had better reason to complain of British ineptitude than their perfidy. King Haakon quickly became a respected and influential figure and his regular public appearances and broadcasts were an important factor in sustaining the spirit of his troops in exile and their countrymen in bondage at home. The government in exile, following one or two judicious personality changes, also established a sound working relationship with the British authorities, and in May 1941 subordinated all Norwegian forces to British operational control.

One priceless asset materialised immediately: control of the major part of Norway's mercantile fleet, the fourth largest in the world, had been transferred to London before the final collapse. Their powerful support, particulary in the carriage of vital oil supplies, proved of inestimable value during the darkest days of the Battle of the Atlantic from 1941 onwards. But very few of the armed forces escaped to Britain, only one or two senior officers without troops under the leadership of General Fleischer and a handful of small ships and light aircraft. Regeneration was surprisingly rapid. In addition to Norwegians conscripted in Britain and the crews of some whalers returning from the Antarctic, a steady trickle of recruits escaping from Norway gradually laid down the foundations of small but effective forces. The Norwegian air arm was reborn in Canada as early as September 1940 and two Norwegian fighter squadrons later fought with great distinction in British skies. By the end of 1941, the Norwegian Navy comprised no less than fifty-five ships, operating mainly in concert with larger British units, the highlight of which was the sinking of the *Scharnhorst* off northern Norway in December 1943. The Army, consisting of a single Brigade, was held in readiness in Scotland for reinvasion of the homeland and thus took a less active role in the subsequent fighting. Nevertheless, a very spirited Independent Company participated in two commando raids on the Lofoten Islands and an attack on Mökøy in the Inner Leads during which their leader, Martin Linge, was unfortunately killed.

The re-possession of their homeland was of course their guiding spirit and inspiration. In this aim, they were frequently uplifted by Churchill's avowed and probably genuine wish to mount an expedition to liberate Norway, but the more cautious Chiefs of Staff were less enthusiastic and managed to sustain their delaying tactics until the war drew to its natural conclusion. The United States also gave sympathetic support to the Norwegians and relationships nurtured during the war undoubtedly paved the way for Norway's later role as a vital constituent of NATO's northern flank.

Quisling's initial reign following his self proclaimed coup of 9 April did not last long and the administration of Norwegian affairs at the end of April passed into the hands of a Reichskommissar, Josef Terboven, lately Oberpräsident of the Rhein Province. He ruled Norway with a mixture of cunning and brutality until his suicide in May 1945. By the end of May 1940, the main Norwegian political parties had agreed to support the Administrative Council which had been set-up in mid April after the dismissal of Quisling, and also agreed to demand the King's abdication in return for influence in the composition of a proposed new ruling council. But Quisling had not readily accepted his downfall and persuaded Hitler during a visit to Germany in August that the entire council should be composed of fascists and their sympathisers. So ended a brief attempt to establish some form of constitutional government within occupied Norway, and the Administrative Council was replaced on 25 September by direct German rule supported only by National Socialist puppets. Before the end of 1940, local democratic government had also disappeared, its power transferred to leaders nominated by the Commissar of the Interior.

But very few countries remain quiescent for long under an alien dictatorship, and by the end of 1940 the first signs of organised unrest emerged. Led by the Supreme Court and the Church, supported by sports clubs, professional organisations and a few of the trade unions, passive resistance slowly began to take root. The Communists, earlier vigorous opponents of the government in exile, were converted to resistance overnight by the German invasion of Russia in July 1941. In February 1942, Quisling was appointed Minister-President over a cabinet of National Socialist ministers and resistance now focalised not only on the German oppressors, but also on their Fascist collaborators.

Active resistance in the early stages was hindered by uncertainty of aim, lack of equipment and lapses of security. The establishment of a dedicated Norwegian Section of the British Special Operations Executive (SOE) and the emergence of a natural leader, a young lawyer named Jens Christian Hauge, gradually brought order and direction to the Norwegian resistance movement by the end of 1942. Nevertheless, success was at best limited and almost invariably brought brutal and ruthless German reprisal. Indeed, the fear of German retaliation was a regular pre-occupation of both the government in exile and the resistance movement in Norway – long years of neutrality and the psychological shock of the invasion had deadened, at least temporarily, the spirit of freedom in the Norwegian breast. The resistance movement, known from its earliest days as Milorg, preferred to wait patiently for direct military intervention rather than indulge in guerilla activity of its own although it gave useful support to the SOE from time to time and provided constant information to London on German military movements. One notable success should be recorded although its significance at the time could hardly have been fully recognised. As early as 1942, in an attempt to produce an atomic bomb, the Germans were developing a heavy water plant at Rjukan, a remote area to the west of Oslo. After an initial plan involving the Royal Engineers had miscarried, a small group of Norwegians successfully destroyed the existing heavy water stock and damaged the plant. They followed this up a year later by sinking a boat carrying essential plant to Germany, thus striking a major blow against Hitler's last desperate attempt to snatch victory in the West. Military training and re-arming continued throughout 1943 and 1944 with increasing boldness and effectiveness, but the expected liberation army did not materialise, and after the invasion of Normandy in June 1944 the prospect of direct action sharply receded. Nevertheless, isolated acts of sabotage continued with varying degrees of success and retribution. The first liberating army, if it may be so described, to enter Norwegian territory was the Russian advance from Finland in October 1944 in pursuit of the retreating German Army. Fortunately for the future peace and stability of Norway and NATO's northern flank in general, they did not advance beyond Kirkenes and the eventual clearance of Finmark was left to a small Norwegian army under Major General Dahl.

At the end of 1944, although the irony could not have been lost on the resistance movement, acts of sabotage were actually stepped up to frustrate the withdrawal of German forces to the Western Front, and in this they were generally successful. When the armistice was eventually signed on 7 May, substantial German forces remained in Norway, sufficient even to encourage Terboven to continue the fight. However, the German troops, still well disciplined, but themselves weary of a long war in an often inhospitable climate chose not to prolong the struggle. Milorg at last came out into the open, and with the help of a small Allied force, completed the disarming of the Germans and the re-possession of their country.

Almost exactly four years to the day after slipping away from Tromso in such undignified haste, King Haakon returned in triumph to his beloved Norway. In between there had been periods when, even in his most optimistic moments, he must have had difficulty envisaging the enthusiastic scenes which would greet his return. But he had served his country well in exile and never faltered from a steadfast belief that the tyranny which had overtaken Norway would itself in due course be defeated.

References

Chapter 2

1 Admiralty Papers 205/4.
2 Field Marshal Lord Ironside, *The Ironside Diaries*, p. 161.
3 Nigel Hamilton, *Monty, The Making of a General*, p. 285.
4 T. K. Derry, *The Campaign in Norway*.
5 Sir Llewellyn Woodward, *British Foreign Policy in the Second World War* – vol 1, p. 34.
6 War Cabinet Paper No. 162 of 1939 – 16 December 1939.
7 Admiralty Papers 116/4471.
8 War Cabinet Paper No. 3 of 1940.
9 Winston Churchill, *Second World War*, vol. 1, p. 438.
10 Sir Llewellyn Woodward, op. cit., p. 74.
11 Winston Churchill, op. cit. p. 429.
12 Eric Morris, *Churchill's Private Armies*, chap. 2.

Chapter 3

1 Later Admiral of the Fleet Sir Philip Vian GCB, KBE, DSO.
2 Winston Churchill, op. cit. p. 444.
3 Vian – *Action This Day*, p. 28.
4 Inspired by a strip cartoon in the *Daily Mirror* containing three characters, Pip, Squeak and Wilfred. Martin Gilbert, *Finest Hour*, p. 179.
5 Derry, op. cit.
6 Adolph Hitler, *Mein Kampf*, p. 652.
7 Ibid., p. 654.
8 Quoted from *To Lose a Battle*, Alistair Horne, Penguin Edition, p. 170.
9 Mr Chamberlain's broadcast to the nation – 27 February 1938.
10 War Cabinet Paper (40) 111 – 27 March 1940.
11 Sir Llewellyn Woodward, op. cit., p. 116.
12 *Esk, Impulsive, Icarus* and *Ivanhoe*.
13 *Hardy, Hotspur, Havock* and *Hunter*.
14 *Inglefield, Ilex, Isis* and *Imogen*.
15 *Greyhound, Glowworm, Hyperion* and *Hero*.
16 F. H. Hinsley, *British Intelligence in the Second World War*, vol. 1.
17 Sir Llewellyn Woodward, op. cit., p. 116.
18 Lord Ironside, op. cit., Part Three.

Chapter 4

1 Order of the Day – 1 April 1940 – Reproduced in Fuehrer Conferences on Naval Affairs, 1940·
2 B. Liddell Hart, *History of the First World War*, p. 101.
3 W. Shirer, *The Rise and Fall of the Third Reich*, p. 676.
4 A. Speer, *Inside the Third Reich*, p. 164.
5 W. Warlimont, *Inside Hitler's Headquarters 1939-45*, p. 79.
6 See p. 24.
7 Shirer, op. cit., p. 680.
8 Shirer, op. cit., p. 680.
9 Documents on German Foreign Policy, vol. 8.
10 Walter Warlimont, *Inside Hitler's Headquarters 1939-45*, p. 68.
11 Shirer, op. cit., p. 683.
12 E. F. Ziemke, *The German Northern Theatre of Operations 1940-45*, p. 20.
13 Warlimont, op. cit., p. 69.
14 Leland Stowe – *Chicago Daily News*.

Chapter 5

1 Henry Longfellow.
2 Vice Admiral Friedrich Ruge, *Sea Warfare 1939-1945*. A German Viewpoint. Comparison in the classification of heavy ships between the Royal Navy and the Kriegsmarine is not always straightforward. In Ruge's comparison, the *Scharnhorst* and *Gneisenau* are classified as battleships although they are generally referred to as battlecruisers.
3 B. H. Liddell Hart, *History of the First World War*, p. 357.
4 Winston Churchill, op. cit., p. 467.
5 War Cabinet Paper 65/6.
6 Ibid.
7 Liddell Hart, op. cit., p. 360.
8 *Bedouin, Eskimo, Punjabi* and *Kimberley*.
9 *Esk, Impulsive, Icarus* and *Ivanhoe*.
10 See p. 195 for a more detailed account of this action.
11 The *Deutschland* renamed.
12 *Möwe, Albatross* and *Konda*.
13 See also p. 193.
14 E. Hauge, *Odds Against Norway*, p. 18.
15 Shirer, op. cit., p. 699.

Chapter 6

1 Seal papers – Quoted in Martin Gilbert, *Finest Hour*, p. 219.
2 War Cabinet No. 86 of 9 April 1940.
3 Harold Nicholson, *Diaries and Letters 1939-1945*, p. 70.
4 Ziemke, op. cit., p. 56.
5 Ruge, op. cit., p. 70.
6 Quoted from S. Roskill, *The War at Sea*, vol. 1, p. 69.
7 Quoted in D. Macintyre, *Narvik*, p. 73.
8 Signal dated 0931/9th.
9 Signal dated 0952/9th.

10 Signal dated 1200/9th.
11 The word 'intend' in this context means that a course of action will be followed unless higher authority invervenes and decrees otherwise. The word 'propose' on the other hand invites a response.
12 P. Dickens, *Narvik, Battle of the Fiords*, p. 95.
13 Lieut Commander Roope's action in the *Gloworm* was actually some 48 hours earlier than Warbuton-Lee's at Narvik, but the facts did not come to light until later, and the latter's was the first to be announced.
14 Signal dated 2012/10th.
15 Signal Forbes to Whitworth 1909/12th.
16 Quoted in S. W. Roskill, *HMS Warspite*, p. 205.
17 Ruge, op. cit., p. 72.

Chapter 7
1 A Carton de Wiart, *Happy Odyssey*.
2 See chapter 12.
3 Signal 1157/14.
4 See also p. 173.
5 *El d'Jezair, El Mansour, El Kantara* and the *Ville d'Oran*.
6 Carton de Wiart, op. cit., p. 169.
7 S4528 Captain's Report of Proceedings.
8 Air Historical Branch Narrative.
9 Ibid.
10 Carton de Wiart, op. cit., p. 170.
11 Gilbert, op. cit., p. 269.
12 Carton de Wiart, op. cit., p. 173.
13 *El d'Jezair, El Kantara* and *El Mansour*.
14 Carton de Wiart, op. cit., p. 174.
15 Air Historical Branch narrative.

Chapter 8
1 Brigadier N. Barclay, *Foreword to the History of the Sherwood Foresters 1919-1957*.
2 Dudley Clarke (later Brigadier) who had a most varied and exciting military career wrote a splendidly vivid account of the campaign in the Gudbransdal in his book *Seven Assignments*.
3 Dudley Clarke, op. cit., p. 97.
4 *Black Swan, Auckland, Flamingo* and *Bittern*.
5 Dudley Clarke, op. cit., p. 110.
6 Quoted from Beckwith, *The 8th Battalion, The Sherwood Foresters, TA*, p. 8.
7 Dudley Clarke, op. cit., p. 120.
8 Ibid., p. 121.
9 *London Gazette*, 37584, 28 May 1940.

Chapter 9
1 Later General Sir Bernard Paget GCB, DSO, MC.
2 Later Brigadier E. E. E. Cass CBE, DSO, MC. Brigadier Smyth had commanded the first K.O.Y.L.I. until immediately before the outset of the campaign.
3 Later Brigadier A. L. Kent-Lemon CBE.
4 Later Major General A. E. Robinson CB, DSO.

5 Expedition Force Instruction No. 1 by Commander 5th Corps dated 22 April 1940.
6 Later Brigadier D. C. Tennet CBE.
7 Citation for the Award of the Military Cross.
8 AHB Narrative.
9 Ibid.
10 Ibid.
11 Captain Pegram, Captain of *HMS Glasgow*. Quoted from *Narvik* – Donald MacIntyre, p. 157.
12 See p. 32.
13 Varying claims for the credit for breaking Enigma codes have been made, notably by General Bertrand, in 'Enigma ou la plus grande enigme de la querre 1939-45' (1973) and Group Captian F. W. Winterbotham, in 'The Ultra Secret' (1974). These are well summarised in *British Intelligence in the Second World War*, vol 1, appendix 1, (HMSO 1979).
14 This was the forerunner of the better known prefix 'Ultra' which was introduced in June 1941.
15 Hinsley, p. 141.
16 AHB Narrative.
17 Ibid.
18 Hansard, 7 May 1940.
19 Ibid.
20 Hansard, 8 May 1949.

Chapter 10

1 War Cabinet No. 3, 5 September 1939. Cabinet Paper 61/1.
2 See p. 20.
3 Report addressed to the War Cabinet on 17 August 1917. Quoted in the *War in the Air*, appendices, p. 8-14, Oxford, Clarendon Press.
4 A. Hendrie, *The Lockheed Hudson in World War II*, William Kimber, 1983.
5 Gron Edwards, *Norwegian Patrol*, p. 52.
6 Later Air Chief Marshal Sir Basil Embry.
7 Quoted from 11 HS 98 – Narrative by Captain Norman MacMillan, Air Historical Branch.
8 Bomber Command statistics are taken from *The Bomber Command War Diaries* by Martin Middlebrook and Chris Everitt, Viking 1985.
9 B. Embry, *Mission Completed*, Methuen & Co. 1957.
10 As DO 17s were not engaged in Norway, this was clearly a misidentification. Two Bf 110s failed to land at Fornebu, so it is possible that they were the aircraft claimed.
11 F. K. Mason, *The Gloster Gladiator*, 1964.
12 Slessor, *The Central Blue* Cassell *1956*, p. 191. For an equally parochial view written at about the same time from the other side, see Fleet Air Arm, Lt Cdr P. Kemp, Herbert Jenkins 1954.
13 *Juno, Fury, Fearless, Hasty, Hyperion* and *Hereward*.
14 William Jameson, *Ark Royal 1939-41* p. 104, Hart Davis 1951.

Chapter 11

1 Quoted in *The War in the Air*, vol 6, p. 136.
2 See chapter 15.
3 Hugh Thomas, *The Spanish Civil War*, Penguin Edition, p. 320.

4 Cajus Becher, *The Luftwaffe War Diaries*, Macdonald 1966, p. 87.
5 AHB Narrative.
6 The two paratroop operations in Denmark on the same morning were actually the first, but no significant opposition was expected or encountered.
7 See p. 79.
8 Air Ministry Weekly Intelligence Summary No. 34.
9 J. R. Smith and A. L. Kay, *German Aircraft of the Second World War*, 1972.
10 See p. 230.

Chapter 12
1 Winston Churchill, *The Gathering Storm*, p. 483.
2 T. K. Derry, *The Campaign in Norway*, appendix A.
3 Major O. J. L. Fitzgerald, *Irish Guards 1939-45*, Gale and Polden, 1949, p. 13.
4 Report by Lord Cork – *London Gazette*, 10 July 1947.
5 Mr Mackesy wrote a convincing article in support of his father's actions at Narvik in the RUSI Journal, December 1970.
6 Theodor Broch, *The Mountains Wait* – Webb Publishing Company 1942.
7 D. Erskine, *The Scots Guards 1919-1955*, p. 29.
8 Fitzgerald, op. cit., p. 19.
9 Ibid., p. 21.
10 W. Warlimonth, *Inside Hitler's Headquarters 1939-1945*, p. 79.
11 Military Committee Memorandum No. 77, 1940.
12 Quoted in MacIntyre – *Narvik*, p. 181.
13 Admiralty Papers 199/1929 – Quoted Gilbert, Ibid., p. 256.
14 Admiralty Papers 199/29.
15 Fitzgerald, Ibid., p. 25.
16 Fitzgerald, Ibid., p. 26.
17 Fitzgerald, Ibid., p. 27.
18 Fitzgerald, Ibid., p. 27. The anniversary of the Gallipoli landings was in fact 25 April, but the comparison in other respects was apt.
19 Admiralty Paper 119/1929.
20 H. L. Graham, Article in Scots Guards Magazine, 1959, p. 54.
21 Fitzgerald, Ibid., p. 36.

Chapter 13
1 T. E. Lawrence, *Seven Pillars of Wisdom* 1935.
2 Defence Committee, DEFE 2/1 dated 1 June 1940.
3 Later Major General Sir Colin Gubbins KCMG, DSO, MC, Commander Special Forces and Special Operations Executive.
4 WO 165/55 dated 2 May 1940.
5 WO 106/1944 dated 30 April 1940.
6 Premier papers 4/32/2 dated 14 May 1940.
7 Premier papers 3/328/4 dated 14 May 1940.
8 Erskine, op. cit., p. 35. The price of whiskey in Norway in 1940 must have been as expensive as it is today.
9 In some histories, including Derry, this location is called Stein after the tiny hamlet on the north side of the bay.
10 There is now a new bridge across the mouth of the estuary, but this was not there in 1940.

11 Erskine, op. cit., p. 38.
12 See p. 252.
13 Fitzgerald, op. cit., p. 465.
14 Ibid., p. 46.
15 Ibid., p. 46.
16 Erskine, op. cit., p. 42.
17 Actually to the north west of Krokstranden as the road follows the winding river valley.
18 Graham, op. cit., p. 58.
19 He had, however, driven down through the area on his arrival in Norway.
20 Erskine, op. cit., p. 45.
21 Erskine, op. cit., p. 46.
22 Fitzgerald, op. cit., p. 58.
23 Ibid., p. 58.

Chapter 14
1 J. Connell, *Auchinleck*, p. 86.
2 *London Gazette*, 10 July 1947.
3 Karol Zbyszewski, *The Fight for Narvik*.
4 Supplement to the *London Gazette*, 10 July 1947. He was to be less happy many years later with Mr Churchill's account in *The Gathering Storm*.
5 Ibid.
6 1129/17 Admiralty to Lord Cork.
7 2217/18 Lord Cork to Chiefs of Staff.
8 Admiralty Papers 199/1929.
9 *London Gazette*, 10 July 1947.

Chapter 15
1 D.P.(P)32 – 1938.
2 Also known as Laksely.
3 P. 248.

Chapter 16
1 Minute to Anthony Eden of 14 June 1940: Churchill papers 20/13.
2 This was an exaggeration as even by 15 June, the Germans had only seven divisions in Norway.
3 Chiefs of Staff W.P. (40) 165.
4 Sereau, *L'Expedition de Norvègo*, p. 84.
5 Facsimile in the Narvik museum.
6 *Karl Galster, Erich Steinbrinck, Hans Lody* and *Hermann Schoemann*.
7 Quoted in Garrett, *Scharnhorst and Greisenan*, p. 45.
8 Leo Cooper in association with Secker and Warburg, 1987.
9 Winton, op. cit., p. 156.
10 Roskill, op. cit., p. 198.
11 *London Gazette*, 10 July 1947.

Chapter 17

1 House of Commons, 20 September 1939.

2 *London Gazette*, 37584, 28 May 1940.

3 In many respects Lord Palmerston's career (and indeed personality) paralleled that of Mr Churchill. Both attended Harrow; both started their ministerial careers in a Service department – Churchill in rather more spectacular fashion than Palmerston; both tended to see Britain's interests in an international and historical context; both were not averse to changing parties when it suited them, and both depended on political cunning and public acclaim to overcome their many enemies in the establishment. Both in the end were acclaimed national heroes.

4 In his recently published book *Bitter Victory* (Collins 1988), Carlo d'Este has comprehensively shown that the lesson had not been learned by the time of the invasion of Sicily in 1943.

Bibliography

Air Historical Branch, AHB/11/117/4, Norway.
Aris, G. *The Fifth British Division* (1959).
Ash, Bernard *Norway 1940* (Cassell, 1964).

Barclay, Brigadier C. N. *The History of the Sherwood Foresters 1919-1957* (Clowes & Sons, 1959).
Beckworth, Colonel E. G. C. *The 8th Battalion, The Sherwood Foresters, TA.*
Bekker, Cajus *The Luftwaffe War Diaries* (Macdonald, 1966).
Bowyer, Chaz *Bristol Blenheim* (Ian Allan, 1984).
Broch, Theodor *The Mountains Wait* (Michael Joseph, 1943).
Buckley, Christopher *Norway, The Commandos, Dieppe* (HMSO, 1952).

Carton de Wiart, Lieut General Sir Adrian *Happy Odyssey* (Jonathan Cape, 1950).
Churchill, Winston *The Second World War, Vol I* (Cassell, 1948)
Clarke, Dudley *Seven Assignments* (Jonathan Cape, 1948).
Colville, John *The Fringes of Power – Downing Street Diaries* (Hodder and Stoughton, 1985).
Connell, John *Auchinleck* (Cassell, 1959).
Cooper, Matthew *The German Army 1933-1945* (Macdonald & Jones, 1978).

Derry, T. K. *The Campaign in Norway* (HMSO, 1952).
—, *A History of Modern Norway 1814-1972* (Clarendon Press, 1973).
Dickens, Captain Peter *Narvik, Battle in the Fiords* (Ian Allen, 1974).

Edwards, Gron *Norwegian Patrol* (Airlife Publishing, 1985).
Embry, Air Chief Marshal Sir Basil *Mission Completed* (Methuen, 1957).
Erskine, David *The Scots Guards 1919-1955* (W. Clowes & Sons, 1956).

Fitzgerald, Major D. J. L. *History of the Irish Guards in the Second World War* (Gale and Polden, 1949).

Garrett, Richard *Scharnhorst and Gneisenau* (David and Charles, 1978).
Gilbert, Martin *Finest Hour* (William Heinemann, 1983).
Green, William *Warplanes of the Third Reich* (Macdonald, 1970).
Graham, Brigadier H. L. *The First Battalion in Norway* (Scots Guards Magazine, 1959).
Griffen, Major General, J. A. A. *The History of the Tenth Foot 1919-1950* (Gale and Polden, 1953).

Hambro, Carl J. *I Saw it Happen in Norway* (Hodder and Stoughton, 1940).
Hauge, E. *Odds Against Norway* (Lindsey Drummond, 1941).
Hendrie, Andrew *Seek and Strike – The Lockhead Hudson in World War 2* (William Kimber, 1983).
Hingston, Lieut Colonel Walter *History of the Kings Own Yorkshire Light Infantry, Vol 5* (1950).
Hinsley, F. H. *British Intelligence in the Second World War, Vol 1* (HMSO, 1979).
Hubatsch, W. *Problems of the Norwegian Campaign 1940* (RUSI Journal, August 1958).

Ironside, General Lord *The Ironside Diaries 1937-1940* (Constable, 1962).

Jameson, William *Ark Royal* (Rupert Hart-Davis, 1957).
Joubert de la Ferté, Air Chief Marshal Sir Philip *Birds and Fishes – The Story of Coastal Command* (Hutchinson, 1960).

Kemp, Lieut Commander P. K. *Fleet Air Arm (Herbert Jenkins, 1954).*

Lapie, Pierre *With the Foreign Legion at Narvik* (Murray, 1941).
Liddell Hart, B. H. *History of the Second World War* (Cassell, 1970).
—, *The Other Side of the Hill* (Cassell, 1951).
Lindbäck-Larsen, O. *Krigen i Norge 1940* (Oslo, 1965).
Lucas, James *Alpine Elite* (Janes, 1980).

Mackesy, P. *Churchill on Narvik* (RUSI Journal, December 1970).
Mason, F. K. *The Gloster Gladiator* (Macdonald, 1964).
Mason, H. M. *The Rise of the Luftwaffe* (Cassell, 1973).
Maund, L. E. H. *Assault from the Sea* (Methuen, 1949).
Medlicott, W. N. *The Economic Blockade, Vol 1* (HMSO, 1952).
Messenger, C. *The Commandos* (1985).
Middlebrook, Martin (and Chris Everitt) *The Bomber Command War Diaries* (Viking, 1985).
Morris, Eric *Churchill's Private Armies* (Hutchinson, 1986).
Moulton, Major General J. L. *The Norwegian Campaign of 1940* (1966).

Raeder, Grand Admiral Erich *The Struggle for the Sea* (William Kimber, 1959).
Richards, Denis *Royal Air Force 1939-1945, Vol 1* (HMSO, 1953).
Roskill, Captain S. W. *HMS Warspite* (Collins, 1957).
—, *The War at Sea, Vol 1* (HMSO, 1954).
Ruge, Vice Admiral Friedrich *Sea Warfare 1939-1945* (Cassell, 1957).

Saundby, Air Marshal Sir Robert *Air Bombardment* (Chatto and Windus, 1961).
Sheffield, Major O. F. *The York and Lancaster Regiment* (Gale and Polden, 1956).
Shirer, William *The Rise and Fall of the Third Reich* (Secker and Warburg, 1959).
Slessor, Sir John *The Central Blue* (Cassell, 1956).

Smith, J. R. (and A. L. Kay) *German Aircraft of the Second World War* (Putnam, 1972).

Smith, Peter *Hit First, Hit Hard, HMS Renown* (William Kimber, 1979).

Speer, Albert *Inside the Third Reich* (MacMillan, 1970).

Stokes, Brigadier R. S. G. *Our Arctic Campaigns – Narvik 1940* (Royal Engineers Journal, September 1975).

Suchenwirth, Richard *Historical Turning Points in the German Air Force War Effort* (Arno Press, New York, 1968).

Synge, Captain W. A. T. *Green Howards 1939-1945*.

Taylor, Telford *The March of Conquest* (Edward Hulton, 1959).

Terraine, John *The Right of the Line* (Hodder and Stoughton, 1975).

Thetford, Owen *Aircraft of the Royal Air Force Since 1918* (Putnam).

—, *British Naval Aircraft Since 1912* (Putnam, 1958).

Thompson, Kenneth *HMS Rodney at War* (Hollis and Carter, 1946).

Underhill, Brigadier W. E. *The Royal Leicestershire Regiment 1928-1956*

Vian, Admiral of the Fleet Sir Philip *Action This Day* (Frederick Muller, 1960).

Waage, John *The Narvik Campaign* (Harrap, 1964).

Warlimont, W. *Inside Hitler's Headquarters 1939-1945* (Wiedenfield and Nicholson, 1964).

Warner, Philip *Auchinleck, the Lonely Soldier* (Buchan & Enright, 1961).

Webster, Sir Charles (and Noble Frankland) *The Strategic Air Offensive Against Germany, Vol 1* (HMSO, 1961).

Winton, John *Carrier Glorious* (Leo Cooper, 1986).

—, *The Victoria Cross at Sea* (Michael Joseph, 1978).

Woodward, Sir Llewellyn *British Foreign Policy in the Second World War, Vol 1* (HMSO, 1970).

Zbyszewski, Karl *The Fight for Narvik* (Lindsey Drummond, 1940).

Ziemke, E. F. *The German Northern Theatre of Operations, Department of the Army Pamphlet* No. 20-271 (1959).

APPENDIX

1. *Engagements of 8 and 9 April*

Destroyer	*Glowworm*	(Lt Cmdr G. Broadmead Roope)
Battle Cruiser	*Renown*	(Captain C. E. B. Simeon) (flagship of Vice-Admiral W. J. Whitworth)

2. *First Battle of Narvik (10 April)*

2nd Destroyer Flotilla

	Hardy	(flotilla leader, Captain B. A. W. Warburton Lee)
	Hunter	(Lt Cmdr L. de Villiers)
	Hotspur	(Cmdr H. F. H. Layman)
	Havock	(Lt Cmdr R. E. Courage)
	Hostile	(Lt Cmdr J. P. Wright)

3. *Second Battle of Narvik (13 April)*

Battleship	*Warspite*	(Captain V. A. C. Crutchley, VC) (flagship of Vice Admiral W. J. Whitworth)
Destroyers	*Bedouin*	(Cmdr J. A. McCoy)
	Cossack	(Cmdr R. St V. Sherbrooke)
	Eskimo	Cmdr St J. A. Micklethwait)
	Punjabi	(Cmdr J. T. Lean)
	Hero	(Cmdr H. W. Biggs)
	Icarus	(Lt Cmdr C. D. Maud)
	Kimberley	(Lt Cmdr R. G. K. Knowling)
	Forester	(Lt Cmdr E. B. Tancock)
	Foxhound	(Lt Cmdr G. H. Peters)

4. *Engagement of 8 June*

Aircraft Carrier	*Glorious*	(Captain G. D'Oyly Hughes)
Destroyers	*Acasta*	(Cmdr C. E. Glasfurd)
	Ardent	(Lt Cmdr J. E. Barker)

PART II
ARMY

1. *'MAURICEFORCE'*

Major General A. Carton de Wiart, VC.

British

146th Infantry Brigade (Brigadier C. G. Phillips):

1st/4th Battalion The Royal Lincolnshire Regiment
   (Lieut-Colonel R. W. Newton)
1st/4th Battalion The King's Own Yorkshire Light Infantry
   (Lieut-Colonel W. S. Hibbert)
The Hallamshire Battalion, The York and Lancaster Regiment
   (Lieut-Colonel C. O. Robbins)

French

General de Division Audet
5th Demi-Brigade Chasseurs Alpins

13th Battalion Chasseurs Alpins
53rd Battalion Chasseurs Alpins
67th Battalion Chasseurs Alpins

2. *'SICKLEFORCE'*

Major General B. C. T. Paget
148th Brigade (Brigadier H. de R. Morgan):

1st/5th Battalion The Royal Leicestershire Regiment
   (Lieut-Colonel G. J. German)
1st/8th Battalion The Sherwood Foresters
   (Lieut-Colonel T. A. Ford)

15th Brigade (Brigadier H. E. F. Smyth):

1st Battalion The Green Howards
   (Lieut-Colonel A. E. Robinson)
1st Battalion The King's Own Yorkshire Light Infantry
   (Acting Lieut-Colonel E. E. E. Cass)
1st Battalion The York and Lancaster Regiment
   (Lieut-Colonel A. L. Kent-Lemon)
168th Light Anti-Aircraft Battery, Royal Artillery
260th Heavy Anit-Aircraft Battery, Royal Artillery
55th Field Company Royal Engineers

3. 'SCISSORSFORCE'

Brigadier C. McV Gubbins

> Nos 1, 2, 3, 4, 5 Independent Companies
> One Section 166th Light Anti-Aircraft Battery, Royal Artillery
> 1st Battalion Scots Guards (Lieut-Colonel T. B. Trappes-Lomax)
> 1st Battalion Irish Guards (Lieut-Colonel W. B. Faulkner)
> 2nd Battalion The South Wales Borderers (Lieut-Colonel W. Gottwaltz)
> One Troop, 203rd Field Battery, Royal Artillery
> One Troop, 55th Light Anti-Aircraft Battery, Royal Artillery
> Detachment 230th Field Company, Royal Engineers

4. 'AVONFORCE'

Major General P. J. Mackesy

24th (Guards) Brigade (Brigadier the Hon W. Fraser):

> 1st Battalion Scots Guards
> 1st Battalion Irish Guards
> 2nd Battalion The South Wales Borderers
>
> 3rd Light Anti-Aircraft Battery, Royal Artillery
> 229th and 230th Field Companies, Royal Engineers
> Detachment 231st Field Park Company, Royal Engineers

5. 'RUPERTFORCE'

Major General P. J. Mackesy

British

24th (Guards) Brigade:

> One Troop 3rd King's Own Hussars
> 203rd Battery, 51st Field Regiment, Royal Artillery
> 193rd Heavy Anti-Aircraft Battery, Royal Artillery
> 55th Light Anti-Aircraft Regiment, Royal Artillery
> 3rd Light Anti-Aircraft Battery, Royal Artillery
> 229th and 230th Field Companies, Royal Engineers

French

General de Brigade Bethouart

27th Demi-Brigade Chasseurs Alpins:

> 6th Battalion Chasseurs Alpins
> 12th Battalion Chasseurs Alpins
> 14th Battalion Chasseurs Alpins

13th Demi-Brigade Foreign Legion:

> 1st and 2nd Battalions
> 342nd Independent Tank Company
> 2nd Independent Group Colonial Artillery
> 14th Anti-Tank Company, 13th Chasseurs Alpins

Polish

Chasseurs du Nord (General Bohucz-szysko):

   1st Demi-Brigade: 1st and 2nd Battalions
   2nd Demi-Brigade: 3rd and 4th Battalions

6. *NORTH WESTERN EXPEDITIONARY FORCE* (1)

British

Lieut General C. J. E. Auchinleck

   24th (Guards) Brigade
   One troop 3rd King's Own Hussars
   203rd Battery, 51st Field Regiment, Royal Artillery
   6th Anti-Aircraft Brigade, Royal Artillery
   55th Light Anti-Aircraft Regiment
   56th Light Anti-Aircraft Regiment
   51st Heavy Anti-Aircraft Regiment
   82nd Heavy Anti-Aircraft Regiment
   No 10 Army Observer Unit, Royal Artillery
   229th and 230th Field Companies, Royal Engineers

French and Polish
(as above)

PART III

ROYAL AIR FORCE

Group Captain M. Moore (Narvik only)

   No 263 Squadron, Gladiators
      (Squadron Leader J. W. Donaldson)
   No 46 Squadron, Hurricanes
      (Squadron Leader K. B. B. Cross)

   (Narvik only)
   No II Observer Screen

Note (1): Admiral of the Fleet the Earl of Cork and Orrery was appointed naval commander on 10 April of the Narvik Expedition and Joint Force Commander on 21 April. This was expanded to include forces in the Bodo area on 7 May.

Index